SLAVERY AND THE MAKING OF EARLY
AMERICAN LIBRARIES

Slavery and the Making of Early American Libraries

*British Literature, Political Thought, and the
Transatlantic Book Trade, 1731–1814*

SEAN D. MOORE

OXFORD
UNIVERSITY PRESS

OXFORD
UNIVERSITY PRESS

Great Clarendon Street, Oxford, OX2 6DP,
United Kingdom

Oxford University Press is a department of the University of Oxford.
It furthers the University's objective of excellence in research, scholarship,
and education by publishing worldwide. Oxford is a registered trade mark of
Oxford University Press in the UK and in certain other countries

First Edition published in 2019

Impression: 3

Published in the United States of America by Oxford University Press
198 Madison Avenue, New York, NY 10016, United States of America

British Library Cataloguing in Publication Data
Data available

Library of Congress Control Number: 2018962582

ISBN 978–0–19–883637–7

Printed and bound by
CPI Group (UK) Ltd, Croydon, CR0 4YY

In Memory of my Father Francis Eugene Moore II (1924–2011), a U.S. Navy veteran whose heroism in two D-Days in the WWII Pacific Theatre was surpassed by his risk-taking over the far greater portion of his life in confronting racism and inequality. He worked for social justice, human rights, and peace during the Vietnam, Afghanistan, and Iraq conflicts and other military misadventures. I took his bravery on civil rights for granted until the difficulties I encountered researching and writing this book. Though he was an engineer by profession, by the time he was raising me, the youngest of his eight children, he viewed writing as the highest calling of humanity, and encouraged me to dedicate my life to it.

Preface

In 1681, a Boston importer of British books by the name of John Usher invested in a slave-trading voyage to Africa. The expedition was organized by Andrew Belcher, a merchant who passed his business to his son Jonathan Belcher, later royal governor of Massachusetts, New Hampshire, and New Jersey, and the official who granted Princeton University its charter.[1] This transaction is the first known example of an early American bookseller also engaging in the trade in enslaved persons. It would not be the last. In fact, books and people were regarded as equally exchangeable commodities throughout the colonial and early republic periods. For example, an advertisement in the *Boston Weekly Newsletter* of 1737 stated that the Massachusetts bookseller Thomas Fleet would auction off "the best Part of the Books which should have been Sold last Night, together with Two likely young Negro Women."[2] The trading relationship between books and slaves was predominant enough that James Madison, himself a Princeton graduate, would complain to his father in 1782 that if he did not receive money from home, he would have to settle a debt with a Philadelphia bookseller by "selling a negro."[3] The personal libraries of men like Madison should therefore be understood as slavery-funded archives from which enslaved Africans, far from being silent, speak to us as people with agency who were founders of the intellectual and cultural infrastructure of the United States. Indeed, as Craig Wilder and researchers at Brown, Yale, Columbia, Princeton, Georgetown, and other colleges have documented, they and their labor were the capital endowing America's early universities, most of which are now part of the Ivy League.[4] This book contributes to that scholarship by establishing that the country's earliest proprietary subscription libraries, institutions that pooled the money of men involved in the trade in slaves and related enterprises to purchase imported British books, were also essentially endowed by African people. These libraries were not "public" in today's sense of taxpayer-funded local

---

[1] Jeffries Papers 1622–1880. MSS MsN-2067 (XT). Massachusetts Historical Society, Boston, Massachusetts, 86; Worthington Chauncey Ford, *The Boston Book Market, 1689–1700* (Boston: the Club of Odd Volumes, 1917), 83–4; C. S. Manegold, *Ten Hills Farm: The Forgotten History of Slavery in the North* (Princeton: Princeton UP, 2010), 111–13.

[2] Quoted in E. Jennifer Monaghan, *Learning to Read and Write in Colonial America* (Amherst: U Massachusetts P, 2005), 241.

[3] James Madison, *The Papers of James Madison Digital Edition*. Accessed June 25, 2014. Ed. J. C. A. Stagg (Charlottesville: University of Virginia Press, Rotunda, 2010). <http://rotunda.upress.virginia.edu/founders/JSMN-01-04-02-0057>.

[4] Craig Steven Wilder, *Ebony and Ivy: Race, Slavery, and the Troubled History of America's Universities* (NY: Bloomsbury P, 2013); Brown University Steering Committee on Slavery and Justice. Accessed December 11, 2017. <http://www.brown.edu/Research/Slavery_Justice/>; Yale, Slavery & Abolition: Yale University and its Legacy. Accessed December 11, 2017. <http://www.yaleslavery.org/>; Columbia University and Slavery. Accessed December 11, 2017. <https://columbiaandslavery.columbia.edu>; Princeton & Slavery. Accessed December 11, 2017. <https://slavery.princeton.edu/>; The Georgetown Slavery Archive. Accessed December 11, 2017. <https://slaveryarchive.georgetown.edu/>.

institutions open to everyone. Rather, they were privately owned joint stock corporations in which each proprietor owned a share or more that entitled him to borrowing rights, much like today's "public companies."[5] That slavery was the basis of that ownership is at the root of this study's larger message that we should not regard the identity politics of race and the issue of economic inequality as such different concerns, given that the cultural philanthropy of these proprietors was rooted in economic exploitation. This book examines these facts by studying libraries and reading across the eighteenth and early nineteenth centuries, especially around the time of the Revolution. It does so by focusing its analysis on the British literary works that colonists were consuming in these libraries for how it related to the non-fiction, particularly in the discipline of political thought, which they also were reading.

From Portsmouth, New Hampshire, where a library called the Athenaeum sprang from families made wealthy by Atlantic trade, to the Savannah Library Society in Georgia, proprietary subscription libraries met the high cost of imported books through the combining of slaveholders' resources. In this regard, Northern and Southern libraries are not so different; indeed, this book's examination of libraries in both regions demonstrates that the cultural development of both was dependent on slavery for capitalization, showing that both the North and the South were implicated not only in the trades in slaves and their products, but also in the cultural capital that these trades created. Crucially, these libraries—slavery-created "reading networks"—were also social networks for their members and for their communities at large.[6] Their function may not have always primarily been reading, but also the furtherance of the businesses of those involved—people whose good taste in books enhanced their reputations and, therefore, their commercial networking prospects. They were therefore an important part of the associational culture sweeping the Atlantic world at the time, and so should be regarded as central to the cultural history of the English-speaking world. As Mark Towsey and Kyle Roberts have pointed out, libraries across this oceanic community served as "venues for conviviality and social networking, and as fulcra for other kinds of civic behavior, including philanthropy, social reform and cultural politics."[7] These institutions' blending of civic, financial, and cultural functions provides the basis for this book's efforts to tie together the analysis of such libraries by reference to their effects on early American civic engagement at the time of the Revolution. The stories that library proprietors were consuming were bound up with the stories that they were telling about their own lives and communities—narratives patterned, in part, on the lives about which they were reading. These early libraries, their books,

---

[5] Tom Glynn, *Reading Publics: New York City's Public Libraries, 1754–1911* (NY: Fordham UP, 2015), 6–7, 15, 18; Mark Towsey and Kyle B. Roberts, "Introduction." *Before the Public Library: Reading, Community, and Identity in the Atlantic World, 1650–1850.* Eds Mark Towsey and Kyle B. Roberts (Leiden: Brill, 2017), 9–10.

[6] Jana Smith Elford, "Recovering Women's History with Network Analysis: A Case Study of the Fabian News." *The Journal of Modern Periodical Studies* 6.2 (2015): 198–208.

[7] Towsey and Roberts, 16.

and their members, in short, were crucial players in the cultural history producing America's stories.

It is in this storytelling sense that the possession of the document proving Usher's involvement in the transatlantic slave trade is bound up with the repressions, revelations, and reburials of the truth that characterize the telling of the history of slavery in America. The version of this document that survives in the Massachusetts Historical Society reads, at the bottom, "Copy of a paper stolen from the office hold in Faneuil Hall, and purchased by Dr. John J.H. Hogg, 481 Broadway South Boston, from Cork a dealer on Washington St. Boston, now in the possession of Dr. Hogg. Walter Lloyd Jeffries Dec. 8ᵗʰ 1886."[8] The fact that an Irishman "from Cork" like Hogg would be in possession of such an accounting would not surprise us today. In the post-Civil War era, however, when the North was at great pains to suppress its slavery history, this possession signals that even recent immigrants were aware of how Northerners, not just Southerners, had profited from the trade. Moreover, it signals that the Irish, a persecuted white underclass to be sure, may have wanted this document to prove the hypocrisy of the heirs of the slave-trading New England founders—"Brahmin" elites—who claimed to have waged war against the South to end slavery. Though it is difficult to prove this motive, Irish political ascendancy in Boston began in the late nineteenth century and culminated in Democrat John F. Kennedy's defeat of Republican Henry Cabot Lodge, a descendant of slave traders and vice-presidential running mate to Richard Nixon, in the US Senate race of 1952.

This book on the slavery origins of American cultural artifacts, in this case imported British and European books, may help explain the reasons that this story of slavery-funded libraries has *not* been told before. Particularly in the Northern states, the role of slavery in the economy has often been obscured, with abolitionist histories of the North such as Joseph Felt's 1849 book, or George Moore's 1866 one, both of which contained critiques of Massachusetts slave trading, becoming less common after the Civil War.[9] From time to time the story of slavery in the North has been revived, notably by Lorenzo Johnston Greene in the 1940s, Edgar McManus, David Brion Davis, and Edmund Morgan in the 1960s and 1970s, and most recently by Joanne Pope Melish, Wilder, Sven Beckert, Seth Rockman, Chrissy Pujara-Clark, and a host of other scholars.[10] Yet even when we include the South in studying the relationship of slavery to American institutions, little work

---

[8] Jeffries, 86.

[9] Joseph B. Felt, *Annals of Salem, Volume 2* (Salem: W & S. B. Ives, 1849); George H. Moore, *Notes on the History of Slavery in Massachusetts* (NY: Appleton, 1866).

[10] Lorenzo Johnston Greene, *The Negro in Colonial New England 1620–1776* (NY: Columbia UP, 1942), 70–1, 58–9; Edgar J. McManus, *Black Bondage in the North* (Syracuse: Syracuse UP, 1973); David Brion Davis, *The Problem of Slavery in the Age of the Revolution, 1770–1823* (Ithaca: Cornell UP, 1975); Edmund Morgan, *American Slavery, American Freedom: The Ordeal of Colonial Virginia* (NY: Norton, 1975); Joanne Pope Melish, *Disowning Slavery: Gradual Emancipation and "Race" in New England, 1780–1860* (Ithaca: Cornell UP, 1998); Wilder; Sven Beckert and Seth Rockman, eds, *Slavery's Capitalism: A New History of American Economic Development* (Philadelphia: U Pennsylvania P, 2016); Chrissy Pujara-Clark, *Dark Work: The Business of Slavery in Rhode Island* (NY: NYU P, 2016).

has been done on the abundant evidence of books being purchased abroad with the wealth generated by slavery in all colonies and states on the Eastern seaboard.

The early American fashion for imported British culture was connected to the role of England in the colonial economy and in the early American imagination. We have to remember that for the majority of the eighteenth century, London, not Washington DC or New York, was the capital of America. London "was the financial centre of Britain's vast trading empire that spanned the globe from America to the West Indies, Africa and Bengal."[11] This metropolis was where Americans' credit accumulated, as most of their business was not done in currency, but in bartering their crops for other items through London merchants and banks. They often employed numerous mercantile bills of credit circulating throughout the Atlantic that drew on those institutions in their trades. The sugar, tobacco, rum, and even slaves that Americans shipped were evident on London's docks, shops, and coffee-houses. In return for their credit in the city, "English textiles, clothing, porcelain, clocks, guns and instruments, books, prints, toys and trinkets of every kind" were imported to America as part of the "consumer revolution that was sweeping the English-speaking world."[12] Indeed, American planters and merchants were appending themselves to a trade network that had been developed over the course of the century by British commercial men. As David Hancock has explained, between 1735 and 1785 London merchants had built an "interconnected chain of shipping and trading routes between London and Calcutta, Madeira, the British West Indies, and the North American mainland colonies." This network "provided the commercial infrastructure for the development of the British Atlantic world."[13] The oceanic trade in wine, for example, "created a common commercial, cultural, and conceptual space that pervaded the Atlantic basin, affecting people in Europe, Africa, the Americas—even India and China."[14] As this book demonstrates, however, wine might be only one of the many goods in a cargo ship trading New England fish to Spain and Portugal, slaves from Africa to the Americas, and sugar and molasses to the North American colonies as it proceeded to and from each port of call.

What Americans were after, particularly after 1750, was "social replication," or the imitation of the lifestyles of the British elite.[15] The roots of American cultural history, accordingly, lie in transatlantic trade, as it was not only in books that colonists trafficked with Britain, but also in the education of many of their leaders. Indeed, slavery was so crucial to the accumulation of this kind of cultural capital that Charles Pinckney's education at the Westminster School in London, Christ Church at Oxford, and the Middle Temple enabled his "spirited defense of slavery that drew on his talents as an orator and classical scholar" at the Constitutional

[11] Julie Flavel, *When London Was Capital of America* (New Haven: Yale UP, 2010), 2–3.
[12] Flavel, 3, 10.
[13] David Hancock, *Citizens of the World: London Merchants and the Integration of the British Atlantic Community, 1735–1785* (Cambridge: Cambridge UP, 1995), 2.
[14] David Hancock, *Oceans of Wine: Madeira and the Emergence of American Trade and Taste* (New Haven: Yale UP, 2009), xxix.
[15] Jack P. Greene, *Pursuits of Happiness: The Social Development of Early Modern British Colonies and the Formation of American Culture* (Chapel Hill: U North Carolina P, 1988), 168–70; Hancock, *Oceans*, xxix.

Convention in 1787.[16] Slavery was supporting this Anglicization of America through abstract commodities like education, taste, manners, and culture; as Simon Gikandi has written, there was "a link between slavery, consumption, and the culture of taste, all-important conduits for understanding modern identity."[17] It is therefore not surprising that most Americans would defend slavery as crucial not only to their economy before and after the Revolution, but also to their sense of themselves as enlightened cosmopolitans.

The existence of anti-slavery advocates among those cosmopolitans is therefore striking, and their writing, counter-cultural at the time, forms an important part of this shared cultural history. "Print culture and the spoken word" in the form of novels, poetry, sermons, and public readings, writes Robin Blackburn, "were eventually to express a generalized humanitarian sentiment that tried to break with the prevailing language of commerce, civilization and racial difference" espoused by enslavers.[18] Teaching slaves how to read, and thereby enabling them to understand these and other works, was not initially considered incompatible with keeping them enslaved. Some colonists, however, particularly in the North, not only would connect literacy to anti-slavery, but also would begin to link abolition to their own movement for liberty from Britain. As Christopher Leslie Brown argues, the British abolitionist movement owes its origins to "the conflicts between colonial and metropolitan elites that commenced with the Seven Years' War and ended with American Independence, the conflicts that forced the British to make sense of their increasingly global empire."[19] Revolution and abolition were linked, with the former providing the context of rights discourse in which the latter could be contemplated. Crucially, this conversation largely took place in the medium of books. The books that were part of the import boom before the Revolution would extend to the hands of slaves. After Britain's 1772 Somerset legal decision, which declared that enslaved persons who escaped to Britain were free, some Americans in the Revolution and post-Revolution period began to pass anti-slavery measures despite persistent racism and continued slave trading. This book's chapters, particularly the final one on the Library Company of Philadelphia, document the development of abolitionist sentiment in the very libraries established on the financial basis of slavery. The story of these libraries is therefore very much a part of the cultural history of the Atlantic world, particularly when we regard the dialectic between pro- and anti-slavery advocacy as central to that history.

This book performs this kind of cultural analysis not from the perspective of a historian, but from the position of a scholar of English literature interested in what the early American circulation and reading of eighteenth-century British literary

[16] Edward Pearson, "'Planters Full of Money': The Self-Fashioning of South Carolina's Plantation Society." *Money, Trade, and Power, the Evolution of South Carolina's Plantation Society.* Ed. Jack P. Greene, Rosemary Brana-Shute, and Randy J. Sparks (Columbia: U South Carolina P, 2001), 306.

[17] Simon Gikandi, *Slavery and the Culture of Taste* (Princeton: Princeton UP, 2011), xiv.

[18] Robin Blackburn, *The American Crucible: Slavery, Emancipation and Human Rights* (London: Verso, 2011), 153.

[19] Christopher Leslie Brown, *Moral Capital: Foundations of British Abolitionism* (Chapel Hill: U North Carolina P, 2006), 26.

works can tell us about the broader transatlantic significance of those works. That is to say, rather than performing a quantitative approach by collecting exhaustive empirical data on the transatlantic book trade in the Digital Humanities vein, this study is more interested in asking what such data can tell us about the period's drama, poetry, and fiction. As such, it is more of a cultural history of early America and the Atlantic world than one solely focused on the book trade and book history, though these latter aspects of this monograph comprise the central methodology through which this cultural history is analyzed. The research questions in which this project is invested, accordingly, are drawn less from the quantitative analysis aspect of book history and more from the problem of the relationship of slavery to American institutions.

The "literary" history of the book in which this study is engaged, accordingly, is more invested in the inquiry into how colonials were using contemporary British literature than the simple fact that it was available from booksellers and libraries. Book history methodology is therefore employed more to inform our understanding of literary works than to serve as an end unto itself. Consequently, this analysis is necessarily a history of reading, a task understood here, in Lisa Jardine and Anthony Grafton's words, as an effort to "reconstruct the social, professional and personal contexts in which reading took place," in this case the early American library.[20] I attempt to establish the foundations of American reading from early library catalogs and circulation records as much as from diaries and correspondence. Rather than documenting reading in every proprietary subscription library formed in this period, of which there were many, I focus on five major libraries founded in the half-century before the Revolution: the Library Company of Philadelphia, 1731; the Redwood Library of Newport, 1747; the Charleston Library Society, 1748; the New York Society Library, 1754; and the Salem Social Library, 1760. I concentrate on these five libraries rather than the others because each of the port cities hosting these institutions was made wealthy by Atlantic trade in slaves and slave-produced commodities, and their libraries therefore form a paradoxical context for the reading of books often objecting to slavery. I also choose to investigate these particular libraries because as institutions formed prior to the Revolution, they became incubators of what Bernard Bailyn calls "the ideological origins of the American revolution," since many of the same people who composed the patriot and loyalist leaders in some of the major cities were also members of them. In addition, unlike most of the proprietary libraries founded in the colonial period, these five survive into the present day. This helps make the type of analysis I conduct possible since they still contain primary source materials explaining their relationship to revolution, slavery, and abolition as well as records documenting reading patterns.

This book's chapters on each of these libraries are paired with a reading of a major literary book available to the respective library members, though readings of other literary and non-fictional works that form the larger print media context around these specific books, expressed in each library's catalog and collections, are

---

[20] Lisa Jardine and Anthony Grafton, "'Studied for Action': How Gabriel Harvey Read His Livy." *Past & Present* 129 (Nov. 1990), 30.

contained within each chapter. These chapters, however, are not sequenced by their dates of founding, but rather by the publication dates for the central literary works, and the careers of their authors, explored in each (*Oroonoko*, 1688 & 1759; *Windsor Forest* and an *Essay on Man*, 1713 & 1733; *Robinson Crusoe*, 1719; *Chrysal, or, the Adventures of a Guinea*, 1760 & 1765; and the *Interesting Narrative of the Life of Olaudah Equiano, or Gustavus Vassa, the African*, 1789). The analyses of each of these books in light of other works that surrounded them, and for their relationship and significance to the contexts of their libraries and cities, will serve as lenses into broader questions. These questions are not limited to why the members of these libraries were reading certain books, or to how they placed these books in service to revolution and abolition. Rather, they are inquiries into how Americans understood themselves as part of an anglophone Atlantic print media market, or imagined community, that was linked to their consumer culture and politics and that helps explain how they behaved financially, intellectually, and politically.

Each chapter is structured in a way that furthers this book's interdisciplinary aims; they each feature an introduction, an explication of its major literary text for analysis, a history of the library it explores, and evidence of reading books in the library's particular socio-cultural context. Sequencing this book around the publication dates of the major literary texts each chapter explores also enables it to track the gradual development of anti-slavery sentiment in British literature over the course of the eighteenth century. By culminating in a chapter on Philadelphia becoming the most abolitionist city in the Atlantic world by the 1760s and 1770s to the extent that it had an appetite for such works as Olaudah Equiano's slave narrative, this book attempts to explain how early American libraries, once outcomes of oppression, became linked to liberation.

Each of the works analyzed in depth in this book tells us something about American attitudes towards slavery. Moreover, the other texts that readers of these works were reading indicate patterns of consumption of imported British books that help determine not only the tastes of readers, but also their political proclivities. Perhaps even more so than the less literary anti-slavery texts of the time, each of the works discussed in each chapter helped elite, white readers to imagine questions of profit and loss, justice and injustice, and liberty versus tyranny in a manner that influenced their approaches to abolition and the American Revolution. Much of the literature and philosophy that early Americans were consuming, I contend, was preoccupied with problems of human rights and liberty, ripening the climate for both revolutionary and abolitionist sentiment. Works on sensibility and sentimentality in relation to politics, in particular, were encouraging the development of fellow feeling in a manner that, in turn, encouraged the extension of rights and liberties to all, and were being avidly read in the colonies. As Jardine and Grafton have established in documenting the reading of political theory and history in the period, early modern readers "persistently envision action as the *outcome* of reading—not simply reading as active, but reading as a target for action," providing "a link between the absorption of information…and public practice."[21] Studying

---

[21] Jardine and Grafton, 40.

reading at the time of the American Revolution, in short, helps us understand how people put ideas into practice for both abolitionist and anti-imperial ends.

In also asking how British and European works of political thought, not just literature, influenced the ideas behind the Revolution, this book is addressing an open research question. As James Raven has noted about existing scholarship on the transatlantic book trade, "What has yet to be resolved... is the broader cultural significance of the book import boom" of the years immediately preceding the Revolution, particularly in light of this seemingly counterintuitive American cult of "Britishness" during "a time of increasing colonial tension."[22] Imported works on law, history, and political theory, I argue, were helping colonials address the specific tasks and questions at hand: What was the proper mode of civic engagement in a British territory struggling to define what its rights were under English constitutional norms and law? How "English" was America and its institutions at the time of the Revolution? What did the assertion of English liberties for white American males mean for African slaves, and did it demand anti-slavery and abolitionist responses? Why were imported British books "lifelines to identity" for Anglo-Americans? How much was the contemporary interpretation of that identity wrapped up with the economic right to participate in the period's new British consumer society and with legal, political, and constitutional "English" rights?[23]

This study's history of the transatlantic book trade provides one answer to these questions. It contends that it is only through work on the multiple genres that colonials were reading together with literature that an interdisciplinary cultural history of the relationship of imported works to early American ideas, patriotic civic engagement, and events can be articulated. As Leslie Howsam and Raven have explained, books were objects of Atlantic exchange "that changed according to the mutations of colonialism, migration, exile, commerce, political independence and nationalism."[24] Put another way, books had a very different civic meaning in the American colonies than they did in Britain. The different interpretations put on them in the colonies helped enforce the boundaries of the social networks reading them to the extent that "political ideas appeared the more focused and supported by new aspirations and orientations," enabling "an empowerment that ranged from the social and economic to the intellectual, scientific and political."[25] Slavery served multiple roles in this interdisciplinary cultural history: (1) the financial means by which culture was acquired; (2) the reason that this culture was leveraged for the independence of a slaveholding republic; (3) a central locus for the articulation of human rights that not only led to anti-slavery discourse and action,

---

[22] James Raven, "The Importation of Books in the Eighteenth Century." *A History of the Book in America, Volume I: The Colonial Book in the Atlantic World.* Eds Hugh Amory and David Hall (Chapel Hill: U North Carolina P, 2007), 196.

[23] Raven, 185.

[24] Leslie Howsam and James Raven, "Introduction." *Books Between Europe and the Americas: Connections and Communities, 1620–1860* (Basingstoke: Palgrave Macmillan, 2011), 3.

[25] Howsam and Raven, 19.

but also to the appropriation of "slavery" by white patriots to claim their own rights; and (4) a means of understanding how value was mediated and collateralized in the period's paper economy of circulating currency, financial instruments, and books. This latter category, in particular, helps explain how the rise of a black author like Equiano signals the fortuitous return of the human, collateralized asset to the imaginary or nominal value of the written paper created upon him and by him. This development helps to produce a cult of the author characteristic not only of modern literature, but also of the people reading him or her as a "free person"— a brand with whom they would like to identify—and who were modeling their own modern "free" personalities as subjects of "free" nations like the United States.

This book is also a cultural history in another sense, for in its analysis of private libraries as multifaceted institutions, it also points towards the question of how such organizations are funded today. As I explained in the outset of this preface, these libraries were not "public," but they played an outsized role in American cultural development and in determining what public policy decisions would be made that affected everybody. They were, first and foremost, exclusive social spaces—private clubs—designed to perpetuate the cultural capital of elite white men involved in the Atlantic slavery economy. Second, much like America's earliest universities, they were the recipients of philanthropy from those men, who maintained libraries' collections and enabled them to also serve non-members like clergymen, who could not afford membership. Third, as the clubs of the slaveholding leadership of their cities and the colonies around them, they performed an important civic function, enabling those leaders to meet together, make business deals regarding shipping, read some of the same books and discuss them, and make decisions influencing the futures of their communities and the country. Consequently, they were inward-facing institutions for their members that were outward-facing when those people wanted public policy altered in one direction or the other; they often performed as private groups who wanted to control the public. The fact that patriot and loyalist slaveholders in most of the libraries disagreed so vehemently on how to preserve their positions of privilege that they could no longer hold board meetings by the middle of the 1770s exemplifies this power, as it meant war for the whole country.

Accordingly, there is a cautionary tale in this book, for it not only explores the beginnings of American culture in imported British books, but also investigates the slavery origins of American cultural philanthropy, that which sustains projects like this one in the waning days of taxpayer support for universities, the humanities, and students who study them. Its lessons about the often unseemly sources of such philanthropy certainly can teach us a set of ethics regarding what gifts we should accept for ourselves and for our institutions. But this history of what many project to be the politically neo-conservative and economically neo-liberal fantasy age of the founding period, an era prior to publicly mandated and supported libraries and universities, may be back where our society is headed if we do not stay awake. As both conservatives and some liberals in many nations attempt to set public policy in the direction of low taxes and charity-only public goods, new questions must be asked about possible agendas that come with charitable gifts and about the sustainability of a post-public society. This book, accordingly, will conclude with reflections on what has been termed "the charitable industrial complex" in both our own moment and in the founding era of the United States, asking how current economic arrangements contribute to a culture that, while very different from the slavery philanthropy past, carries its ghosts.

Durham, New Hampshire
June 16, 2018

Acknowledgments

I may be said to be fulfilling what is called the "author-function" for this book; it is really the product of many people, groups, and institutions who have taught me much about book history, American studies, slavery, and the other topics herein and who have supported me in the pursuit of this project. *Slavery and the Making of Early American Libraries* has been in development for quite a long time, and I would like to thank students who participated in seminars that I have taught on its subjects, colleagues who advised me on applications for fellowships to research it, institutions that have funded it, and scholars who helped me to compose it.

This book received its initial inspiration from a National Endowment for the Humanities (NEH) Summer Institute for school teachers entitled "The Role of Slavery in New England Commerce, Industry, and Culture to 1860" that my spouse, Jessica Angell Moore, attended at Brown University in 2009 under the direction of Morgan Grefe and Joanne Pope Melish. I deepened my reading in Early American Studies by taking the 2011 Summer Seminar in the History of the Book on loyalism at the American Antiquarian Society (AAS) taught by Philip Gould and Edward Larkin, who also wrote letters of support for some of my fellowship applications. Eric Nelson's 2012 Folger Library seminar on the "Royalist Revolution" formed the political thought argument of this book. I was able to participate in these seminars while serving as Director of the University Honors Program with the permission of my supervisor, University of New Hampshire (UNH) Provost Lisa MacFarlane. The support of the Assistant Director of the Honors Program, Kate Gaudet, whose expertise is Early American and Atlantic Studies, led to many helpful conversations and readings. I have been teaching UNH graduate seminars on its topics for over ten years, and I thank the following participants for reading, writing about, and discussing the material with me: Maija Birzulis, Jordan Fansler, James Finley, Bill Gallagher, Jacqueline Houseman, Timothy Johnson, Christopher Lampron, Lin Nulman, Ashley Benson, Gerald Cournoyer, Lucas Dietrich, Jeremy Hicks, Michael Luz, Patrick Spears, Michael Haselton, Ryan Sherwood, Kimberly Young, Solimar Collado, Sherard Harrington, Meghan Hill, Shannon Miller, Kathleen Shaughnessy, and Ashlee Thomas. The observations of undergraduates Edith Allard, Patrick Breitenbach, Kayla Keeley, Marissa Moore, Kristiana Packard, Sophie Ruesswick, Will Silverstein-Belden, Sarah Slack, Eliza Sneeden, and Hannah Vagos, who took a senior seminar on slavery and culture with me in 2017, helped with the closing arguments of this book. Particular thanks are due to Bill Ross of the UNH Library's Special Collections division for helping me to teach several of these seminar students the material aspects of our early editions of Chaucer's Works. Ross and Louise Buckley of the UNH libraries are also to be thanked for advice about the founding of the first taxpayer-supported public libraries in the US. Further references from Srinivas

Aravamudan, Briggs Bailey, Simon Gikandi, Eliga Gould, Suvir Kaul, and David Watters helped me to secure funding and time to perform this work.

Funding for this project was initiated with a summer grant writing stipend from the UNH College of Liberal Arts in 2011, and I found out about other opportunities by subscribing to the UNH Research Office's "S.M.A.R.T.S" listserv. A 2014 UNH Graduate School Summer Faculty Fellowship allowed me to commute to and work in several libraries. A New England Regional Fellowship Consortium grant in 2014–15 enabled me to work at the Massachusetts Historical Society (MHS), the Rhode Island Historical Society (RIHS), and the John Hay Library at Brown University, and I would like to thank Kate Viens and Conrad Wright for the opportunity to present my research at a brown bag lunch at the MHS. I was aided not only by the curators, archivists, and librarians of these libraries in this work, but also by my research assistant, Moira Wright, who was sponsored by UNH's Research Experience and Apprenticeship Program (REAP). In the fall of 2014, I worked in residence in Worcester under the auspices of an AAS/NEH fellowship. There, I was helped by Paul Erickson and fellows in residence like Claudia and Richard Bushman, Carol Faulkner, Trenton "Cole" Jones, Melanie Kiechle, and Heather Kopelson. Specific conversations with Ashley Cataldo, Molly O'Hagan Hardy, Thomas Knowles, and Nan Wolverton led me to many sources important to this project, I had much help with housing from Cheryl McCrell and Andy Cariglia, and Nick Conti helped me with Information Technology challenges. A brown bag luncheon they organized in December 2014 helped me to work through aspects of the introduction of this book with other scholars, as did a talk I gave to graduate students that semester at Clark University, to which I was invited by SunHee Kim Gertz. The Preservation Society of Newport County (the Newport Mansions museum) awarded me a fellowship for the spring of 2015, where I was aided by Museum Director Laurie Ossman, CEO Trudy Coxe, Brittany Hullinger, Elizabeth Warburton, Abigail Stewart, Colleen Breitenstein, and fellows Aimee Keithan and Arabeth Balasco. Special thanks to Paula McCrady, Curt Genga, and Pat Emery for housing me in the butler's quarters of the Chepstow Mansion, and to Andrea Carneiro for photography promoting my work. While in Newport, I performed research and gave a presentation at the Redwood Library and Athenaeum's "Life of the Mind Salon" that was organized by Doug Riggs, a member of the library, and gave a lecture at Rosecliff mansion in May organized by Ossman. I thank Redwood colleagues Benedict Leca, Executive Director of the library, Lori Brostuen, Director of Library Systems, and Elizabeth Delmage for information on Redwood holdings in slavery and abolition. Particular thanks are due to special collections librarians Whitney Pape, Robert Kelly, Maris Humphreys, and Chelsea Ordner, who were instrumental early in this project. Ordner, in particular, helped me locate in the Redwood's boardroom the painting, discussed in Chapter 2, of Abraham Redwood holding a book by Alexander Pope. Provost Scott Zeman of Salve Regina University was kind enough to give me McKillop Library access while I was living in Newport. B. Anthony Bogues and Shana Weinberg invited me to give a talk at the Brown Center for Slavery and Justice in 2015, the responses to which, and the advice of Seth Rockman and Justin Pope, were quite helpful in developing my second chapter. I thank Phoebe Bean of the Rhode Island Historical Society and Timothy Engels, Raymond Butti, Ann Dodge, Allison Bundy, Robin Wheelwright Ness, James Moul, Jennifer Betts, Christopher Geissler, and Holly Snyder for access to papers related to the Rhode Island slave trade at the Hay Library of Brown University. Neil Bleicken of The Civic-Minded group at the Algonquin Club in Boston gave me the opportunity to present my work on the critique of the charitable industrial complex to a diverse group in June 2015.

The National Endowment for the Humanities awarded me a fellowship for the 2015–16 academic year, and thanks are due to many of the above-mentioned individuals and Burt Feintuch for reading drafts of the application for it. During that year I worked on my first chapter at the Phillips Library of the Peabody Essex Museum. There, I was aided by Anne Deschaine, Catherine Robertson, and Jennifer Hornsby, who awarded me Visiting Researcher status for the 2015–16 academic year. I am also grateful to the Library Company of Philadelphia and Historical Society of Pennsylvania, institutions that awarded me a one-month American Society for Eighteenth-Century Studies (ASECS) fellowship for the summer of 2016 to research my fifth chapter. Jim Green was particularly helpful in directing me to manuscript sources and secondary works at both of these libraries, and while I was there, Cathy Matson pointed out who were the merchants among the first subscribers to the New York Society Library. I would also like to thank the readers of essay-length versions of Chapters 1 and 2 at *PMLA*; though these essays made it as far as the editorial board at that journal and were ultimately declined, the readers' reports and work that I did to revise for that journal helped make this a better book. I am also grateful to Mark Towsey, Kyle Roberts, Tessa Whitehouse, and the AHRC-funded "Community Libraries: Connecting Readers in the Atlantic World, *c.*1650–1850" network for allowing me to present a portion of this book at their "Libraries in the Atlantic World" colloquium in Liverpool in 2014. Colloquium members John and Sherylynne Haggerty of the University of Nottingham, and Laura Miller of the University of West Georgia, are particularly to be thanked for introducing me to social network theory and the concept of a "reading network." I also would like to thank the *Humanities to Go* program panel assembled by the New Hampshire Humanities Council (NHHC) in June 2016, for recommending that this book project "should be abandoned," a verdict that assured me that I was on the right course and that this work has a message that the people of New Hampshire need to hear. Indeed, I am most grateful for the colleagues who, on the contrary, invited me to be their speaker for the Karmiole Lecture on the History of the Book Trade at UCLA's Clark Library in November 2017. The sponsor, Kenneth Karmiole, Library Director Helen Deutsch, Professor Christopher Looby, and colleagues like Kathy Sanchez, Erich Bollman, and Alastair Thorne were instrumental in organizing the lecture. The success of that well-attended talk, and feedback from the audience, helped me to revise the book and to see its potential.

For my work towards my Salem chapter (Chapter 1), I am grateful to Ginevra Morse of the New England Genealogical Society, who gave me the genealogy of the Gardner family of Salem mentioned in that chapter. Particular thanks are due to Jean Marie Procious and Carolyn McGuire of the Salem Athenaeum for investigating their library's holdings of original editions of Alexander Pope's *Works*. I am also grateful to those who were able to give me references for Salem's historical involvement in slavery: Vincent Carretta, Thomas Knowles, Dane Morrison, Emily Murphy, Elizabeth Kenney, Kirsten Silva Gruesz, and Jessica Lanier. For information about authors like Samuel Clarke and Henry Grove who were read in the Salem Social Library, I thank Don Nichol. For references to the reading of Aphra Behn's *Oroonoko* and its adaptations in colonial America, I thank John Sullivan, Laura Mielke, and Anne Greenfield. I am also grateful to Scott B. Guthery for informing me of the digitization of the Boston Library Society's "Books Borrowed Ledger (1793–1797)" at the Boston Athenaeum, and for directing me to the pages of that ledger recording Paul Revere's borrowings. In addition, I must acknowledge that my discussion in Chapter 1 of the reception of Jonathan Swift's works in Salem, in part, was reprinted from my article in *Early American Literature*, Vol. 52, Number 2 (2017).

For Chapter 2 on Newport, Ruth S. Taylor, Bertram Lippincott III, CG, Brigitte Sullivan, and Molly Bruce Patterson were particularly helpful in helping me identify the Newport Historical Society's relevant holdings, as was John Parillo. For this chapter's argument about books in early American art, I am grateful to Philip Weimerskirch, Simone Murray, David Szewczyk, Jean Lee Cole, Eric White, Will Slauter, Beth Knazook, Steven Van Impe, Mindell Dubansky, Yuri Cowan, Barbara Hochman, Andrew Greg, Claire Bruyere, Vivienne Dunstan, Eric White, Paul Wright, Jennifer Lowe, Patrick Goossens, Maureen Mulvihill, Toni Bunch, and Karen Reeds. For help in identifying the Redwood's earliest editions of the works of Alexander Pope and Jonathan Swift, I thank Katherine Quinsey, Stephen Karian, Catherine Ingrassia, Tom Jones, Don Nicholl, Edward Griffin, Zach Hutchins, James Egan, Nicole Eustace, Anna Foy, Carla Mulford, Hugh MacDougall, Christopher Beyers, Joel Berson, Robb Haberman, Christopher Phillips, Helen Littman, and Edward White. Special thanks are due to Farley Grubb and Rob Tye for helping me to understand shipping routes and monetary flows between and across the Atlantic World. Jordan Goffin's *Atlas of the Rhode Island Book Trade* was also very helpful in my initial forays into its subject.

Erin Schreiner and Jenny Furlong of the New York Society Library were very helpful in emailing me documents and training me to use the *City Readers* database for Chapter 3 on that library. Craig Wilder was able to supply me with many references to New York's slavery history, and J. A. Downie, Kevin Jordan, and Carolyn Williams supplied me with references to scholarship on Defoe's engagement with slavery.

For Chapter 4's assessment of information on Eliza Lucas Pinckney, I thank David Dillard, Kacy Tillman, Todd Hagstette, Kathy McGill, Kirsten Iden, Kathryn Duncan, Maryann O'Donnell, Linda Troost, Darcy Fryer, Susan Parrish, Debra Ryals, Sören Fröhlich, Sharon Finch, Elizabeth Ferszt, Jodi Schorb, and Robby Koehler. That chapter is also the product of help from Anna Smith of the Charleston Library Society, who supplied me with many scans of the pages of its 1811–14 borrowing ledger. I also thank Isabelle Lehuu, who gave me references to her research on this ledger.

For Chapter 5, Carretta, Gregory Pierrot, Steven Thomas, and Nicole Aljoe were particularly helpful in my discussion of Olaudah Equiano.

For help with the cumbersome process of obtaining images and permissions for the illustrations in this book, I thank Erin Beasley of the National Portrait Gallery of the Smithsonian Museum, John Mckee, Mia Magruder Damman, Susan Stein, and Jim Dreesen of Monticello (Thomas Jefferson Foundation), Claire Blechman at the Peabody Essex Museum, Anne Marie Gallagher and Kyna Hamill of the Medford Historical Society and Museum, Jean Marie Procious and Carolyn McGuire of the Salem Athenaeum as well as Hornsby of the Phillips, Patrick Crowley and Michelle Farias of the Redwood, Carolyn Cruthirds of the Museum of Fine Arts in Boston, Tom Clark, Jessica Steytler, and Sara Trotta of the Congregational Library and Archives in Boston, Louis Jordan and Sara Weber of the Rare Books and Special Collections at the Hesburgh Libraries at the University of Notre Dame, and Ann McShane of the Library Company of Philadelphia. Jaclyn Penny of the AAS and Karie Diethorn of the National Park Service and Independence National Historic Park in Philadelphia helped me with the difficult task of tracking down a usable and rare digital image of Anthony Benezet.

My UNH colleagues on the pre-1800 British Literature faculty, Rachel Trubowitz, Doug Lanier, Cristy Beemer, Dennis Britton, Reginald Wilburn, and Samantha Seal, were very supportive of this project, not only in rearranging course schedules so that I could take the leaves necessary for it, but also in allowing me to move into Early American and Atlantic Studies. Wilburn is especially to be thanked for recommending the epigraph from W. E. B. Dubois that introduces Chapter 5. The UNH Eighteenth-Century Interdisciplinary Seminar permitted me to bring in speakers related to this book's topics and fields, and gave me the opportunity to present my fifth chapter. I would particularly like to thank seminar members Nadine Berenguier, Heidi Bostic, Willem De Vries, Michael Ferber, Jan Golinski, Edward Larkin, Janet Polasky, and Susie Wager. Matthew Wyman-McCarthy has been tremendously helpful not only in managing things at the journal *Eighteenth-Century Studies* in such a way as to permit me time to write, but also in copyediting this manuscript before I submitted it to Oxford University Press.

I am grateful to Oxford University Press editor Jacqueline Norton and her colleagues Amy Wright, Verity Rimmer, Catherine Owen, and Elakkia Bharathi, as well as copy-editors Edwin Pritchard and his wife Jackie, who have shepherded this manuscript through the publishing process.

For the child care that allowed me time to travel and to work on this manuscript from home and campus, I thank Bianca Bonani, Au Pair in America, and the staffs of Knoll-Edge Preschool and the Young Women's Christian Association (YWCA) of Newburyport, Massachusetts. My brother Frank Moore and his children Sam, Madeleine, and Anne, and my in-laws Jack and Lea Angell, also have provided support for my family's home life while I have been away. The friendship of Marcus and Amy Belanger, Mary Burke, Derek Cameron, Maurice Conroy, Nat and Elena Coughlin, Dan Edson, Richard French, Gus Harrington, John Kiernan,

Tom Lochhaas, Tom McCarty, Leon Morse, Malcolm Nason, Jerry Sullivan, Danielle Sutton, Michael Updike, and many others has been a breath of fresh air and respite from the more difficult aspects of this project.

Most of all I would like to thank my wife Jessica and children James and Nancy for their patience as I have traveled researching and writing this book.

Contents

List of Illustrations

Introduction

> There is no document of civilization which is not at the same time a document of barbarism. And just as such a document is not free of barbarism, barbarism taints also the manner in which it is transmitted from one owner to another.
>
> Walter Benjamin, "Thesis on the Philosophy of History"

Early American libraries stood at the nexus of two major branches of transatlantic commerce: the book trade and the slave trade. British book prices were so high in the eighteenth century that Jonathan Swift's *Gulliver's Travels* would have cost £85–125 in today's money, so one would have to be in the top 0.5 percent income bracket to own a collection of any size; reading literature was "elite culture with a vengeance" and not a middle-class phenomenon.[1] Consequently, colonial Americans seeking to purchase multiple books had to be quite wealthy, and as the Atlantic economic system was based on slavery, those readers most likely would be deriving their purchasing power from the trade in slaves, the products of their labor, or home-grown provisions they sold to slave plantations.[2] These colonials were aware that "the staging of reading as an act of cultural distinction" or "refinement" was a facet of art and the book market in England, and sought to replicate that refinement in North America, where slavery was more palpable. Anglo-American readers were therefore seeking "to affirm the distinctiveness of an English identity that had to account for its presence and prescience in zones of displacement and enslavement."[3] The act of reading an imported work of British literature in the colonies, accordingly, would help produce a strategic cultural difference between the white beneficiary of the slavery economy and enslaved Africans. That beneficiary's taste in reading could be one measure of his or her attitude towards racial differentiation and its justification.

This book asks how such difference is negotiated when there is evidence of a colonial taste for works on slavery, and renegotiated when it is apparent that some of these readers consumed anti-slavery texts. The practice of the material docu-

---

[1] Robert D. Hume, "The Value of Money in Eighteenth-Century England: Incomes, Prices, Buying Power—and Some Problems in Cultural Economics." *Huntington Library Quarterly* 77.4 (Winter 2014): 384–5, 415; Richard D. Altick, *The English Common Reader: A Social History of the Mass Reading Public, 1800–1900.* 2nd edn (Chicago: U Chicago P, 1998), 39, 41, 51–2.

[2] Barbara L. Solow, *The Economic Consequences of the Atlantic Slave Trade* (Lanham: Lexington Books, 2014), 47–8, 55–6.

[3] Simon Gikandi, *Slavery and the Culture of Taste* (Princeton: Princeton UP, 2011), 57, 32; Richard Bushman, *The Refinement of America: Persons, Houses, Cities* (NY: Vintage, 1993), xii.

mentation of the reading of such volumes might thereby be transformed when we begin to see slavery as both a cause of dissemination and a subject of books circulating in the eighteenth-century Atlantic world. Postcolonial book history of the kind that this study is performing, focusing both on how the dispossessed funded the British and transatlantic book market and on the reception of those books in the colonies of an empire, is therefore also a cultural history of the development of the American reader and his or her tastes *in* these material objects and their contents.

In engaging in this analysis of the American dissemination of British books, this study is intervening in this field of postcolonial book history from the perspective of Atlantic and African-American studies. This approach has its roots in D. F. McKenzie's work on the New Zealand colonial contact zone, Matt Cohen's critique of that work, and Hugh Amory's concept of "ethnobibliography" in early American material culture.[4] It is also informed by theorists like Srinivas Aravamudan, who have seen English attempts to implant Christian concepts into Hindu and Islamic scripture as part of the book history of South Asia, a "translation zone" in which cosmopolitanism or "translational transnationalism" occurs between many cultures.[5] A postcolonial, Atlantic, and African-American book history like I am imagining here, in Robert Fraser's words, is "transcending" the allocation of "writers and their texts to separate geopolitical spheres."[6] The fact that communities of readers like the English migrate into contact zones indicates that we must focus on the "power of the consumer," or reader, as an index to the portability of British taste in colonies like early North America, where print was often turned against the English diaspora by Native Americans and others.[7] Examining that reader as funded by slavery may demonstrate "the advantages to be gained from an alliance between book historians and scholars of African American cultures of print," and how such an alliance might inform critical race theory.[8]

In short, exploring slavery's relationship to early American libraries partakes of Matt Cohen's prescription that the history of the book in America should "involve the material instantiation of communication as much as its ethnohistorical context."[9] This study's documentation of how the Anglo-American reader obtained books via slavery, while performing this instantiation and contextualization, aims

---

[4] Donald F. McKenzie, *Bibliography and the Sociology of Texts* (Cambridge: Cambridge UP, 1999), 107; Matt Cohen, *The Networked Wilderness: Communicating in Early New England* (Minneapolis: U Minnesota P, 2010), 16; Hugh Amory, *Bibliography and the Book Trades: Studies in the Print Culture of Early New England*. Ed. David Hall (Philadelphia: U Pennsylvania P, 2005), 11–33.

[5] Srinivas Aravamudan, *Guru English: South Asian Religion in a Cosmopolitan Language* (Princeton: Princeton UP, 2006), 33–5; Emily Apter, *The Translation Zone: A New Comparative Literature* (Princeton: Princeton UP, 2006), 6, 87.

[6] Robert Fraser, *Book History Through Postcolonial Eyes: Rewriting the Script* (London: Routledge, 2008), 187–8.

[7] Fraser, 186; Phillip H. Round, *Removable Type: Histories of the Book in Indian Country, 1663–1880* (Chapel Hill: U North Carolina P, 2010), 5.

[8] Leon Jackson, "The Talking Book and the Talking Book Historian: African American Cultures of Print—the State of the Discipline." *Book History* 13 (2010): 292–3; Lara Langer Cohen and Jordan Alexander Stein, "Introduction: Early African American Print Culture." *Early African American Print Culture*. Eds Lara Langer Cohen and Jordan Alexander Stein (Philadelphia: U Pennsylvania P, 2012), 3.

[9] Matt Cohen, 20.

to break new ground by blending close literary analysis, an examination of slavery philanthropy's role in the history of libraries, and an interrogation of the reading patterns and tastes of men involved in slavery. In doing so, it asks how British books were received and adapted to the needs of colonial communities in the era of the American Revolution, how they influenced thinking about abolition, and how libraries helped enable civic engagement concerning these issues.

The methodological implications of this study's model of interpreting British texts read in a colonial contact zone, accordingly, are of great significance to Atlantic and early American cultural historiography. The question of how one economically interprets the archive of reading, or the question of how a scholar thinks about the historical efficacy of anti-slavery writing that counters a dominant economy and culture, affects how we tell the story of what cultural capital Americans had in the founding period, and how that capital was formative of identity. If inscription produces differentiations like race, an interrogation of how reading writes back to inscription requires that we understand the economies that supported the dissemination of the books that shaped modern ideas of race and subjectivity.[10] This understanding, in turn, helps explain why the negotiation of such differences is desirable to the tasteful purchaser and to his or her period's book market. Historians have explained that this market in printed commodities was part of a larger British and transatlantic consumer society, yet little attention has been paid to how the reader obtained the money, in this case through racial slavery, to meet prices and support the trade.[11] Whether colonists were importing books in unbound sheets, as the Library Company of Philadelphia planned for its first collection, or bound, as the Salem Social Library did with its initial purchase, costs of production and consumption remained high enough to require the support of a slavery economy.[12]

This book argues that a necessary corollary of Eric Williams's thesis that eighteenth-century slavery created the surplus capital necessary for investment in the industrial revolution of the nineteenth is that it also provided the consumer

[10] Jacques Derrida, *Of Grammatology*. Trans. Gayatri Chakravorty Spivak (Johns Hopkins UP, 1997), 44, 65.

[11] John Brewer, *The Pleasures of the Imagination: English Culture in the Eighteenth Century* (NY: Farrar Straus Giroux, 1997), 92–3; John Feather, *A History of British Publishing*. 2nd edn (London: Routledge, 2006), 51–68; T. H. Breen, "'Baubles of Britain': The American and Consumer Revolutions of the Eighteenth Centuries." *Past and Present* 119 (May 1988): 87; T. H. Breen, *The Marketplace of Revolution: How Consumer Politics Shaped American Independence* (Oxford: Oxford UP, 2004), 79–80; David Hancock, *Citizens of the World: London Merchants and the Integration of the British Atlantic Community, 1735–1785* (Cambridge: Cambridge UP, 1995), 33–4; James Raven, *London Booksellers and American Customers: Transatlantic Literary Community and the Charleston Library Society, 1748–1811* (Columbia: U South Carolina P, 2002); James Raven, "The Importation of Books in the Eighteenth Century." *A History of the Book in America, Volume 1: The Colonial Book in the Atlantic World*. Eds Hugh Amory and David Hall (Chapel Hill: U North Carolina P, 2007), 183–98; Hugh Amory, "Printing and Bookselling in New England, 1638–1713." *A History of the Book in America, Volume 1: The Colonial Book in the Atlantic World*. Eds Hugh Amory and David Hall (Chapel Hill: U North Carolina P, 2007), 83–116.

[12] Dorothy F. Grimm, "A History of the Library Company of Philadelphia, 1731–1835" (Philadelphia: U Pennsylvania dissertation, 1955), 64–5, 142–3; Dr. H. Wheatland, "Sketch of the Social and Philosophical Libraries." *Proceedings of the Essex Institute* 2 (1856–60): 142–3.

foundation for the rise of the "industrial book" as an aspect of that revolution.[13] Steam presses and other mechanical means of reproducing texts may have emerged to help disseminate books to more people at lower prices, but the capital to create those machines, and the book market into which their products were inserted, would be built on the prior slavery-for-books arrangement.[14] Even the schooling in how to use books—literacy—was in many cases funded by the Atlantic slavery economy because America's earliest colleges and universities were attended and endowed by people with investments in that economy.[15] This study of the transatlantic book trade of the eighteenth century, in the period in Britain when there was an expansion of print due to the lapsing of censorship restrictions and technological developments in hand-printing, therefore places slavery as a historical pillar for the international book market that we have today.

Establishing this fact by reference to every transatlantic book transaction in this era is impossible, which is why the parameters of this monograph are narrowly focused on what America's five major pre-revolutionary proprietary subscription libraries can teach us about these foundations. These "social libraries" exemplified and displayed the intellectual, cultural, and social capital created by slavery, and we can cross-reference their proprietors' reading habits with their activities in the slave trade and related businesses like shipbuilding, tobacco, sugar, molasses, and rum. This process also reveals that it was not only these agricultural and industrial activities that were brought into being by the trade; colonial professionals' paperwork of news, insurance, banking, and law was also connected to slavery-related commerce. The books in these libraries created "reading networks," or what reader-response theorist Stanley Fish calls "interpretive communities," within these central spaces of reading for Atlantic port cities engaged in transoceanic commerce.[16] In such communities, texts are not as important as readers; "there are no fixed texts, only interpretive strategies for reading them"; those strategies are "not natural, but learned"; "meanings are not extracted but made"; and these meanings are created by a reading network like the library's proprietors.[17] The remarkable consistency, across all five libraries, of which titles were most frequently stocked and borrowed indicates that the period's imported British books were not only creating reading networks in their individual cities, but also a shared English-speaking imagined community across the Eastern seaboard. These libraries thus serve as examples of Michael Warner's observation that the early American reader saw him- or herself

[13] Eric Williams, *Capitalism and Slavery* (Chapel Hill: U North Carolina P, 1944), 98–107; David Finkelstein and Alistair McCleery, *An Introduction to Book History* (London: Routledge, 2005), 78–80; Scott E. Casper, Jeffrey D. Groves, Stephen W. Nissenbaum, and Michael Winship, eds, *A History of the Book in America, Volume 3: The Industrial Book, 1840–1880* (Chapel Hill: U North Carolina P, 2007), 4.

[14] Abigail Williams, *The Social Life of Books: Reading Together in the Eighteenth-Century Home* (New Haven: Yale UP, 2017), 98.

[15] Craig Steven Wilder, *Ebony and Ivy: Race, Slavery, and the Troubled History of America's Universities* (NY: Bloomsbury P, 2013).

[16] Jana Smith Elford, "Recovering Women's History with Network Analysis: A Case Study of the Fabian News." *The Journal of Modern Periodical Studies* 6.2 (2015): 198–208; Stanley Fish, "Interpreting the Variorum." *Critical Inquiry* 2.3 (Spring 1976): 484–5.

[17] Fish, 484–5.

"becoming part of an arena of the national people that cannot be realized except through such mediating imaginings" as books.[18] Early American libraries, in short, were crucial to the intellectual and ideological formation of the continental network that was to become the Republic.

It is not possible to overstate the significance of these centers of reading to the consolidation of the economic, cultural, and political leadership of the colonies and the wider Atlantic world. The "library books represented an important thread in the social fabric and helped cement the social elite of the seaport city," creating a common set of values, assumptions, and, at the very least, topics of conversation that served to reinforce the shared economic interests of library proprietors.[19] Being accepted as a member of one of the libraries, and being able to afford a share and pay periodic fines and assessments, was a sign of one's citizenship in such an elite. In South Carolina, where a share in the library cost a whopping £50 (about $10,000 in today's money), "membership secured entry into the ruling class of Charleston." In Massachusetts, the first proprietary subscription library was considered a "veritable Social Register of Salem."[20] In this regard, the prestige of belonging to one of these American institutions mirrored developments within Britain itself, where library membership had become a sign of respectability.[21] Early American libraries, in short, were "philanthropic but exclusive" in their capacity as "elite institutions promoting a liberality that also represented freedom from material need."[22] Slavery, ironically, created that freedom for shareholders, enabling them to become philanthropists to the learned societies, schools, and other organizations that served them and their families.

An example of this development is the Social Library of tiny Portsmouth, New Hampshire, which was founded in 1750 by thirty-four such men. The town had been involved in the slave trade since the middle of the seventeenth century, and by 1750, it traded in slave-grown crops from the Caribbean like sugar, and some Portsmouth families even owned plantations there and in South America.[23] This commerce contributed to the wealth of merchants so much that it is unsurprising that all but one of the library's founders were the town's top taxpayers.[24] The town's reliance on slavery-related commerce is evident in the fact that Parliament's Sugar Act of 1764, a tax on certain West Indian sugar transactions, caused a local

---

[18] Michael Warner, *The Letters of the Republic: Publication and the Public Sphere in Eighteenth-Century America* (Cambridge: Harvard UP, 1990), xiii.

[19] Isabelle Lehuu, "Reconstructing Reading Vogues in the Old South: Borrowings from the Charleston Library Society, 1811–1817." *The History of Reading, Volume 1: International Perspectives, c.1500–1900*. Eds Shafquat Towheed and W. R. Owens (London: Palgrave Macmillan, 2011), 79.

[20] Lehuu, 65; cited in James Raven, "Social Libraries and Library Societies in Eighteenth-Century North America." *Institutions of Reading: The Social Life of Libraries in the United States.* Eds Thomas Augst and Kenneth Carpenter (Amherst: U Massachusetts P, 2007), 34.

[21] David Allan, *A Nation of Readers: The Lending Library in Georgian England* (London: The British Library, 2008), 70–1.

[22] Raven, "Social," 29, 50.

[23] Mark J. Sammons and Valerie Cunningham, *Black Portsmouth: Three Centuries of African-American Heritage* (Durham: U New Hampshire P, 2004), 16–17.

[24] Jim Piecuch, "Of Great Importance Both to Civil and Religious Welfare': The Portsmouth Social Library, 1750–1786." *Historical New Hampshire* 57 (2002): 67.

recession, as did the decline of such commerce during the War of 1812.[25] Unlike most libraries, this library's books weren't used much, as membership in it was "primarily a community status symbol."[26] Members were so reluctant to admit new members to their elite circle that they would often raise the price of a share in the library to unattainable heights; they were as interested in "black-balling" new membership applications to "maintain exclusivity" and their cultural leadership as their counterparts in British proprietary subscription libraries.[27] Even after the Social Library closed in 1786 and the Portsmouth Athenaeum opened in 1817, three-quarters of the latter institution's proprietors were in the top 10 percent of taxpayers.[28] The Athenaeum, consequently, "gained a solid claim on the attention and affections of almost all of Portsmouth's wealthiest merchants."[29] As this book argues through its close-reading of archival evidence of the business affairs, consumer habits, and reading patterns of the proprietors of the five major libraries, this creation of exclusive learned and social institutions, serving an incestuous white elite made wealthy by slavery, was even truer in the most prominent American port cities.

The libraries thus served an important social, cultural, and civic function, creating a network of leaders who would become patriots or loyalists in the Revolution, providing the reading matter that would constitute them intellectually and ideologically, and planting the seeds for discourse on the slavery that facilitated early American cultural capitalization. This study examines these developments by reference to the deeply interrelated problems of possessive individualism and slavery in Anglo-American political thought. It also investigates the motives and means for American participation in the British consumer revolution and book market, the history of American reading, and the rise of Atlantic abolitionism. In doing so, it focuses on the colonial consumption of volumes of British literature as the foundation of American cultural history, demonstrating how the empire's preoccupation with its economic underpinnings was worked out in the genres of drama, poetry, and fiction. That this history is rooted in slavery-financed institutions like universities and libraries, and is itself a legacy of the eighteenth century's attempt to divorce the spheres of the aesthetic, literary, and cultural from that of the economic, affects how we read literature and constitute it as a discipline today.

CIVIC ENGAGEMENT, POLITICAL THOUGHT, AND POSSESSIVE INDIVIDUALISM IN A SLAVERY SOCIETY

Slavery was not only funding the libraries and book collections themselves, but also their proprietors' civic engagement, particularly around the discourses and

---

[25] Piecuch, 78; Michael A. Baenen, "Books, Newspapers, and Sociability in the Making of the Portsmouth Athenaeum." *The New England Quarterly* 76.3 (Sept. 2003): 388.

[26] Piecuch, 82, 76.

[27] Mark Towsey and Kyle B. Roberts, "Introduction." *Before the Public Library: Reading, Community, and Identity in the Atlantic World, 1650–1850*. Eds Mark Towsey and Kyle B. Roberts (Leiden: Brill, 2017), 8–9.

[28] Baenen, 390.   [29] Baenen, 392, 398.

events surrounding the American Revolution. Members of the Portsmouth Social Library and Athenaeum served on the governor's council, in the legislative assembly, and as aldermen both before and after the Revolution. This pattern was similar to that in the rest of the colonies, where only propertied white men would be allowed to vote and serve in such offices. In this political activity, some patriotic and some loyalist, colonial leaders were aided, ironically, by those very same British books that the libraries and bookseller-printers supplied. For example, one of the most popular, easily accessible vernacular books on liberty and rights in the colonies was Henry Care's *English Liberties: or, the Freeborn Subject's Inheritance.* An American edition of it published in 1774 by John Carter of Providence was his bestselling book, with thirty-eight copies sold to Rhode Islanders in 1774 and 1775, complementing at least one prior English edition sold as early as 1769.[30] This book contained reprints and commentary on many English legal texts that would become patriotic emblems, including the Magna Carta, the Charter of the Forest, and the Habeas Corpus Act. It also contained histories of the Ship Money controversy, of the privileges and elections of parliaments, of the Civil War and 1688 Revolution settlement outlining the relationship of Crown and Parliament in the seventeenth century, and of "the liberties of the subject."[31] Given that it also contained texts on the practical application of the law, explaining how Justices of the Peace and coroners should function, in addition to legal and theoretical readings, Care's book was basically a handbook on how to perform civic engagement in the English-speaking world. Often, *English Liberties* was ordered together with school books, law books like Blackstone's *Commentaries on the Laws of England*, and Oliver Goldsmith's *The Vicar of Wakefield*, indicating that the ideation of what rights an English colonist should expect was packaged for colonists together with law and literature explicating them.

This American "Britishness" in the area of rights and liberties should therefore not be surprising when we see that a figure like the "Goose Creek planter and patriot John Mackenzie" of South Carolina, who bequeathed his books to the Charleston Library Society, was described at his death as "'that jealous, disinterested and unshaken Patriot—that true Friend to *America* and the *English Constitution.*'"[32] Patriotic Americans saw no inconsistency between their advocacy for, and action on behalf of, their own country and their upholding of the English constitutional rights and values that they felt a corrupt, London-based empire had abandoned. Indeed, up until the Revolution, they had developed, in Mary Bilder's words, a "transatlantic constitution" in which they would pass laws for themselves as long as they were not "repugnant" to the laws of Great Britain.[33] Slavery might be regarded as a central example of how the laws of colonies like Virginia might

---

[30] John Carter ledger #1 1768–1775. Rhode Island Historical Society, Providence, Rhode Island. RIHS MSS 336 Vol. 2.

[31] Henry Care, *English Liberties, or, the Freeborn Subject's Inheritance* (Providence: Carter, 1774), title page.

[32] Raven, *London*, 35, 156.

[33] Mary Sarah Bilder, *The Transatlantic Constitution: Colonial Legal Culture and the Empire* (Cambridge: Harvard UP, 2004), 1–11.

differ from the laws of Britain. But in general, even the most patriotic Americans believed themselves to be operating in an English jurisprudence from which they would occasionally diverge on the basis of different "histories, local economies, and social structures."[34] Americans, in short, wanted the same rights that their English brethren had in a manner that paralleled their pursuit of the right to be the same kind of consumers, and imported books were both products to buy in that British and transatlantic consumer society and bearers of ideas about those rights. Slavery, however, as it did for Mackenzie, was funding their participation in that consumer society, its marketplace of books and ideas, and the very economy that their quest for British legal, political, and governmental rights was seeking to protect.

Indeed, as Edmund Morgan pointed out long ago in his study of the British political thought appropriated for American uses by prominent Virginians of the period, the patriots were paradoxically asking for a republican form of freedom from Britain for themselves while enslaving three-fifths of their population.[35] They "cherished civic freedom as a central value," writes Robin Blackburn. "That this English freedom coexisted with, or even depended upon, colonial slavery was a paradox rarely addressed."[36] As Christopher Leslie Brown has observed, British counter-propagandists were quick to point out the "self-evident hypocrisy of American slaveholders," helping them "fix the meaning of such contested terms as *slavery* and *liberty* in ways that validated British rule and invalidated colonial resistance."[37]

Morgan's paradox of white Americans claiming English liberties for themselves while enslaving Africans has been expanded upon more recently by Blackburn and Gerald Horne. They have argued that what patriots were trying to preserve in their conservative "counter-revolution of 1776" were the civic privileges—like voting and serving in office—that slave ownership, inasmuch as it meant both chattel and real property rights in land, conferred upon them. Abolition "was rising in London not least because Britain was becoming increasingly dependent on African soldiers and sailors."[38] Legal cases such as the Somerset case, in which the Chief Justice of the King's Bench, Lord Mansfield, ruled that a slave who escaped to British soil would be free, began to be seen by Americans as a threat to their economy and privileges. This case "unnerved the powerful slaveholders of North America—and was followed by others—all of which aided in lighting a fuse of revolt that detonated on 4 July 1776."[39] At stake was their understanding of citizenship or subjectivity, built on the British model that the imported books that they were imbibing sketched out.

[34] Bilder, 6.

[35] Edmund Morgan, *American Slavery, American Freedom: The Ordeal of Colonial Virginia* (NY: Norton, 1975), 4–6.

[36] Robin Blackburn, *The American Crucible: Slavery, Emancipation and Human Rights* (London: Verso, 2011), 145.

[37] Christopher Leslie Brown, *Moral Capital: Foundations of British Abolitionism* (Chapel Hill: U North Carolina P, 2006), 126.

[38] Gerald Horne, *The Counter-revolution of 1776: Slave Resistance and the Origins of the United States of America* (NY: NYU P, 2014), 9, 11; Blackburn, 134.

[39] Horne, 2; Blackburn, 134.

By the American inheritance of their colonial customs about law, property, political theory, and history up until the Revolution, this understanding meant that slave ownership was that which was constitutive of the virtuous white male subject or citizen. The British ideology of republicanism that inspired patriots, accordingly, may have become altered when transplanted into a continuously slavery-based economy that had governed social life since English settlement. This is not to overstate the case for American exceptionalism in this matter—there is every reason to believe that people in Britain who shared their library-building pursuits, particularly in slave-trading centers like Liverpool and Bristol, also were developing the same attitudes.[40] It was the War of Independence, however, that made the American case different, as slavery was not only at the root of their reading about English liberties, as it was in Britain, but also a reason for their rebellion that would go on to influence the founding documents of the Revolution and Early Republic.

Slavery is therefore the ghost that stalks the study of the history of eighteenth-century Anglo-American political thought. Theories of republicanism that have dominated this field of study for fifty years, such as Caroline Robbins's *The Eighteenth-Century Commonwealthman*, Bernard Bailyn's *The Ideological Origins of the American Revolution*, and J. G. A. Pocock's *Virtue, Commerce, and History*, have found this property basis for citizenship in a classical civic humanist tradition. As Pocock summarized, contemporaries located English citizenship in an "ancient constitution" in which "the form determining politics was land, whose stability—as opposed to the mobility of goods and money—set men free to be the rational political creatures which they were by nature" (Pocock, 61). Accordingly, says Pocock, they idealized the yeoman farmer on his freehold of a small portion of land as the ideal of virtuous citizenship. These three scholars, in advocating for a disinterested and communitarian form of citizenship nonetheless based on land ownership and agrarian "civic virtue," were reacting to a prevailing consensus of the middle of the twentieth century. This doctrine was that the dominant understanding of political personhood in the period was a "Lockean liberal" one in which individualism and self-interest were formative of political communities. According to Bailyn, American patriots had the classics, the thinkers of the European Enlightenment, and "the great figures of England's legal history" to help them articulate a very different form of government than one based on individualism. They also had New England Puritans' political and social theories, and, most of all, seventeenth- and eighteenth-century British political philosophy "at their fingertips" to support their ideation of what would become a republican form of citizenship.[41]

The crisis of the Revolution had brought these various strands of thought together, a development, I will argue, that was the consequence of the transatlantic book market on the eve of the Revolution. Republicanism was made thinkable in

[40] David Allan, *A Nation of Readers: The Lending Library in Georgian England* (London: The British Library, 2008), 62, 66, 79, 91, 99; Mark Towsey and Kyle B. Roberts, "Introduction." *Before the Public Library: Reading, Community, and Identity in the Atlantic World, 1650–1850.* Eds Mark Towsey and Kyle B. Roberts (Leiden: Brill, 2017), 3–10.

[41] Bernard Bailyn, *The Ideological Origins of the American Revolution* (Cambridge: Harvard UP, 1992), 22–54.

America due to "the spread of independent landholding" and a "broad electorate" due to that ownership. The availability and possession of land created "the moral basis of a healthy, liberty-preserving polity" that "seemed already to exist in the unsophisticated lives of the independent, uncorrupted, landowning yeoman farmers who comprised so large a part of the colonial population."[42] The consensus of Robbins, Pocock, and Bailyn, accordingly, was that eighteenth-century republicans had an agrarian vision of who the virtuous citizen would be, and that this vision could be realized, perhaps only, in North America. In this view, early American libraries would be venues for reading eighteenth-century republican political thought without regard to slavery.

Now, however, "The Robbins/Pocock/Bailyn thesis...has itself hardened into an orthodoxy as stultifying as the paradigm which it unseated."[43] In attempting to decouple the political ideology of the eighteenth century from its economic basis to the extent that it could be reclassified as political "thought," this orthodoxy had an "'ideological' axe to grind" itself.[44] Separating politics from economics was itself an ideological act, and though claiming to contextualize Enlightenment ideas, this school often overlooked the actual economic activities—such as slaveholding and slave trading—in which political actors and thinkers were engaged that might characterize them as less than "virtuous." The immediate target of these scholars was the work of C. B. MacPherson, who, at about the same time, had written a social history of ideas that successfully synthesized the period's political ideology with its pursuit of individual wealth through a critique of Lockean liberalism from the democratic socialist perspective.

The MacPherson thesis is centrally relevant to slavery in that it posits that modern individuality is derived from proprietorship of one's person and labor, ownership that slaves did not have. MacPherson explains that seventeenth-century political philosophers from Thomas Hobbes, to James Harrington, to the Levellers, and to John Locke argued that Englishmen were living in a "possessive market society" in which an individual's labor was a commodity and therefore his property before he sold it.[45] Locke's *Two Treatises of Government*, for MacPherson, was the culmination of this thought, establishing that labor was both the unquestionable property of the individual and alienable or exchangeable in possessive market society.[46] Crucially, however, Locke removes natural law limits on the accumulation of private property, and eliminates any debt that the laborer has to society for the skills that go into that labor or its products, and the laborer joins with others in a social contract to defend and expand that property.[47] In short, in MacPherson's reading of the history of seventeenth- and eighteenth-century

[42] Bailyn, 51–2.

[43] Pamela Edwards, *The Statesman's Science: History, Nature, and Law in the Political Thought of Samuel Taylor Coleridge* (NY: Columbia UP, 2004), 6.

[44] Edwards, 6.

[45] C. B. MacPherson, *The Political Theory of Possessive Individualism: Hobbes to Locke*. Ed. Frank Cunningham (Oxford: Oxford UP, 2011), 48.

[46] MacPherson, 239.   [47] MacPherson, 199, 221, 269.

British political theory, "To be an individual is to be an owner."[48] The consequence for law is that "Locke's constitutionalism is essentially a defence of the supremacy of property—and not that of the yeoman only, but more especially that of the men of substance to whom the security of unlimited accumulation was of first importance."[49] The Lockean social contract, therefore, is "a defence of the rights of expanding property rather than of the rights of the individual against the state."[50] As Eric Slauter has contended, this very problem of the preservation and expansion of individual property ownership was at the cultural origins of the social contract known as the United States Constitution.[51] In MacPherson's view, then, it would be appropriate to ask how the accumulation of books of political thought in early American libraries was connected to slavery. He would consider it entirely natural to ask how the reading of that political thought by slaveholders in those libraries may have aided arguments for the preservation of slavery as that which enabled possessive individualists to keep accumulating.

There has been considerable debate about the influence of Locke on the political theory of the Revolution, some of which echoes the Robbins/Bailyn/Pocock critique of MacPherson's possessive individualism thesis. Much of it, however, partakes of a broader philosophical dispute over MacPherson's presentist projection of his own middle-twentieth-century liberal concern for "democratizing the present" onto the past.[52] It takes issue with his selective use of early English political thought to focus on the problems of labor and individualism (more the products, they say, of the later Adam Smith and Karl Marx). It also objects to his idealism in suggesting that democratic socialism and other liberal means of resolving inequality are possible, and outlines numerous other problems with his theory.[53]

A central objection from critics inspired by Michel Foucault is that early modern political thought was about the "nature of political (not economic) power" and not about "the economic conception of the self" that MacPherson posits.[54] Consequently, they contend that MacPherson's anachronism is also taking for granted a more voluntary system of labor than that which really existed within the

---

[48] Joseph Carens, "Possessive Individualism and Democratic Theory: MacPherson's Legacy." *Democracy and Possessive Individualism: The Intellectual Legacy of C.B. MacPherson.* Ed. Joseph H. Carens (Albany: SUNY P, 1993), 2.

[49] MacPherson, 257–8.

[50] John Locke, *Two Treatises of Government.* Ed. Peter Laslett (Cambridge: Cambridge UP, 1996), 353; MacPherson, 257.

[51] Eric Slauter, *The State as a Work of Art: The Cultural Origins of the Constitution* (Chicago: U Chicago P, 2009), 223, 232.

[52] John Keane, "Stretching the Limits of the Democratic Imagination." *Democracy and Possessive Individualism: The Intellectual Legacy of C.B. MacPherson.* Ed. Joseph H. Carens (Albany: SUNY P, 1993), 108.

[53] James Tully, "The Possessive Individualism Thesis: A Reconsideration in the Light of Recent Scholarship." *Democracy and Possessive Individualism: The Intellectual Legacy of C. B. MacPherson.* Ed. Joseph H. Carens (Albany: SUNY P, 1993), 24–31; Keane, 108; William Leiss, "The End of History and Its Beginning Again; or, The Not-Quite-Yet Human Stage of Human History." *Democracy and Possessive Individualism: The Intellectual Legacy of C. B. MacPherson.* Ed. Joseph H. Carens (Albany: SUNY P, 1993), 265; Jane Mansbridge, "MacPherson's Neglect of the Political." *Democracy and Possessive Individualism: The Intellectual Legacy of C. B. MacPherson.* Ed. Joseph H. Carens (Albany: SUNY P, 1993), 155.

[54] Tully, 26–7.

mercantilist economic policies of the time. They argue that, in fact, it was to the *Two Treatises'* conception of the voluntary surrender of one's labor, over which one was said to have rights, which critics of capitalism turned.[55] Civic humanist scholars of republicanism in the Robbins/Pocock/Bailyn camp claim that MacPherson was anachronistic in thinking that eighteenth-century ideas of an "independent economic realm" were true in the seventeenth century's "authoritative allocation of work by government." Therefore "liberalism is a tradition which emerged in the eighteenth, not the seventeenth, century."[56] MacPherson, they say, does not realize that eighteenth-century writers were theorizing a divide between "an economic realm and a political-civil realm."[57] In keeping with their interest in divorcing politics from economics, these scholars contend that Hobbes and Locke were usually left out of the language of contemporary reflections on capitalism. The kinds of regulation characteristic of seventeenth-century mercantilism, they argue, gave way to a more private and self-regulating commercial society in which "the practices of the division of labor in economic, political, and military life" led to greater political stability.[58] In sum, these critics of the possessive individualism thesis attempt to prove that MacPherson's utopian theory may have been appropriate at his moment of publication, but that the time of liberalism's three main branches— liberal, socialist, and national liberation—is over and that those possibilities have been "unmasked" as "illusions."[59]

The history of the application of the MacPherson thesis to the study of the ideological origins of the American Revolution, particularly in regards to the influence of Locke, has not been without controversy, though recently there has been a trend of recuperating Locke's influence and the theory of possessive individualism. Until the middle of the twentieth century, "the prevailing scholarly consensus suggested that we needn't go beyond the *Second Treatise* in order to understand American Revolutionary Thought."[60] Then, however, revisionist historians like Bailyn, Pocock, Stanley Katz, and John Dunn preferred to see the civic republicanism of figures like the Trenchard and Gordon of *Cato's Letters*—libertarian advocates for limited government and the virtuous citizenship of landowners—as more dominant than Lockean liberalism. They suggested that Locke was a negligible influence at best, and perhaps "the Revolution's foremost ideological nemesis."[61] There has been, however, a "comeback" of Locke and liberalism in the late twentieth and early twenty-first centuries by the recuperative school: scholars like Lee Ward, Steven Dworetz, Joyce Appleby, Isaac Kramnick, Thomas Pangle, John Patrick Diggins, and John Simmons.[62] Most of these scholars, particularly Dworetz and Pangle, argue that the heroes of civic republican theorists like Trenchard and

---

[55] Tully, 32, 34.   [56] Tully, 38.   [57] Tully, 39.
[58] Tully, 35, 36.   [59] Leiss, 265.

[60] Steven Dworetz, " 'See Locke on Government': The Two Treatises and the American Revolution." *Studies in Eighteenth Century Culture* 21 (1992): 101–27, 101 n. 1.

[61] Dworetz, 101–2.

[62] Lee Ward, *The Politics of Liberty in England and Revolutionary America* (Cambridge: Cambridge UP, 2004), 1–6.

Gordon were actually Lockeans because the topics on which they dwelled—liberty, taxation, and consent—are drawn from Locke's treatises on government.[63]

For both the revisionists and some members of the recuperative school, however, MacPherson's theory of Lockean possessive individualism was anathema. Dworetz claims that the reason that the revisionists could credibly make their claim is rooted in their response to their immediate predecessors in political theory, MacPherson and Leo Strauss. The two of them had a "hostile interpretation of Locke, seeing his liberalism at its worst, as 'possessive individualism' and the corrupt apology for the 'spirit of capitalism.'"[64] Yet Dworetz, too, rejects the MacPherson thesis, saying that chapter 5 of the *Second Treatise*—the one on property—was rarely cited by the patriots, so "the Revolutionists did not call upon the bourgeois Locke to justify unlimited appropriation."[65]

Most of the recuperative school, however, concurs with MacPherson. Appleby, in particular, sees in the ideological origins of the Revolution "the rise of the thoroughly Lockean liberal philosophy of individualism and capitalism."[66] Kramnick identified a liberal strain in American political thought from the 1760s onwards, and Diggins "firmly confirms the centrality of Locke's teaching of economic individualism for the shaping of American political discourse."[67] In short, it seems that most of these disciples of the recuperation of the liberal Locke, excluding Dworetz and perhaps Simmons, embrace the possessive individualism thesis.[68] It is not ahistorical to make this claim, as Jack Greene, in his "social simplification" formulation, has contended that, particularly after 1760, the evidence indicates that colonists were valuing, above all, individualism and personal acquisition.[69] The recuperative school's view of MacPherson's relevance to the American revolutionary context also has been affirmed by Barbara Arneil, who writes that though the "historical realities of seventeenth-century England" made possessive individualism difficult to actualize there, those obstacles "are overcome by the very close and tangible connection between Locke and the American plantation."[70] Indeed, the reading of Locke on such a plantation, and in the early proprietary subscription libraries, may have amounted to an embrace of his endorsement of the view of property ethically enabling possessive individualism.

This slave plantation context, the economic enabler of unlimited individual accumulation, may be the best evidence for possessive individualism as a major motive for revolution. The centrality of this context has been affirmed by David Armitage, who cites a provision from Locke's *Fundamental Constitutions of Carolina* that declares that "Every Freeman of Carolina shall have absolute power and Authority over his Negro slaves of what opinion or Religion soever."[71] The plantation context

---

[63] Dworetz, 102.   [64] Dworetz, 102–3.   [65] Dworetz, 105.

[66] Ward, 5.   [67] Ward, 5–6.

[68] John Simmons, *The Lockean Theory of Rights* (Princeton: Princeton UP, 1992), 302.

[69] Jack P. Greene, *Pursuits of Happiness: The Social Development of Early Modern British Colonies and the Formation of American Culture* (Chapel Hill: U North Carolina P, 1988), 167–8.

[70] Barbara Arneil, *John Locke and America: The Defence of English Colonialism* (Oxford: Clarendon P, 1996), 209.

[71] David Armitage, "John Locke, Carolina, and the *Two Treatises of Government*." *Political Theory* 32.5 (Oct. 2004): 609.

of Locke's thinking about property, due to his work as a secretary and treasurer for South Carolina proprietors like his patron, the Earl of Shaftesbury, was foremost in his mind in the summer of 1682 when he was writing both the *Constitutions* and the property chapter of the *Two Treatises*.[72] "There is therefore no mistaking either his tacit commitment to this brutal provision," Armitage writes, "or to the hold the master–slave relationship had over his political imagination both before and during the composition and revision of the *Two Treatises*."[73] This relationship was also in the imaginations of many early Americans, particularly in the South, and especially in South Carolina. Indeed, one of the Charleston Library Society's principal proprietors, Henry Laurens (see Figure 0.1), spoke of himself as " 'an absolute monarch' who governed 'his subjects' with an iron fist hidden in a velvet glove. Designating himself as a king, Laurens felt obliged to behave accordingly, fashioning his conduct in a style befitting such an exalted position."[74] This governmental and civil sense of

Figure 0.1 *Henry Laurens* (1724–92). By John Singleton Copley (1782). Oil on canvas. National Portrait Gallery, Smithsonian Institution; gift of the A.W. Mellon Educational and Charitable Trust, 1942.

[72] Armitage, 615–16.   [73] Armitage, 619.
[74] Edward Pearson, " 'Planters Full of Money': The Self-Fashioning of South Carolina's Plantation Society." *Money, Trade, and Power: The Evolution of South Carolina's Plantation Society*. Eds Jack P. Greene, Rosemary Brana-Shute, and Randy J. Sparks (Columbia: U South Carolina P, 2001), 301.

the self was being produced, in part, by the books and reading of the proprietary subscription libraries like that of Charleston to the extent that some proprietors were quite conscious that their civic engagement in the Revolution was for the purpose of tyrannizing over their slaves. It follows that those who by the Revolution embraced Locke's property doctrine were leaning on him to help legitimize their already-existing slave constitutions as well as absolutist control over the people whose labor financed their sophistication and political behavior.

In short, the African slave was *the* property that created the sovereign, virtuous agrarian white civic republican. Therefore, there appears to be justification for arguing that the modern European and American self was economically constructed rather than purely politically constituted in the manner imagined by Foucauldians. This position is not necessarily inconsistent with that of the civic humanists, who see that "landed property provides the independence necessary for citizenship" in republicanism and that therefore property was the basis of the political personality.[75] The existence of slave-owning civic republicans like Thomas Jefferson proves this point (see Figure 0.2). The difference between this position

Figure 0.2 *Portrait of John Locke* (1632–1704). 1789 copy by Stewart (or "Stuart") after Sir Godfrey Kneller (1646–1723), photography by Edward Owen. © Thomas Jefferson Foundation at Monticello.

[75] Tully, 34.

and that of the civic humanists, however, lies in how it connects political expression to the standing in possessive market society of those articulating it. The problem is that the civic humanists, by focusing solely on the discourse of the period's political philosophers and the contextual texts surrounding their books, have taken them at their word.

Philosophers of this period like them, as Simon Gikandi has written, were engaged in an effort to "quarantine one aspect of social life—the tasteful, the beautiful, and the civil—from a public domain saturated by diverse forms of commerce, including the sale of black bodies."[76] If we divorce the period's political discourse from its economy, then we fail to see that "the project of modernity was premised on the search for rules in which the larger concerns of the world, including the slavery that reached its zenith in the period of the Enlightenment, would be sublimated to an idealistic structure."[77] British political thought was attempting to make such rules to govern social relationships; however, it is the job of the scholar to archaeologically recover how those relationships were constructed, and who was included in them. Slaves, clearly, were not included in the community imagined by most of these thinkers or by current civic humanist historians, a fact that puts pressure on the civic republican consensus in such a way as to validate the possessive individualism thesis's reconciliation of the period's political ideology with its economic realities. In this view, the eighteenth-century America of "virtuous" agrarian citizens was the template upon which this slavery-based republican subjectivity and its capacity for unlimited accumulation could be actualized. Westward expansion and slavery, exemplified as early as in the seventeenth-century colonial charters and as late as in Jefferson's Louisiana Purchase, intimated the possibility of unlimited acquisition of land and people.

It is in the discipline of English and American Literature that this interpretation of the slavery basis for the property constituting the eighteenth-century republican citizen has gained the most legitimacy, for scholars of literature, unlike the dissenters from MacPherson's view among historians, have never given up on the possessive individualism thesis. For example, Judith Butler and Athena Athanasiou recently have critiqued the idea that Lockean possessive individualism—proprietorship—has provided the legitimacy of the modern subject by discussing dispossession, or the loss of personal property, as a form of social death. Dispossession, for them, incorporates, among other things, "ownership of one's living body by another person, as in histories of slavery," an observation relevant to many other forms of dispossession involving race, gender, sexuality, and nationality.[78] Christian Ravela recently has explained Butler and Athanasiou's position, writing that "the ideology of possessive individualism worked to simultaneously occlude the subject's constitutive interdependence and historically rationalize dispossession in settler colonial regimes."[79] Possessive individualism may be a philosophy that is the very constituent of the

---

[76] Gikandi, 6.   [77] Gikandi, 7.

[78] Judith Butler and Athena Athanasiou, *Dispossession: The Performative in the Political* (Cambridge: Polity P, 2013), 2.

[79] Christian Ravela, "'Turning Out' Possessive Individualism: Freedom and Belonging in Samuel R. Delany's *The Man Man*." *Modern Fiction Studies* 62.1 (Spring 2016): 92.

apology for the modern nation and empire; "possessive individualism works ideologically to naturalize the state's maintenance of unequal property relations by rendering the state's protection of property as both natural and universally ethical, even though those property relations formed out of histories of dispossession."[80] *Bildungsromane* novels like Daniel Defoe's *Robinson Crusoe* and Samuel Richardson's *Pamela*—stories of individual growth over time—have linked property to citizenship and belonging.[81] The slave, of course, is left out of this belonging; indeed, as in Robinson Crusoe's slave Friday, he may be the property formative of that sovereign individual.

Accordingly, Butler, Athanasiou, and Ravela are drawing on a long tradition of critique in which MacPherson's possessive individualism thesis has been central to our understanding of eighteenth-century literature, particularly of the rise of the novel. As early as 1957, Ian Watt argued that the new Lockean mode of subjectivity was modeled on eighteenth-century possessive individualist characters like Robinson Crusoe and Pamela, as their life stories reveal them to be successful acquisitors of capital and social mobility.[82] There was some dissent from this view by critics like Max Novak and John Richetti, but as several of this book's chapters cite, many of the most current eighteenth-century critics take the concept of possessive individualism for granted as one of the most well-established prisms through which to examine the period's literature.[83]

Lynn Festa, for example, sees in the period's autobiographies a patterning of "the proprietary possessive individual."[84] Most recently, Ramesh Mallipeddi has shown Crusoe to have "a privatized, hermetic possessive individualism" and Olaudah Equiano to be one who "overcomes dispossession by becoming a possessive individual."[85] As this book argues, because "the specific, developed, individualized identity of the teller" of the stories in eighteenth-century novels like *Robinson Crusoe* "becomes the subject of the book," and "novels' characters become the imaginative resources on which readers drew to make themselves individuals," early American readers, like the British ones these critics discuss, were patterning their behavior around imported British literature.[86] As Chapter 3 of this book explains, their quest for the unlimited accumulation of capital and things for themselves through enslaving others, consequently, seems to be the most obvious behavioral trait American republicans shared with the fictional Crusoe. This study

---

[80] Ravela, 94.   [81] Ravela, 93–4.

[82] Ian Watt, *The Rise of the Novel: Studies in Defoe, Richardson and Fielding* (Berkeley: U California P, 1957), 65, 170, 174.

[83] Maxmillian Novak, "Robinson Crusoe's Original Sin." *SEL* 1.3 (1961): 19–29; John Richetti, *Philosophical Writing: Locke, Berkeley, Hume* (Cambridge: Harvard UP, 1983), 29; John Richetti, "Introduction." *Cambridge Companion to the Eighteenth-Century Novel*. Ed. John Richetti (Cambridge: Cambridge UP, 1996), 8.

[84] Lynn Festa. *Sentimental Figures of Empire in Eighteenth-Century Britain and France* (Johns Hopkins UP, 2006), 134.

[85] Ramesh Mallipeddi, *Spectacular Suffering: Witnessing Slavery in the Eighteenth-Century Atlantic* (Charlottesville: U Virginia P, 2016), 204–5, 183.

[86] J. Paul Hunter, *Before Novels: The Cultural Contexts of Eighteenth-Century Fiction*. (NY: Norton, 1992), 327; Deidre Lynch, *The Economy of Character: Novels, Market Culture, and the Business of Inner Meaning* (Chicago: U Chicago P, 1998), 126.

is therefore claiming that eighteenth-century British fiction, poetry, and drama was popular among early Americans because it was not only validating their behavior, but also creating models of individuals who were negotiating the early capitalism of the Atlantic slavery economy, in some cases succeeding, and in others becoming enslaved.

The transatlantic book trade, best expressed in the foundation of early American libraries, therefore enabled an early American, possessive individualist form of civic engagement based in slavery and the pursuit of the English rights and liberties that would protect the individual and his property. It is as if individual rights, as MacPherson explains that late seventeenth-century philosophers had posited, had become a commodity in this period. The immanence of these rights—the sense that they were just out of the patriots' grasp—marshaled desire that could be channeled into the marketing of a variety of products, including cultural, intellectual, and abstract ones that both created desire and fulfilled it, albeit incompletely. The rights that early Americans were seeking in the Revolution, in short, were perhaps unintentionally being marketed to them, packaged in works of literature and political thought that promoted possessive individualism as a consumer identity that was also a political one. They wanted the rights that their fellow British consumers in England had. The patriots' pursuits of the rights to both consume and be sovereign, individual subjects required a form of political sovereignty that could guarantee that Americans could have these British liberties. As Sarah Knott has written, "the possession of the individual, autonomous self spread ahead of, and rather alike, possession of the political franchise."[87] Imported British books were the central means by which this self-fashioning, franchise-seeking, and national sovereignty were being imagined.

Yet, if the colonial desire for rights in the liberal Lockean mode was paradoxically asserted within the context of slavery, the social contract that patriots were seeking in establishing that sovereignty was actually what Charles Mills has called a "racial contract" that simultaneously denied those rights to non-whites. Locke had legitimized slavery, or at least naturalized it, in several places in the *Two Treatises*, most clearly in the *Fundamental Constitutions*.[88] As Mills has argued, "In the *Second Treatise*, Locke defends slavery resulting from a just war, for example, a defensive war against aggression . . . Yet Locke had investments in the Royal Africa Company and earlier assisted in writing the slave constitution of Carolina."[89] As Laura Doyle has written, this Lockean social contract combined inclusion with exclusion; it was formative of a racial contract embracing pre-1066 Anglo-Saxonism and excluding all other ethnicities, races, and nationalities from inclusion in the Englishness of the social contract.[90] Because Locke's social contract is economic in that the chief reason that men unite into commonwealths is the preservation of their property, "the Racial Contract is calculatedly aimed at economic exploitation" that creates

---

[87] Sarah Knott, *Sensibility and the American Revolution* (Chapel Hill: U North Carolina P, 2009), 21.
[88] Locke, 177, 237, 284–5.
[89] Charles Mills, *The Racial Contract* (Ithaca: Cornell UP, 1997), 67–8.
[90] Laura Doyle, *Freedom's Empire: Race and the Rise of the Novel in Atlantic Modernity, 1640–1940* (Durham: Duke UP, 2008), 2, 11–12.

"global European economic domination and national white racial privilege."[91] In short, the racial contract facilitates MacPherson's unlimited accumulation of property, but for whites only, and slavery was the basis for that contract and for the financing of that accumulation.

It is for this reason that some of the founding documents guiding United States civic engagement, particularly the Declaration of Independence and the Constitution of 1787 (before the thirteenth amendment), have been viewed as racial contracts, or covenants that white men were making with each other for the preservation of slavery and their property in it. The Declaration, though it "made a strong appeal to what was owed to natural rights and human nature," was "easier to reconcile with enslavement than might be thought" because it embodied the desires of patriots to rebel against Britain in order to preserve their slave interests.[92] Indeed, as Pauline Maier has pointed out, the Declaration's contradictions on equality and slavery were unresolved and debated over the course of the nineteenth century by notables like William Lloyd Garrison, Frederick Douglass, and Abraham Lincoln.[93] The Constitution of 1787, though it never used the term "slave," "provided critically important political protection for slave property (or its then functional equivalent, the political economies of slave states) through the three-fifths clause."[94] It might even be said to have been backsliding from the ideals of the Revolution, which had witnessed some states banning slavery, by "limiting the power of the federal authorities, by recognizing white representation of slaves in the Southern states and by requiring all states to respect each other's slave property."[95] The Revolution actually strengthened slavery because the South had a bigger share of the economy and population in union with the North than it had had as part of the British empire, leading debate towards what would become "slavery's constitution."[96] The possessive individualists who needed property in slaves to propel their pursuit of unlimited accumulation of capital, accordingly, made use of the British political thought that would best preserve their "slaveholder's union." The transatlantic consumer culture of which they were a part provided the books that they required for this task.

SLAVERY, TRANSATLANTIC CONSUMER SOCIETY, AND THE BRITISH BOOK TRADE

Though not all aspects of MacPherson's theory have been retained in recent research on early American and transatlantic consumer society, it has helped open the door towards this study's analysis of slavery's relationship to the accumulation of books

[91] Mills, 31–2.   [92] Blackburn, 137–8.

[93] Pauline Maier, *American Scripture: Making the Declaration of Independence* (NY: Vintage, 1997), 197–200, 204–9.

[94] George William Van Cleve, *A Slaveholders' Union: Slavery, Politics, and the Constitution in the Early American Republic* (Chicago: U Chicago P, 2010), 9.

[95] Blackburn, 141.

[96] Van Cleve, 41; David Waldstreicher, *Slavery's Constitution: From Revolution to Ratification* (NY: Hill and Wang, 2009).

as an aspect of cultural history linked to possessive individualist consumer behavior. This consumer research is important to our understanding of reading, and the people doing it, because, as Leah Price has argued, there is a new scholarly consensus in the field of book history that not only the author, but "the consumer also produces meaning."[97] This research informs this study because it is clear that early Americans were financing their consumerism through the proceeds of slavery, the commercial facts of which also help us understand London not only as their financial center, but as their cultural one. Early Americans were not purchasing cast-off or discarded books from Britain, but were rather pursuing the latest London literary fashions. Consequently, early American proprietary subscription libraries were engaged in a parallel acquisitions policy to their British counterparts, a context that provides a fruitful opportunity for the synthesis of early American and British library history. The consequence for the methodology of the history of the book is that we therefore might regard the Atlantic book trade as not divided so much by geography in terms of nations, but by language in terms of identity.

Early American consumer behavior is manifest in some of the most civically engaged early Americans—George Washington, Thomas Jefferson, and James Madison—who, all evidence indicates, had metropolitan, London tastes. As Kariann Yokota writes, "Throughout Washington's adult life, his extant records show, he purchased chinaware from abroad. His correspondence reveals his careful deliberations about the various objects that would help transform him into a cultured gentleman," and he bartered his crops for these imported luxuries.[98] This was true even during the War of Independence, despite the movement for non-importation and even non-consumption. In 1776, when he was planning his defense of New York City, Washington ordered "elegant British and Chinese goods for his home" through loyalist merchants, and in 1779 he bought "Queens China" to entertain French military officers in the field.[99] Jefferson returned from his diplomatic post in France with "eighty-six crates of goods and large debts" acquired from dealings with the merchants of Paris and London.[100] British officers who occupied the White House during the war of 1812, before they burned it, found that Madison and Washington had imported furniture, silverware, and china to entertain in the highest cosmopolitan fashion.[101]

The Americans were exchanging the agricultural goods that they found in nature, and cultivated, for British goods, which represented civility for them.[102] They were importing vast amounts of commodities from London, which were cheaper and of higher quality than American products, and were a major market for British manufacturers: "by 1773 the colonists purchased almost 26 percent of all domestically produced goods that were exported out of the mother country."[103] In doing so, these colonists were "purchasing identity" of a particularly British, individualist kind, and their consumer behavior amounted to an embrace of individualism in a

[97] Leah Price, "Reading: The State of the Discipline." *Book History* 7 (2004): 311.
[98] Kariann Akemi Yokota, *Unbecoming British: How Revolutionary America Became a Postcolonial Nation* (Oxford: Oxford UP, 2011), 88.
[99] Yokota, 86, 88.   [100] Yokota, 63.   [101] Yokota, 226–7.
[102] Yokota, 64–5; Breen, *Marketplace*, xi–xii.   [103] Breen, *Marketplace*, 61.

manner that suggests that the form of individuality that they were being sold in cultural products itself may have been invented to sell other commodities.[104] Indeed, one of the more popular imported educational texts read by Americans, Locke's *The Child's New Play-Thing*, "is a metaphor for consumption" in which "the individual is depicted as in charge of his own fate," indicating that Americans were absorbing these behavioral norms.[105] The "transatlantic migration of arts and culture...fulfilled the promise of civility and the development of high culture in the distant colonies," and imported books, I argue, were the leading and most ideological mark of that international, Enlightenment civility.[106] Clearly, early Americans were living in a transatlantic version of a possessive market society, and cultural products were on the high end of that market, with colonial proprietary subscription libraries being some of the largest purchasers.

Slavery was an economic engine for this kind of acquisition of culture and taste-fulness all over the Atlantic, and was particularly important in fueling the consumer habits of early Americans.[107] In the Virginia of Washington, Jefferson, and Madison, that fuel was best expressed in the tobacco industry, which required intensive slave labor. Indeed, the increased production of tobacco in Virginia has been docu-mented as the principal reason the population of African slaves increased there over the course of the seventeenth and eighteenth centuries.[108] The role of slavery in trade was therefore often at one remove; Virginians would barter with London agents in tobacco, and later, wheat and other slave-cultivated crops. It is evident, for example, that some of Madison's most wealthy and influential Virginia con-stituents were dependent on English markets for exporting their tobacco, and that they relied on cargo ships from the northern colonies to get it to Britain.[109] During and after the War of Independence, there were hopes that France would replace England as a market for it.[110] Because Virginians could pay their taxes in it, there were even attempts to export government tobacco in exchange for financing and arms from France. There was a "tobacco contract" sealed in March 1777 that the Americans had negotiated with the French tax collectors, in which the collectors advanced the patriots money in exchange for a monopoly on importing it, and there is evidence of at least one exchange of it for French military material through Virginia's agent at Nantes.[111] In short, tobacco was financialized, with the plant

---

[104] Phyllis Whitman Hunter, *Purchasing Identity in the Atlantic World: Massachusetts Merchants, 1670–1780* (Ithaca: Cornell UP, 2001), 1–13.

[105] Ross W. Beales and E. Jennifer Monaghan, "Literacy and Schoolbooks." *A History of the Book in America, Volume 1: The Colonial Book in the Atlantic World*. Eds Hugh Amory and David Hall (Chapel Hill: U North Carolina P, 2007), 386.

[106] Yokota, 75.   [107] Gikandi, 50–96.   [108] Williams, *Capitalism & Slavery*, 26.

[109] James Madison, *The Papers of James Madison Digital Edition*. Ed. J. C. A. Stagg (Charlottesville: University of Virginia Press, Rotunda, 2010). Accessed December 10, 2014. <http://rotunda.upress.virginia.edu/founders/JSMN-01-06-01-0006>.

[110] Madison, Accessed December 10, 2014. <http://rotunda.upress.virginia.edu/founders/JSMN-01-09-02-0116>.

[111] Madison, Accessed December 10, 2014. <http://rotunda.upress.virginia.edu/founders/JSMN-01-06-02-0150>; Madison, Accessed December 10, 2014. <http://rotunda.upress.virginia.edu/founders/JSMN-01-07-02-0004>; Frederick L. Nussbaum, "American Tobacco and French Politics, 1783–1789." *Political Science Quarterly* 40 (1925): 502–3.

and even slaves themselves being used as security for money advanced to Americans from Europe.[112]

Invoices from Washington, Jefferson, and Madison to their London and Liverpool agents show how they would enclose a list of goods to be acquired in London together with every shipment of their tobacco to those agents. Their London agent, or factor, would sell the tobacco to other merchants and retailers; "thus was established a credit line on which colonial planters could draw in a variety of ways."[113] This mechanism of exchange was related to the lack of circulating British currency in the American colonies; in lieu of that monetary medium, commodities were used as money in transactions, particularly between merchants, farmers, and other dealers in a broad array of goods, who knew how to sell what they received in barter. Slave-cultivated goods like tobacco and sugar were frequently used in payments for other goods within a colony, between colonies, and all across the Atlantic.

The transatlantic book trade was no exception to these trading customs, and might be regarded as the branch of commerce most connected to the slavery-for-taste pattern of exchange. The vast majority of the early American book market consisted of imports from Britain, counting for as much as 4 percent of total British book output and 60 percent of all British book exports in the 1770s.[114] The American purchase of British cultural capital only accelerated as 1776 approached, indicating that British political thought and the literature that expressed it in a more vernacular, fictional manner were helping to produce the ideology of the Revolution.[115] In short, Americans were paradoxically seeking high British culture and taste at the moment they were rejecting British rule. The transatlantic book trade, in this view, might be seen as facilitating the political and revolutionary mobilization of early Americans.[116] This potent discourse of liberty, being almost entirely imported from England, however, put American patriots in the position of "taking sides against a place that, in terms of cultural influence, meant the world to them"; they were "making war against the Land of Literature and of Books."[117] That this English land of culture was in the process of extending that liberty to Africans in such rulings as the Somerset case, as Blackburn and Horne have contended, ironically, may have been the signal for the Americans to rebel.

Imported books about British liberties are therefore part of a cultural history in which even their production and circulation were made possible by forms of slavery that, in some cases, they sought to overcome. Accordingly, the technical and logistical details of their dissemination are aspects of the methodology of the

---

[112] Thomas Jefferson, *The Papers of Thomas Jefferson Digital Edition*. Ed. Barbara B. Oberg and J. Jefferson Looney (Charlottesville: University of Virginia Press, Rotunda, 2008). Accessed June 27, 2014. <http://rotunda.upress.virginia.edu/founders/TSJN-01-15-02-0620-0001>.

[113] Calhoun Winton, "The Southern Book Trade in the Eighteenth Century." *A History of the Book in America, Volume 1: The Colonial Book in the Atlantic World*. Eds Hugh Amory and David D. Hall (Chapel Hill: U North Carolina P, 2007), 231.

[114] Raven, *London*, 3–18; Raven, "Importation," 184–5.

[115] Raven, "Importation," 196, 195.

[116] Raven, *London*, 8; Breen, "'Baubles of Britain,'" 87.

[117] Kevin Hayes, *The Road to Monticello: The Life and Mind of Thomas Jefferson* (Oxford: Oxford UP, 2008), 173.

history of the book that bear on this cultural history. Calhoun Winton has described what the shipping aspect of such book transactions would look like, using the example of how the Glasgow merchant partners James Lawson and John Semple would trade with Maryland tobacco growers: "Approximately twice a year a ship, owned or leased by the partners, departed Port Tobacco [in Maryland] laden with tobacco or other commodities such as sugar and rum being transshipped. Approximately twice a year a similar ship cleared Port Glasgow for Maryland, laden with virtually anything, but always including books."[118] Washington, Jefferson, and Madison had many similar exchanges of tobacco and other crops for books. They dealt with English, Scottish, and French agents like Robert Cary and Co. (Washington's preferred factors), Perkins, Buchanan and Brown, Donald and Burton, John Stockdale, Foulis of Glasgow, and Philip Mazzei of Paris (Jefferson's agents), and often with Americans abroad, as Madison did with James Maury, American consul in Liverpool.[119] Their private library collections were therefore quite similar to those of their British counterparts, some of whom "would have acquired their books for their intellectual content, and others, as status symbols—the two are not mutually exclusive."[120] The domestic library of the plantations of these Virginians resembled, intentionally, that of the English gentleman's in his country house.[121] As this study establishes, proprietary subscription libraries followed this private library pattern of modeling both knowledge and status.

American cultural history is therefore not solely American, as transactions in cultural products closely mirrored other patterns of economic exchange in an imperial British Atlantic world. The British book trade did not, for most of the eighteenth century, regard other English-speaking territories outside of the British

[118] Winton, 231.
[119] George Washington, *The Papers of George Washington, Digital Edition.* Ed. Theodore J. Crackel (Charlottesville: U Virginia P, Rotunda, 2008). Accessed June 23, 2014. <http://rotunda.upress. virginia.edu/founders/GEWN-02-07-02-0103-0002>; <http://rotunda.upress.virginia.edu/founders/ GEWN-02-07-02-0119>; <http://rotunda.upress.virginia.edu/founders/GEWN-02-09-02-0268>; <http://rotunda.upress.virginia.edu/founders/GEWN-02-06-02-0189-0002>; <http://rotunda.upress. virginia.edu/founders/GEWN-02-06-02-0217>; <http://rotunda.upress.virginia.edu/founders/GEWN-02-06-02-0166-0001>; Mark Dimunation, "'The Whole of Recorded Knowledge': Jefferson as Collector and Reader." *The Libraries, Leadership, & Legacy of John Adams and Thomas Jefferson.* Eds. Robert C. Baron and Conrad Edick Wright (Golden: Fulcrum, 2010), 117–18; Jefferson, Accessed June 27, 2014, <http://rotunda.upress.virginia.edu/founders/TSJN-01-02-0022>; <http://rotunda. upress.virginia.edu/founders/TSJN-01-02-0040>; <http://rotunda.upress.virginia.edu/founders/TSJN-01-03-02-0411>; <http://rotunda.upress.virginia.edu/founders/TSJN-01-23-02-0007>; <http://rotunda. upress.virginia.edu/founders/TSJN-01-24-02-0431>; <http://rotunda.upress.virginia.edu/founders/ TSJN-01-24-02-0711>; <http://rotunda.upress.virginia.edu/founders/TSJN-01-25-02-0313>; <http:// rotunda.upress.virginia.edu/founders/TSJN-01-25-02-0471>; <http://rotunda.upress.virginia.edu/ founders/TSJN-01-26-02-0167>; Eric Stockdale, "John Stockdale, London Bookseller and Publisher of Adams and Jefferson." *The Libraries, Leadership, & Legacy of John Adams and Thomas Jefferson.* Eds. Robert C. Baron and Conrad Edick Wright (Golden: Fulcrum, 2010), 45–8; Madison, Accessed December 10, 2014. <http://rotunda.upress.virginia.edu/founders/JSMN-02-05-02-0016>; <http:// rotunda.upress.virginia.edu/founders/JSMN-02-04-02-0050>; <http://rotunda.upress.virginia.edu/ founders/JSMN-02-08-02-0064>; <http://rotunda.upress.virginia.edu/founders/JSMN-02-04-02-0223>; <http://rotunda.upress.virginia.edu/founders/JSMN-02-05-02-0440>; <http://rotunda.upress. virginia.edu/founders/JSMN-04-01-01-0006>.
[120] Williams, *Social Life of Books*, 50. [121] Williams, *Social Life of Books*, 50.

Isles as separate cultural spheres any more than publishers in the international book trade of our own time see any contradiction between having both London and American headquarters. The politics, and, eventually, sovereignties of Britain and America were different, but readers in both maintained a desire for "Britishness" in its book form.

Explaining Washington, Jefferson, and Madison's practice of trading slave-cultivated crops for books gives a material culture affirmation both to Morgan's paradox and Bailyn's explication of what texts were influencing American founders, informing us about what the most civically engaged early Americans were reading. This evidence shows that some of these early figures were not only arguing for their liberty while enslaving others, but were also using the proceeds of that very enslavement to purchase the ideological origins of their cause. Accordingly, this study, rather than debating whether the Revolution had ideological, economic, or cultural roots, focuses on the possession of books through slavery itself as the synthesis of these views. That is to say, the transatlantic book trade may be taken as evidence that the American pursuit of the possession of ideas in their imported book forms was the dissemination of ideology enacted in pursuit of individual economic advantage in the marketplace of the Revolution—a marketplace funded by the economic fact of slavery.

The cultural history made possible by this analysis of the transatlantic book trade—our understanding of the Revolution's ideological, intellectual, and literary sources in relation to its economy—is manifest in what the five major libraries stocked. Strikingly, the titles that they bought were not significantly different from what British proprietary subscription libraries were shelving. American librarians and the proprietors giving them their orders, like their British counterparts, were mostly drawing on "the advice offered by the major contemporary periodicals" like the *Monthly Review*, the *Critical Review*, the *Gentleman's Magazine*, the *European Magazine*, and the *Annual Register* for clues about what to order.[122] Indeed, as detailed in this study's chapters, the popularity of such periodicals in the colonies was such that a couple of Boston booksellers sold more British magazines "than any other genre of print."[123] British libraries also felt that "in order to ensure that a respectable collection would be in place as soon as possible, block purchases should be made of some of the age's canonical texts."[124] Libraries across Britain were consistent in wanting reference works, scholarly and philosophical publications, "uplifting works by didactic moralists like Addison, Shaftesbury, Johnson and Blair, as well as serious works of theology, history, and politics, supplied by the pens of formidable thinkers like William Warburton, Edward Gibbon, and Baron Montesquieu."[125] The most popular historians were David Hume, William Robertson, Gilbert Burnet, and Gibbon, and most libraries thought it important to have copies of Adam Smith's *Theory of Moral Sentiments* and *The Wealth of*

[122] Allan, 86.
[123] Elizabeth Carroll Reilly and David D. Hall, "Customers and the Market for Books." *A History of the Book in America, Volume 1: The Colonial Book in the Atlantic World*. Eds Hugh Amory and David Hall (Chapel Hill: U North Carolina P, 2007), 389–90.
[124] Allan, 86.   [125] Allan, 99.

Nations.[126] All of these works were in every one of the American libraries studied in this book at some point in the eighteenth century; Hume's histories, in particular, have been proven to have circulated widely in America and helped colonists articulate their grievances with Britain.[127] British libraries were weakest in fiction, but "the most distinguished and 'respectable' novels of the eighteenth century, as opposed to the so-called 'trashy' fiction, were routinely found in the subscription libraries by 1800."[128]

Colonial libraries mirrored their British counterparts in such orders, though there were variations. For example, the Redwood did not stock as many novels in its original collection as the Salem Social Library did, but the acquisitions policy for all generally followed what was popular in London, as the policy of the Charleston Library Society makes clear. That Charlestonians requested "new, talked-about literature (as distinct from embarrassment about orders for fashionable belles lettres) remains an outstanding feature of the library's wants list, but it clearly co-existed with another, entirely different sense of literary currency, that of a corpus of publications contributing to a debate and intellectual canon irrespective of their age of publication."[129] It should not be surprising that the proprietors of the other early American proprietary subscription libraries wanted the same books for the same reasons, as London was their cultural center and they wanted what was most popular and current there.

Therefore, we should not be too worried about the question of why Americans were reading the books that they did; they simply were buying books from the same British booksellers as metropolitan Britons were, using the same booksellers' catalogs and magazines to determine what they should order. In terms of the travel and shipping time it took books to reach their destinations, "the far-flung parts of the British Isles were as remote from London as were Massachusetts and Barbados," indicating that we should consider the British book market, holistically, as an Atlantic market. Indeed, we might regard the American book market as an extension of what John Feather and Jan Fergus have identified as Britain's internal "provincial book trade." The American trade had identical arrangements to the internal trade in the dissemination of London-published books—a process that Robert Darnton has called the "communications circuit" of books from author, to bookseller, to printer, to shipper, to retailer, and to reader.[130] It was the societal difference created jointly by British economic and political policy in North America, and by the American reaction to it, that made for the very different receptions of the same works in both places. The American libraries, accordingly, had become laboratories and communities for the mediation of reading that gave this cultural capital a distinct, revolutionary civic meaning.

---

[126] Allan, 101–3.

[127] Mark G. Spencer, *David Hume and Eighteenth-Century America* (Rochester: U Rochester P, 2005).

[128] Allan, 99, 105.   [129] Raven, *London*, 161.

[130] John Feather, *The Provincial Book Trade in Eighteenth-Century England* (Cambridge: Cambridge UP, 1985); Jan Fergus, *Provincial Readers in Eighteenth-Century England* (Oxford: Oxford UP, 2007); Robert Darnton, "What is the History of Books?" *The Book History Reader*. Eds David Finkelstein and Alistair McCleery (London: Routledge, 2002), 11.

EARLY AMERICAN READING: TRAVEL, HISTORY, LAW, POLITICS, AND LITERATURE

The study of colonial reading, accordingly, is of central relevance to understanding how the same British books had a different impact in America than they did in the imperial metropole. In undertaking such a study for the purpose of understanding early American libraries, I am much indebted to the essays in Hugh Amory and David Hall's *A History of the Book in America, Volume 1: The Colonial Book in the Atlantic World*, recent scholarship on reading in Britain by David Allan and Abigail Williams, and much work by Jennifer Monaghan and others. Mindful of Leah Price's observation that the term "the history of reading" is one that encompasses "enterprises as various as the social history of education, the quantitative study of the distribution of printed matter, and the reception of texts or diffusion of ideas," this study attempts to unite those enterprises by studying the colonial library as both a social and reading network.[131] The advantages of doing so are that this field's history of calling attention to how reading is socially mediated in the eighteenth century by communities of religion, profession, schools, and the household can be supplemented by analyses of the rising "polite" forms of private associational culture. The proprietary subscription library is the most representative example of that culture. The genres of books stocked and circulated by early American libraries were in a variety of disciplines, with readers often borrowing several from different fields over the course of the same loan period, indicating that colonial reading was an interdisciplinary affair related to members' diverse interests. The civic meanings of these books, crystalized, as Bailyn says, by the particular circumstances of the years leading up to the Revolution, are best captured in our understanding of how members read non-fiction like voyages, histories, and political thought. The British literature they read that offered examples of how those books' lessons could be lived, however, was probably more compelling.

As in Britain, literacy was first spread in the colonies by Protestantism; Puritans, in particular, placed a high value on the ability to read the Bible, and were skeptical of pleasurable and popular literature and ballads.[132] Religious revivals like the Great Awakening underscored the fact that catechisms, hymn books, Bibles, and works "devotional or evangelical in nature" were bestsellers, and "the largest share of books retained at death remained those dealing with religion."[133] Many people learned to read through chanting aloud and memorizing primers and catechisms, and ministers were encouraged to speak their sermons from memory.[134] Religious radicals complained that "the privileging of learnedness" was setting up a class system between the clergy and laity among the settlers, an argument not far wrong in that elite early American colleges like Harvard were founded to produce more

---

[131]   Price, 304.

[132]   David D. Hall, "Readers and Writers in Early New England." *A History of the Book in America, Volume 1: The Colonial Book in the Atlantic World.* Eds Hugh Amory and David Hall (Chapel Hill: U North Carolina P, 2007), 118.

[133]   Reilly & Hall, 395, 399, 387–99.   [134]   Hall, "Readers," 122.

ministers.[135] Consequently, even though the Protestant ethic of reading was oriented towards liberating people from " 'popish tyranny,' " in most of the religiously orthodox Protestant colonies, "literacy, catechizing, and print were means of buttressing a moral order premised on the authority of parents, magistrates, and ministers."[136]

Establishing rates of literacy either in Britain or colonial America with any definitive accuracy would be to partake of "irresolvable debates," which, in keeping with this study's skepticism of statistical approaches to cultural history, "render quantification extremely problematical."[137] However, it has been argued that the rate of people, particularly white men, being able to sign their name increased over the course of the eighteenth century, though signature literacy rates for women (and even more so for blacks) were lower.[138] Evidence of increased literacy is manifest in the burgeoning sales of spelling books from Britain like Thomas Dyche's *A Guide to the English Tongue*, Henry Dixon's *The English Instructor*, and Thomas Dilworth's *New Guide to the English Tongue*, as well as the American *New England Primer* and Noah Webster's *American Spelling Book*.[139] These assisted with household instruction, which was considered the most important form of teaching literacy to the extent that in New England, laws were passed requiring home schooling of children and servants.[140]

Like the British, Americans partly learned their critical reading skills from sermons and reading aloud at home.[141] Complementing home schooling and church was an expansion of the establishment of both public and private schools after 1750, particularly focusing on grammar and elocution. There was growth in the number of British books imported as well as in domestic printing by the Revolution, which, together with the proliferation of newspapers, indicates that a much larger readership in America existed in the 1760s and 1770s than before, and much of this market was for the poor in the form of chapbooks and almanacs.[142] Consequently, in New England, the majority of households owned books, but usually fewer than five in total.[143] The fact that white male literacy, particularly in New England, was nearly universal by the Revolution may help prove that, in America as in Britain, "the average eighteenth-century novel reader...was more likely to have been a respectable middle-aged man."[144] Evidence from the circulation records studied in this book indicates that this was the case in the colonies. In short, as in Britain, "people's behaviour as consumers of texts" was shaped by the expansion of printing, the extension of literacy, and the coming of age of criticism. The performance of the latter, as we shall see in Chapter 4's discussion of the reading of Eliza Lucas Pinckney, was indicative of high cultural literacy and social class.[145]

---

[135] Hall, "Readers," 138–41, 131.   [136] Hall, "Readers," 121.   [137] Allan, 3–4.
[138] Beales & Monaghan, 380–2.   [139] Beales & Monaghan, 383–6.
[140] Beales & Monaghan, 382; Hall, "Readers," 119–21.
[141] Williams, *Social Life of Books*, 11–63.
[142] E. Jennifer Monaghan, *Learning to Read and Write in Colonial America* (Amherst: U Massachusetts P, 2005), 235–9; Reilly & Hall, 391–2.
[143] Hall, "Readers," 124.   [144] Monaghan, 3; Williams, *Social Life of Books*, 3.
[145] Allan, 9.

This class dimension to the pursuit and rise of literacy in the period cannot be underestimated, as going hand in hand with the ability to engage in criticism were the ideologies of taste and politeness, initially espoused by Whig cultural theorists like the Earl of Shaftesbury and the authors of the taste-making periodicals the *Tatler* and the *Spectator*: Joseph Addison and Richard Steele. "Politeness" became a sign of literacy—the enhancement of the "individual's own conversation" and sociability—and was associated with the desire for social mobility; it was believed that reading honed and burnished "not only one's intellect and conversation but also one's outward performance and conduct."[146] In America, secular spaces of reading like gentlemen's clubs, literary coteries, taverns, and stores, as well as public performances, reading circles, singing schools, colleges, and meetings of organizations like the American Philosophical Society, "embodied a form of sociability characterized by politeness and 'refinement.'"[147] People judged people not only by "how well someone else read, but by the kinds of books that a person was reading," writes Abigail Williams. In this sense, one's place in the social hierarchy was indexed by both skill and evidence of their acquisition of cultural capital.[148] That social world tended to take place in associational cultures like clubs and societies, where these skills and knowledge could be displayed and shared.[149] The practice of reading, accordingly, was not only usually mediated by family, community, and other socio-cultural contexts like ethnicity and religion, but also by these specific social networks located in the particular cultural history of the eighteenth century all over the British Atlantic.[150] Libraries were among these polite networks, and as such, places where reading not only was done, but where the social fruits of that reading were appreciated, valued, and converted into social capital that helped advance the lives and social standing of readers.

Accordingly, any study of early American reading must account for the role of early American libraries as places not only for the cultivation of literacy, but also for the social life literacy created and maintained, both of which can be understood best through surviving circulation records. In undertaking research on the five major early American proprietary subscription libraries as examples of where and how slavery-enabled reading took place, I am bringing to American library history the goal of Priya Joshi's study of the borrowing records of Calcutta's Public Library and Bagbazar Library. In her work, Joshi makes "an educated assessment of what circulated in colonial India, and, perhaps even, to whom," an approach I am applying to the study of reading in colonial America.[151] Along with Joshi and Isabelle Lehuu, rather than accept the methodological orthodoxy in book history studies that circulation records are circumstantial evidence and do not tell us whether a book was actually read like diaries or letters would, I instead contend that they tell

---

[146] Allan, 11–12, 2.

[147] David D. Hall and Elizabeth Carroll Reilly, "Practices of Reading: Introduction." *A History of the Book in America, Volume 1: The Colonial Book in the Atlantic World.* Eds Hugh Amory and David Hall (Chapel Hill: U North Carolina P, 2007), 379; Reilly & Hall, 397.

[148] Williams, *Social Life of Books*, 63.   [149] Allan, 14.   [150] Hall & Reilly, 379.

[151] Priya Joshi, *In Another Country: Colonialism, Culture, and the English Novel in India* (NY: Columbia UP, 2002), 52–3.

us more than traditionally has been believed.[152] *Sequential* borrowings of volumes of a work, the *velocity* of borrowing (how quickly a book changes hands), and other details in library records can inform us of at least the popularity of certain titles and literary tastes in an interpretive community, if not also how their contents were read. They can also tell us something significant about how what we regard as "canonical" now may not have been what was actually read then. As Williams reminds us, such "Piecemeal sources remind us of some important aspects of book circulation at this time: that some of the most loved works are now little known."[153] As the circulation records analyzed in this book demonstrate, though many books that we still read now were being borrowed, others, like the it-narratives discussed in Chapter 4, are today only known to a tiny percentage of the professoriate.

What is striking about how the cultural history of reading in this period is connected to the book trade is not only that the kinds of books that borrowers at the five libraries were checking out were in a variety of genres paralleling the contents of British libraries, but also that non-fiction ones dominated. The most frequently stocked category of book in American libraries followed the pattern in British ones, with "the overlapping disciplines of geography, travel, topography and natural history" often treated "as part of a broader domain of knowledge that also included history, biography, and antiquities."[154] These genres were dominant not only because the vast majority of proprietors of libraries were men, but also because they were connected to their business affairs. These books could help them figure out where to trade and the history and customs of trading nations, and were generally regarded as "useful knowledge" for that reason.

Voyages and travels were the most important type of books for port cities for these reasons, as were those that contained information on mathematical and scientific matters necessary for navigation, shipbuilding, and other aspects of getting ships and men to places around the world. As described in greater detail in Chapters 3 and 5, voyages to Africa were important reading for both slave traders and antislavery advocates, as were those to the West Indies and the rest of the central and south Atlantic. One book that all five libraries stocked, and which circulated frequently from them, was Commodore George Anson's *A Voyage Round the World, in the Years MDCCXL, I, II, III, IV*, published in 1748 with such success that double-digit numbers of succeeding editions were printed over the course of the century, including in Boston.[155] Focused mostly on the Pacific and swashbuckling adventures against the Spanish there, such as the capture of a treasure galleon, this story of a British naval expedition "offered more than just information, adventure, and prestige to subscribers. It was the authorized story from the squadron's leader, a

---

[152] Isabelle Lehuu, "Reconstructing Reading Vogues in the Old South: Borrowings from the Charleston Library Society, 1811–1817." *The History of Reading, Volume 1: International Perspectives c.1500–1990*. Eds Shafquat Towheed and W. R. Owens (NY: Palgrave, 2011), 64–5.

[153] Williams, *Social Life of Books*, 9.   [154] Allan, 102.

[155] Phyllis Whitman Hunter, "Transatlantic News: American Interpretations of the Scandalous and Heroic." *Books Between Europe and the Americas: Connections and Communities, 1620–1860* (Basingstoke: Palgrave Macmillan, 2011), 76.

respected and now celebrated naval officer."[156] American library proprietors may have been reading this book not only for its pull-out nautical charts and descriptions of how to navigate to Pacific destinations and the cultures found there, but also for its very human stories of survival and triumph in difficult circumstances. For this reason, its adventure aspects were central to its appeal:

> Over time, the tone of the narrative could change as well, in this case from a respected voyage account with navigational value to an adventure story targeted especially at young boys. John Barrow explained in 1839 that the Anson story was, "a voyage which, is still about the most delightful of any with which we are acquainted; and we believe, has sent more young fellows to sea, than even the renowned *Robinson Crusoe*."[157]

Seaport cities like Salem, Newport, New York, Philadelphia, and Charleston needed such accounts to help motivate their sons and others to do the hard work of seafaring for their enterprises, perhaps indicating a broader readership beyond just the proprietors themselves. What is most interesting here, however, is how non-fiction and fiction like *Crusoe*, which in some of these libraries circulated to some of the same people who borrowed Anson's *Voyages*, could be blended in the imagination, with Anson's account taking on a novelistic quality in its reception and the novel's realism making it appeal as a true story. There were many such narratives of travels and voyages circulating in early American libraries, compelling not only for their navigation and anthropology, but also for their tales of the exploits of men who made a living out of working the world's oceans.

The genre of history was valued for similar reasons. Library proprietors were reading not only about the geography and pasts of far-flung places for trade like the Middle East and Asia, but also of those of many European countries. Histories of England were by far the most important for the colonists, as their description of the conflicts, events, and writings of the previous centuries provided them with information about how they should go about their own civic engagement. As mentioned above, Hume's and Robertson's histories were among the most popular titles in these libraries. Colonists were, however, also reading a variety of histories that were also stocked in the personal libraries of Washington and Jefferson like those of Tobias Smollett, Thomas Fuller, William Camden, and John Baxter. Clarendon's *History of the Rebellion*, John Phillips's *The Secret History of the Reigns of K. Charles II and K. James II*, Thornagh Gurdon's *History of Parliaments*, and John Reeves's *History of the English Law* were among the most important to their political interests.[158]

---

[156] Hunter, "Transatlantic," 76–9; Katherine Parker, "London's Geographic Knowledge Network and the Anson Account (1748)." *The Global Histories of Books: Methods and Practices*. Eds Elleke Boehmer, Rouven Kunstmann, Priyasha Mukhopadhyay, and Asha Rogers (London: Palgrave Macmillan, 2017), 29.

[157] Parker, 34.

[158] Washington, Accessed June 23, 2014. <http://rotunda.upress.virginia.edu/founders/GEWN-02-07-02-0103-0002>; Library Thing: George Washington, Accessed March 3, 2015. <http://www.librarything.com/catalogue/GeorgeWashington>; Jefferson, Accessed June 23, 2014. <http://rotunda.upress.virginia.edu/founders/TSJN-03-02-0001-0002>; Accessed June 24, 2014. <http://rotunda.upress.virginia.edu/founders/TSJN-01-02-0022>; <http://rotunda.upress.virginia.edu/founders/TSJN-01-37-02-0195-0002>.

Moreover, these works also cast historical individuals as role models for how to be a "British" subject or citizen. Like voyages, they were also of interest to the education of sons.

In the genre of political philosophy, as Bailyn established and Chapters 1–5 demonstrate, early Americans like the libraries' proprietors were reading broadly. However, no figure was as central as Locke; even Bailyn, despite his critique of the Lockean liberal thesis, makes a special place for Locke as a "dominant" and "wholly determinative" source for both patriot and loyalist sides of the dispute over what action to take towards Britain.[159] Ministers had been preaching Locke from early in the eighteenth century, and protesters in the 1760s and 1770s were citing him, to the extent that, "In ratifying a new government based on Locke's principle that no one can be 'subjected to the Political Power of another without his own Consent,' Americans were legislating their childhood convictions."[160] The *Two Treatises* was also widely available for reading in both imported and domestic imprints. Demonstrating that there was no edition of the *Treatises* reprinted in America until the Boston radical printers' Edes and Gill abridged edition of 1773, Slauter stresses that the book was mostly available as an import with one Boston bookseller importing seventy-six student orders for it in the 1750s and 1760s, another selling twenty, and a New York bookseller advertising many copies.[161] The five major early proprietary subscription libraries, too, thought it important to have an imported copy of Locke's *Two Treatises*. The Salem Social Library's Catalogue and Donation Book of 1761 had what was most likely the 1759 London three-volume folio edition of Locke's *Works* that contained these treatises in volume two.[162] A 1764 London edition of the *Two Treatises* was included in a 1767 book order from the Charleston Library Society to its agents in London, an order that also included a 1751 folio edition of Locke's *Works* that contained the *Two Treatises* in the second volume.[163] The 1789 catalog of the New York Society Library lists an undated three-volume quarto edition of Locke's works that most likely contained the treatises, given that previous three-volume formats did.[164] The Redwood Library lists a 1740 folio fourth edition of Locke's "Works and Pieces" in its original 1747 catalog. This is most likely the London Parker edition of 1740, the second volume of which contained the treatises.[165] The 1741 catalog of the Library Company of Philadelphia lists the same three-volume 1740 folio edition

---

[159] Bailyn, 30.

[160] Dworetz, 104, 106; Gillian Brown, *The Consent of the Governed: The Lockean Legacy in Early American Culture* (Cambridge: Harvard UP, 2001), 3.

[161] Eric Slauter, "Reading and Radicalization: Print, Politics, and the American Revolution." *Early American Studies* 8.1 (Winter 2010): 16, 17, 36.

[162] "Catalogue and Donation Book, 1761–1782." Salem Athenaeum Records, MSS 56, Phillips Library, Peabody Essex Museum, Salem, Massachusetts.

[163] Raven, *London*, 156.

[164] New York Society Library, *The Charter, Bye-laws, and Names of the Members of the New-York Society Library: With a Catalogue of the Books Belonging to the Said Library* (NY: Gaine, 1789), 46.

[165] Marcus McCorison, ed., *The 1764 Catalogue of the Redwood Library Company at Newport, Rhode Island* (New Haven: Yale UP, 1965), 10.

containing the *Two Treatises* in the second volume, as well as a separate and distinct 1698 London octavo edition.[166]

The philosophy of individualism and property that Locke preached, however, was more popularly available in the imported literature that these libraries were stocking, a fact that is the basis of this book's original contribution to English literary scholarship and to our understanding of what books were read in early America. As the chapters herein demonstrate, works like Behn and Hawkesworth's *Oroonoko*, Pope's *Essay on Man*, Defoe's *Robinson Crusoe*, Johnstone's *Chrysal, or, the Adventures of a Guinea*, and Equiano's *The Interesting Narrative* circulated extensively throughout the colonial and early Republic periods. They, and others that the same readers were borrowing, indicate that early Americans had moved beyond the Protestant, or particularly, Puritan, skepticism of reading for pleasure and towards the kind of literature compatible with transatlantic consumer society.

As Chapter 1 indicates, there was a particular taste for sentimental literature on the eve of the Revolution in the Salem Social Library, a development all the more important for understanding how both independence and anti-slavery could claim hold of the affections of so many not just in Massachusetts, but across British America. The hypocrisy of slaveholding patriots is evident in Chapter 2's analysis of the Redwood Library, which reads Pope's poems, particularly those concerning Britain's newly acquired monopoly over the slave trade to Spanish America, and how these writings reflected a conservative skepticism about banning it. Robinson Crusoe's unapologetic possessive individualism is the subject of Chapter 3, which examines how many people at the New York Society Library read it and what else they were reading in order to establish that he and his acquisitiveness were models that early Americans sought to emulate. Chapter 4 analyzes the significance of a work about a coin being read in the Charleston Library Society, given that South Carolina's monetary system had long made a connection between currency and the slave property backing it, and establishes that this connection is relevant to our understanding of the Atlantic slavery economy. Anti-slavery is the subject of the final chapter (Chapter 5) on Equiano, as his book was informed by the very Library Company of Philadelphia context that had produced some of the abolitionist books that he cites. Individualism, in these chapters, is understood in many ways: as the impulse of economic men implicated in slavery like Crusoe and American merchants, as an aspect of the individual human rights that people were claiming to defend in the Revolution, and as the basis for the humanistic extension of those rights to the enslaved and dehumanized African diaspora.

It is clear, then, that early American readers like the kind found among the proprietors of the libraries had internalized the messages of this literature as well as Locke's view of property in the construction of individualism. The questions about taxation and consent with which they were obsessed were ultimately ones about the disposition of what they owned and who had the right to tax it. As Cathy Davidson has established in *Revolution and the Word: The Rise of the Novel in*

---

[166] Library Company of Philadelphia, *A Catalogue of Books Belonging to the Library Company of Philadelphia* (Philadelphia: Franklin, 1741), 33.

America, it is not anachronistic to say so, as American novelists after the Revolution led the way in critiquing the possessive individualism and slavery not only characteristic of the motives of some patriots, but also unleashed by the arrival of independence.[167] As if anticipating MacPherson, Gothic novels paying homage to Charles Brockden Brown like Adelio's *A Journey to Philadelphia* (1804), Caroline Matilda Warren's *The Gamesters; or, The Ruin of Innocence* (1805), and George Watterston's *Glencarn; or, The Disappointment of Youth* (1810) and *The Lawyer* (1808) "are all concerned with the very way in which evil can be rooted in the concept of individualism." Moreover, their characters "lack any sense of social responsibility that might act as a check upon individual desire."[168] Slavery was excoriated in works like William Hill Brown's *The Power of Sympathy* (1789), sometimes regarded as the first American novel.[169] Similarly, Royall Tyler's *The Algerine Captive* (1797) argues that "The Constitutional compromise on slavery was itself un-American and must be undone."[170] Dorcasina, Tabitha Gilman Tenney's heroine in *Female Quixotism* (1801), resolves to marry a Virginian in the hope that she will convince him to free his slaves.[171] Such original American works seemingly aimed to be a corrective to eighteenth-century British literature's possessive individualism and the slavery with which it was compatible, with the objective, perhaps, of reprogramming an American readership that, paradoxically, had been politically mobilized by it.

The Anglo-American cultural history in which this book is engaged, accordingly, is difficult to separate from the early American civic engagement that was influenced by it, with the reading and sociability of libraries playing such a strong role in building the interpretive and political communities involved in the colonial period, the Revolution, and the Early Republic. This engagement was obviously inflected by Locke and others in the tradition of British history, law, and political philosophy, but it was also informed by the great variety of literary texts that colonists imported. All of these works, regardless of genre, could be considered ones that were about furthering their possessions (particularly non-fiction like travels and histories), modeling norms of individual behavior (such as conduct books, works on aesthetics and politeness, and literature), and other concerns centering on one outcome: the creation of the possessive individualist reader. Books *were* consumer society, and they fundamentally taught people how to be good consumers, how to behave in an individualist society, and, most fundamentally, how to survive as an individual in modernity. It is not surprising, then, that human rights and anti-slavery texts like many of those discussed in this book would be appealing in this sphere of printed books, as individual rights were something to possess in a possessive individualist Anglo-Atlantic world. Yet this cultural history of what early Americans were reading is difficult to disentangle from slavery as economic history, and therefore from eighteenth-century book history as both an inquiry into an area of business and an expression of what was valued in that economy.

---

[167] Cathy N. Davidson, *Revolution and the Word: The Rise of the Novel in America* (Oxford: Oxford UP, 2004), 313.

[168] Davidson, 333–4.   [169] Davidson, 183.   [170] Davidson, 291, 259.

[171] Davidson, 277.

SLAVERY AND ABOLITION IN THE AGE
OF REVOLUTIONS

A central argument of this book is that anti-slavery sentiment—a significant aspect of American cultural history expressed in the late eighteenth century—arose, paradoxically, on the foundation of slavery-created spaces of reading and the books within them. Given the context of anti-slavery in the age of revolutions, however, this is not an entirely surprising conclusion. As Brown has pointed out, "No one in Britain could campaign against colonial slavery or the Atlantic slave trade without also confronting fundamental questions about the structure, character, and purpose of empire."[172] As Chapter 2 illustrates, the trope of "slavery," so often appropriated in patriot rhetoric, also worked in reverse, with the American rebellion influencing the movement for abolition in Britain as it problematized the moral authority of the British government.[173] Even though one of the causes of the Revolution may have been the preservation of slavery, in harnessing political ideology for that cause, a few patriots realized that "By pairing anti-slavery initiatives with challenges to imperial sovereignty" they could encourage the British "to think of abolitionism as an aspect of patriot politics," as Chapter 1 contends.[174]

The larger stakes of the relationship between the Revolution and abolition, consequently, lay in the propaganda for and against the patriots. Benjamin Franklin worried that colonial slavery would "'encourage those who would oppress us, by representing us as unworthy of the Liberty we are now contending for.'"[175] The British did make those representations; no less an authority than author and critic Samuel Johnson would ask, in a work of counter-propaganda entitled *Taxation No Tyranny*, "How is it that we hear the loudest yelps for liberty among the drivers of Negroes?"[176] Indeed, this kind of rhetoric, especially after losing the War of Independence, may have influenced the British to develop "moral capital" for their empire afterwards that actually helped expand it.[177] The American Revolution was the crucible in which this British moral consensus was forged, and as this book contends, the relationship between slavery-enabled reading and anti-slavery sentiment is therefore central to understanding early America's economy, cultural history, and relationship with the empire.

The British, however, had seeded anti-slavery attitudes in America in the century before the Revolution, manifest mostly in their cultivation of black literacy. As Monaghan has proven, British evangelists like George Whitefield, leader of the "Great Awakening," had converted many slaves to various denominations of Protestantism.[178] The first efforts to instruct slaves were led by British organizations like the Society for the Propagation of the Gospel (SPG) and the Associates of Thomas Bray, which opened Negro grammar schools in Savannah, Charleston,

---

[172] Brown, *Moral Capital*, 26.   [173] Brown, *Moral Capital*, 27.
[174] Brown, *Moral Capital*, 143.   [175] Quoted in Brown, *Moral Capital*, 118.
[176] Samuel Johnson, *Taxation No Tyranny: An Answer to the Resolution and Address of the American Congress* (London: Cadell, 1775), 89.
[177] Brown, *Moral Capital*, 29, 12.   [178] Monaghan, 242–3.

Williamsburg, Philadelphia, New York, and Newport.[179] Significantly, "only reading could be legally taught," not writing, which makes the fact that the Charleston school had a Negro teacher, Andrew, all the more remarkable.[180] The British efforts were supplemented by American ones, as women like Eliza Lucas Pinckney of South Carolina, discussed in Chapter 4, and Philip Fithian of Virginia offered reading lessons to a handful of slaves.[181] Most of these efforts, however, though intending to make slaves better Christians, were not oriented towards their emancipation.

British and American anti-slavery writing, explored in every chapter of this book, may have been producing more of an imagination of a day when slaves would be emancipated rather than always instigating action. As Brown writes, "anti-slavery ideas could and did exist without generating comprehensive anti-slavery initiatives," and Blackburn says that instead of these initiatives, "there is a rhetorical radicalism combined with marginal, protracted, or unconvincing ameliorations."[182] As Chapter 4 indicates, even the New York Manumission Society was not necessarily in favor of the abolition of slavery; some members continued to own slaves, and others developed white racial supremacist attitudes despite being opposed to slavery. Nonetheless, religious groups like the Quakers had begun to ban their members from slaveholding, and some of the newly independent states passed laws banning the trade in slaves as well as ones providing for gradual emancipation within their jurisdictions. As Chapters 3 and 4 contend, however, men in states like New York and South Carolina continued to engage in the slave trade well into the middle of the nineteenth century, despite Jefferson's and Congress's 1807 federal ban on this commerce. Slavery continued to fund cultural philanthropy to institutions like universities and libraries, indicating its enduring connection to the cultural history of the United States.

BOOK HISTORY, ECONOMICS, AND THE FAILURE OF THE ENLIGHTENMENT IN EARLY AMERICA

This book's contribution to eighteenth-century cultural history, and to the postcolonial and African-American book history of McKenzie, Matt Cohen, Amory, Aravamudan, Apter, Fraser, Jackson, Lara Cohen and Jordan Stein, Joshi, and others through which it is examined, is relevant to the study of reading, literature, and culture in all periods. By using a blend of methodologies, this book shows how the economic enabling of the reader's book acquisitions, in this case through slavery, connects his or her taste to the ordering of a society and economy. It also establishes that while circulation records have traditionally been interpreted as only circumstantial evidence that a book was read, sequential borrowing of works and the velocity of books circulating to patrons enhances the prospect that these records may be taken as documentation of actual reading. Reading in any period or geographical context may be said to sublimate its discrepant relationship to

---

[179] Monaghan, 247–71.   [180] Monaghan, 254–6, 271.   [181] Monaghan, 243.
[182] Brown, *Consent*, 29; Blackburn, 149.

the economy—its "quarantining" of culture from the commerce that makes it possible—but we are heirs to how that practice begins in the eighteenth century.[183]

The study of America's first major proprietary subscription libraries, however, desublimates this relationship. We not only can see the traces of slaves' lives in these archives—"the archive of the masters." We can also observe how, particularly in Northern cities, the relative distance from slavery-intensive areas like South Carolina and the West Indies helped merchants "'absent' themselves from the complex of sugar and slavery" to achieve this quarantining physically.[184] The Charleston Library Society, though an exception to this geographic separation, also bears witness to how its proprietors attempted to distance themselves by literacy and class from very proximate slaves, even poorer whites. America's East Coast states, which contain the most universities founded with slave-trade fortunes, consequently, continue to be accorded "cultured" status based on this intellectual, social, and geographic distancing. That development has been enabled intellectually by a long historical process of acts of reading that have separated tasteful culture from the worldly concerns of commerce.[185] The methodology of book history, by separating the aesthetic object of the book from the untidy story of its readers' business affairs and funding, has for too long perpetuated this separation. This study's documentation of how reading is always mediated by the communities and institutions to which readers belong and which give texts meaning holds implications for how we read today. It promises to make us conscious of how our time and expense in reading is often constructed on the labor of others. It is my hope that this volume's documentation of reading in slavery-produced archives will inform studies of reception that include attention to the consumer aspect of the sociology of the text and, in doing so, contribute to our understanding of the cultural history of America and the British Atlantic.

What connects the chapters that follow in this book—the narrative unification of the cultural history of America's earliest libraries and their impact on culture and politics—is the understanding that libraries were civic institutions for the mediation of reading that constructed interpretive communities based on local, regional, and national needs. These needs were, in the first place, economic, which required political action in the form of revolutionary events like non-importation agreements and other protests of the Sugar Act of 1764 (a principal danger to West India traders in these port cities), the Stamp Act of 1765, the Declaratory Act of 1766, the Townshend Duties of 1767, and many other measures. The political ideas and legal texts available in the libraries helped ideologically motivate patriots, with works of literature also modeling the kinds of possessive individualism, individual rights, and other aspects of "British" subjectivity and citizenship for which they were fighting. Problems in economics and politics, accordingly, were at the root of why American library proprietors who were civic activists were reading certain works differently than their British counterparts.

The fact that the libraries up and down the East Coast were stocking the same titles helped create a more unified continental interpretive community than had

---

[183] Gikandi, 6.   [184] Gikandi, 36, 114.   [185] Wilder, 47–111.

existed before the crisis with Britain, or indeed, before these libraries were founded. This community formation took place upon the basis of unified economic interest in the face of Parliament regarding the colonists as "others" to British liberties and constitutional rights. Though the libraries of Salem, Newport, New York, Charleston, and Philadelphia had idiosyncrasies having to do with the ethnic and religious makeup of their cities' populations, they were united by a secular interest in trading in the Atlantic slavery economy. Slavery was central to the economic and political rights that they were claiming, so it is not surprising that they would put a revolutionary interpretation upon, and put to use, the ideas and attitudes modeled for them in imported books during the Atlantic crisis of the 1760s and 1770s. Slavery, and the civic engagement to preserve it, are therefore the economic and political basis for American cultural history in the colonial era, though moves to abolish it in the Early Republic period and afterwards aimed to correct and revise this history, an effort particularly manifest in America's first novels.

The story that this book is telling, accordingly, is of the human rights problems presented by the motives for Revolution, and the halting attempts to overcome them in the late eighteenth and nineteenth centuries. The moral of this story is that the eighteenth century failed to deliver the Enlightenment that its books imagined to the extent that even some of the founding documents of the age of revolutions were tainted by slavery. It was probably not until the social programs following the Great Depression and Second World War that many of the Enlightenment's goals in the arena of human rights were realized. The libraries where these imaginings took place are still with us today, however, and are important archives for understanding the eighteenth century's failure. They also help us appreciate how the nineteenth- and twentieth-century revolutions in political thought, human rights, and activism have improved the world enough for us to see how far this earlier past fell short of what many of its writers idealized.

1

Buying *Oroonoko* in Salem
Sentimentality, Spectacle, Slavery, and the Salem Social Library

I have, through my whole life, held the practice of slavery in such abhorrence, that I have never owned a negro or any other slave, though I have lived for many years in times, when the practice was not disgraceful, when the best men in my vicinity thought it not inconsistent with their character.

John Adams, letter to Robert J. Evans, June 8, 1819

Nowhere can the relationship between slavery, colonialism, and the transatlantic book trade be made more visible than in a study of the receptions of Aphra Behn's *Oroonoko* and other sentimental works like it in Salem, Massachusetts. *Oroonoko* is the most foundational narrative in our understanding of slavery and colonialism in early English literary history, being set both in West Africa and Surinam, and it has often been regarded as one of the first anti-slavery accounts of what life was like on a plantation. The presence of this story in colonial Massachusetts, in this case in the form of John Hawkesworth's 1759 stage adaptation of Behn's 1688 novel, indicates both a provincial investment in the slave-trade financing of the book trade and the rise of nascent anti-slavery opinion. To study this play in the context of eighteenth-century Salem is therefore to engage in a unique form of postcolonial book history that intervenes both in recent theoretical approaches to this story and in methodological innovations in the study of the material culture of the period. Scholarly work on the book trade in early America is a thriving example of how colonialism has been important in this methodology, yet it may be furthered by examining that trade in the context of the broader Atlantic slavery economy as it was experienced in Salem. This local book trade was centered on the Salem Social Library that was established there in 1760—a proprietary library with expensive shares owned by people engaged in the commerce of slavery and related enterprises. The foundation of this institution in an Atlantic slave-trade port shows how the history of American libraries, and the history of slavery that we receive from those libraries, are deeply connected.

The cultural history of Anglo-American engagement with the problems of race is therefore also one of libraries—both as distributors of the books constituting this history, and as institutions for the social mediation of reading that were themselves rendered possible by the philanthropy of people profiting from slavery. The Salem library was no exception, and is an example of how the cultural philanthropy of such people enabled this cultural history to begin to take form in the founding era of the United States. As a group of scholars has noted, though the wealthy of Salem donated to build roads, bridges, and schools, "Philanthropy in Salem was not always altruistic... While the library certainly enhanced Salem's cultural life, it was restricted by the founders to 'the sole use of ourselves, Heirs or assigns.'"[1] The slavery philanthropy that went into founding the library, in short, was self-interested, and though there was one woman proprietor of the library in the 1760s, membership was mostly restricted to wealthy white men. The moment of the founding of the library in the 1760s must therefore be understood as one in which the British empire's cultural capital in the form of books was available in America only to a small elite. Their civic engagement, in this chapter demonstrated in such activities as the non-importation agreements, or boycotts of British imports, was, in part, propelled by their reading about their English rights and about the history and success of such activism in other parts of the empire like Ireland.

The Salem Social Library is of value to this book's analysis of slavery's relationship to this engaged reading not only because it has the most thorough extant record of pre-revolutionary book borrowing of any of America's earliest proprietary subscription libraries, but also because its records indicate heavy borrowing in the category of "literature." Established in 1760, and becoming the Salem Athenaeum in 1810, its "charge book" for 1764 to 1768—crucial years in the development of American political attitudes and literary taste—survives in the Phillips Library of the Peabody Essex Museum. Circulation is recorded by patron, all of whom were proprietors, or shareholders in the library, and we have information about the business dealings of many of those proprietors because many of their families' papers are also located at the Phillips Library. The charge book therefore not only informs us of the reading network surrounding individual books and the tastes of those books' readers in other volumes, but of the social network constituting the leadership of Salem's slavery economy and political activism in the years leading up to the Revolutionary War.

Oroonoko was only one of many books with a social justice theme doing its work on this readership. When we regard it as a sentimental text that creates sympathy for the royal slave hero of the story, the African prince Oroonoko, we can see how it was like similar texts that were circulating in the zeitgeist of sentimentality in the Atlantic book market of the middle and late eighteenth century. Hawkesworth's most explicitly sentimental edition of 1759 was published and produced on stage just as that movement and its appetite for books with affective impact was getting off the ground. As Lynn Festa has written, "the massive expansion of colonial enterprise fostered a blossoming of sentimentality during the 1760s and 1770s."[2] This relationship between capital and affect should not be surprising; as Deidre Lynch has written, each had to take on a transferable and communicable form, and

---

[1] National Park Service, *Salem: Maritime Salem in the Age of Sail* (Washington: US Department of the Interior, 1987), 25.

[2] Lynn Festa, *Sentimental Figures of Empire in Eighteenth-Century Britain and France* (Johns Hopkins UP, 2006), 68.

books of sentimental literature circulated emotive characters in much the same way as money, helping to create the Atlantic as an affective network of exchange.[3] Even as the sentimental literature early Americans received encouraged them to locate, humanistically, an intrinsic self in their affections and to resist being a commodity, it also spread the appetite for goods circulating in transatlantic consumer society that were paradoxically about commodification.[4] Sentimental literature, in short, was telling Anglo-American readers not to be slaves to the transatlantic marketplace, which may have influenced them to enact anti-market activities like the non-importation agreements in order to claim their human rights.

The way that this literature was constituting the self, accordingly, had implications for feelings about slavery. Reading literature, particularly novels like Behn's, as Lynn Hunt has written, "created a sense of equality through passionate involvement in the narrative." The period of the rise of the novel "coincides with the birth of human rights," so it is not surprising that literary genres "played their part in promoting and sustaining anti-slavery feeling."[5] The message of sentimental literature like Hawkeworth's theatrical adaptation of Behn's novel, accordingly, also had implications for the anti-slavery movement, which specifically targeted slavery as a commercial, rather than a natural condition.

This chapter will first explore contemporary and recent receptions of *Oroonoko*'s sympathetic effects upon readers and audiences, focusing on book reviews in British magazines that Americans were reading. Here, it will claim that Hawkesworth and his Massachusetts readers, like current critics of our universities' historical relationships to slavery, were exposing the discrepancies and misrecognitions by which culture obfuscated its connections to the slave trade. Next, the chapter will examine the telling of the history of slavery in Massachusetts, and Salem in particular, as well as how that historiography relates to the activities of the Social Library's proprietors in slavery and slavery-related commerce. Third, it will use the charge book to assess which books library proprietors were borrowing and analyze how contemporaries were understanding spectacle, the emotions, and how they should feel about slavery. In doing so, it will place the purchase of *Oroonoko*'s anti-slavery sentiment in the context of the Salem interpretive community. Finally, it will conclude that Salem's patriot activity, manifest in actions like boycotts, would not have been possible without the sentimental construction of this interpretive community. It will also show how the trope of "slavery," so often appropriated by Anglo-American patriots to describe their relationship with Britain, also pointed in the direction of abolition, at least in Massachusetts.

The cultural history that this chapter explores, I contend, is essentially what Hayden White famously called a "literary artifact," shaped as much by the circumstances and priorities of Massachusetts in different phases of its development as by

---

[3] Deidre Lynch, *The Economy of Character: Novels, Market Culture, and the Business of Inner Meaning* (Chicago: U Chicago P, 1998), 81, 112.

[4] Festa, 68.

[5] Lynn Hunt, *Inventing Human Rights: A History* (NY: Norton, 2007), 39–40; Robin Blackburn, *The American Crucible: Slavery, Emancipation and Human Rights* (London: Verso, 2011), 154.

the availability of evidence regarding its trade in the Atlantic slavery economy.[6] Why historians have sometimes avoided and sometimes embraced the topic of colonial Massachusetts' connections to slavery is a historiographical challenge—a story in and of itself, as those I cite, from different periods in the last three centuries, bear witness. The ambivalent status of slavery in the Massachusetts imagination stems from how the colony and state regarded works like *Oroonoko* and anti-slavery efforts at the moment of the Revolution, attitudes that have shaped how British and American writers have engaged with this subject. How *Oroonoko* and works like it were read in Salem, accordingly, places the study of reading at the center of cultural history, bringing archival evidence and cultural materialist methodology to bear on that history.

I

Oroonoko, originally published by Behn in 1688 as a short novella, has received much scholarly attention in recent years because of its blend of the themes of race, gender, and colonialism. She was the first English woman to make her living by her pen; Virginia Woolf wrote that "All women together ought to let flowers fall upon the tomb of Aphra Behn...for it was she who earned them the right to speak their minds."[7] The novel's narrator, a woman who journeys to the English colony in Surinam, is supposed to be based on Behn herself, who traveled there as a girl. The plot centers on Oronooko, an African man of royal lineage who has received a European education and manners from a French tutor. Oroonoko is in a love affair with a woman, Imoinda, in their own African country, Coromantien. Their love is forbidden because his grandfather, the King, is interested in her. Oroonoko then secretly enters into the King's seraglio to make love to her, for which act Imoinda is sold into slavery. Oroonoko then continues his role as a war hero, beating other tribes in battles and capturing some of them as slaves. Unfortunately, when he boards an English ship to sell these slaves to its captain, he himself is captured, enslaved, and shipped to be sold in Surinam. Once there, his new owner rechristens him "Caesar," and treats him as a "royal" or "noble" slave who is more an ornament than a worker, which has led one critic to consider him a kind of "pet" similar to the African boys adopted by fashionable people in England at the time.[8] As luck would have it, Imoinda has also been enslaved and sent to Surinam, and their owners allow them to live as a couple and as "pets" to the English colonial community. After several adventures, some involving the Native Americans there, Imoinda becomes pregnant, and resolves that she doesn't want her child to be born a slave and urges Oroonoko to lead a slave rebellion. After he is defeated, captured, and

---

[6] Hayden White, "The Historical Text as Literary Artifact." *Narrative Dynamics: Essays on Time, Plot, Closure, and Frames.* Ed. Brian Richardson (Columbus: Ohio State UP, 2002), 191–210.

[7] Virginia Woolf, *A Room of One's Own* (London: Vintage, 1996), 61.

[8] Srinivas Aravamudan, *Tropicopolitans: Colonialism and Agency, 1688–1804* (Durham: Duke UP, 1999), 29–70.

tortured upon the failure of this rebellion, he kills Imoinda to let her die with dignity, and then himself is burned to death, drawn, and quartered.

This story maintained durable popularity over the course of the eighteenth century; it was never out of print, there were several adaptations of it, and it often has been taken have been an inspiration to the abolitionists. Thomas Southerne was the first to turn the novel into a play, which was first staged in 1695, published in 1696, and performed very frequently in the period. He altered the story in several ways. First, he made it appealing within the genre of the Restoration comedy's marriage plots by having Behn's narrator and another woman, one cross-dressing, traveling to Surinam to get husbands and having love intrigues doing so. Also, Imoinda is no longer African in his version, but rather a white woman who was the daughter of an English mercenary working for the Coromantien king; the scenes of inter-racial love helped heighten interest in the play. Jane Spencer has explained that Southerne's adaptation was "not designed to make a slaving nation uncomfortable," possibly because Southerne was seeking the patronage of the wealthy absentee Barbados plantation owner and patron of the arts Christopher Codrington, and it was generally received as a story more about love and heroism than slavery.[9] There were numerous translations of the novel and play into other languages, but it did not receive significant modification in English until about 1760, when Hawkesworth's adaptation (1759), Francis Gentleman's version (1760), and an anonymous edition that was not staged (1760) were published.[10] John Maxwell's *The Royal Captive* version was performed in 1767, but Southerne's adaptation continued to be performed even as these newer versions claimed audiences' attention. John Ferriar's new version of 1787, *The Tragedy of Oroonoko; or, The Royal Slave*, was a "deliberate attempt to create abolitionist propaganda," and was published in Manchester as *The Prince of Angola* (1788).[11]

Hawkesworth's adaptation, the one purchased in Salem, sets out from the preface to "render *Oroonoko* a regular Tragedy of five Acts" and omit Southerne's more comic elements in the play.[12] Southerne's choice to introduce the play with the comedic marriage plot is, in Hawkesworth's view, "loose and contemptible," leading to "Immorality" and undermining the "Merit of the tragic Scenes in this play."[13] Oroonoko and Imoinda are intended, in this version, to be sentimental figures.[14] They "are so connected as to make but one Object, in which all the Passions of the Audience, moved by the most tender and exquisite Distress, are concentered."[15] Hawkesworth also changed Southerne's music in the play to render sympathy for the enslaved. "It was thought," he writes, "that the Songs supposed to be sung by

[9] Jane Spencer, *Aphra Behn's Afterlife* (Oxford: Oxford UP, 2000), 232.

[10] Spencer, 244.   [11] Spencer, 257–8.

[12] John Hawkesworth and Thomas Southerne, *Oroonoko, a Tragedy, as it is Now Acted at the Theatre-Royal in Drury Lane* (London: Bathurst, 1759), front matter.

[13] Hawkesworth & Southerne, front matter.

[14] Aravamudan, 49, 63; Spencer, 244, 247, 249, 257; J. R. Oldfield, "Ties of Soft Humanity: Slavery and Race in British Drama, 1760–1800." *Huntington Library Quarterly* 56.1 (Winter 1993): 4; Brycchan Carey, "To Force a Tear: Anti-Slavery on the Eighteenth-Century London Stage." *Affect and Abolition in the Anglo-Atlantic, 1770–1830*. Ed. Stephen Ahern (Aldershot: Ashgate, 2013), 112.

[15] Hawkesworth & Southerne, front matter.

the Slaves on this Occasion, should, though amorous, be plaintive, the Expression of Beings at once capable of Love, and conscious of a Condition in which all its delicacies must become the Instruments of Pain."[16] In addition, scenes between Oroonoko and his co-conspirators in the play's slave rebellion are altered so that Oroonoko is able to detect an informer, Hotman—who betrayed his friend Aboan and the rebellion—and act accordingly. "His superior Sagacity," Hawkesworth says, "had detected the Artifice by which his Friend had been deceived to their mutual ruin."[17] Hawkesworth's adaptation, in short, is claiming to be a more enlightened version of Southerne's play that both harkens back to Behn's original text and renders a version of the tragic hero compatible with 1759's episteme of sentimentality.

The dissemination of Hawkesworth's *Oroonoko* play to the American colonies and its reading there was facilitated, in part, by the paratexual apparatus of book reviews, at least three of which appeared in the December 1759 editions, respectively, of the *London Magazine*, the *Gentleman's Magazine*, and the *Critical Review*. It may have been from one of these magazines that George Gardner, a Harvard student from Salem who was the son of a merchant, Samuel Gardner, heard about the play. The elder Gardner was also a Harvard graduate and leading trader in slaves and the products of slavery, who, like other Salem businessmen involved in that commerce, was wealthy enough to afford a share in the Salem Social Library. George, when he graduated in 1762, would resist going into his father's business, and would become a liquor store owner instead, dying at the age of thirty in the early 1770s. On January 22, 1760—well within the time the December reviews could have arrived from London—he ordered an imported copy of Hawkesworth's play from the leading Boston importer of London books, the Reverend Jeremy Condy, who would become the purchasing agent for the Salem Social Library.[18] Priced at 1 shilling 2 pence, it was highly likely an individual play text, as George bought William Congreve's tragedy *The Mourning Bride* on the same day for the same price; it also could not have been Behn's novel because a contemporary booksellers' catalog had novels going for at least three shillings.[19] It was most likely Hawkesworth's version because colonists tended to import the latest fashions. Though I have not been able to trace with any exactitude George's reading and interpretation of the book, the fact that it was purchased by someone from a town that made its living through the slavery-based Atlantic economy suggests at least an incipient taste for books that objected to, or at least engaged with, the ethics of that trade.

This seemingly incongruous discovery of such a utopian book in Salem follows the cultural logic of what Fredric Jameson and Pierre Bourdieu term "discrepancy," or the dialectical conflict between the privileged and excluded that is resolved in culture's misrecognitions and in habits that render such contradictions

---

[16] Hawkesworth & Southerne, front matter.   [17] Hawkesworth & Southerne, front matter.
[18] Jeremiah Condy, "Account book, 1759–1770," MSS Folio Vol. C, 17, American Antiquarian Society. Worcester, Massachusetts.
[19] Thomas Lowndes, *A New Catalogue of Lownds Circulating Library* (London: Lowdes, 1761), 49, 74.

unconscious.[20] That other readers like Gardner were both questioning and participating in such discrepancies is evident in the fact that a Harvard colleague, Peter Atherton, purchased *Oroonoko* a month later on February 21, 1760, perhaps indicating that their ambiguous relationship to slavery and abolition was characteristic of Harvard as a whole.[21] Indeed, cultural "discrepancy" is what recent works by Craig Wilder and others on American universities' connections to slavery seek to expose; Hawkesworth and readers like Gardner and Atherton, similarly, were rendering such misrecognitions visible in their own moment.[22]

As Hawkesworth's prologue had signaled, the central concern of all three periodical reviews is how Hawkesworth had transformed Southerne's play by removing the comedic plot of women arriving in Surinam to find husbands in order to focus on the tragedy of Oroonoko and Imoinda's deaths due to their foiled attempts to free themselves from slavery. The *London Magazine* and *Gentleman's Magazine* supported the changes Hawkesworth made, and both encouraged attention to the play by, in separate sections of the magazines from the book lists, including an excerpt from the prologue.[23] It was a review, later attributed to Samuel Johnson, which appeared in the December 1 edition of the *Critical Review*—a magazine that New Englanders such as the Salem Customs Collector James Cockle were buying from Condy—that made a more pronounced case for the play's anti-slavery effects.[24] James Basker notes that though the majority of the review is a formalist literary take on the playwright's techniques, at the center of it is a "radical insight into Hawkesworth's central achievement, his development of the play as an expressly anti-slavery vehicle, an aim that neither Southerne nor Behn before him can be said to have pursued unequivocally, if at all."[25]

Johnson focuses on two scenes, the first the slave rebellion begun in Act 1 Scene 3, which is "important in the play for shifting the focus from one man's fate onto a whole people suffering in captivity and for humanizing these people, granting them inner lives, emotional depth, and psychological complexity."[26] Johnson's second comment is on the songs in Act 2 Scene 3, in which "the lovers' duet is thus quietly transformed into a protest against the dehumanizing effects of slavery."[27] Hawkesworth and Johnson thereby skewer the myth of "'the happy Negro' and what already by the end of the eighteenth century was emerging as a trope in the works of apologists for slavery."[28] Johnson may have been particularly inclined to give this play a review favorable to abolition because of several events and publications

[20] Fredric Jameson, *The Political Unconscious: Narrative as a Socially Symbolic Act* (Ithaca: Cornell UP, 1981), 288–99; Xudong Zhang, "Modernity as Cultural Politics: Jameson and China." *Fredric Jameson: A Critical Reader*. Eds Sean Homer and Douglas Kellner (NY: Palgrave, 2004), 183; Pierre Bourdieu, *Distinction: A Social Critique of the Judgment of Taste*. Trans. Richard Nice (Cambridge: Harvard UP, 1984), 86.

[21] Condy, 79; Bourdieu, 366.

[22] Craig Steven Wilder, *Ebony and Ivy: Race, Slavery, and the Troubled History of America's Universities* (NY: Bloomsbury P, 2013), 47–111.

[23] *London Magazine, or Gentleman's Monthly Intelligencer* 28 (Dec. 1759), 688, 677; *Gentleman's Magazine, by Sylvanus Urban, Gent* 29 (Dec. 1759), 666.

[24] Condy, 66.

[25] James Basker, "Intimations of Abolition in 1759." *Age of Johnson* 12.1 (2001): 54–5.

[26] Basker, 55.   [27] Basker, 58.   [28] Basker, 58.

in the previous and current years. He had witnessed an African prince weeping at a London performance of Southerne's play in 1749. Also, his London black friend Francis Barber had disappeared (presumed kidnapped into slavery) in 1758–9. In addition, Johnson had objected to slavery in 1759 in his introduction to *The World Displayed*, two new issues of the *Idler*, and even in earlier works like *The Life of Francis Drake* and the *Life of Savage*, and would later do so most famously in *Taxation no Tyranny*.[29] Despite this account of how contemporaries were reading the story, current critics like Suvir Kaul, Anne Widmayer, and Mita Choudhury lament the way Behn's novella and Southerne and Hawkesworth's plays "naturalize slavery as a transcultural condition" in that Oroonoko accepts the practice in his own country of enslaving prisoners of war.[30]

The status of the emotions in the play—of the situating of Hawkesworth's anti-slavery in tropes of sentimentality and sympathy—is perhaps the locus for the most contestation about whether the play is ambivalent to slavery and the relation between races. For some critics, it is uncontroversial to say that creating sympathy for the enslaved helped fuel anti-slavery advocacy. Srinivas Aravamudan has acknowledged that the attitude towards pathos changed by the time Hawkesworth adapted the play and that his version was written with heightened sentimentalism.[31] Hawkesworth's revisions have led Spencer to argue that "his play uses sentimental discourse to present black slaves as fully human by virtue of their finer feelings," which made for good anti-slavery propaganda.[32] Brycchan Carey concurs, writing that altering the play in this direction "marks Hawkesworth's project as sentimental," an argument in which he is joined by J. R. Oldfield.[33]

Kaul, however, sees a problem in Hawkesworth's pathos, and argues that Hawkesworth is actually worse than Southerne, discussing a speech by Blandford to Maria—both sympathetic towards the slaves—about the slave trade being a "mercy" for those who would otherwise be killed after losing a battle: "This recasting of the slave trade as a potentially life-saving intervention on behalf of Africans is only an egregious instance of Hawkesworth's larger effort to emphasize the redeeming possibilities of sympathy without seriously questioning the structure or function of slavery."[34] Similarly, Joyce McDonald is concerned that the play makes "Hawkesworth's slaves enclose themselves within a culture of pathos and sensibility."[35] This authorial strategy is made problematic by an incongruous scene of the rage over an attempted rape of Imoinda by the lieutenant governor being ameliorated with a sentimental musical interlude where male and female slaves sing that "Love, Love and Joy must both be free, | They live not

---

[29] Basker, 48–51.

[30] Suvir Kaul, "Reading Literary Symptoms: Colonial Pathologies and the *Oroonoko* Fictions of Behn, Southerne, and Hawkesworth." *Eighteenth-Century Life* 18.3 (Nov. 1994): 84; Anne F. Widmayer, "The Politics of Adapting Behn's *Oroonoko*." *Comparative Drama* 37.2 (Summer 2003): 207; Mita Choudhury, "Race, Performance, and the Silenced Prince of Angola." *A Companion to Restoration Drama*. Ed. Susan J. Owen (Oxford: Blackwell, 2001), 167.

[31] Aravamudan, 63.   [32] Spencer, 247, 249, 257.

[33] Carey, "To Force a Tear," 112; Oldfield, 4.   [34] Kaul, 93.

[35] Joyce Green McDonald, "The Disappearing African Woman: Imoinda in 'Oroonoko' after Behn." *ELH* 66.1 (Spring 1999): 81.

but with Liberty."[36] One should be suspicious of sympathy, sensibility, and sentimentality in regard to slavery fictions, Kaul contends, as in Hawkesworth we see "a final cleansing of the excesses of the *Oroonoko* story, so that it safely, *rationally*, reaffirms the superiority of English self-conception in the language of transcultural empathy—an empathy that enacts a Eurocentric aristocracy of refinement and appropriate emotion."[37]

If early Americans were indeed seeking European refinement in their consumer yen for imported books and other luxuries, then George Gardner's consumption of Hawkesworth's staging of white refinement in opposing slavery is simultaneously solipsistic, possessively individualistic, and potentially liberating for others. The play's sympathetic effects may have been appealing, in Festa's terms, because Oroonoko, as a royal slave, was an aristocrat who was supposed to be standing apart from the market, not in it as a commodity. This transference to a similarly stoic white reading subject of the black prince's humiliation at being marketed is accomplished, Ramesh Mallipeddi says, through a sentimental process of spectacle. As Ramesh Mallipeddi argues, Behn's female narrator's "sexualization of, and her identification with, Oroonoko is abetted by his polished, tapering body," turning his life and death into a spectacle that imbricates his body in "new ideologies of empire" and the "commodity form."[38] He is "a typical romance hero whose feats of valor are untouched by the vagaries of slavery and servitude," but that heroism is conflated with blackness and exoticism to the extent that Oroonoko becomes "fetishized as an exotic commodity."[39] Sympathy for him may have been solipsistic for white Americans in the 1760s seeking rights because he stands for the inalienable, not fungible nature of humanity: "the suffering slave is an embodied self, a particular person—in fact, a royal one—endowed with certain inalienable rights such as bodily self-possession."[40] Possessive individualism, here, is not only the right to consume in the marketplace, but to own oneself in that marketplace. The scandal for early American white readers is that it is Oroonoko's body that is placed as the bulwark against anyone, white or black, being alienable, but it is only the spectacle of Oroonoko's death that renders that inalienability sacred.

It is in this way that the sympathy for the suffering black hero in *Oroonoko* and other writing is almost immediately appropriated and put into service to a white American patriotism that positioned those whites as slaves in search of this sentimentally induced idea of liberty. Despite this mirroring effect of sympathy for the use of the individual in the white audience, however, there is evidence to suggest that many whites, including citizens of Salem and Massachusetts who were arguing for their freedom from Britain, were also becoming abolitionists. The divided nature of Americans' attitude towards slavery may well have emerged from the very different effects on readers of sympathetic, and, in some cases, sentimental, writing

[36] J. R. Oldfield, *Transatlantic Abolitionism in the Age of Revolution: An International History of Anti-slavery, c. 1787–1820* (Cambridge: Cambridge UP, 2013), 81.

[37] Kaul, 81.

[38] Ramesh Mallipeddi, *Spectacular Suffering: Witnessing Slavery in the Eighteenth-Century British Atlantic* (Charlottesville: U Virginia P, 2016), 36.

[39] Mallipeddi, 37, 39, 41.   [40] Mallipeddi, 48.

about slavery. Mapping the taste in sentimental literature, and reading habits related to it, in a colonial slave port like Salem provides a case study not only of the role of slavery in the northern colonies, but also of the importance of early proprietary subscription libraries like the Salem Social Library in helping to establish colonial interpretive communities.

II

That someone in Salem purchased *Oroonoko* seems counter-cultural, as the town's life revolved around the Atlantic slave trade, and it was wealth from that trade that financed the central space of reading, the library. Most of the original proprietors of the library—the philanthropists/shareholders who funded it—were either directly involved in the shipping of slaves or derived their wealth from shipping provisions to plantations in return for slave-produced commodities. Even if they were not merchants, they might invest in voyages or insure them, and due to the barter nature of the economy in an environment where there was a limited amount of circulating currency, they might use plantation products like sugar and rum in payments with each other. Surviving papers of some of these proprietors add documentation to the very limited information that we have about the history of the slave trade in Massachusetts, and Salem in particular, and provide an understanding of the slavery basis for literary taste in the colony. Further, these papers help explain why this story has not been told before, and are therefore of central importance to understanding how eighteenth-century cultural historiography has gone through phases of the repression, recovery, and reburial of aspects of this story for centuries.

The Salem Social Library owes its beginning to a society for "improvement in literature and philosophy"—Salem's "Monday Evening Club."[41] This club was "comprised of more than thirty of Salem's most affluent citizens"—gentlemen who "possessed literary attainments of a high order," and which had been meeting since 1750. They met at a local tavern on March 31, 1760, and invested a total of 175 guineas for the establishment of the library.[42] There were twenty-seven original subscribers who ventured anything from five to twenty pounds.[43] Half of the subscribers were Harvard graduates, and there were three clergymen, two doctors, a port official, and many others, most of whom were merchants. Many of these men donated their own books to the library, which was regarded as "one of the most important libraries in the Colonies."[44] Many of the subscribers owned slaves, who were elliptically classified as "servants for life" in the 1771 Massachusetts tax assessment.[45]

---

[41] H. Wheatland, "Sketch of the Social and Philosophical Libraries." *Proceedings of the Essex Institute* 2 (1856–1860): 140–6, 140; Cynthia B. Wiggin, *A Short History of the Salem Athenaeum* (Salem: Forest River P, 1972), 4.

[42] Wiggin, 4.   [43] Wheatland, 141.   [44] Wiggin, 5–6.

[45] Bettye Hobbs Pruitt, *The Massachusetts Tax Valuation List of 1771* (Boston: G. K. Hall, 1978), 130–54.

Condy, Boston's major seller of books imported from England, was selected to be the agent by whom the library would acquire British books, and he would do so by travelling to London personally and buying them from booksellers there. He was probably chosen because he had a reputation of catering to educated men and professionals, some of whom were affiliated with Harvard.[46] Condy arranged for a total of 182 books, in 415 volumes, which were obtained by London bookseller Joseph Richardson and shipped aboard a ship called the *Hawke* for an order totaling £104.5.1, and which arrived in Salem in the spring of 1761.[47] These were added to 124 volumes donated by proprietors, making for a total original catalog of 539 volumes.[48] As in Britain, where the initial premises of a library was often a pub, residence, or other building, the library was kept in a local brick schoolhouse. In addition to the subscription for membership, proprietors usually paid an annual assessment to obtain new books.[49] The cost of proprietorship in the Social Library limited the number of owners mostly to those involved in shipping, though historians like James Duncan Phillips have said that there may have been times when ordinary people could obtain a book.[50] The charge book shows no such extension of privileges, however, and the National Park Service has cast doubt on the shareholders' generosity.[51] Consequently, lack of sympathy for the enslaved as depicted in *Oroonoko* would seem consistent with the shareholders' tribal attitude towards charity, at least until their reading, described later in this chapter, worked upon the emotions of some of them.

The story of Salem's involvement in slavery is not often told, but why it has sometimes been revealed or repressed over the course of close to three centuries may be as interesting as the fact of its existence, and is central to the maritime history of this seafaring New England city. Massachusetts was the first English colony on the continent to legalize slavery. Historians conventionally agree that the first evidence of a slave ship arriving in Boston was the *Desire* in 1638, the government-sponsored voyage of which had traded captive Native Americans from the Pequot War to the West Indies in exchange for African slaves.[52] This event prompted a clarification in law, and in 1641 the legislature passed "The Massachusetts Body of Liberties," which declared that bond slavery would be illegal unless it applied to "lawful captives taken in just wars. And such strangers as willingly sell themselves. Or are sold to us."[53] This law was upheld "through the whole colonial period," and

---

[46] Elizabeth Carroll Reilly and David D. Hall, "Customers and the Market for Books." *A History of the Book in America, Volume 1: The Colonial Book in the Atlantic World.* Eds Hugh Amory and David D. Hall (Chapel Hill: U North Carolina P, 2007), 389.

[47] Wheatland, 143.   [48] Wheatland, 143.

[49] David Allan, *A Nation of Readers: The Lending Library in Georgian England* (London: The British Library, 2008), 88; Wiggin, 6–7; Wheatland, 143–4.

[50] James Duncan Phillips, *Salem in the Eighteenth Century* (Boston: Houghton Mifflin, 1937), 265.

[51] *Salem: Maritime Salem in the Age of Sail* (National Park Service, Washington: US Department of the Interior, 1987), 25.

[52] George H. Moore, *Notes on the History of Slavery in Massachusetts* (NY: Appleton, 1866), 9; Lorenzo Johnston Greene, *The Negro in Colonial New England 1620–1776* (NY: Columbia UP, 1942), 16–17; C. S. Manegold, *Ten Hills Farm: The Forgotten History of Slavery in the North* (Princeton: Princeton UP, 2011), 45; Joseph B. Felt, *Annals of Salem, Volume 2* (Salem: W & S.B. Ives, 1849), 2:230–1.

[53] Moore, *Notes*, 11–30; Felt, 2:415; Manegold, 46.

was expanded to include provisions for the slave status of children born to slaves.[54] Boston alone had 1,693 African American slaves and sixty-nine Native American slaves mentioned in probate documents from 1647 to 1770.[55] Nineteenth-century scholarship claimed that there were approximately 650 African slaves in Massachusetts in 1708, 2,000 in 1720, 2,600 in 1735, 4,489 in 1754, 5,779 in 1764–5, 5,249 in 1776, 4,377 in 1784, 4,371 in 1786, and 6,001 in 1790.[56] Isaac Royall of Medford, himself an owner of a plantation in Antigua and a slave trader, held the most slaves of anyone in the colony, having sixty-nine slaves at one time or another, though Alexandra Chan estimates that the number might have been double that.[57] There was enough of a slave trade within the colony of Massachusetts for 1,487 slave-for-sale advertisements to be taken out in the *Boston Newsletter* and *Boston Gazette* between 1704 and 1781.[58]

To be sure, however, the wealth Massachusetts colonials obtained through slavery was not due primarily to the comparatively few slaves they owned, but was rather derived from shipping slaves from Africa and related parts to the West Indies and southern colonies, with slaves occasionally brought from thence north. As the librarian of the New York Historical Society, George Moore, wrote at the close of the Civil War, Massachusetts products like fish, lumber, and other wood products were often exported on ships to the Eastern Atlantic that would return to the Western Atlantic with slaves in a triangular, in some cases square, trade:

> The ships which took cargoes of staves and fish to Madeira and the Canaries were accustomed to touch on the coast of Guinea to trade for negroes, who were carried generally to Barbadoes or other English Islands in the West Indies, the demand for them at home being small. So far, however, from any protest being made, the first code of laws in Massachusetts established slavery, as we have shown, and at the very birth of the foreign commerce of New England the African slave-trade became a regular business.[59]

This detailing of how a Massachusetts slave-trade transaction and shipping route would take place may have been controversial at a time when the North was celebrating its triumph in the Civil War, but it was not unheard of for contemporaries writing before the end of the Civil War to speak on the subject.

For example, a historian of abolitionist sympathies writing the *Annals of Salem* in 1849, Joseph Felt, referred to several eighteenth-century slave-trading voyages out of Salem, lamenting the plight of so many like Oroonoko. He established that on December 21, 1763, "One of our vessels sails for Guinea" and that on

---

[54] Moore, *Notes*, 18.

[55] Peter Benes, "Slavery in Boston Households, 1647–1770." *Slavery/Anti-slavery in New England, the Dublin Seminar for New England Folklife Annual Proceedings*. Ed. Peter Benes (June 2003), 15.

[56] Moore, *Notes*, 50–1; Charles Deane, "The Connection of Massachusetts with Slavery and the Slave Trade." *Proceedings of the American Antiquarian Society*. New Series, Vol. 4. Oct. 1885–Apr. 1887 (Worcester: AAS, 1888), 216.

[57] Manegold, 192.

[58] Robert E. Desrochers, Jr, "Slave-for-Sale Advertisements and Slavery in Massachusetts, 1704–1781." *The William and Mary Quarterly* 59.3 (July 2002): 623–64, 624.

[59] Moore, *Notes*, 28–9.

October 29, 1771, "one of our vessels had arrived at Barbadoes from Guinea. She had lost one of her mates."[60] In an expression of his anti-slavery feelings, he comments on his note about a 1773 shipboard slave insurrection: "July 13. One of our vessels had reached the West Indies from the river Gambia, with slaves. All her crew had died except the mate and one hand. Such deadly havoc among dealers in human flesh has ever been one of its retributive consequences."[61] He indicts both New Englanders and Africans for engaging in the Guinea trade:

> Of the instructions, long given in our country, relative to the Guinea trade, we have the following. They come to our own threshold. They were indicted by men of otherwise respectable standing. They hold a language as though no human right was violated, even if those of our race were bartered for the liquid of perdition [rum], torn from the dearest connections, home and nation, and sold into perpetual bondage. This, too, when slavery was terminated in our Commonwealth. Strange, that ever the lust of gain should have presented such a caricature of nice care for tithing mint, and flagrant omission of the weightier matters of equity. It is well, that revolution in opinion, long ago cleansed out from our commercial reputation, such a deep moral leprosy.[62]

Felt prints the only known Salem order to one of its ships bound for Africa, though he is careful to omit the names of the writer (likely the owner) and the captain, no doubt to spare their descendants. Dated November 12, 1785, it orders the brig *Favorite* to "make the best of your way to the coast of Africa, and there invest your cargo in slaves" and "touch at St. Pierre's, Martinico" to trade the slaves.[63] He writes of the *Favorite* and another vessel being active in slaving at the same time: ". . . Thus were orders given to convert the vessel [the *Favorite*], which had recently been a refuge to a considerable number of our shipwrecked countrymen, into a pandemonium for many more of down trodden Africa. The brig *Gambia* was reported the same month, as bound on the like nefarious traffic."[64] The *Favorite* was again reported as making the triangular route in 1787: "Nov. 27: News from the brig *Favorite*, that she had arrived at Martinico from her voyage to the coast of Guinea, and, as the usual result of such enterprises, that disease had swept away a large number of her crew, as well as of the poor Africans, with which she was crowded."[65] Another Salem ship had stopped at Goree Island, a slave port in Senegal, the same year: "May 13. A brig arrives from Goree, with the loss of her mate and mainmast in a gale."[66] He writes of one of the Crowninshields, George, helping a ship with 50 slaves to port in 1790.[67] Felt mentions a voyage in 1791: "Sept. 6. Reported that another of our vessels, the St. John, had arrived at Surinam from Africa. This shows, that a few of our merchants, like others in various sea ports, still loved money more than the far greater riches of a good conscience,—more than conformity with the demands of human rights, with the law of the land and the religion of their God."[68] Though most of these records of voyages are for the period after 1776,

---

[60] Felt, 2:261, 2:264.   [61] Felt, 2:265.   [62] Felt, 2:288–9.   [63] Felt, 2:289–91.
[64] Felt, 2:291.   [65] Felt, 2:292.   [66] Felt, 2:292.
[67] Felt, 2:294.   [68] Felt, 2:296.

it is highly probably that the surviving 1785 orders for the *Favorite's* Africa expedition were quite common before the Revolution. Felt's account, in short, is one that is closest both to the eighteenth century and to slavery debates in his own time; there seems to be no similar abolitionist history of Massachusetts slave trading, other than George Moore's, like it in his own century.

Indeed, many historians seemed to be engaged in a defense of Massachusetts on this count, particularly after the Civil War, suggesting a pattern of erasure and reburial of the story of slavery in the state and rest of the North that still affects how we tell this history today. Charles Deane, in a paper for the American Antiquarian Society of 1879, made the argument that the British were the main profiteers in the slave trade, that Rhode Islanders were the only Americans to trade slaves, and that Massachusetts only had slaves due to commerce with Rhode Island. Buried in a footnote, however, are interviews that Jeremy Belknap, founder of the Massachusetts Historical Society, had performed with eighteenth-century men before their deaths that suggest varying memories as to whether Massachusetts vessels sailed to Africa on slave purchasing missions. Among the testimony is that of Dr. John Eliot, born in 1754:

> The African trade was carried on; and commenced at an early period; to a small extent compared with Rhode Island, but it made a considerable branch of our commerce (to judge from the number of our still-houses, and masters of vessels now living who have been in the trade). It declined very little till the revolution. Some excellent writings were diffused previously to this, and the sentiment of the people was against it; but the merchants who had been engaged in the business still continued sending their vessels for slaves, till the trade was prohibited by act of the court, 1788.[69]

Similarly, Thomas Pemberton, born 1728, responded to Belknap with an affirmation of this commerce's existence:

> We know that a large trade to Guinea was carried on for many years by the citizens of the Massachusetts colony, who were the proprietors of the vessels and their cargoes, out and home. Some of the slaves purchased in Guinea, and I suppose the greatest part of them, were sold in the West Indies, some were brought to Boston and Charlestown, and sold to town and country purchasers by the head... This business of importing and selling negroes continued till nearly the time of the controversy with Great Britain. The precise date when it wholly ceased I cannot ascertain, but it declined and drew to a period about the time the British Parliament attempted to enslave the colonists by arbitrary acts.[70]

Other witnesses said that Massachusetts engaged in slavery to a lesser extent than these two excerpts suggest. Accordingly, though he acknowledges some trade in slaves and profits from rum distilleries fueled by the sugar trade with the West Indies, Deane says that "The African trade was never prosecuted to a great extent by the merchants of Massachusetts," a conclusion that seems to contradict some of the testimony buried in his footnote.[71]

[69] Deane, 209–10 n. 1.   [70] Deane, 209–10 n. 1.   [71] Deane, 210.

It is difficult to find histories that avow eighteenth-century Massachusetts slavery from the time Moore wrote until the middle of the twentieth century. For example, James Duncan Phillips's *Salem in the Eighteenth Century* of 1937, a great deal of which discusses the commerce of the city, does not mention slavery at all. Yet Lorenzo Greene, writing just a few years later in 1942, confirmed this primary role of Massachusetts in the trading, not just the ownership, of slaves.[72] Though they were not alone among New Englanders in entering the Atlantic network of trade in this way, Bostonians were the leaders. "Boston was preeminent as the port of departure for slave ships," wrote Greene, "with Newport, Rhode Island, as its closest rival; but Salem, Newburyport, Charlestown and Kittery," and other towns in New England also participated in the slave trade.[73] Edgar McManus's *A History of Negro Slavery in New York* (1966) and *Black Bondage in the North* (1973) were also crucial in reviving this history. More recently, the work of Joanne Pope Melish, Craig Wilder, and many other historians has pushed this history to the center of scholarly debate, paralleling the renewed interest literary critics have had in the story of *Oroonoko* and its problems of slavery, race, and colonialism.[74]

Records obtained by the Historical Society of Medford, Massachusetts provide some of the little surviving primary documentation of the Massachusetts trade in African bodies in this period. The "Medford Slave Letters" are a series of correspondences between the years 1759 and 1769—exactly at the time that the Salem Social Library was established—documenting the trade in slaves and connected commodities by Timothy Fitch (see Figure 1.1), a Medford man who also did business in Salem and other nearby towns. Fitch was also connected to Salem through his second wife Eunice Brown Plaisted, the widow of Ichabod Plaisted of Salem (see Figure 1.2), and he and his wife kept a house in Salem as well as in Boston and Medford. It is worth analyzing the Medford Slave Letters in detail not only because they show how slaving voyages worked, but also because they are part of the story of how the history of slavery in Massachusetts has been both repressed and recovered.

The first letter, dated Boston, January 14, 1759, is from Fitch to William Ellery (see Figure 1.3). Ellery, who later represented Rhode Island at the signing of the Declaration of Independence, captained a vessel for Fitch called the *Caesar*. In the letter, Fitch instructs Ellery to sail to Senegal and other places on Africa's coast to sell his cargo and "to purchase a Cargo of slaves with which you are to proceed to South Carolines." Fitch also lists backup ports such as St Christopher's and St Eustatia in the West Indies should events like a cessation of the Seven Years War happen, and orders that the slaves be exchanged for the produce of those ports or "undoubted Bills of Exchange, Otherwise Cash." He also orders Ellery to meet with other ships in which he has invested, the schooner *Bachus*, captained by Walter Rand, and the sloop *Peggy*, captained by Elias Ellery, in Sierra Leone and to sell these ships and to put their slave cargoes and their crews on his ship in the

[72] Greene, 20.   [73] Greene, 27–8.
[74] Joanne Pope Melish, *Disowning Slavery: Gradual Emancipation and "Race" in New England, 1780–1860* (Ithaca: Cornell UP, 1998); Wilder.

Figure 1.1 Joseph Blackburn (English, c. 1700–78) *Portrait of Timothy Fitch*, 1760–75. Oil on canvas. Boston, Massachusetts, United States. 48 ½ × 39 ½ inches (123.19 × 100.33 cm). Peabody Essex Museum, Bequest of Miss Caroline R. Derby, 1878. Photo 1961.

hopes of transporting 200 slaves.[75] Another document dated August 21, 1759 lists the sale of slaves in Barbados, likely the cargo of this voyage.[76]

Fitch gives similar instructions to Captain Peter Gwinn of the schooner *Phillis* on January 12, 1760, even providing for the slaves to be brought to Boston, and on November 8, 1760, in which Gwinn is told to go to Africa in convoy with another of Fitch's ships.[77] The Boston goods to be traded by Gwinn in Africa include rum, sugar, wine, snuff, coffee, flour, bread, pork, beef, gunpowder, pitch, turpentine, tar, tools, and furniture.[78] A letter of September 4, 1761 orders Gwinn on a voyage in which he is to travel to Africa and bring slaves to South Carolina or

[75] Timothy Fitch, *The Medford Slave Trade Letters, 1759–1765*. Medford Historical Society & Museum. Accessed May 2, 2016. <http://www.medfordhistorical.org/collections/slave-trade-letters/voyage-one-capt-william-ellery-behalf-timothy-fitch/>.

[76] Fitch, <http://www.medfordhistorical.org/collections/slave-trade-letters/bridge-town-barbados-list-slaves-auctioned/>.

[77] Fitch, <http://www.medfordhistorical.org/collections/slave-trade-letters/peter-gwinns-first-voyage-record-behalf-timothy-fitch/; http://www.medfordhistorical.org/collections/slave-trade-letters/voyage-timothy-fitch-peter-gwinn/>.

[78] Fitch, <http://www.medfordhistorical.org/collections/slave-trade-letters/invoice-sundry-merchandize-shipt/>.

Figure 1.2 Joseph Blackburn (English, c. 1700–78) *Portrait of Eunice Brown Fitch* (d. 1799), c. 1760. Oil on canvas. Boston, Massachusetts, United States. 48 ½ × 39 ½ inches (123.19 × 100.33 cm). Peabody Essex Museum, Bequest of Miss Caroline R. Derby, 1878. Photo 1962 Jeffrey R. Dykes/PEM.

Montecristo and buy sugar, molasses, or rice, or if they cannot be obtained, gold or bills of exchange, all of which were to be shipped back to Boston.[79] A similar order has Gwinn going on a triangular trade mission in October 1762 with a similar cargo of Boston items.[80] A March 5, 1764 mid-voyage letter has Gwinn sailing for Havana via Africa to exchange slaves for sterling, Spanish milled dollars, and sugar in Cuba, and a June 5, 1765 letter orders Gwinn to take slaves from Africa to Montecristo and St Eustatia and bring cash and molasses back to Boston.[81] In October 1765, he is ordered to take slaves from Africa to Surinam, Anguilla, St Eustatia, St Martens, or St Croix, and to bring back cash and sugar; a 1766

[79] Fitch, <http://www.medfordhistorical.org/collections/slave-trade-letters/voyage-capt-peter-gwinn-senegal/>.
[80] Fitch, <http://www.medfordhistorical.org/collections/slave-trade-letters/capt-peter-gwinn-makes-another-voyage/; http://www.medfordhistorical.org/collections/slave-trade-letters/invoice-sundry-merchandize-shipped/>.
[81] Fitch, <http://www.medfordhistorical.org/collections/slave-trade-letters/mid-voyage-letter-contract-capt-peter-gwinn/; http://www.medfordhistorical.org/collections/slave-trade-letters/correspondence-mid-voyage-timothy-fitch-peter-gwinn/>.

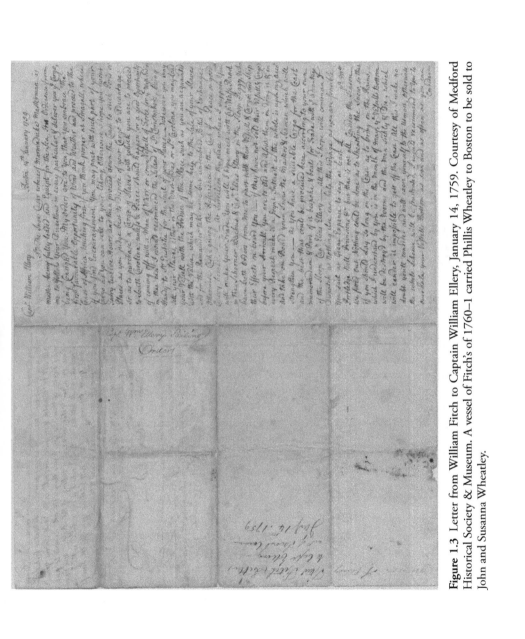

Figure 1.3 Letter from William Fitch to Captain William Ellery, January 14, 1759. Courtesy of Medford Historical Society & Museum. A vessel of Fitch's of 1760–1 carried Phillis Wheatley to Boston to be sold to John and Susanna Wheatley.

account of the sale of slaves, likely from that voyage, shows that they were sold for the value of £3,660.2.6, though the surviving bill of sale doesn't say where they were sold.[82] The final document in the Medford Slave Papers is dated November 27, 1769, and orders Gwinn to go to Anamobo in Ghana and to bring the slaves he purchases there to Hampton, Virginia.[83] Throughout these letters, Fitch expresses anxiety about war, privateers, and hurricanes; he also fears that Bostonians and British authorities might seize his ships and/or their cargo for reasons he does not disclose.

In addition to, and complementing, Fitch's and Felt's evidence, *The Transatlantic Slave Trade Database* lists seventeen slave voyages from Salem before 1860, including what Felt described as the two by the *Favorite* of 1785 and 1787, the voyages of unnamed ships in 1763 and 1773, and one by the *St John's* of 1791. In 1782, the *Anthony*, owned by Joseph and Joshua Grafton and captained by George Nelson, travels to Gambia in what must have been a slave-trade mission. In 1785, the Grafton's ship *Africa*, captained by Robinson Revell, makes for the Gold Coast, and their ship *Gambia*, captained by Robert Champlin, goes from Salem to Anamobu in Ghana and sells the slaves in Charleston. The *Polly and Sally*, owned by George Crowninshield and captained by Thomas Thomas, travels from Salem to Africa in 1787. In 1791, the ship *Felicity*, owned by John White and captained by William Fairfield, travels to Sierra Leone to trade for slaves bound for Surinam. According to the National Park Service, this same ship had witnessed a slave mutiny in 1789: "In 1789, Captain William Fairfield was killed by a slave uprising on the *Felicity* as the ship was sailing from the Ivory Coast to Cayenne in South America. The surviving crew members were able to regain control of the ship and eventually sold the Africans."[84] The year 1791 also saw the *Speedwell*, captained by a man named Burdet, taking a similar itinerary, and the *Abeona*, captained by John Sinclair and owned by him and John Waters, does a Salem–Sierra Leone–Havana triangle. The *Favorite* makes another trip in 1794, the *Ruth* and the *St John* do so in 1795, and the *Hope*, captained by Stephen Smith, journeys to Africa and sells slaves in Cuba in 1796. Finally, an unnamed ship captained by G. Ropes and owned by him and men by the name of Prince and Phillips makes a voyage to Gambia in 1802. There were doubtless many more voyages before, during, and after these dates, but there is little remaining evidence of them.[85]

Regardless of whether the people of Salem were directly engaged with voyages to Africa, they profited from the trade of fish and other New England products for slave-produced goods, particularly West Indian sugar, molasses, and the rum that they either distilled in Salem or purchased in the islands and in the Surinam depicted in Behn's novel and Hawkesworth's play. The nineteenth-century scholars Osgood and Batchelder, who also, tellingly, omit Massachusetts involvement in the

---

[82] Fitch, <http://www.medfordhistorical.org/collections/slave-trade-letters/correspondence-mid-voyage-timothy-fitch-peter-gwinn-2/; http://www.medfordhistorical.org/collections/slave-trade-letters/accountinvoice-sale-slaves/>.

[83] Fitch, <http://www.medfordhistorical.org/collections/slave-trade-letters/voyage-peter-gwinn-behalf-timothy-fitch-snow-fair-lady/>.

[84] National Park Service, *African-American Heritage Sites in Salem: A Guide to Salem's History* (Washington: US Department of the Interior, 1998), n.p.

[85] "Voyages." *The Transatlantic Slave Trade Database*. Accessed May 2, 2016. <http://www.slavevoyages.org/voyage/search>.

slave trade from their history of Salem, said that in the early part of the eighteenth century, witnesses reported that Salem sold:

> Dry Merchantable Codfish for the markets of Spain, Portugal and the Straits. Refuse fish, lumber, horses and provisions for the West Indies. Returns made directly to England are sugar, molasses, cotton-wool, logwood and Brasiletto wood, for which we depend on the West Indies. Our own produce a considerable quantity of whale and fish oil, whalebone, furs, deer, elk and bear skins are annually sent to England.[86]

Felt's *Annals* reports that much of this fish was used for feeding slaves in the West Indies: "The merchantable cod were exported to Spain, Portugal and Italy; and the refuse to the West Indies, for negro slaves. The last clause of this account implies a shameless neglect of the obligation which justly demands reciprocal beneficence among human beings."[87] Rum, in particular, was "New England's largest manufacturing business before the revolution" as "immense quantities of the raw liquor were sent to Africa and exchanged for slaves."[88] In short, Salem participated in provisioning slave voyages and plantations to its south while trafficking in what those plantations produced: "Salem merchants were involved in the slave trade between Africa and the West Indies directly, and also indirectly by supplying salt cod for the plantations and for the purchase of slaves in Africa."[89] Even when Salem vessels were dealing in tobacco and rice grown in southern regions, they were supporting slave labor arrangements both before and after the Revolution.[90]

There is also evidence that the coastal trade with the southern colonies and West Indian islands in slave-produced commodities, however, also regularly included slaves themselves, which merchants and ship captains might buy and sell in order to fill out the rest of their cargo. The major western Atlantic ports receiving slaves directly from Africa, "Bridgetown, Barbados; Kingston, Jamaica; Charleston, South Carolina; and Roseau, Dominica—were not just end points of the translatlantic slave trade. They were entrepots, gateways through which African captives passed en route to a host of colonies."[91] Whereas the traders from Africa dealt in large cargoes of slaves, "Intercolonial traders, by contrast, could operate on a smaller scale because they incorporated slave trading into a mixed commerce."[92] Salem merchants were very much involved in this kind of trade, often shipping their most famous product—fish—to exchange for "mixed cargoes of return voyages" that included slaves.[93]

The surviving papers of some of the Salem men who were proprietors of the Social Library show that they were not exceptional among local residents in profiting from the trade in slavery and the products connected with it. The case of Timothy Orne, "probably the richest merchant of the time," is an exemplary one for this complexity, as he was not only dealing in slaves and the goods of Salem and

[86] Charles S. Osgood and H. M. Batchelder. *Historical Sketch of Salem 1626–1879* (Salem: Essex Institute, 1879), 127.

[87] Felt, 2:218.　　[88] Greene, 25–6.

[89] Aviva Chomsky, "Salem as a Global City, 1850–2004." *Salem: Place, Myth, Memory.* Ed. Dane Anthony Morrison, Nancy Lusignan Schultz (Northeastern UP, 2004), 230.

[90] Greene, 23–4.

[91] Gregory E. O'Malley, *Final Passages: The Intercolonial Slave Trade of British America, 1619–1807* (Chapel Hill: U North Carolina P, 2014), 6.

[92] O'Malley, 10.　　[93] O'Malley, 201.

the West Indies, but also investing in and insuring the slavery-related voyages of others.[94] He is said to have owned interest in thirty-five or forty vessels, working with captains like John Crowninshield, Richard Derby, George Dodge, John Gardner, and Joseph Grafton and trading to the West Indies, Barbados, Surinam, Jamaica, and other southern ports, in addition to Spain, Gibraltar, and the Western Islands.[95] In an act that also shows the connection of shipbuilding to slavery, Orne in 1758 contracted with "Able Merril of Newberry in the County of Essex in New England Shipright" to build a 140-ton brig, the *Cicero*, to which many of Orne's papers refer, for £3,450.[96] A letter from Orne to Capt. John Gardner of the *Cicero* dated "Salem N. England Nov 5 1762" included an order for an enslaved person to be purchased along with other merchandise like molasses, cocoa, coffee, cotton, and rum. Orne paid for this person with 45 pounds worth of fish and mackerel that he was using as a practice trade for his children:

> Below is Invoice of my children's adventure aboard the Brigg Cicero, which I desire you to dispose of in the West Indies to the best advantage & to Remit me the Neat proceeds of it & of the sixteen Johannes in Molasses Cacao Coffee Cotton Rum, or any other Goods that you think will yield here the most profit. As I am in want of a Negro Boy if you can get One that's very likely and Cheap I would have you buy one for me, more Especially if you can't lay out the Money to Advantage in produce or should have Effects of the Owners to fully load the Brigg. I should chuse to have a boy from the Gold Coast somewhat spry & abt. 12 years old I am yours Tim. Orne.[97]

This kind of unexceptional enumeration of a human being to be cargo with other products of the slave trade indicates how regular this type of transaction could be. A poorly spelled letter to Salem merchants Messrs Jonathan Gardner & Company (presumably a company including Orne as an owner, as it is in his papers) from Captain Israel Lovitt of the *Cicero*, dated Eustatia, November 30, 1764 shows the *Cicero* traded 16 slaves:

> St. Eustatia the 30 of Novemr. Gentlemen these may serve to acquaint you of my proceedings as I wrote you by Cap. Ingersoll that I had Chartred my vessel to Gorge for One Johannes for thee merch and to Account men for less as the time shall be I carey on Mr. Osborn acct 16 Negroes and to prevent Disputes I have been to St. Kitts with my schooner and cleared them but with expence of & all other is at Mr. Osborn's Excepting the vesell and your Interest witch I have on board witch is the holl of my Cargo & as I have but just had an opertunity of carrying it all into Dolors as it is winter and no emidate vessel coming home I think it will be best to carey it with me and bring it out in goald on my Return witch may yeald sum small profit. I am goin under saile this evening at my arrival at Gorge shall indeavor to send you letters from there.[98]

In fact, there is evidence that the *Cicero* shipped 500 slaves on a 1761 voyage.[99] At around the same time, Orne is named in a summons to the Court of Admiralty in Boston for the *Cicero* "Landing Contrary to Law" twenty-one hogsheads and

[94] Phillips, 242.   [95] Phillips, 243.
[96] Orne Family Papers, MSS 41 Box 3 Folder 4, Phillips Library, Peabody Essex Museum, Salem, Massachusetts.
[97] Orne, MSS 41 Box 3 Folder 7.   [98] Orne, MSS 41 Box 3 Folder 9.
[99] Orne, MSS 41, B3 F4, B3 F7.

fifty-four tierces of molasses and other goods totaling £1,080 sterling at Salem.[100] A letter dated "Salem N. England Jan 13 1755" from Orne to Mr. Joshua Grafton, master of another of Orne's ships, the *Rebecca*, orders Grafton to sell fish from Salem at Barbados and buy a slave, sugar, and rum: "However, Dispose of it when & how you think best for my Interest & make me Returns in a Negro Boy if you can get one reasonable about 11 or 12 year old that is active Nimble of a good Disposition & spare make & not over cunning sutable for a House Negro, & the Remainder in Good Muscovado Sugar & good Rum."[101] A year later, Orne instructed Grafton to trade his cargo in North Carolina for "Returns in good porck, Tallow, Skins & Furs, Wheat, Corn, good Hard Pitch, Thin Tar, bb Staves & heading, or any other goods that you are well assured will be most profitable to us."[102] Orne was involved in insuring his own and other vessels, and a notation in a 1761 almanac of his has an account he kept of "John Nuting Jr. [a library proprietor] for Thirteenth Quarter" that records insuring a voyage of the sloop *Industry* from Africa to the island of St Kitt's.[103] Other almanac notations show him keeping track of the weather, ships heading out of port, lists of loans made to other people, and other business information. One can see from all this evidence how one person could be standing at the nexus of many different kinds of Atlantic trade, all based on slavery, all while operating out of a Massachusetts port like Salem.

Other members of the Salem Social Library, some of whom were readers of sentimental literature similar to *Oroonoko*, had high levels of involvement in this trade. Francis, Joseph, and Andrew Cabot, all Harvard graduates, had complex transatlantic transactions mostly based in their sales of fish to Bilbao, Spain, and other nearby ports like Cadiz, Lisbon, and Gibralter. Blacks are mentioned at least twice in these papers. The first is a January 14, 1772 reference to a free man named "Tom" who is on the list of crew as a cabin boy on the ship *Premium* making 30 shillings a month, a bit less than the forty-five other crew members were paid. The *Premium*'s orders were to exchange an unnamed cargo at James River in Virginia "for as much Wheat as your hold will contain."[104] The second reference is in a letter to Andrew Cabot from his Captain Putnam in Philadelphia, April 14, 1772, reporting a lack of success in selling sugar and successfully selling "Fortune the Negro boy."[105]

There is evidence that the Cabots were also trading with the West Indies, as proven by a Portledge Bill of 1765–6, a letter from Josiah Orne to the Cabots dated Montecristo July 15, 1767, and many other documents.[106] There is a sales receipt for seven boxes of Lemons and twenty Casks of Raisins for the account of Captain Joseph Cabot to Kittery dated October 5, 1767, indicating he was getting these kinds of West India goods for the New England market.[107] There is also an account dated Salem May 31, 1772 between the Cabots and Joseph Bowditch for a trip to Carolina on the schooner *Dolphin*, an account with Stephen Cleveland of

---

[100] Orne, MSS 41 Box 3 Folder 9.
[101] Orne, MSS 41 Box 8 Folder 9.   [102] Orne, MSS 41 Box 8 Folder 9.
[103] Orne, MSS 41 Box 16 Folder 6.
[104] Cabot Family Papers, MSS 161 Box 1 Folder 1, Phillips Library, Peabody Essex Museum, Salem, Massachusetts.
[105] Cabot, MSS 161 Box 1 Folder 1.   [106] Cabot, MSS 161 Box 1 Folder 3, Box 1 Folder 4.
[107] Cabot, MSS 161 Box 2 Folder 2.

the schooner *Neptune*'s trip to Carolina, and Henry Higginson from Salem to the West Indies on the schooner *Two Brothers*.[108] Sometimes trade with Bilbao also involved the West India trade, as a merchant in Bilbao wrote the Cabots in 1772 that fish was not selling well, and that they should try shipping "good French sugars" from the West Indies instead; they fulfilled this sugar order on July 21, 1773, a fact that indicates that slave-produced goods were part of the Bilbao fish trade.[109] The Cabots also were doing a lot of shipping to London, and a receipt dated March 16, 1748 in an elegant hand lists that they sold some products there, including those derived from slavery: "pitch, whalefins, tarr [*sic*], rum, staves, Indico [*sic*], Cotton, Gold Coin and Pieces of 8."[110] A receipt dated September 25, 1773 to one of the Mr. Cabots on a printed form from Solomon Marriott, Weaver and Mercer, "near the corner of St. Paul's in Cheapside," for 23 yards' Rich White Brocade for a total of £12.1.6 indicates that the Cabots were obtaining some British fashions from the proceeds of their trade.[111] The Cabots were not only dealing in their own ships, but were investing in shares of those of others in Salem, as a list survives of their shares in nineteen other ships.[112]

The Cabots' shipping papers, though suggesting that most of their profits were from fish to Spain, omit a great deal of what else they profited in. Their surviving ledger and waste book of sales show that they sold massive amounts of molasses and sugar to distillers in and around Salem. For example, one entry is a sale dated Salem June 30, 1768 to Joseph Sprague, Distiller of "6 Hogshead Molasses" worth £622.22, a massive amount of money at the time. Numerous other entries show rum and sugar sales to others, presumably in Salem. This evidence indicates that products and tools of exchange in the slave trade like sugar, molasses, and rum were being handled by the Cabots, with the likely outcome that rum was being exported to be exchanged throughout the Atlantic, perhaps in the West Africa trade.[113]

Similarly, library member Benjamin Pickman, son of a merchant who had "gilt codfish carved on the stairways" of his Salem house to testify as to the source of his wealth, seemed to have earned his main profits from selling molasses and sugar to distillers and others in the Salem area, as did many other library affiliates. One of Pickman's shipping ledgers indicates that in the early 1760s, he sold fish for sugar in the West Indies and other places, and that he outfitted ships like the *Adventure* with rum to sell in the West Indies.[114] His waste book indicates sales of a variety of items—from sugar and rum to buttons—to a wide range of individuals.[115] His "Distillery Account Book" has the frequent label "By Distill House Parr Acct" in each facing page of the ledger, indicating that he may have owned his own distillery even while selling molasses and sugar to other distillers.[116] Richard Derby's ledger for 1744–56 has such extensive sales of rum, sugar, molasses, and related goods

[108] Cabot, MSS 161 Box 2 Folder 2.   [109] Cabot, MSS 161 Box 1 Folder 1.
[110] Cabot, MSS 161 Box 2 Folder 2.   [111] Cabot, MSS 161 Box 2 Folder 2.
[112] Cabot, MSS 161 Box 2 Folder 2.   [113] Cabot, MSS 161 Box 1 Folder 5, Box 2 Folder 1.
[114] Benjamin Pickman Papers, MSS 5 Vol. 24: 87, 92, 166, 197, Phillips Library, Peabody Essex Museum, Salem, Massachusetts.
[115] Pickman, MSS 5 Vol. 25.   [116] Pickman, MSS 5 Vol. 25.

that it is safe to say that he, too, was connected to the slave trade.[117] The papers of Samuel Barton, who was in business with other library shareholders like Joseph Blaney and Pickman, also show extensive dealings in shipments of molasses, sugar, and rum, mostly from Surinam, but also in a coastal trade with colonies like North Carolina.[118] Samuel Curwen, a merchant who later became Commissioner for Tonnage and Imposts for Essex County and a Justice of the Peace, has several surviving documents illustrating his involvement in Atlantic trade, particularly in rum, sugar, molasses, fish, rice, wine, and flour.[119] The papers of Jonathan Gardner, a merchant and proprietor of the library, show ships like the schooner *Postillion* and the schooner *Outfest* going to West Indies and/or Gibraltar. Gardner's papers contain numerous documents on his dealings in sugar, Barbados rum and limes, molasses, and beef; one 1762 import of molasses totaled 1,089 ¼ gallons, for a total value of £2,610.10.1.[120] Most of this molasses would be distilled into rum to be sold to African slave traders like Oroonoko himself is said to have been.

Local shopkeepers, who purchased goods from ships, but who were not necessarily involved in shipping directly, also benefited from the slave trade. Library proprietor Nathaniel Ropes and his wife Abigail, for example, kept a shop in Salem near the wharves. From 1740 to 1750 their ledger shows people purchasing rum, sugar, molasses, and indigo.[121] This ledger also shows how they charged their customers fees for "Cato," presumably their slave, to deliver these goods.[122] Another document, the Ropes' waste book for 1753–74, shows them selling sugar, indigo, pork, and cotton to several individuals.[123] Ropes also used the profits from his business to insure vessels, as he did for a voyage by the schooner *John* from Salem, to North Carolina, to Kittery, Maine. Ropes signed this contract on February 8, 1771, and it was co-signed by fellow insurers Francis Cabot and George Dodge. He underwrote another voyage the same year for the schooner *Sally* to travel from Rhode Island to North Carolina. The former insurance policy, interestingly, has a clause in it that the premium payment for the voyage shall be raised if "War or hostilities should be commenced against the English during the abovementioned voyage," suggesting that insurers were pricing-in the Revolution ahead of its arrival.[124]

Even the eminent physician, library proprietor, and son of a Harvard University President, Dr. Edward Augustus Holyoke, was not above writing insurance policies for various kinds of Atlantic voyages from 1757 to 1773. He has a list of policies for many voyages to West Indies ports like Barbados, Surinam, Anguilla, as well as trips to Gibraltar, Lisbon, Bilbao, Carolina, and Virginia. Many of these policies

---

[117] Derby Family Papers, MSS 37 Vol. 23, Phillips Library, Peabody Essex Museum, Salem, Massachusetts.

[118] Barton Family Papers, MSS 110 Box 1 Folder 3, Phillips Library, Peabody Essex Museum, Salem, Massachusetts.

[119] Curwen Family Papers, MSS 45 Box 5 Folder 2, Phillips Library, Peabody Essex Museum, Salem, Massachusetts.

[120] Gardner Family Papers, MSS 147 Box 1 Folder 5, Phillips Library, Peabody Essex Museum, Salem, Massachusetts.

[121] Nathaniel Ropes Papers, MSS 190 Vol. 2: 8, 9, 10, 12, 21, 37, Phillips Library, Peabody Essex Museum, Salem, Massachusetts.

[122] Ropes, MSS 190 Vol. 2: 3, 21.   [123] Ropes, MSS 190 Box 1 Folder 3.

[124] Ropes, MSS 190 Box 1 Folder 5.

are for ships owned by John Crowninshield and the Cabots.[125] At various points he invests in a shipment of slave-grown rice to Gibraltar, orders clothes from London via the Cabots' voyages to Bilbao, deals with London and Amsterdam bankers on currency exchange in mercantile bills and continental dollars, and orders drugs and books directly from London.[126]

Professionals and government officials were not fully exempt from participating in the trade in slaves and the products they produced or consumed. Thomas Pynchon, a lawyer, Timothy Pickering, who eventually became a revolutionary general and U.S. Secretary of State in the early Republic, and Joseph Bowditch, who served as sheriff of Essex County, dealt at various times in their lives in this trade. Part of that involvement was certainly related to slave-produced goods often being used in lieu of currency to pay for things like government services. As professionals and officials dealing in legal matters, however, they had cases and situations that came before them on Atlantic trade that required them to become embroiled in the slavery economy.

Pynchon, for example, took payments in a variety of commodities for his legal services. His ledger shows that in 1750, Stephen Higginson, Robert Mackentire, and Joseph Allen paid their fees in sugar, and in 1761 Thomas Eden did the same.[127] Sometimes slaves themselves were used in payment; in 1760 Benjamin Waters pays his fees, or perhaps a legal settlement, in the money's "cost in Negroes."[128] Clients like Jeremiah Condy and Nathan Goodale paid part of their costs in books, and there are several notations of payments received from people in the West Indies, presumably for shipping cases they had before Salem and Boston courts.[129]

Pickering, like Pynchon, did not seem to be directly involved in the slave trade, though some documents show that he had investments in shipping. For example, there are many extant lists of inventory on ships, and invoices of cargo for ships like the *Wyoming* in his papers.[130] A June 1, 1769 document protesting a sale of fish for molasses at Dominica by the schooner *Brinia* that had actually not gone according to plan, suggests that Pickering was embroiled in some maritime law case regarding West India shipping at that time.[131] In addition, an invoice dated September 7, 1779 of merchandise for a voyage of the schooner *Benjamin* from Salem to Kennebunk and the West Indies, captained by William Woodberry, shows that Pickering was trading to the West Indies during the War of Independence.[132] His papers also include a receipt for his share of the prize money won by the privateers "Lexington, Santapee, & St. John" during that war.[133]

[125] Holyoke Family Papers, MSS 49 Box 20 Folder 3, Phillips Library, Peabody Essex Museum, Salem, Massachusetts.

[126] Holyoke, MSS 49 Box 20 Folder 1.

[127] William Pynchon Papers, MSS 236 Box 3 Folder 2, Phillips Library, Peabody Essex Museum, Salem, Massachusetts.

[128] Pynchon, MSS 236 Box 3 Folder 2.　　　[129] Pynchon, MSS 236 Box 3 Folder 2.

[130] Pickering Family Papers, MSS 400 Box 9 Folder 1, Phillips Library, Peabody Essex Museum, Salem, Massachusetts.

[131] Pickering, MSS 400 Box 6 Folder 9.　　　[132] Pickering, MSS 400 Box 9 Folder 1.

[133] Pickering, MSS 400 Box 9 Folder 1.

Bowditch's case is somewhat different. He was a merchant before he was sheriff, and in the 1730s, dealt with a variety of West Indian shipping on his own account. An October 27, 1731 letter from a merchant in Barbados, the New Yorker Gedney Clarke, contains a receipt for two hogsheads of fish for which he will pay in a later shipment of rum.[134] Another from Clarke dated April 4, 1733 acknowledges receipt of fish and a return shipment of rum.[135] An August 1732 invoice from Clarke shows a similar exchange.[136] In November 1731, writing for his company "Bowditch and Hunt," Bowditch tells one of his captains bound for Virginia or Maryland to be careful not to ship contraband.[137] A 1732 customs receipt shows him contracting with Captain John Crowninshield, master of the *Benjamin and Sarah*, for a shipment of rum and oil to Barbados.[138] Many other invoices show him shipping to and from Barbados, other ports in the West Indies, Virginia, Maryland, and the Carolinas, trading mostly rum for sugar, molasses, and other agricultural products.[139] Rum and sugar were such commodities that Bowditch used them as currency to pay for a renovation of his schooner *Adventure* that cost £81.17.8.[140] He apparently owned at least one slave in Salem, as in 1762 and 1764 he has receipts from a tailor, Ephraim Ingalls, for "making ye negro" various items of clothing. Indeed, even someone like a tailor was profiting from slavery.[141] Perhaps the most intriguing document in Bowditch's papers is one relating to his son Thomas's stake in a 1795 voyage from Belfast, Ireland, carrying linens to trade on the coast of Africa.[142]

Clearly, even through something as small as purchasing a bag of sugar, the entire Salem economy rode on the backs of the slavery economy of the Atlantic in the eighteenth century, and it touched the lives of all who were involved in the library. This story is hard to recover, but the papers of the library proprietors, together with the accounts of nineteenth- and twentieth-century historians, indicate that the pursuit of the story is as much a part of our cultural history as our understanding of slavery's role in our libraries. In this way, slavery was not only the economic basis for the library to the extent that it was underwriting literary taste in the latest imported British books; it was also the scandal affecting how this history would—or would not—be told. The reading habits of people made wealthy by slavery, manifest in the surviving library charge book from the 1760s, indicate that they were not only reading to further their businesses, but also to display their status through access to fashionable imported cultural capital.

---

[134] Joseph Bowditch Papers, MSS 156 Box 2 Folder 3, Phillips Library, Peabody Essex Museum, Salem, Massachusetts.

[135] Bowditch, MSS 156 Box 2 Folder 3.   [136] Bowditch, MSS 156 Box 2 Folder 2.

[137] Bowditch, MSS 156 Box 2 Folder 3.   [138] Bowditch, MSS 156 Box 2 Folder 4.

[139] Bowditch, MSS 156 Box 2 Folder 4, Box 2 Folder 3.

[140] Bowditch, MSS 156 Box 2 Folder 4.   [141] Bowditch, MSS 156 Box 2 Folder 6.

[142] Bowditch, MSS 156 Box 2 Folder 2.

III

The Salem context of reading *Oroonoko* and other books was shaped by this history of local involvement in slavery. The books in the library's first catalog show that it held literary works in a range of genres, but I would like to focus on the sentimental titles in philosophy and literature, as well as books of political theory, that the library's charge book from this period says were checked out most frequently. Doing so may help us analyze the role of Salem and slavery in what Sarah Knott has identified as the "reconstitution of self and society" that men and women engaged in the "sentimental project" were imagining in the era of the American Revolution.[143] It may also help us understand the appropriative uses of sympathy for the enslaved for the project of American independence, as well as the split between those slaveholders using the trope of slavery to describe their relationship with Britain and those patriots who also became abolitionists. Further, it may demonstrate that circulation records not only "deserve to be mined for evidence of reading vogues," a task that requires the kind of "careful trailing of individual books and library users" that I do below, but also may lead us to judge them as potential documentation of books actually being read.[144]

The library's borrowing policies were quite liberal, as a proprietor could take out one folio, or two quartos, or four of smaller format out for eight weeks, and he could write out a ticket for one of his family members to enter the library and do the same. There was a fine of one shilling for every two weeks a book was late, and though the charge book indicates that some were fined, there were very few overdue books. Preference on lending a title was given to one who had not borrowed that title before, and all books were to be returned to the library by the time of its annual meeting. Local clergymen, who could not afford to be members of the library, were allowed the use of the books from time to time under the same rules. The fine for a damaged book was set by agreement between the Librarian and the member checking it out. No one was allowed to carry a book out of town under penalty of five shillings, and a member could not lend the book to a non-member. If a member lost a book, he had to pay a fine equal to its value within a month, with a further fine of one shilling a month if he was late it making this payment. Money from fines and membership fees was to "be laid out in Books agreeable to the Determination of the Society," and if a member did not pay his fines and other fees, his share in the library was to be forfeited to the other members.[145] As the charge book reveals, readers' tastes could be quite interdisciplinary, with a reader often borrowing a work of fiction at the same time he took out a book of non-fiction. The sheer number of entries with a member taking out three or four books at once

[143] Sarah Knott, *Sensibility and the American Revolution* (Chapel Hill: U North Carolina P, 2009), 3.
[144] Isabelle Lehuu, "Reconstructing Reading Vogues in the Old South: Borrowings from the Charleston Library Society, 1811–1817." *The History of Reading, Volume 1: International Perspectives c.1500–1990*. Eds Shafquat Towheed and W. R. Owens (Basingstoke: Palgrave Macmillan, 2011), 65.
[145] Charter, Rules, & Regulations of the Social Library, Salem Athenaeum Papers, MSS 56 B2 F1, 4–6. Phillips Library, Peabody Essex Museum, Salem, Massachusetts.

indicates the predominance of the smaller octavo and duodecimo editions, which were the formats in which most literary works were published.

There is no evidence that *Oroonoko* in any of its formats was stocked in the library, though it is obvious that at least some people like Gardner were aware of it, and it was performed in the American colonies. Eighteenth-century accounts establish that some Americans viewed *Oroonoko* as a dangerous play because of its sympathetic and sentimental anti-slavery message: "the enslaved black body that appeared on stage in the figure of Oroonoko in London and galvanized a weeping public there had a far different stage life when (re) transported to the New World."[146] A production in New York in 1783 was sustained for only four nights, when it was not well received.[147] In Charleston, South Carolina, in 1795, a performance of the play was advertised, but then cancelled.[148] As Elizabeth Maddock Dillon has contended, "the 'firmness and resolution' that Oroonoko shows in his refusal to live as a slave or to be separated from his wife might be viewed, among slave-holding Charlestonians, as sentiments not suitable for emulation."[149] The story was different in the more abolitionist-leaning states of Pennsylvania and Massachusetts, however, as a 1792 production in Philadelphia was popular, and a 1799 Boston production received a sympathetic response.[150] In the earlier period, around the time of the library's founding, however, Gardner's 1760 purchase of Hawkesworth's play would have been prescient, indicating that he was ahead of his community in understanding the evils of slavery. The sentimental books in the Social Library that he had access to through his father's membership there might have given him a taste for an anti-slavery work like this, and they may have had an influence on how Salem readers and civic leaders regarded slavery in the period of the Revolution.

The library had many titles in sentimental philosophy that were being borrowed quite frequently between 1764 and 1768, the years encompassed by the charge book that were also active years in the dispute between Britain and the colonies. Adam Smith's *Theory of Moral Sentiments* was borrowed seventeen times, Edmund Burke's *Philosophical Enquiry into the Origins of our Ideas of the Sublime and Beautiful* four times, William Smith's translation of Longinus' *On the Sublime* three times, Alexander Gerard's *An Essay on Taste* four times, Voltaire's *Letters* sixteen times, and Locke's *Works*, containing the theory of affections *An Essay Concerning Human Understanding*, twice. Philosophy of a more political bent was also popular in an age of constitutional dispute with Britain. Rousseau's *The Social Contract* was borrowed four times, Puffendorf's *Introduction to the History of Europe* five times, Hume's *History of England* eighty times, Hume's *Essays* twenty-one times, Montesquieu's *Spirit of the Laws* six times, Montesquieu's *Miscellanies* eight

---

[146] Elizabeth Maddock Dillon, *New World Drama: The Performative Commons in the Atlantic World, 1649–1849* (Durham: Duke UP, 2014), 131.

[147] John Daniel Collins, "American Drama in Anti-slavery Agitation, 1792–1861." Ph.D. dissertation, State University of Iowa, 1976, 218–20.

[148] Dillon, 42.   [149] Dillon, 42.

[150] Thomas Clark Pollack, *The Philadelphia Theatre in the Eighteenth Century* (Westport: Greenwood P, 1968), 185; Heather S. Nathans, *Early American Theatre from the Revolution to Thomas Jefferson: Into the Hands of the People* (Cambridge: Cambridge UP, 2003), 82–3, 98; Collins, 21; Isaac Goldberg, *Tin Pan Alley: A Chronicle of American Popular Music* (NY: F. Ungar, 1961), 36.

times, Burlemaqui's *Principles of Law* nine times, *Memoirs of the Count of Brandenburg* five times, and Vattel's *Law of Nations* ten times. More literary versions of political thought were also popular, such as John Trenchard and Thomas Gordon's *Cato's Letters*, which was borrowed sixteen times, Bernard Mandeville's *Fable of the Bees* or William Law or Francis Hutcheson's response to it, borrowed seventeen times as a whole, and works by Jonathan Swift, which were borrowed seventy times in these years.[151]

Literary works that we would classify today as sentimental fiction were in high demand. Eliza Haywood's *Betsy Thoughtless* was the most popular of these works, being borrowed on thirty-eight occasions. Samuel Richardson's *History of Sir Charles Grandison* was borrowed thirty-six times, followed by Frances Sheridan's *Memoirs of Sidney Bidulph* on twenty-four occasions. Richardson's *Pamela* was borrowed seventeen times.[152]

The borrowing records of Timothy Orne and of George Gardner's father Samuel Gardner are perhaps the best gauge of the Salem interpretive community's engagement with these genres. The tastes of the city's largest slave trader were omnivorous (see Figure 1.4). In politics, Orne borrowed *Cato's Letters* and *The Fable of the Bees* in 1764, checking out two volumes of the former work again in 1767. He checked out *Tom Jones* in 1765, Voltaire's *Letters*, *Betsy Thoughtless*, and Gerard's *Essay on Taste* in 1767, and *Don Quixote* and *Sir Charles Grandison* in 1768. Throughout these years, he also was interested in Alexander Pope, Jonathan Swift, Charles Mouhy's *The Fortunate Country Maid*, Charles Johnstone's *Chrysal, or the Adventures of a Guinea*, and Shakespeare's *Works*. Though he was active in shipping, there is no record of him borrowing books of astronomy, navigation, geography, or travels, suggesting that rather than reading such works to support his business acumen, he was recycling his profits from the trade into British cultural capital by contributing to the library and checking out its books. Slavery, in short, was supporting his taste in high British culture.[153]

Samuel Gardner expressed far more interest in books about travel related to his shipping business, and in this period borrowed *Tour Thro' Great Britain*, *Piratical States of Barbary*, *Lives of the Admirals*, *Collection of Voyages*, *Adventurer*, *Grand Tour*, *Shaw's Travels*, *Gage's Travels*, *Ultoa's Voyages*, and *Anson's Voyages*. He was also deeply invested in works of law and politics, borrowing Vattel, *Fable of the Bees*, *Cato's Letters*, Montesquieu's *Spirit of the Laws*, Puffendorf's *Introduction*, Hume's *History of England*, and Voltaire's *Letters*. From 1764 through 1767, he borrowed sentimental fictions like *Betsy Thoughtless*, *Sidney Bidulph*, *The Fortunate Country Maid*, *The Female Quixote*, and François Fenelon's *Telemachus*. These, especially if borrowed from the library under the auspices of his membership by his son, might have helped form the appetite for sentimental works leading to the purchase of Hawkesworth's *Oroonoko*. Through the entirety of this period, the elder Gardner was also taking literary works like Shiells's *Lives of the Poets*, Dodsley's poems, James

---

[151] All of this borrowing data comes from "Charge Book, 1760–1768," Social Library Records, MSS 56, Phillips Library, Peabody Essex Museum. Salem, Massachusetts.
[152] "Charge Book."   [153] "Charge Book."

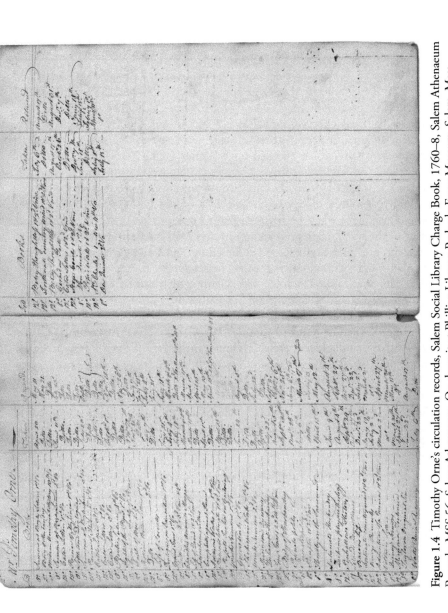

Figure 1.4 Timothy Orne's circulation records, Salem Social Library Charge Book, 1760–8, Salem Athenaeum Records, MSS 56, Salem Athenaeum. On deposit at Phillips Library, Peabody Essex Museum, Salem, Mass.

Thomson's works, Matthew Prior's poems, John Dryden's poems, Jonathan Swift's works, Samuel Butler's *Hudibras*, and Richard Steele's plays. British literature was clearly top-shelf reading for Gardner, and he was fully immersed in the sentimentality movement being imported into his shores.[154]

The borrowings of Orne and Gardner present the possibility of a provisional theory that circulation records may tell us more about whether borrowed books were actually read than we have hitherto thought, particularly when we account for volumes of a work being read sequentially over several borrowing periods. For example, it is highly likely that Orne read at least the first two volumes of *Cato's Letters* in 1764 because he checked out volume 1 from June 11 to July 23, returned it, and immediately checked out volumes 2 and 3 from July 23 to October 1. He then returned these and immediately checked out volume 3 again from October 1 to November 12. Gardner checked out volumes 1 and 2 of *Sidney Bidulph* on October 1, 1764, and immediately borrowed volume 3 upon returning them on October 15, indicating that the first two volumes were probably read. He borrowed the first volume of *Fortunate Country Maid* July 21, 1766, and immediately took out volume 2 when he returned it on August 4. In 1767, he repeated his reading of the novel, taking out volumes 1 and 2 on June 8. He returned the first volume on June 22, and the second volume July 3, indicating that he had read the first volume and was retaining the second one to finish. This pattern is particularly evident with Swift's *Works* in 1765, when Gardner took out volume 1 on September 16, 1765, volumes 2, 3, 4, and 5 on September 30 when he returned volume 1, volume 6 on October 14 when he returned volumes 2, 3, 4, and 5, and volume 7 on October 8 when he returned volume 6. Gardner read the five volumes of *Lives of the Poets* in a similarly sequential fashion in the winter of 1765 and again in the summer of 1766. Even if we can account for other readers' demand for the same books leading to returning them, it only enhances the possibility that the contents of these books were indeed being read by a proprietor.[155]

Surviving evidence of the personal collections of Salem residents supports this view of their appetite for British books. The Revd John Prince's collection of books, sold to his son in 1810, included several books of law, history, and philosophy such as Puffendorf's works, Lord Coke's reports, and Paul de Rapin's *History of England*.[156] The Pickering Family Papers at the Peabody Essex Museum document an estate sale of the books of Samuel Orne, a relative of Timothy Pickering, dated November 1774. This list includes serious legal and political works like Blackstone's *Commentaries on the Laws of England*, *Cato's Letters*, and Tobias Smollett's *History of England*. There are, however, many sentimental works of philosophy and literature such as the Earl of Shaftesbury's *Characteristics of Men, Manners, Opinions, and Times*—perhaps the most significant work to launch theorizing of sentimentality—and John Locke's *Essay Concerning Human Understanding*, also a theory of the affections. Popular sellers like Oliver Goldsmith's *The Vicar of Wakefield* and

---

[154] "Charge Book."   [155] "Charge Book."
[156] Prince Family Papers, MSS 72, B7 F6, Phillips Library, Peabody Essex Museum, Salem, Massachusetts.

Fenelon's *Telemachus* are only the most sentimental of literary works on a list that also included Edward Young's *Night Thoughts* and James Thompson's *The Seasons*.[157]

A shipment of books to Timothy Pickering dated February 7, 1772, however, shows just how much sentimental, and even erotic, literature had penetrated into an old Puritan town like Salem. This "Catalogue of Books Ship'd on Board the Vesuvius, Ichabud Lovelace, Commander," included standard titles like Richardson's *Clarissa*, Tobias Smollett's *Ferdinand Count Fathom* and *Roderick Random*, and Sterne's *Sentimental Journey*. It also contained more obscure romance novels known only by the titles *Adventures or Memories of a Man of Pleasure, Charles Careless Esq. His Amours, Cassandra a Romance, Memoirs of a Coquette, History of the Amours of Miss Kitty, Jilt or Female Fortune Hunters, Adventures of a Rake of Taste*, and *Venus Unmasked*. This move from sentimentality to erotic work, I argue, is in the spirit of spectacle as Mallipeddi describes it, transforming sentimentality from a resistance to commodification in the post-Seven Years War Atlantic marketplace into the full commodification of the body. It is apparent that on the eve of the Revolution, then, some readers—in this case a Salem man who would go on to become a colonel in the continental army and future US Secretary of State—were not resisting the pull of the British consumer society their non-importation agreements, detailed below, putatively scourged.[158]

The most relevant sentimental work for a reading of *Oroonoko's* sympathetic spectacle, however, was a hybrid Social Library title borrowed only a little less frequently than *Betsy Thoughtless, Tom Jones*, or *Grandison*: *Yorick's Sermons* by the sentimentalist Laurence Sterne, the famous author of *Tristram Shandy* and *A Sentimental Journey* (see Figure 1.5). This semi-satirical set of sermons was borrowed diffusely by many different readers at different times, suggesting that it had both a high velocity—often being checked out by a patron the same day it had been returned by another—and high impact.[159] This book was so popular that four editions were produced in 1760 and 1761 alone, when the Social Library began. However, because the book is not mentioned in the 1761 catalog, the library may later have bought the 1764 London sixth edition. One particular sermon, "Sermon III: Philanthropy Recommended," posits a theory of spectacle that is redeeming rather than solipsistic. On the theme of the Good Samaritan, Sterne urges charity and taking care of one's neighbor. He says that we are innately disposed to compassion when we see misfortune, especially when it is tragic: "But where the spectacle is uncommonly tragical, and complicated with many circumstances of misery, the mind is then taken captive at once, and were it inclined to it, has no power to make resistance, but surrenders itself to all the tender emotions of pity and deep concern."[160] Sterne, in working out a theory of how the mind and affections operate in such a situation, urges that this charity should extend to others beyond one's own nation, as the Samaritan treated the suffering Jew who had been left for dead by thieves.[161] Sterne's theory of the working of sympathy

---

[157] Pickering, B2 F9.   [158] Pickering, B9 F1.   [159] "Charge Book."
[160] Laurence Sterne, *The Sermons of Mr. Yorick* (London: Dodsley, 1764), 59–60.
[161] Sterne, 70–2.

Figure 1.5 Joshua Reynolds. *Laurence Sterne* (1713–68), c. 1760. © National Portrait Gallery, London.

around spectacle, I contend, was planting the seeds for sympathy for African slaves, especially in its focus on the charitable duty to have sympathy for someone of another tribe or nation. Indeed, Sterne was part of an incipient abolitionist movement, having corresponded about his opposition to slavery with the British abolitionist Ignatius Sancho.

Most theorists of sentimentality in the period did not view the sympathy generated by tragic spectacle as suspicious. In *The Theory of Moral Sentiments*, Adam Smith writes: "Our joy for the deliverance of those heroes of tragedy or romance who interest us, is as sincere as our grief for their distress, and our fellow-feeling with their misery is not more real than that with their happiness."[162] As mentioned above, Smith's book was borrowed seventeen times by twelve individuals from 1764 to 1768. The high velocity of its circulation—the book was almost always borrowed by a patron on the same day it was returned by another, such as Barton to Jeffry on June 24, 1765, Jeffry to M'Gilchrist on August 5, 1765, M'Gilchrist to Ropes on September 2, 1765, Ropes to Holyoke on October 14,

---

[162] Adam Smith, *The Theory of Moral Sentiments*. Library of Economics and Liberty. Accessed April 30, 2016. <http://www.econlib.org/library/Smith/smMS1.html.>

and so forth—indicates that it actually was being read.[163] And considering that the passages quoted above were in the first pages of the book, the odds are that many Salem Social Library readers were engaged with the relationship between tragedy, spectacle, and sympathy.

In short, though Kaul, McDonald, and Mallipeddi argue that the spectator of a tragic death like Oroonoko's may be experiencing sympathy selfishly, it is clear that contemporaries like Smith, Sterne, and many others argued that sympathy was a positive good, leading to a more moral society. Sympathy for spectacular suffering may have pointed in both directions, of course, and as this chapter has been arguing, the suffering associated with slavery was both appropriated by Anglo-Americans to describe their own condition and leveraged for the anti-slavery cause.

There is no evidence that either Samuel or George Gardner read *Yorick's Sermons* or Smith. However, Samuel's repeated borrowing of a collection of tragedies, and George's purchase of the tragedies *Oroonoko* and *The Mourning Bride* in January 1760, indicates that spectacle of the kind that was generating sympathetic responses was making its way to a slave port like Salem. George, like many sons of fathers who are ruthless businessmen, may have been more liberal than Samuel, even going so far as to reject his father's profitable business. George Gardner's consumption of Hawkesworth's staging of white refinement in opposing slavery is simultaneously solipsistic for whites and potentially liberating for African slaves. This potential, however, is almost immediately withdrawn and put into service to a white American patriotism that positioned those whites as slaves to Britain who were in search of this sentimentally induced idea of liberty. Nonetheless, particularly in Massachusetts, there were patriots who were also abolitionists.

IV

The use of the term "slavery" to describe white Americans'—particularly Massachusetts people's—relationship with Britain stems from about the time George Gardner acquired his copy of *Oroonoko*. Near Gardner in both time and place, the lawyer James Otis of Boston began the Revolution by objecting to British Writs of Assistance—warrants allowing customs officials to search for smuggled goods—in terms that appropriated the trope of slavery. In February 1761, a year after Gardner received his copy of the play, Otis wrote, "I will to my dying day oppose, with all the powers and faculties God has given me, all such instruments of slavery on the one hand and villainy on the other as this Writ of Assistance is."[164] This epithet would be included in patriot rhetoric over the next two decades, levelled at measures like the Stamp Act, the Townshend Acts, and other tax measures from the British Parliament. Accordingly, we can see how it is possible that patriots were appropriating anti-African slavery sentiment for their own pursuit of equal refinement and rights,

---

[163] "Charge Book."

[164] James Otis, "Against Writs of Assistance." National Humanities Institute. <http://www.nhinet.org/ccs/docs/writs.htm>. Accessed May 2, 2016.

and that anti-slavery texts like *Oroonoko* might have been paradoxically making whites feel like slaves.

Salem was very much involved in this revolutionary activity, and some of its leaders who were members of the Social Library took leading roles. The Boston Merchants' Society that was behind lawyers like Otis had consulted Salem merchants for details on their fishing business as early as 1764 in the lead-up to protests against the Sugar Act, and Salem articulated opposition to that Act in a memorial to the Massachusetts legislature that was forwarded to London.[165] Salem agreed to non-importation—a boycott—to protest the Stamp Act in 1765, and adopted the Boston resolutions for non-importation to object to the Townshend Acts in September 1768.[166]

As I have argued elsewhere, nowhere is Salem people's appropriation of the term "slavery" to describe their relationship with Britain more apparent than in their reading of the Irish writings of Jonathan Swift, an advocate for boycotts who wrote that "all government without the consent of the governed is the very definition of slavery."[167] This slave epithet in these works—considered not so much in relation to African chattel slavery as political servitude—would come to govern his reputation among patriots in America. Books by him or about his Irish writings circulated in Salem at high velocity to such prominent Salem patriots and loyalists as Samuel Barton, Joseph Dowse, Timothy Pickering, Joseph Bowditch, William Jeffry, Samuel Gardner, Ebenezer Putnam, Timothy Orne, and others.[168]

These activists' engagement with Swift's use of the term "slavery" to describe the condition of colonials in relation to the mother country was all the more ironic considering that at least three of them—Jeffry, Gardner, and Pickering—had borrowed the library's copy of Montesquieu's *Spirit of the Laws*, which had many passages questioning the history and ethics of slavery.[169] While Montesquieu was surely thinking of African slavery, it is apparent that most American patriots were applying his feelings about slavery to their own colonial situation and not recognizing themselves as the despots.[170]

If politically engaged Salem men had an appetite for Swift's biting political satire, they also, for the most part, had a taste for experiencing the finer emotions. In this period, Barton borrowed *Yorick's Sermons*, Smith's *Theory of Moral Sentiments*, *Fortunate Country Maid*, and a collection of tragedies. Dowse took out *Female Quixote*, *Sidney Bidulph*, and *Fortunate Country Maid*. While the patriotic Pickering's sentimentalism is well documented above, the loyalist-leaning Bowditch was

[165] Charles M. Andrews, "The Boston Merchants and the Non-importation Movement." *Publications of the Colonial Society of Massachusetts* 19 (Transactions 1916–17): 166–7.

[166] Andrews, 198–200, 206.

[167] Sean Moore, "The Irish Contribution to the Ideological Origins of the American Revolution: Non-importation and the Reception of Jonathan Swift's Irish Satires in Early America." Reprinted from *Early American Literature* 52.2 (Spring 2017): 341; Jonathan Swift, *The Prose Works of Jonathan Swift*. Ed. Herbert Davis. 14 vols. (Oxford: Blackwell, 1939–68), 10:63.

[168] Phillips, 253–98; Moore, "Irish Contribution," 352–5; "Charge Book."

[169] Baron de La Bréde et de Montesquieu. *Spirit of the Laws* (London: Nourse & Vaillant, 1758), 1:336.

[170] "Charge Book."

having none of it, borrowing no sentimental titles in the 1760s. William Jeffry read *Fortunate Country Maid, Telemachus, Yorick's Sermons*, many works on the philosophy of the sublime and beautiful, *Grandison, The Theory of Moral Sentiments, Sidney Bidulph*, and a collection of tragedies. As discussed above, Timothy Orne and Samuel Gardner were not averse to borrowing sentimental titles. Putnam seems to have been interested in a collection of tragedies, *Grandison*, works on the sublime and beautiful, *Yorick's Sermons, Sidney Bidulph*, and Shaftesbury's *Characteristics*. Diman was also a reader of *Fortunate Country Maid* and Smith's *Sentiments*, and Jonathan Orne borrowed *Pamela, Betsy Thoughtless, Telemachus, Yorick's Sermons*, and *Fortunate Country Maid*.[171]

It should be noted that Massachusetts patriots after the Revolution like Paul Revere continued to read works of both sentimentality and political thought, indicating both continuity and development of the regional discourse on rights. The borrowing ledgers (1793–7) of the Boston Library Society, which was founded in 1792, chartered in 1794, and eventually merged with the Boston Athenaeum after its establishment in 1807, bear witness to Revere's reading habits. He was sequentially reading volumes of Edward Gibbon's *The History of the Decline and Fall of the Roman Empire*—an important work in the history of British political thought—in 1794, and continued to check out similar non-fiction like Charles Rollin's *Ancient History* in the years encompassed by the ledgers. In the genres that composed sentimentality, he read *Lord Chesterfield's Letters* in 1795 and a book on tragedy in the same year. His record shows that he read travel books, other literary works like Samuel Johnson's *Lives of the Poets*, Tobias Smollett's *Peregrine Pickle*, Francis Burney's *Cecilia*, a collection of romances, and many, many magazines throughout this period. Perhaps signaling his interest in the anti-slavery position, the last title in his record was Royall Tyler's *The Algernine Captive* (1797), one of the most abolitionist of the American novels of the 1790s.[172]

In short, if American independence was contemplated in books of both political theory and sentimental literature, and consummated by both literates aware of these books and the illiterate, abolition of slavery clearly was also. Many American patriots like Otis were also abolitionists, indicating that anti-slavery sentiment such as that held by Hawkesworth was helping to produce the idea of liberty for both whites and blacks.[173] In short, creating sympathy for the enslaved in fictions like *Oroonoko* was certainly about cultivating a refined, liberal sensibility of superiority in whites, and the fact that the trope of slavery, as I have argued, was appropriated for white colonists does not necessarily mean that this was always self-serving or that non-whites could not possess this refinement as well. Indeed, the banning of slavery that would take place in Massachusetts in the 1780s drew

---

[171] "Charge Book."

[172] Boston Library, "Books Borrowed Volume 1, 1793–1797," Archives of the Boston Library Society. Boston Athenaeum, Boston, Massachusetts. Accessed September 9, 2018. <http://cdm16057.contentdm.oclc.org/cdm/ref/collection/p16057coll21/id/7>, 99, 196, 280, 368, 428, 474, 518, 539.

[173] James Otis, "Rights of the British Colonies." *Am I Not a Man and a Brother: The Anti-slavery Crusade of Revolutionary America, 1688–1788*. Ed. Roger Bruns (NY: Chelsea House Publishers, 1977), 104.

upon a long abolitionist tradition in the state. As early as 1700, Samuel Sewall's pamphlet *The Selling of Joseph*, written to build opposition to a slaveholder suing to cancel a contract to free his slave, made a religious argument against slavery.[174] Court cases in the 1760s rode the tide of sentimental anti-slavery, with the case of Jenny Slew of Ipswich gaining her freedom in 1766.[175] In 1767, Boston's Nathaniel Appleton wrote *Considerations on Slavery*, which reminded the white patriots that their cause for liberty was one with anti-slavery; he was trying to "shame slaveholding patriots into reform."[176] The preacher John Allen of Boston published *On the Beauties of Liberty* in 1773, which linked American patriotism to anti-slavery.[177] Reverend Nathaniel Niles of Newburyport, near Salem, also preached *Two Discourses* in 1774 to link the liberty of the colonists with the need to liberate slaves, as did Benjamin Coleman of Newbury in another sermon in the same year.[178] In Salem itself, Allen, in the *Watchman's Alarm to Lord N____* (1774), both attacked British policy and turned on Salem's "pretended votaries for freedom" for participating in the business of slavery.[179] By 1790, Massachusetts could report on the federal census that it held no slaves.[180]

V

This kind of empirical evidence of the various valences and uses of the suffering associated with slavery unifies the postcolonial interrogation of spectacle and its sympathetic effects with the history of reading, for as the history of the book in Salem attests, contemporaries were very much engaged in inquiring into sympathy and spectacle themselves. While the appropriation of "slavery" by some Anglo-American patriots clearly supports Kaul, McDonald, and Mallipeddi's view of the solipsism of the spectators of slave suffering, abolitionist writings concerned with this suffering suggest that sentimentality also was performing good works. The solidarity created by sentimentalism in building affective interpretive communities in which liberty both from Britain and from slavery could be articulated cannot be underestimated. The fellow feeling created by sympathetic, anti-slavery fictions like Hawkesworth's adaptation of *Oroonoko*, or any of the other available sentimental fictions, was not always about creating difference, but also about creating the consensus necessary to actualize the emancipation of many groups from oppression of all kinds. Performing the history of reading in eighteenth-century Salem—the examination of how a reading network or interpretive community was created in a slave port in the 1760s—thereby brings the postcolonial focus on problems of race together with the methods and concerns of book history. That the slavery-financed Social Library was at the center of this community certainly lends credence to some postcolonial theorists' contentions that the book is complicit in

---

[174] Roger Bruns, ed., *Am I Not a Man and a Brother: The Anti-slavery Crusade of Revolutionary America, 1688–1788* (NY: Chelsea House Publishers, 1977), 11.
[175] Bruns, 105–7.   [176] Bruns, 128.   [177] Bruns, 257.
[178] Bruns, 316–24, 325–7.   [179] Bruns, 329.   [180] Bruns, xxix.

imperialism.[181] Yet books, as I have argued, also helped contemporary Anglo-Americans to imagine liberty for those Africans who were, as Sterne signaled in the tale of the Samaritan and the Jew, outside their tribe.

Massachusetts was not alone in New England in trading slaves; in fact, Rhode Island, particularly in the city of Newport, is regarded as the most significant slave-trade hub in the eighteenth-century North American colonies. Those made wealthy by the trade, like their Salem counterparts, had expensive tastes in imported British merchandise, with British books being among the most prized commodities to the extent that they would form, in 1747, the second major library in America after Philadelphia's Library Company. Explaining the history of this Redwood Library in connection to slavery also requires extensive analysis of archival material, though historians of Rhode Island have been among the leaders in documenting this paper trail. As this chapter has explained, the act of excavating such a trail is itself a story within the cultural history of America and the British Atlantic, showing how slavery is not only the basis for much of this culture, but also how it continues to help produce the story of America.

---

[181] Homi K. Bhabha, "Signs Taken for Wonders: Questions of Ambivalence and Authority under a Tree Outside Delhi, May 1817." *Critical Inquiry* 12.1 (Autumn 1985): 149.

2

"Whatever Is, Is Right"
The Redwood Library and the Reception of Pope's Poetry in Colonial Rhode Island

"I was surprised to find that no matters of philosophy were brought upon the carpet. They talked of privateering and building of vessels."

> Alexander Hamilton on meeting some proprietors
> of the Redwood Library

Poor Pope philosophy displays on
With so much rhyme and little reason,
And though he argues ne'er so long
That all is right, his head is wrong.

> Lady Mary Wortley Montagu, "The Reasons that Induced
> Dr. S. to write a Poem called 'The Lady's Dressing Room.'"

A painting located in the boardroom of the Redwood Library of Newport, Rhode Island—the second oldest proprietary library in America—presents to the viewer an image and context of display in which slavery, the library, and the reading of Alexander Pope's poetry are imbricated (see Figure 2.1a). The portrait is of Abraham Redwood, Jr (1709–88), an absentee Antigua plantation owner and slave trader residing in Newport who donated £500 sterling to fund the book collection of the library that still bears his name today. Like the Salem Social Library and early American universities, the library partook of the philanthropy of slave traders like Redwood and many others, as Newport was the most significant triangular trade port in British North America.[1] This Redwood Library was established in 1747 by the Newport Literary and Philosophical Society, an association that was organized, in part, by the Anglo-Irish philosopher George Berkeley in 1730 during his stay in Rhode Island. The books that it collected, due to the fact that early Americans were eager for British cultural capital, were imported from London.[2] Many of these

---

[1] Craig Steven Wilder, *Ebony and Ivy: Race, Slavery, and the Troubled History of America's Universities* (NY: Bloomsbury Press, 2013), 24–32, 65–111; Simon Gikandi, *Slavery and the Culture of Taste* (Princeton: Princeton UP, 2011), 97–144; Jay Coughtry, *The Notorious Triangle: Rhode Island and the African Slave Trade 1700–1807* (Philadelphia: Temple UP, 1981), 25, 36–7.

[2] For recent scholarship on the American appetite for British imports, including books, see T. H. Breen, *Marketplace of Revolution: How Consumer Politics Shaped American Independence* (Oxford: Oxford UP, 2005); James Raven, "The Importation of Books in the Eighteenth Century." *A History of the Book in America. Volume 1: The Colonial Book in the Atlantic World.* Ed. Hugh Amory and David

Figure 2.1a Samuel King. *Abraham Redwood* (1709–88), c. 1780. Redwood Library and Athenaeum, Newport, Rhode Island. The painting was completed and hung in the Redwood family home in Portsmouth, Rhode Island. The painting was given to the library by a direct descendent of Mr. Redwood, Mrs. Edward Grossman, in 1949, and now hangs at the head of the library's boardroom.

books were about liberty, indicating that the Redwood may have been a laboratory for the paradox that some Americans were arguing for their freedom from Britain while simultaneously enslaving others.[3]

The book Redwood is holding in the portrait—"Pope Essay on Man," a poem that reflects on the providential limiting of human freedom—is a salient example of the kinds of books Rhode Islanders were reading to come to terms with their implication in this paradox (see Detail of Figure 2.1b). Its conservatism, most strongly manifest in its line "Whatever is, is Right," I argue, expressed a sympathy with slavery that helped imaginatively resolve this paradox for readers in this northern slave-trading colony.

Hall (Chapel Hill: U North Carolina P, 2007), 183–98; Julie Flavell, *When London was Capital of America* (New Haven: Yale UP, 2010).

[3] Edmund S. Morgan, *American Slavery, American Freedom: The Ordeal of Colonial Virginia* (NY: Norton, 1975), 4–6.

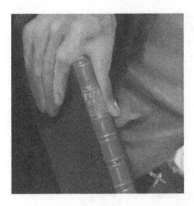

Figure 2.1b Detail of Abraham Redwood painting. Redwood is holding a book—the gilt-lettering spine of which indicates that it is a copy of "Pope Essay on Man." Redwood Library and Athenaeum, Newport, Rhode Island.

This chapter asks whether the British books read by colonial Rhode Islanders—some of whom were Redwood proprietors and patrons—in their pursuit of "British" taste and identity were not only symptomatic of this paradox, but also naturalizations of slavery that rendered this paradox invisible to them. The work of Pope was ubiquitous in the colonies, and evidence from early Rhode Island shows it being read by many; the Redwood even possessed a nine-volume scholarly edition of his works published in 1751 that circulated quite well in the late 1750s and early 1760s. While we may never know precisely how the books that this Newport archive lent were interpreted, the fact was that its formation, and the purchases of British books by Rhode Islanders in general, were symptomatic of the disavowal of the Enlightenment's relationship to the accumulation of capital through the slave trade.[4] At the very least, the evidence that we have of specific books circulating and being commented upon serves as an index to the metropolitan tastes of readers living in a Rhode Island—and indeed continental—economy based on slavery. The Rhode Island case, like the Virginia and Massachusetts ones that I have documented, demonstrates that slavery, in short, was supporting the early American pursuit of good taste in literature.[5] Further, it shows that slavery was the means by which Americans were learning the political ideas and modes of civic engagement enabling their project for independence and the preservation of slavery, as manifest in actions like the Stamp Act protests and the burning of the British revenue ship the *Gaspee* in Rhode Island in 1772.[6] If the Revolution was fought to preserve slavery against British efforts to abolish it with the 1772 Somerset case and the recruitment of blacks for the British military, as Blackburn and Horne have contended, then Rhode Island, the most significant American slave-trade center, was in the vanguard with this kind of civic action. The cultural history of Rhode Island and the other colonies in this period thus appears interdisciplinary, with literary taste and political thought working together to form a distinctive brand of American

---

[4] Gikandi, 4–10.   [5] Gikandi, *passim*.
[6] Mary Sarah Bilder, *The Transatlantic Constitution: Colonial Legal Culture and the Empire* (Cambridge: Harvard UP, 2004), 180–3.

civics—and the economy on which that civics was based—that this cultural capitalization underwrote and facilitated.

This chapter will first analyze the passages on slavery in some of Pope's poems, particularly *Windsor Forest*, a juvenile propaganda poem in which he first articulates the paradox of African slavery within anglophone liberty, and *An Essay on Man*, a later, more mature, and popular work that naturalizes this disavowal. Second, it will study the history of the Redwood Library's foundation, explaining its relevance to Slavoj Zizek's critique of charity to intervene in the study of what I am calling slavery philanthropy while showing Newport to be a central slave-trade port. Here, I will connect the library to the larger Rhode Island book trade of which it was a part and to its main rival, the Providence Library Company and Athenaeum. Third, it will examine the Redwood's circulation receipt books—borrowing records—as evidence of the tastes of readers involved in slavery and of the fact that these readers were thinking of slavery in terms of their relationship to foreign, and later British, powers rather than to the Africans who they were enslaving. Fourth, it will show clear evidence of the receptions of *Windsor Forest*'s disavowing lines " 'Till Conquest cease, and slav'ry be no more" in George Washington's correspondence and of *An Essay on Man*'s acceptance of slavery—"Whatever is, is Right," in the records left by Rhode Island readers. Finally, it will explain that there were anti-slavery advocates among the Redwood Library's readers, establishing that Rhode Island law soon turned in an abolitionist direction during and after the Revolution even as figures like Redwood never freed their slaves.

In the sequence of documenting these facts, I will claim that for Rhode Island readers at least, British poetic discourse on slavery pointed in two directions: first to their own potential condition as a "British" people who might become subject to a foreign sovereign, and only second to the condition of the Africans they were enslaving. This disavowal, characteristic of the anglophone rhetoric of liberty, would also become constitutive of colonists' own revolutionary movement, specifically leveraged against enslavement by those very same Britons who invented this discourse—a discourse purchased for the Redwood with slavery philanthropy. I also will make the methodological claim that reader reception, the most difficult node in Robert Darnton's concept of the "communications circuit"—the journey of a book from author, to bookseller, to printer, to shipper, to retailer, and to reader—may also be established through evidence from the visual arts.[7] Portraiture with books, as Garratt Stewart explains, is a "fertile wedding of scribal and visual culture" that adds the temporal space of reading to the visual place of a painting, creating a "drama of reader plus book" reflecting a depth of interiority in the reader.[8] In this case, the painting of Abraham Redwood with Pope's book, together with evidence from book advertisements, library catalogs, borrowing records, diaries, and commonplace books, proves that Rhode Islanders in the library were familiar with Pope's tacit acceptance of slavery. In doing this analysis, I hope to show how transatlantic

---

[7] Robert Darnton, "What is the History of Books?" *The Book History Reader*. Ed. David Finkelstein and Alistair McCleery (London: Routledge, 2002), 11.

[8] Garrett Stewart, *The Look of Reading: Book, Painting, Text* (Chicago: U Chicago P, 2006), 33, 77.

literary history may be performed by multi-disciplinary reference to almost all available print, manuscript, and visual sources on the reception of a British author like Pope in a small place like Rhode Island. Even as it calls attention to the slavery financing of culture, however, this chapter presents only one layer in an archaeology of Rhode Island history. Put another way, eighteenth-century slavery exists beneath a more progressive, late eighteenth- and nineteenth-century stratum of abolition in the northern United States in which Redwood readers were intimately involved.

I

When close-reading *Windsor Forest* and *An Essay on Man*, it is difficult to avoid the pitfalls of seeing only race when the term "slavery" is uttered; indeed, that reading is part of the disavowing gesture at the root of the period's British and American discourse on liberty.[9] In eighteenth-century anglophone poetry and political thought, "slavery" was "an idiom in English political discourse" associated as much with qualities such as foreign domination, absolute monarchy, and Roman Catholicism as with the state of African bondage.[10] In articulating English Protestantism-as-liberty, champions of the new British state that had emerged with the 1688 Revolution and their counterparts a few generations later in America viewed themselves as the opposites of both European foreigners and the Africans who their societies were enslaving. The Treaty of Utrecht of 1713, the settlement of the War of the Spanish Succession that granted Britain the Asiento—the monopoly over the transatlantic shipping of slaves to Spanish colonies—was the context within which this simultaneous celebration of the victory of British liberty and the enslavement of others was staged. *Windsor Forest* was the most literary of the publications promoting the Treaty to the English public and endorsing the Tory ruling party, which had negotiated the Treaty, and with which Pope was affiliated (see Figure 2.2). *An Essay on Man*, a more widely disseminated work, developed *Windsor Forest*'s articulation of this endorsement of African slavery to the point of a refusal to reform it.

Pope's articulations of his approval of slavery were available all across the Atlantic, as the dissemination of Pope's writing in America was so extensive that writers like James Kirkpatrick, Mather Byles, Henry Brooke, and James Ralph both imitated and satirized him.[11] Pope's *Iliad*, *Odyssey*, and *Universal Prayer* were popular with American women, and writers like Phillis Wheatley and Annis Stockton read him and appropriated his style.[12] Agnes Sibley's foundational book *Alexander Pope's*

    [9] Srividhya Swaminathan and Adam R. Beach, eds, *Invoking Slavery in the Eighteenth-Century British Imagination* (Farnham: Ashgate, 2013), 1–18.

    [10] Christopher Leslie Brown, *Moral Capital: Foundations of British Abolitionism* (Chapel Hill: U North Carolina P, 2006), 127.

    [11] David S. Shields, *Civil Tongues and Polite Letters in British America* (Chapel Hill: U North Carolina P, 1997), 77; David S. Shields, *Oracles of Empire: Poetry, Politics, and Commerce in British America, 1690–1750* (Chicago: U Chicago P, 1990), 179–80; Austin Warren, "To Mr. Pope: Epistles from America." *PMLA* 48.1 (Mar. 1933): 61–73.

    [12] Caroline Winterer, *The Mirror of Antiquity: American Women and the Classical Tradition, 1750–1900* (Ithaca: Cornell UP, 2007), 29–34; Carla Mulford, ed., *Only for the Eye of a Friend: The Poems of Annis Boudinot Stockton* (Charlottesville: UP of Virginia, 1995), 28–40.

Figure 2.2 Jonathan Richardson, English, 1667–1745. *Alexander Pope*, about 1736. Oil on canvas. 76.5 × 63.2 cm (30 1/8 × 24 7/8 in.). Framed: H. 43 in.; W. 38 in. Museum of Fine Arts, Boston. James T. Fields Collection 24.19.

Prestige in America is the most thorough treatment of his influence in the colonies, and she notes that Pope's *Works* was listed more frequently than the books of any other British writer in the catalogs of early Virginians' private libraries.[13] It is clear that the complexity of Pope's motif of slavery was shared by Britons in both England and America, and libraries like those of these Virginians and the Redwood itself were both founded upon slavery and invested in the forms of disavowal of it that were available in poems like Pope's.

There are three passages in *Windsor Forest* that contain the terms "slaves" or "slavery," and each has a different resonance. The first, expressed early in lines 43–52, valorizes England's liberty under the reigning Stuart dynasty, especially the current monarch Queen Anne, by contrasting it with the tyranny and slavery in what England was like before her. Pope writes that in that past, "…wiser brutes were backward to be slaves.) | What could be free, when lawless beasts obey'd, | And ev'n the elements a Tyrant sway'd?"[14] A few lines later in the second passage concerning

[13] Agnes Marie Sibley, *Alexander Pope's Prestige in America, 1725–1835* (NY: Columbia UP, 1949), 9.

[14] Alexander Pope, *Windsor Forest*, lines 50–2. <https://andromeda.rutgers.edu/~jlynch/Texts/windsor.html>

slavery, we are told that if Pope is not specifically citing the pre-1688 old regime, he is at least referring to the Norman Conquest, begun in 1066 at the Battle of Hastings, as the origin of this tyranny over English liberties. Pope writes: "Our haughty *Norman* boasts that barb'rous name, | And makes his trembling slaves the royal game."[15] Here, it is important to remember that in eighteenth-century British political poetry, the term "Norman" was code for England's principal enemy, France. As Laura Doyle has written, celebrants of the victory of William of Orange in the Glorious Revolution of 1688 were at great pains to revise English history to capture a pure "Englishness" that existed before the Norman Conquest. This strategy was part of distancing the nation from eighteenth-century "Frenchness" and was formative of a racial contract embracing pre-1066 Anglo-Saxonism and excluding all other ethnicities, races, and nationalities from inclusion in the Englishness of the social contract.[16] Part of this effort was to deflect accusations that 1688's new conqueror, William of Orange, was a tyrant by arguing that King Louis XIV of France and other Catholic monarchs were the real tyrants who enslaved their people. In this kind of poetry, Protestantism is shown to be the native religion of English liberty, even though King William was a foreign Dutchman, and Catholicism the foreign religion of slavery.

These two passages on English history and Anglo-French relations do much to invent an English subjectivity that is the opposite of a slave, but Pope haltingly intimates an extension of this rhetoric to the current issue of the transatlantic trade in African bodies in his third passage.

Here, he argues that the Treaty of Utrecht would lead to Britain ending slavery worldwide. He writes,

> Oh stretch thy reign, fair Peace! from shore to shore,
> 'Till Conquest cease, and slav'ry be no more;
> 'Till the freed *Indians* in their native groves
> Reap their own fruits, and woo their sable loves,
> *Peru* once more a race of Kings behold,
> And other *Mexico's* be roof'd with gold.[17]

Here, Pope is intimating that the end of the war—"Conquest['s] cease"—will make "slav'ry...no more." These lines seem to be trying to deliver on the earlier ones about the Norman Conquest being associated with slavery by saying the time of that Conquest will be over; yet, their association of that ending with a Treaty of Utrecht that promised new slave profits is very problematic.

Scholars have long noted this problem in the poem. Laura Brown, for example, was among the first to note Pope's implicit endorsement of the African slave trade, given the context of the Treaty.[18] Later, Howard Erskine-Hill, drawing on Vincent Carretta's essay about the poem's discourse on English liberty, critiqued Brown's

---

[15] Pope, *Windsor Forest*, lines 63–4.
[16] Laura Doyle, *Freedom's Empire: Race and the Rise of the Novel in Atlantic Modernity, 1640–1940* (Durham: Duke UP, 2008), 2, 11–12.
[17] Pope, *Windsor Forest*, lines 405–10.
[18] Laura Brown, *Alexander Pope* (Oxford: Blackwell, 1985), 40.

African valence of the term "slavery" by arguing that "slavery" was a contemporary trope in English poetry and political thought that was used in discussions about Britain's internal political condition. He argued that English rulers like Charles I, Oliver Cromwell, the Protestant William of Orange, and the Catholic James II were referred to at various times by their enemies as "tyrants" who were "enslaving" the English people.[19] Erskine-Hill refers to other poems on the Treaty of Utrecht by the Whig Thomas Tickell and the Jacobite Catholic Bevil Higgons as exercising in this tradition.[20] Because Pope was Catholic, Erskine-Hill concludes that "Pope's repudiation of 'slavery' is the affirmation of one whose community and values had been drastically marginalised by the events of 1689" that removed the Catholic James from the throne.[21] Contrary to Erskine-Hill, John Richardson argues that "it is possible to detect a euphemistic avoidance in the writing of Pope and others that betrays an unease about the slave trade and possibly about slavery as a whole" given the poem's context of the Treaty.[22] Richardson further contends that Pope's original unpublished draft of the poem had contained references to the Asiento, but he edited them out: "By removing the Atlantic and the Caribbean from his poem, Pope removes all trace of that [slave] traffic." Doing so "reproduces public avoidance of the business of the South Sea Company."[23] Richardson also mentions the Catholic context of the poem, attributing Pope's weakening of his reference to the end of slavery to the poet's need to not alienate either Whig or Tory potential subscribers for his translation of Homer's *Iliad*, a financial necessity given that Catholic writers like Pope could not legally be awarded sinecures by political patrons.[24]

The favorable reception of Pope's *Windsor Forest* in America has long been noted.[25] Joseph Roach argues that part of Pope's vision is a "Pax Britannica" in which Native Americans are freed from the tyrannical rule of the Spanish empire and become what Pope terms a new "Race of Kings" for Peru and other regions.[26] The poem's "premature proclamation of emancipation" for Native Americans, in Roach's view, serves as a strange "surrogate" superimposed on the elided image of "enslaved Africans."[27] Roach calls attention to how while it is "triumphantly proclaiming the end of slavery, *Windsor Forest* omits mention of the Asiento clause of the Treaty of Utrecht" and therefore erases the slave trade from the poem.[28]

Though some of these interpreters of *Windsor Forest* have stressed the African provenance of the term "slavery," there is room for Erskine-Hill's focus on the anti-Catholic valence of "slavery" in American political thought and poetry when we consult early American imprints. One of the earliest in this vein is a Boston reprint of an address from William of Orange, which references the reign of James

[19] Howard Erskine-Hill, "Pope and Slavery." *Alexander Pope: World and Word.* Ed. Howard Erskine-Hill (Oxford: Oxford UP, 1998), 30–2; Vincent Carretta, "Anne and Elizabeth: The Poet as Historian in Windsor Forest." *SEL* 21.3 (Summer 1981): 425–37.

[20] Erskine-Hill, 38.   [21] Erskine-Hill, 45.

[22] John Richardson, "Alexander Pope's 'Windsor Forest': Its Context and Attitudes Towards Slavery." *Eighteenth-Century Studies* 35.1 (Fall 2001): 1.

[23] Richardson, "Alexander," 5.   [24] Richardson, "Alexander," 9, 12.

[25] Sibley, 14, 96; Warren.

[26] Joseph Roach, *Cities of the Dead: Circum-Atlantic Performance* (NY: Columbia, 1996), 121, 142.

[27] Roach, 140, 144.   [28] Roach, 144.

as a time when the English were "kept under Arbitrary Government and Slavery."[29] A related Declaration by Maryland Protestants of the same year refers to the "Slavery and Popery" from which William has delivered them.[30] By the 1760s and 1770s, the patriots had internalized this Whig linkage of Catholicism to slavery, and frequently complained that taxation without representation was slavery to the extent that it resembled some sort of Franco-Catholic rule. The most famous example of this commonplace is in Thomas Paine's *Common Sense*, where he not only refers to the failure of "republican virtue" under Britain's monarchical system government as "slavery," but also considers British tyranny in the colonies to be a "low papistical design."[31] Edmund Morgan referred to this rhetorical tradition long ago when describing Virginian patriots: "in that 'Land of Liberty'…two-fifths of all the people were in fact already enslaved, under the iron rule of masters who were 'Protestants and Britons.'"[32] Indeed, as Philip Gould has argued, loyalists in places like Newport were quick to notice this hypocrisy and "pointed out the excesses of the patriotic language of liberty."[33]

An Essay on Man represents a further development of *Windsor Forest's* disavowal of the slave trade, was more widely read, and was articulated in a rhetoric of paradox.[34] This poetic essay was the most influential of Pope's works in America, and there are numerous citations of it in early American writing.[35] There were forty-five editions of the poem reprinted in America from 1747 to 1799.[36] It appeared in at least two dozen booksellers' advertisements for imported books in Philadelphia alone in the four decades prior to the Revolution, and there are two dozen references to the poem in contemporary Pennsylvania letters and diaries.[37] It has been described as "a conservative meditation on the ordering of the world," particularly for the often-quoted line about how we should be reluctant to transform existing natural, divine, and social institutions: "One truth is clear: Whatever is, is right."[38]

"Slavery" is mentioned seven times over the course of the poem's four essays in reference to being owned (lines I:68 and I:107), to being the victim of tyranny (line III:246–478), or to being morally weak (lines II:191, III:241, IV:215–16,

---

[29] William III, *The first declaration of His Highness William Henry, by the grace of God Prince of Orang. &c.* (Boston: B. Harris, 1689), 14–15.

[30] *The Declaration of the reasons and motives for the present appearing in arms of Their Majesties Protestant subjects in the Province of Maryland. Licens'd, November 28th 1689* (London, 1689), 6.

[31] Thomas Paine, *Common Sense: Addressed to the Inhabitants of America* (Philadelphia: Bell, 1776), 16, 19.

[32] Morgan, *American,* 3.

[33] Philip Gould, *Writing the Rebellion: Loyalists and the Literature of Politics in British America* (Oxford: Oxford UP, 2013), 37.

[34] Paul Giles, *Transatlantic Insurrections: British Culture and the Formation of American Literature, 1730–1860* (Philadelphia: U Pennsylvania P, 2001), 26.

[35] Giles, 15; Eric Slauter, *The State as a Work of Art: The Cultural Origins of the Constitution* (Chicago: U. Chicago P, 2009), 27–8.

[36] James D. Hart, *The Popular Book: A History of America's Literary Taste* (NY: Oxford UP, 1950), 27.

[37] Nicole Eustace, *Passion is the Gale: Emotion, Power, and the Coming of the American Revolution* (Chapel Hill: U North Carolina P, 2008), 18, 21.

[38] Slauter, 27; Alexander Pope, *Essay on Man.* Ed. Tom Jones (Princeton: Princeton University Press, 2016), line I:294.

and IV:331).[39] The poem's only reference to the institution of transatlantic slavery itself is I:104–I:108, lines about a "poor Indian" who has been given "an humbler heav'n; | Some safer world in depth of woods embrac'd, | Some happier island in the wat'ry waste, | Where slaves once more their native land behold, | No fiends torment, no Christian's thirst for gold." Here, Pope borrows from *Windsor Forest*'s formal strategy of substitution to articulate the disavowal of English involvement in slavery in that an emancipated Indian is a surrogate for the African slave. As Richardson has contended, through this strategy the *Essay*'s "choice of gold over sugar as the motive for violent conquest and enslavement of the conquered emphasizes Spanish rather than English oppression," a gesture that acknowledges African slavery, yet elides it with a palimpsest of the Native American.[40] Once again, the liberty associated with Englishness is insulated by transferring associations of slavery to continental Catholic powers, who are read as more complicit in Native American slavery than in African.

The only other reference to slavery as being owned comes in lines I:61–8, in which animals are transformed, by divine intervention, into masters to explain to humanity its condition: "Why doing, suff'ring, check'd, impell'd; and why | This hour a slave, the next a deity." These lines, especially when put together with the phrase that ends the first essay, "Whatever is, is right," "show slavery being explained, and possibly justified, by its place in a divine plan."[41] This explanation, part of *An Essay on Man*'s attempt to "vindicate the ways of God to man," is part of the poem's effort to advance a "philosophy of resignation" that is "a covert justification" of the slave trade.[42] In fact, Nicole Eustace, in critiquing the poem's advancement of the idea that selfish passion could have positive social consequences, has shown that some pacifist, anti-slavery Quakers thought that "passion's promoters lacked the capacity to feel for any but themselves, to imagine either the sufferings inflicted by war or the evils endured by the enslaved."[43] James Logan even went so far as to refute Pope's *Essay* line by line in a poem entitled *On Reading Pope* (1735).[44] *An Essay on Man*'s conservatism, in short, appealed to slaveholding elites for its implicit endorsement of the institution of slavery.[45] Indeed, this covert acceptance did not go unnoticed by other contemporaries. The Swiss critic Jean-Pierre de Crousaz's *An Examination of Mr. Pope's Essay on Man* (1739) upbraids Pope, saying that lines 61–8 conclude that slavery is not a consequence of humanity's choices, but rather natural in that providence requires it for "the Good of the whole."[46] In short, it has long been known that the problem of slavery is a central motif in the *Essay*, which resigns itself to the necessity of slavery in the divine plan.

Accordingly, when we consider the paradox that early Americans were articulating the importance of their own freedom from British "slavery" while continuing

---

[39] John Richardson, *Slavery and Augustan Literature: Swift, Pope, Gay* (London: Routledge, 2004), 35. Pope, *Essay on Man.*

[40] Richardson, *Slavery*, 102.   [41] Richardson, *Slavery*, 105.

[42] Pope, *Essay on Man*, line 16; Richardson, *Slavery*, 102, 101.   [43] Eustace, 37.

[44] Eustace, 22–4.   [45] Eustace, 39.

[46] Jean Pierre de Crousaz, *An Examination of Mr. Pope's Essay on Man*. Trans. Elizabeth Carter (London: Dodd, 1739), 65.

to hold African slaves, we can see how that discourse may originate in the literature that memorialized the 1688 revolutionary event, the Treaty of Utrecht, and further English achievements. If 1776—an event that Horne says was a defense of slavery—was the third British revolution after 1641 and 1688, as J. G. A. Pocock and Eric Nelson have contended, then it makes sense that the genealogy of this disavowing American patriotic rhetoric includes *Windsor Forest* and *An Essay on Man* as antecedents.[47] Editions of Pope's *Works*, almost all of which contained the poem, were widely available in America, so it should be no surprise that the Redwood owned one. That this library was emblematic of the colonial book market and the American archive in general thereby leads us to consider the Enlightenment's marketplace of ideas—one in which slave-trading Americans seeking imported books were participating. The financing of purchases within this market, as the importation of Pope's books makes clear, was perpetuating a disavowal that problematizes our knowledge of the American reception of that Enlightenment.

II

The history of the origins of the Redwood Library can tell us much not only about how Rhode Islanders imported books, how they paid for them, and the state of the colony's book trade. Specifically, it can also tell us about the literary tastes and civic orientation of the colony's population as a whole. While there is evidence that there were at least four other major specialized booksellers and one other proprietary library in Rhode Island in this period—Benjamin West and John Carter in Providence, George Gibbs and David Hopkins in Newport, and the Providence Library Company—the Redwood, due to its survival into the present day, has the best-preserved history of the colonial Rhode Island book trade. Before discussing these booksellers and some of what they stocked, an explanation of the existing archival material and scholarship on the Redwood may help us index the tastes of Rhode Island's elite—the Newport slaveholders who were proprietors of the library. Doing so provides a context for the colony's reading of Pope's works, and the slavery theme of some of them, which I detail in Section IV.

The study of the origins of the library is one that encompasses the fields of library history, book history, Rhode Island history, the construction of race and slavery, and the critique of philanthropy. Its story is part of recent trends in scholarship on both the roles of Rhode Island in the slave trade and of philanthropists who derived their income from slavery in endowing churches, universities like Brown, and other charitable institutions.[48] It is therefore also a historical discourse anticipating Slavoj Zizek's recent critique of the ethics of capitalism's charity as

    [47] J. G. A. Pocock, *Three British Revolutions: 1641, 1688, 1776* (Princeton: Princeton UP, 1980); Eric Nelson, *The Royalist Revolution: Monarchy and the American Founding* (Cambridge: Belknap P, 2014).
    [48] For these endowments see Joanne Pope Melish, *Disowning Slavery: Gradual Emancipation and Race in New England, 1780–1860* (Ithaca: Cornell UP, 2000); Thomas Norman DeWolfe, *Inheriting the Trade: A Northern Family Confronts its Legacy as the Largest Slave-Trading Dynasty in American History* (Boston: Beacon P, 2008); and Wilder.

one in which we have included it in the cost of doing business, and that by doing so we are encouraging corporate vices by working forgiveness of them into these ethics.[49] The biography of Abraham Redwood, his Newport social network, and the kinds of books that they collected in the library all demonstrate how the circulation of British knowledge to the colonies was underwritten by slavery philanthropy and the labor of the African diaspora.

Abraham Redwood (1709–88) was the third son of a Quaker and Antigua slave plantation owner, also named Abraham (1665–*c*.1717). The younger Abraham was born on his father's slave plantation in Antigua in 1709 and immigrated to Salem, Massachusetts, in 1712 with his family, who eventually moved to Newport. Due to the death of his two older brothers, Abraham Jr became sole heir to the plantation. He was probably educated by the Society of Friends in Philadelphia before he married Martha Coggeshall, a descendant of one of Newport's first settlers, in 1727. The couple had six children. He joined his father's business in 1720, which consisted not only of the Antigua plantation, but also of a bilateral trade in which he sent timber and fish to the Caribbean in exchange for molasses and cash.[50] In the 1730s and 1740s, Redwood Jr expanded his trade into slavery and worked the triangle for which Newport was infamous, using his ships like the *Martha and Jane* on slave voyages.[51] The *Dictionary of National Biography* reports that, "Without a doubt the slave trade provided Redwood with the enormous profits that allowed him to become, as he was described at his death, 'the greatest public and private benefactor on Rhode Island.'"[52] In addition to his gift to Newport's library, Redwood made major contributions to the College of Rhode Island (Brown University) and to a school in Newport for the education of Quakers.[53]

Redwood is a clear example of a slave profiteer reinvesting his profits in the cultural capital available from Britain in the era of the Enlightenment. Redwood's interest in books was probably derived from his Anglophilia and pursuit of the trappings of an Enlightenment English gentleman. His love for imports was manifest in such things as his desire to have an English garden; he even imported an English gardener, Charles Dunbar, and Redwood's correspondence shows that he ordered several plants from London through an agent.[54] His membership in Newport's Literary and Philosophical Society was the driving force behind the founding of the Redwood.[55] An Act of the Rhode Island Assembly dated August 22, 1747 incorporated the library, and there were forty-six original proprietors.

---

[49] Slavoy Zizek, *First as Tragedy, Then as Farce* (London: Verso, 2009), 53.

[50] "Abraham Redwood." *Dictionary of National Biography*. Accessed June 16, 2018. <http://www.oxforddnb.com.libproxy.unh.edu/view/article/68736>.

[51] "Abraham Redwood"; Gladys E. Bolhouse, "Abraham Redwood: Reluctant Quaker, Philanthropist, Botanist." *Redwood Papers: A Bicentennial Collection*. Ed. Lorraine Dexter and Alan Pryce-Jones (Newport: Redwood Library and Athenaeum, 1776), 3.

[52] "Abraham Redwood."　　　[53] "Abraham Redwood."

[54] "Abraham Redwood"; Bolhouse, 2.

[55] Arthur S. Roberts, "Redwood Library: Two Centuries: Excerpts from an article written in 1946." *Redwood Papers: A Bicentennial Collection*. Ed. Lorraine Dexter and Alan Pryce-Jones (Newport: Redwood Library and Athenaeum, 1776), 15.

Redwood pledged £500 sterling to found the library's original book collection, and the books were ordered through an agent in London, John Thomlinson, scion of another Quaker Antigua plantation family.[56] Arthur Roberts has argued that the books were ordered by "a committee on selection," though according to Wilmarth Lewis, we still do not know who exactly the committee members were and whether they were ordering from the catalogs of London booksellers or from another source.[57] Lewis has contended that the Rector of Newport's Trinity Church, James Honyman, must have been on this committee, and that many men who we know donated books must have been able to make recommendations of other books for the library to order.[58] Editions of Homer, Herodotus, Xenophon, Chaucer, Calvin, and Descartes were donated by Thomas Ward, the works of Vossius and Pliny were given by Dr. John Brett, and many books were given by the leader of the Philosophical Society and first Redwood Librarian, Edward Scott.[59] Marcus McCorison has said that there were 751 titles in the original shipment of books from London, totaling 1,338 volumes, and that they were probably shipped in a boat owned by one of the proprietors.[60] McCorison actually reprinted the 1764 printed catalog of the Redwood in 1965, and went so far as to indicate in his indexing whether the library still had the original copy, if the Redwood librarians replaced it with the same edition, or whether the volume was never replaced. Many books disappeared from the library in the late eighteenth century, and though legend has it that the British officers who occupied the library during the Revolution were the culprits, there is plenty of evidence to prove that the library's own members failed to return volumes.[61]

The books that were ordered from Redwood's £500 donation were from a variety of disciplines. As Lewis succinctly described it, they ranged from the classics to theology, medicine, law, mathematics, natural history, and literature, the latter mostly in octavo and duodecimo format. The library catalog had two sections of literary works that included:

> Dryden, Pope, Addison, Gay, Prior, Thomson, Garth, and Young. Shakespeare is represented only by Warburton's edition, 1747, and Milton only by *Paradise* [xi] *Lost*, 1746, and *Paradise Regained*, 1743. We look in vain for Congreve and the novels of Defoe and Richardson, but we find *Joseph Andrews*, which first appeared in 1742. It is the only book of its kind bought with Redwood's £500, but presently *Roderick Random*, 1748, joined it. *Tom Jones*, 1749, was not admitted by the Company. That Dodsley's *A Collection of Poems*, the outstanding book of 1748, was not acquired suggests that Thomlinson or his agent did not go to Dodsley, the leading bookseller of the day, to supply the books.[62]

As we can see from this description, British literary works were there, though they did not dominate the collection. As Lewis has noted, the founders of the library were businessmen more interested in non-fiction: "The section on history and

[56] Marcus A. McCorison, ed., *The 1764 Catalogue of the Redwood Library Company at Newport, Rhode Island* (New Haven: Yale UP, 1965), ix.

[57] Arthur Roberts, *Redwood Library and Athenaeum Newport, Rhode Island* (Providence: Privately Printed, 1948), 22–3; McCorison, ix.

[58] McCorison, xii.   [59] McCorison, xii.   [60] McCorison, xviii.
[61] McCorison, xiii.   [62] McCorison, x–xi.

current affairs catered to a library patronized by men who owned ships: the latest histories of Europe and the latest voyages; books on Russia, Persia, and the Turks."[63] In my research at the Redwood, however, I have found that the literary works, particularly in octavo and duodecimo editions, are the most likely of any genre to have disappeared from the library, a fact that shows just how popular British literature was in Newport.

Newport shipping wealth helps explain the town's library patronage because one had to be quite wealthy to borrow books at the Redwood in the late eighteenth century. A member could borrow one book a month, and would have to leave a deposit with the librarian for the value of the book. Even some of the octavo editions had prices above ten pounds, which was a considerable amount at that time. In fact, poorer intellectuals like clergymen, some of whom would become involved in abolition, could not afford proprietorship in the library and were usually made "honorary members."[64] The costs of library membership and borrowing affirm Roberts's view that "the residence of an unusually large variety of men of wealth in Newport in the early eighteenth century meant that books from English and Continental presses were both prized and used."[65]

Book historians traditionally have been elliptical about the relationship of this wealth and the slavery behind it to this archive, though Lewis wrote that "The possibilities of the coast of Guinea were always present in Newporters' minds."[66] Gladys Bolhouse mentioned Redwood's slave wealth in writing a history of the library, and Arthur Roberts indicated that even nineteenth-century library officers like Robert Johnson owned West Indian estates.[67] Historians of slavery, however, have not been elliptical about this topic and have pointed to just how powerful a social network Newport slave traders and owners were. Jay Coughtry, for example, argued that "Rhode Island merchants controlled between 60 and 90 percent of the American trade in African slaves" in the eighteenth century in his research on Rhode Island's role in the triangular trade, and that he "rarely found a slaver owned outside of Newport."[68] Some involved in the trade, like the Lyon family, vertically integrated the business, with the son, William, living in Newport and sending ships out on slave voyages, and the father, Joseph, living in Charleston South Carolina where many of those slaves disembarked.[69] Coughtry identifies Newport grandees in the trade, "the Champlins; Aaron Lopez and Jacob Rivera; John Malbone; the Vernons; and the Wantons."[70] Interestingly, George Champlin Mason, compiler of the *Annals of the Redwood Library* during the Victorian period, was descended from one of these families. Even more compelling is that some of these names are on the

---

[63] McCorison, xi.

[64] George Champlin Mason, *Annals of the Redwood Library and Athenaeum* (Newport: Redwood, 1891), 45, 56, 75–6.

[65] Roberts, "Redwood Library: Two Centuries," 15.   [66] McCorison, xi.

[67] Bolhouse, 7–8; Roberts, *Redwood Library and Athenaeum*, 17.

[68] Coughtry, 25, 36.

[69] Joseph Lyon Family Papers. Hay Library MS A2012.031. Brown University, Providence, Rhode Island.

[70] Coughtry, 37.

list of the original forty-six proprietors of the library. William Vernon and Samuel Vernon are listed, as is Stephen Wanton.

This evidence proves that it was not only slave ownership, but also active slave trading that went into the philanthropic foundation of the library. Indeed, Lorenzo Greene, in *The Negro in Colonial New England*, documents the large-scale philanthropy of New England slave traders and shows that many Wantons held Rhode Island governorships and that William Vernon was a prominent patriot.[71] Like Gikandi has done in the case of West Indian slaveholders living in eighteenth-century Britain, Greene shows how New England slavers were the wellspring of colonial learning, writing, "From the Negro trade, likewise, came a great part of the wealth that afforded slave trading magnates the necessary leisure for cultural and intellectual leadership."[72] Greene specifically cites the slaving foundations of the Redwood as a principal example of this connection between slavery and intellectual life.[73] More recently, Rachel Chernos Lin has shown how Newport slavers diversified their investment portfolios, becoming "active in banking, insurance, and real estate" and branching into manufacturing.[74] Even America's first cotton mill in Pawtucket was founded, in part, with the slave capital of Moses Brown.[75] It is clear, then, that the business of human trafficking was at the root of the economic success that gave rise to cultural and intellectual life in the form of libraries and other institutions of learning.

The 1774 Rhode Island census gives us some clues to how pervasive slave ownership in New England was, listing every household in Rhode Island by the categories of white, Indian, and black. In mapping the social network of Redwood members, I have cross-referenced the names of the original proprietors of the Redwood with this census and found that some of them can be identified as owning slaves. The Reverend James Honeyman had six, Simon Pease six, William Paul five, Jaheel Brenton three, David Cheesebrough two, William Vernon five, Joseph Jacob three, Samuel Wickham two, Josias Lydon four, John Tillinghast one, and Redwood himself lists three. Even where many of the other original proprietors are not listed in the census, perhaps due to death or having been loyalists driven out of town by patriots by 1774, many people with the same family names seem to have had blacks living in their households.[76]

By 1790, the *Annals of the Redwood Library* show that most of the major slave-trading families were represented at the Redwood as proprietors or members. William Vernon and Gideon Wanton are listed, as are Christopher Champlin, John Malbone, and Abraham Rodriguez Rivera.[77] In fact, William Vernon and

[71] Lorenzo Johnston Greene, *The Negro in Colonial New England 1620–1776* (NY: Columbia UP, 1942), 70–1, 58–9.

[72] Gikandi, *Slavery*, 109–44; Greene, 70.   [73] Greene, 71.

[74] Rachel Chernos Lin, "The Rhode Island Slave Traders: Butchers, Bakers, and Candlestick Makers." *Slavery and Abolition* 23.3 (Dec. 2002), 30, 31.

[75] Lin, 31.

[76] John R. Bartlett, *Census of the Inhabitants of the Colony of Rhode Island and Providence Plantations, Taken by Order of the General Assembly, in the Year 1774; and by the General Assembly of the State ordered to be Printed* (Providence: Knowles, Anthony & Co., State Printers, 1858).

[77] Mason, 71.

John Malbone were chosen as directors of the Library in October 1785, indicating that they may have had a say in book acquisitions.[78] One Moses Lopez, brother of Aaron Lopez, the wealthiest man involved in Newport slavery, was voted a director as early as September 1749.[79] The presence in the Redwood membership of so many members of families who derived at least part of their wealth from the slave trade shows how hard it is to disentangle the relationship of slavery to book acquisitions and reading in the eighteenth century.

The history of the Redwood, accordingly, sheds light on the rest of the period's Rhode Island book trade, including that trade's manifestation in the Providence Library Company, which similarly partook of the slavery economy of the colony. There had been printers in Newport for many years, such as James Franklin, Benjamin Franklin's brother, and his family and descendants, but there is little evidence of their bookselling. Of George Gibbs of Newport we know nothing, except that he opened a bookstore in 1764 and was a member of the Redwood as early as 1749.[80] We know that David Hopkins of Newport, however, was a book retailer who had business dealings with one of the major Boston importers of British books, Henry Knox, who later became a general in the continental army. As early as April of 1772, Hopkins was ordering literary books from Knox that were by then classics such as Defoe's *Robinson Crusoe*, Samuel Richardson's *Pamela*, and Joseph Addison and Richard Steele's magazines *The Tatler* and *Spectator*. He also retailed many histories, religious books, and school books. In addition, he seemed to stock the latest novels, such as Oliver Goldsmith's *The Vicar of Wakefield*, Tobias Smollett's *Humphrey Clinker*, Henry MacKenzie's *The Man of Feeling*, and many works by Laurence Sterne. Further, as detailed below, Hopkins ordered books by Pope for his Newport customers, as well as the latest London magazines that advertised books for his customers to order. What is interesting about his orders is that, by virtue of barter being the dominant means of payment in business-to-business transactions in this period, Hopkins's payments to Knox are in goods from the triangular trade that came to Newport, some of them produced by slaves, such as sugar. For example, on June 11, 1773, Knox received a payment from Hopkins worth £165 consisting of 105 loaves of sugar, 546 pounds of coffee, and a "cask of Tenerife wine."[81] The slave trade, of which the Newport-based triangular trade was very much a part, was therefore helping to pay for the importation of British books to Rhode Island, as Hopkins was clearly obtaining these goods to barter from his seafaring customers.

In Providence, the records of the booksellers Benjamin West and John Carter are fairly sparse, only occasionally indicating that they ordered particular books for their customers. West was selling books like John Bunyan's *Pilgrim's Progress*, *Robinson Crusoe*, Gessner's *The Death of Abel*, Pomfret's poems, Henry Brooke's

---

[78] Mason, 66.   [79] Mason, 38.

[80] Jordan Goffin, *Atlas of the Rhode Island Book Trade in the Eighteenth Century*. <http://www.rihs. org/atlas/>; Mason, 38.

[81] Henry Knox, "Henry Knox Papers II, 1736–1823," Microfilm P-467, Massachusetts Historical Society, Boston. This account book is cited by date, in-text, rather than by page.

sentimental novel *The Fool of Quality*, and works by Pope (described below).[82] His accounts with Jeremy Condy, the bookseller to the Salem Social Library, however, indicate that he was mostly ordering mathematical, navigational, and scientific works.[83] As for Carter, the only book besides the *Vicar of Wakefield* and *Arabian Nights Entertainment* he seemed to sell—and in massive quantities—was his own 1774 reprint of Henry Care's 1721 *English Liberties: or the Free-Born Subject's Inheritance*. The large circulation of Carter's reprint of this book to Rhode Islanders— forty copies in 1774 and 1775 alone—indicates just how much early Americans were thinking about their liberties vis-à-vis the British Parliament in these years, despite their enslavement of others.[84]

The Providence Library Company, similarly, offered opportunities to reflect on these liberties, with its members sometimes engaging in revolutionary civic activity based on the understanding of their rights that they were getting from books. It was the central rival to the Redwood and the main space for reading in this more northerly Rhode Island city. It had been formed in 1753 by men, most of whom were involved in the Atlantic slavery economy like the Brown family, whose links to slavery have been explored in full by Brown University.[85] "Eighty-five men and one woman signed their names and promised to pay twenty-five pounds to become shareholders," writes Jane Lancaster, a substantial sum in that period.[86] The city had a large number of Indian and African slaves—about 10 percent of the entire population.[87] The books for the library—345 volumes—were shipped from London in Obadiah Brown's vessel *Elizabeth* in 1756, together with "chests of tools, door hinges, pots and pans, spices, men's felt hats, and ladies' lambskin gloves."[88] The titles the library stocked were very similar to those of the Redwood and the other libraries discussed in this volume, with works by John Milton, Thomas More, Cervantes, and, of course, Addison and Steele filling out the literary section.[89] Nicholas Brown was appointed the first librarian, and the library was stored in the Town House, showing just how central it was to the civic life of local government.[90] The library burned in the winter of 1758–9, and all but seventy-one books were lost in the fire.[91] A lottery was started to fund a new library, subscriptions were taken out that added fifty-six new members, and new books arrived from London in 1762. These were stored initially at Esek Hopkins's shop and later in the rebuilt state house.[92] The library, as in other cities, became central to Rhode Island civic engagement during the Revolution, as so many people were involved in rum distilling

---

[82] Benjamin West, Account Book 1758–1773, MSS 794, Rhode Island Historical Society, Providence, Rhode Island.

[83] Jeremiah Condy, Account book, 1759–1770. MSS Folio Vol. C, American Antiquarian Society, Boston, Massachusetts.

[84] John Carter, "John Carter Ledger #1 1768–1775," MSS 336 Vol. 2. Rhode Island Historical Society. Providence, RI. Citations from this ledger will be cited, in-text, by date rather than by page.

[85] Brown University Steering Committee on Slavery and Justice. Accessed June 16, 2018. <http://www.brown.edu/Research/Slavery_Justice/>.

[86] Jane Lancaster, *Inquire Within: A Social History of the Providence Athenaeum Since 1753* (Providence: The Providence Athenaeum, 2003), 4.

[87] Lancaster, 5.   [88] Lancaster, 12.   [89] Lancaster, 12.
[90] Lancaster, 12–13.   [91] Lancaster, 13.   [92] Lancaster, 17–19.

and other aspects of the Atlantic slavery economy that they protested the Sugar Act and the Stamp Act to the extent that the new librarian, Silas Downer, "became a leader in the Sons of Liberty."[93] The Sons were quite active civically, their most notable act being burning King George's tax revenue ship the *Gaspee* as a protest against the new taxes in 1772. Libraries and their members like Downer, it seems, were central to Rhode Island civic organization and mobilization.[94]

Newport and Providence bookselling, and early Rhode Island libraries, demonstrate just how much meaning was mediated by interpretive communities economically based in slavery, and libraries, in particular, were able to form such communities based on their city's civic needs. What we know of the borrowing of works by Pope helps us understand the slavery-for-liberty paradox in which early Americans were engaged. The Redwood's circulation receipt books are the best evidence we have of the reading of Pope's conservatism on the topic of slavery.

III

Establishing how *Windsor Forest* and *An Essay on Man* were interpreted in Rhode Island, as I shall in Section IV, first requires an assessment of the circulation patterns of the Redwood as the only Rhode Island library for which we have borrowing records in this period. The Redwood's circulation receipt books are silent on African slavery, largely due to the fact that its original collection included no books on the subject. But they do document that readers were considering "slavery" to be a term relevant to themselves in the face of potential foreign, Catholic domination. The study of reader reception is an inexact art, to be sure, but records of library circulation can tell us much about which British books were popular in America. Though borrowing records are not always evidence that a book was actually read, evidence of the dissemination of particular works to specific people at the very least can help us understand the tastes and habits of members of the library as a social network led by enslavers. Surprisingly, given the preponderance of non-fiction in the Redwood's original collection, many of the most heavily borrowed books were works of literature or entertainment. The original copies of most of the library's literary books are missing, and what remain of them today are only replacement copies obtained decades and centuries after this period. The Redwood's circulation receipt books, however, give hints as to how those original books were used by showing evidence that many economic and political leaders of Rhode Island wanted to borrow British literary works.

These ledgers are fragmentary, as it was the custom for the librarian to tear out the name of the borrower from the receipt when he returned a book, but several borrowers' names and the books they borrowed from 1756 to 1761 are still discernible. If we look for the names of the major Newport slave traders Coughtry describes, we can see that Vernon and Wanton checked out literary, travel, and religious books. Vernon borrowed volume two of the 12mo *British Apollo* and/or

---

[93] Lancaster, 19.   [94] Lancaster, 20–1.

an octavo edition of *The Entertaining Correspondent* on August 18, 1747.[95] He is also listed as returning a book in 1761, but the only part of the title that is discernible is "James." *The British Apollo,* published in London for T. Sanders in 1726, seems like light reading of the cultural trivia and popular science variety. *The Entertaining Correspondent,* a book of polite letters and travels, was printed in London for G. Smith in 1738. Whether borrowing this book is evidence of Vernon's slave-trading interests is difficult to tell, but one could see how a book of travels might be of interest to a merchant, for it describes several ports in the Atlantic and Mediterranean and some of the customs of those countries.

Wanton borrowed volume one of an octavo edition of *The Jewish Spy* on October 30, 1760, a book that was popular enough to be borrowed five times between 1757 and 1761. This book was an epistolary novel attributed to Jean Baptiste de Boyer, Marquis d'Argens. It purports to be correspondence between rabbis in several European cities and reads as part anthropology, part intelligence report. Perhaps Wanton was reading this to get information necessary for European trade, but this cannot be known for certain. On May 13, 1761 Wanton borrowed the second volume of William King's *Essay on the Origin of Evil,* but what that would have to do with the slave trade is uncertain unless Wanton was examining his conscience.

The most visible name in the Redwood's receipt books (and therefore likely the most prolific borrower) is John Easton. He was connected to slavery in that he married Abraham Redwood's sister Patience in April 1735. His parents were Stephen and Sarah Hazard Easton of Newport. According to Bert Lippincott of the Newport Historical Society, who wrote an unpublished manuscript on the Redwood family, John Easton "was a master mariner and a descendent of one of the oldest families in Newport. He died after falling overboard from his ship and drowned."[96] That Easton was involved in shipping is evidenced by court cases in 1743 and 1748, the first of which concerned the unlawful seizure of his ship the *South Kingstown* by a privateer. Because the ship was carrying a "cargo of 50 gallons of rum, 14,000 gallons of molasses, sugar, and indigo," one possibility is that it was on the final leg of a triangular mission to West Africa and the West Indies, and therefore had carried slaves in the middle passage.[97] Yet even if the ship had been on a bilateral New England/West Indies trade instead of a slave voyage, Easton was still economically benefiting from trading in slave-produced sugars.

From 1756 to 1757, Easton borrowed such books as Defoe's *A Tour Through Great Britain,* Camden's *Brittania,* a Polish history called the *History of Peter Alexiowitz,* Buckingham's *Works,* Hutchinson's book on witchcraft, Voltaire's *Letters,* Bishop Cambray's *Tables,* Burnet's *Travels,* Perry's *Memoirs,* Ray's *Collected Travels, Lives of the Admirals,* the *History of the Late War,* Stanley's *Lives of the Philosophers,* and many

[95] "Circulation Receipt Books, 1756–1761," Redwood Archives, Newport, Rhode Island. This account book is cited by date, in-text, rather than by page.

[96] Bertram Lippincott III, ed., *Genealogy of the Redwood Family.* Unpublished Manuscript Property of the Author and the Board for Certification of Genealogists, Washington, DC (Jamestown, RI, 1986), 20–1.

[97] Jane Fletcher Fiske, *Gleanings from Newport Court Files 1659–1783* (Boxford: Self-Published, 1998), 755.

more that are difficult to identify.[98] While this reading list certainly suggests an Anglophile and Francophile imagination, the works on travel and history suggest that there might have been a utilitarian purpose in this reading, namely to aid in overseas trading in slave-produced commodities. Because many of the books might be classified as more learned and academic, however, I would speculate that Easton might not have been reading only for his slave business, but rather using his slave business to support his pleasure reading and his desire for cultural capital, not just information.

Henry Collins, an original proprietor who donated the land upon which to build the library, was also a prominent slave merchant (see Figure 2.3). He was known in his time as the "Lorenzo de Medici of Rhode Island."[99] He had been educated in England and it was said that "He loved literature and the fine arts; he had taste; the sense of the beautiful in nature, conjoined with the impulse to see it imitated and surpassed by art."[100] The Redwood receipt books show that he borrowed

Figure 2.3 John Smibert. *Henry Collins* (1699–1765), 1736. Redwood Library & Athenaeum, Newport, Rhode Island.

[98] "Circulation."

[99] Hugh Thomas, *The Slave Trade: The Story of the Atlantic Slave Trade: 1440–1870* (NY: Simon & Schuster, 1997), 260–1; Mason, 26–7 n. 23.

[100] Mason, 26–7 n. 23.

a *Collection of Voyages* on January 28, 1757, and Mallet's *Life of Lord Bacon* on April 2, 1761.[101] The *Collection of Voyages* might have been relevant to his slave trading, but the life of Lord Bacon was probably more to the taste of a man of learning like Collins, again indicating that slavery, as Gikandi has established, might have been supporting taste, not only the reverse in which the books were supporting the furtherance of the slave trade.

A more famous Newporter and proprietor of the Redwood, Dr. Thomas Moffat, is shown to have borrowed several more literary books. On December 30, 1756 he borrowed volume 9 of a 12mo edition of Jonathan Swift's *Works*, and on May 12, 1757 he borrowed *The London Magazine* for the year 1743. He also took out *The History of Douglas* on July 7, 1757. This book seems to be *A summary, historical and political, of the first planting, progressive improvements, and present state of the British settlements in North-America*, which was published by William Douglas in 1755.[102] Moffat's taste for literary titles like Swift's works and his desiring of a popular magazine suggest that his reading was not confined to non-fiction like the Douglas book, and Gould has documented how he and his loyalist Newport allies appropriated the rhetoric of Tory Scriblerian writers like Pope and Swift to critique the patriots.[103] In short, Moffat was very much interested in British cultural capital of the literary variety.

Connecting his tastes to certain political views and events in his life is problematic. Moffat was famous as a stamp collector during the Stamp Act Crisis of 1764–6, and as a British loyalist, who was driven out of his Newport home by an angry mob in 1765.[104] He took shelter on a British navy vessel in Newport Harbor and set sail for England on the first available ship.[105] When the mob arrived to sack his house, they found its contents reflected a man of taste with paintings of literary characters like "Polly Peachum," scientific gadgets, fine china, and "a library of valuable books, some of which splashed at the bottom of the well, while others enlarged the libraries of those who themselves had a taste for collecting."[106] Whether any of the books the mob found in Moffat's house were borrowed from the Redwood is uncertain, but this list of paintings and other objects of art and science echoes what we know of his Redwood borrowing. He was clearly an Anglophile, but we should not attribute that purely to his loyalism, for Gould has recently pointed out that both patriots and loyalists were making use of British literature in this period to satirize each other.[107]

Other readers at the Redwood, like Moffat, also had an interest in politics. A prominent Rhode Island family, the Wards, has a borrowing record reflecting taste in literary works. Henry Ward, who served as secretary of the colony then the state of Rhode Island 1760–97, was reading Pope's 12mo translation of Homer's *Odyssey* in the summer of 1757, having borrowed two volumes sequentially in June. He borrowed a book called *A Description of Greenland* on July 7, 1757 and

---

[101] "Circulation."   [102] "Circulation."
[103] Gould, 30.   [104] Gould, 30, 50 n. 43.
[105] Edmund S. Morgan and Helen M. Morgan, *The Stamp Act Crisis: Prologue to Revolution* (Chapel Hill: U North Carolina P, 1953), 145–8.
[106] Morgan & Morgan, *Stamp*, 146–7.   [107] Gould 31, 52–3, 18–19, 35, 53, 36.

Matthew Prior's poems on July 28, though I have no evidence of other reading.[108]
Thomas Ward, a proprietor of the library, donated many books to the Redwood,
including "Greek and Latin versions of Homer, Seneca, Dionysius, Keill and
Calvin," though his tastes in the books that he gave also reflected canonical British
literature, such as folio editions of Chaucer and Spenser.[109] Samuel Ward, who was
governor of Rhode Island and the state's representative to the first and second
Continental Congresses, is listed as the moderator of the Redwood's annual meeting as early as September 1764.[110] The Redwood receipt books, consequently,
make clear that literary works may have been requisite to preparing young men for
public life.

Though African slavery does not seem to have been on the reading list of Redwood
readers, aside from anything they might have gleaned from books on travel, the
receipt books do show instances of literary works on the theme of Britain's liberty
or slavery vis-à-vis Catholic powers being borrowed. For example, Joseph Addison
was a writer of odes to liberty in such poems as *To the King* and *The Campaign,
A Poem, to His Grace the Duke of Marlborough*, the latter of which celebrates the
Duke of Marlborough's victory over "The haughty *Gaul.*" His works were borrowed
three times between March 1757 and September 1761.[111] Volume one of this work
prints the "Campaign" poem, proving that Newport readers had access to such odes
to liberty. It was borrowed on March 31, 1757 by George Gibbs, who, as discussed
above, was a bookseller and Redwood library director at one point. His borrowing
record, accordingly, can be taken as evidence that a leader in the Newport book
and library trade was familiar with the British discourse on liberty and slavery,
at least as Erskine-Hill describes it. This fact underscores other evidence from
the library's catalog of other poems in this discourse being available to Newport
readers, such as James Thomsons's *Winter* and *Liberty*, as well as Edward Young's
Night Thoughts. The catalog also included Matthew Prior's propagandistic *A Letter
to Monsieur Boileau Despreaux; occasion'd by the Victory at Blenheim, 1704* and *On
the Taking of Namur, 1695*, the latter of which was borrowed at least four times
between April 1757 and July 1761.[112]

In short, the fact that these poems were available and sometimes borrowed by
Redwood readers shows that they were at least unconsciously disavowing their own
relationship to African slavery. They seemed to have little interest in reading about
slavery and abolition, even as they were absorbing the anti-foreign slavery rhetoric
of British liberty poetry. As I shall explain, Pope's writings were part of that rhetoric
and read extensively both in the library and in the colony of Rhode Island at large.

IV

It is possible to trace the reception of *Windsor Forest* and *An Essay on Man* in
eighteenth-century Rhode Island in order to establish their relevance to slave traders

---

[108] "Circulation."   [109] Mason, 18–19 n. 12.   [110] Mason, 52.
[111] "Circulation."   [112] "Circulation."

and individuals involved in related enterprises by consulting book advertisements, library catalogs, the Redwood's circulation receipt books, diaries, correspondence, and painting. While I have found some evidence of the reading of *Windsor Forest* in the receipt books, proof of *An Essay on Man*'s dissemination is far more abundant. Nonetheless, documentation of the reading of *Windsor Forest* contained in George Washington's correspondence tells us that the poem's line "Till Conquest Cease and Slav'ry be no more" was received as an articulation of the paradox of African slavery in exclamations of English liberty. Letters to Washington also help guide the interpretation of the very strong evidence that *An Essay on Man* was read widely in Rhode Island.

The reception of *Windsor Forest*'s disavowal of African slavery is manifest in two footnotes in George Washington's papers that discuss the case of John Church, a Philadelphian working in the slave trade who was imprisoned by the Spanish in Cadiz on suspicion of being a spy in Cuba. In a letter from October 1791, he tells Washington his complicated tale of how he ran into trouble with the Spanish authorities. He explains how his itinerary included a return to Havana while working as mate on a slave ship and how he was arrested.[113] A second letter from Church dated February 22, 1792 begs Washington to free him using literary allusions to Joseph Addison's *Cato*, and specifically cites *Windsor Forest* in claiming that he was one of the first patriots to take up arms against the British. He praises "Liberty thou sacred priviledge [*sic*] of Americans," and asks Washington to:

> draw that Fatal sword that is the Scourge of Tyranny and never return it to its Scabbard untill the Southern World enjoy the sweets of Liberty "Till the freed Indians in their Native groves Reap their own fruits and woe [woo] their sable loves Then stretch thy Reign fair Peace from Shore to Shore Till conquest cease and slavery be no more." Pope[114]

That Church would emotionally appeal to Washington by citing the President's favorite play, *Cato*, and follow that with a quotation from *Windsor Forest*, indicates that both of these literary works were associated with American patriotic rhetoric about liberty in the eighteenth-century Atlantic world. This evidence of an American prisoner's reception of Pope's poem again underscores that readers may have been thinking of slavery more in terms of European sovereigns than Africans—as a condition of living under Spanish or French rule. That Church seemed to have no regard for the Africans he was trading, even as he himself complained of his lack of liberty, indicates how unconscious Pope's disavowal was to readers in this period. That the trade continued to be elided in the discourse on liberty, even by a man claiming to be a veteran of the Revolution, indicates just how durable and continuous the transmission of *Windsor Forest*'s disavowing rhetoric from Britain to postcolonial America had become.

---

[113] George Washington, *The Papers of George Washington Digital Edition*, ed. Theodore J. Crackel (Charlottesville: University of Virginia Press, Rotunda, 2008), n. 1. Accessed December 23, 2015. <http://rotunda.upress.virginia.edu/founders/GEWN-05-10-02-0180>.
[114] Washington, n. 2.

The evidence of an *Essay on Man*'s reception in Rhode Island in particular makes an even stronger case for the Redwood Library as an institution for the disavowal of African slavery. The colony's institutional library catalogs and personal inventories of individual household's books show that copies of Pope's *Works* containing the poem, as well as freestanding editions of it, were widely available. The Redwood Library's catalog contained an octavo edition of Pope and Warburton's *Shakespeare*, two separate duodecimo and octavo editions of Pope's *Iliad* and *Odyssey*, a small octavo edition of a nine-volume copy of his *Works*, and an octavo edition of his *Letters*. The Redwood also possessed Pope criticism: a duodecimo edition of Crousaz's *Examination* and another of the second edition of William Warburton's 1740 *A Vindication of Mr. Pope's Essay on Man, from the Misrepresentation of Mr. De Crousaz*.[115] The Providence Library, which was established in 1753 and burned down in 1758, possessed octavo editions of Pope's nine-volume *Works* and multi-volume copies of the *Iliad* and *Odyssey*.[116] A "neatly bound" six-volume copy of Pope's *Works* tops the 1784 list of books ordered directly from the London firm of Champion and Dickason, belonging to James Brown, son of the major slaver John Brown who helped endow the university.[117] Zuriel Waterman, a Rhode Island surgeon related to the Providence printer-bookseller John Waterman, had a list of books from 1778 containing a stand-alone copy of *An Essay on Man* and volumes 3 and 4 of an unnamed edition of Pope's *Works*.[118] The Newport bookseller David Hopkins ordered one copy of a six-volume edition of Pope's *Works* and two copies of stand-alone editions of Pope's *Essay on Man* from the Boston book importer Henry Knox on July 2, 1772.[119] Knox also sold a copy of Pope's *Elegy to the Memory of an Unfortunate Lady* to the Providence bookseller Benjamin West on March 15, 1773. Pope is mentioned or cited at least fifty-five times in the extant Newport and Providence newspapers between 1760 and 1789, nineteen of them being advertisements of imported books by or about him, and ten of those being for single or multiple copies of stand-alone editions of *An Essay on Man* specifically.[120]

The reception of Pope's writings in Rhode Island has been noted to be extensive, most recently by Gould, who demonstrates that both patriot and loyalist writers in Newport imitated him to satirize each other.[121] Ezra Stiles, the librarian of the Redwood, Newport Congregationalist minister, and future president of Yale, mentions Pope several times in his literary diary (see Figure 2.4). In the first week of April 1771, he discusses models of style, writing, "If a stranger was to learn English,

---

[115] McCorison.

[116] Providence Library, *Catalogue of all the Books, Belonging to the Providence Library* (Providence: Waterman and Russell, 1768).

[117] James Brown, "Papers of James Brown (1761–1834)," MSS 310, B1 F1, Rhode Island Historical Society (RIHS), Providence, Rhode Island.

[118] Zuriel Waterman, "Zuriel Waterman Memorandum Book," "Benoni and John Waterman Family Papers," MSS 787, Rhode Island Historical Society (RIHS), Providence, Rhode Island.

[119] Henry Knox, "Henry Knox Papers II, 1736–1823." Microfilm P-467. Massachusetts Historical Society, Boston, Massachusetts.

[120] *America's Historical Newspapers*. Accessed July 1, 2015. <http://infoweb.newsbank.com.libproxy.unh.edu/>. All newspaper articles in this database will be documented in-text by newspaper name and date of publication.

[121] Gould, 31, 34, 33, 74–5, 166.

he would not learn an English book wrote by a German or Italian, but by a Pope or an Addison."[122] On a visit to England, he records going to a church service where "Pope's Universal Prayer was sung."[123] It is likely that Stiles was familiar with *An Essay on Man* because many editions of it, especially American ones, were bound in with this prayer.[124] He also describes the life of a Newporter to whom he gave last rites in February 1773, Pollipus Hammond, a "Guinea Captain" who had "no doubt of the Slave Trade" but who "would not chuse to spend [his life] in buying and selling the human species" if he had it to live over again. Stiles, for his part, "imported slaves while president of Yale," so he probably was not outright condemning Hammond or slavery.[125] Stiles says that Hammond had a "pretty Library" which contained works by Pope and other British writers.[126]

Figure 2.4 Samuel King, American, 1749–1819. *Ezra Stiles* (1727–95), B.A. 1746, M.A. 1749. 1771. Oil on canvas. 34 × 28 × 1 ¼ in. (86.4 × 71.1 × 3.2 cm) framed: 40 ½ × 34 ½ × 2 ½ in. (102.9 × 87.6 × 6.4 cm). Bequest of Charles Jenkins Foote, B.A. 1883, M.D. 1890. Ezra Stiles College, Yale University Art Gallery.

---

[122] Ezra Stiles, *The Literary Diary of Ezra Stiles, D.D., LL.D.* Ed. Franklin Bowditch Dexter. 3 vols (New York: Scribner's Sons, 1901), 1:99.
[123] Stiles, 1:306.   [124] Sibley, 29; Eustace, 30.
[125] Edgar J. McManus, *Black Bondage in the North* (Syracuse: Syracuse UP, 1973), 19.
[126] Stiles, 1:340–1.

The circulation receipt books of the library show that volumes of Pope's *Works* were popular, having been checked out at least thirteen times between December 16, 1756 and December 24, 1761.[127] The Redwood Library's catalog from the period says that the edition was a nine-volume one, and because McCorison lists it as a "small octavo," it is most likely the first nine-volume edition ever published: Warburton's edition, published by Lintot, Tonson, and others in 1751, which had *Windsor Forest* in the first volume and *An Essay on Man* in the third volume.[128] Even if it was not the 1751 edition, all London nine-volume octavo editions in the following decade had the poems in these respective volumes, and because the library possessed many works by Warburton, it was most likely a London edition, as the Dublin piracies of the edition excluded his name and editorial content.[129] Evidence that *Windsor Forest* may have been read by Redwood readers is that volume one was checked out on May 26, 1757 by one Alexander Grant, and again on October 30, 1760 by another member whose name remains illegible.[130] *An Essay on Man*, the first work in the third volume, was checked out on December 16, 1756 and on September 1, 1757.[131] This evidence of borrowing, though not necessarily indicative of reading, at least demonstrates that these poems' complex repulsions and attractions to the slave trade would have been familiar to Newport readers and would have been read as part of what elite Rhode Islanders considered tasteful literature.

Marginalia, diaries, and correspondence, in this case of a Rhode Islander, Theodore Foster, who would go on to become a US Senator, also bear witness to the reception of *An Essay on Man* and other writings by Pope. While a student at Brown, Foster kept diaries in the form of notes tipped-in to almanacs and marginalia in those same almanacs. These constitute a record of his reading, and there are many entries such as schoolboy rhymes about morality, citations of the poetry of Matthew Prior, and doggerel songs. Such annotations suggest, as Anthony Grafton has said, that "reading was, among other things, a way for ambitious, powerful men to assemble cultural capital for themselves," and notes like Foster made served to reprocess and rework the texts that such individuals read.[132] Indeed, it was common for eighteenth-century readers in the English-speaking world to keep such commonplace books, as Abigail Williams explains: "Such collections illustrate the way in which contemporaries initiated creative relationships with their reading matter, culling notable pieces to create the literary equivalent of a modern playlist" consisting of "bon mots, sententiae, and aphorisms, often taken from longer poems."[133] On June 22, 1768, for example, in an almanac published by Mein and Fleeming

---

[127] "Circulation."

[128] McCorison, Item 720; *ESTC (English Short Title Catalogue)*. Accessed July 16, 2015. <http://estc.bl.uk/F/?func=file&file_name=login-bl-estc>.

[129] *ECCO (Eighteenth-Century Collections Online)*. Accessed July 16, 2015. <http://find.galegroup.com.libproxy.unh.edu/ecco/start.do?prodId=ECCO&userGroupName=durh54357>.

[130] "Circulation."   [131] "Circulation."

[132] Anthony Grafton, "Is the History of Reading a Marginal Enterprise? Guillaume Budé and His Books." *The Papers of the Bibliographical Society of America* 91.2 (June 1997): 156–7.

[133] Abigail Williams, *The Social Life of Books: Reading Together in the Eighteenth-Century Home* (New Haven: Yale UP, 2017), 129, 131–2.

of Boston, Foster scribbled marginal comments between pages of *An Essay on Man*, the fourth epistle of which was excerpted in the almanac and ran across the top of the page for each month in the almanac's calendar. Mein and Fleeming may have borrowed this strategy from Benjamin Franklin, who excerpted the poem in the 1736 edition of *Poor Richard's Almanack*.[134] The selection from *An Essay* had begun on the January page of Foster's copy, the first couplet of which read, "Know then this truth, (enough for man to know) | Virtue alone is happiness below." These lines kept with the poem's recommendation of a conservative conformity with a providential order. The lines quoted on the June page upon which Foster wrote are a continuation of a stanza that contained Pope's famous line about "that chain which links the immense design," the great chain of being in which every being has its place in a proper order of subordination.[135] Foster's marginalia quote both Horace in Latin and in Pope's English translation, a work that Richardson has said to be about slavery in that Horace was "surrounded by people persuading him to sell himself and to comply with the world."[136] This compliance or resignation, the central philosophical theme of *An Essay on Man*, as this chapter has argued, is complicit with slavery. This problem is underscored by a citation of *An Essay on Man* that Foster made in a letter he wrote in 1777 during the Revolution, where he quotes Pope's line "Whatever is, is Right" to justify the actions of the patriots.[137] Foster's performance of literary criticism of Pope, in this instance being applied to how patriots should conduct themselves, seems to apologize for any of their actions in the name of Pope's philosophy of acceptance of whatever happens. That these patriots may have been defending slavery, as Blackburn and Horne have written, contextualizes the use of Pope's lines to justify both the war and the institution of slavery for which, in part, it was being fought.

It would be a mistake, however, to assume that written material—marginalia, correspondence, diaries, book catalogs and advertisements, borrowing records, and imitation—constitutes the sole bases for evidence of the reception of literary works. Other media such as painting, in the case of Redwood holding Pope's book, have promise for a more interdisciplinary practice of the study of reading. A portrait of a person reading a book helps to create the impression of an interior persona in the sitter that constitutes him or her as the product of the books that they are reading in the painting, especially when the author and title of the book are evident. This effect essentializes the status of their interior life as one of a person of taste. As Stewart writes:

> The genre of reading is exactly that format of figure painting that forgoes, in light of its theme, those implicit vectors of action natural to the mobile body in painted capture. But even while such latent action elsewhere pervades and animates the space of pictorial art, its vectors are curtailed in this case with no loss of energy. This is in part because the figure of textual attention is able to convey them, the invisible somatic and

---

[134] Eustace, 24.
[135] Theodore Foster, "Theodore Foster Papers," MSS 424, Series 2, B5 F1, Rhode Island Historical Society (RIHS), Providence, Rhode Island.
[136] Richardson, *Slavery*, 96.   [137] Foster Series 2, Box 1, Folder 14.

affective motions of the organic body in reading: impulses not just psychological but neural, sensorimotor, respiratory, and so forth, the whole inner churn of reading insulated from view. Hence the strange redoubling of paintings' own temporal doubleness that gets mounted, on reading's inner stage, by the drama of reader plus book...In respect at once to text and reception, to both discursive time and body time, the image of reading's inner duration thus comes to prominence in the most defiant of ways.[138]

The reading person in the portrait comes across as seemingly more embodied by engaging in inner action, registering a realism to that person's character beyond what the two-dimensional impression creates. The painted book directs the viewer elsewhere than in the painting itself, towards an interior world of the posing reader, which, in turn, alters the way in which we view and critique the painting as a whole; "what happens is that the painted act of deciphering text operates at base as a recast scenario for the seeing of painting."[139] The painting of reading—"the first-born and longest-lived progeny of the genre study"—therefore should be counted as evidence of the reception of a book.[140] By creating the eye's "distance between even registered wording and the scenes it summons," the lettering on a book like Pope's directs the viewer towards another kind of space for which the title is a hint.[141] The deliberate choice of the slaveholding founder of the library to pose with a book entitled *An Essay on Man*, instead of any other book he could have chosen, indicates that he embraced its philosophy of resignation in the face of such institutions as the slavery from which he derived his wealth and doled out philanthropy. Particularly for Redwood, the "book as prop" was a sign of how "held but presently unattended books are the insignia of authority and stability in the male portrait,"— patriarchal authority and stability representing the preservation of slavery.[142] Perhaps Redwood embraced the poem's philosophy because by this time, he had refused the Society of Friends' demand in the 1770s that all Quakers should reject slavery, which led them to " 'Disown him to be any longer a member of our Society' " in 1775.[143] Redwood's choice to pose with a copy of *An Essay on Man*, it would appear, reflected an attitude compatible with the toleration of slavery; "Whatever is, is right," in this context, must be understood as an affirmation of slavery as something that "is" and therefore should be.

V

Ironically, the history of Rhode Island establishes that slavery provided the books that would lead to its undoing. Even as we document how the Redwood Library was an archive imbricated with the institution of slavery, we must be conscious that, as Gikandi put it, this was what the library "was," not what it came to be.[144] Not all Redwood readers were involved with slavery, and some, like the Reverend

---

[138] Stewart, 77.   [139] Stewart, 56.   [140] Stewart, 56.   [141] Stewart, 56.

[142] Stewart, 46.   [143] Bolhouse, 8.

[144] Simon Gikandi, "Editor's Column: The Fantasy of the Library." *PMLA* 128.1 (Jan. 2013): 12–14.

Doctor Samuel Hopkins of the First Congregational Church of Newport, were actively against it (see Figure 2.5). He was the first Congregational minister in America to denounce slavery from the pulpit, and as a consequence several wealthy slave traders left his church. In his 1776 book *A Dialogue Concerning the Slavery of the Africans, Showing it to be the Duty and Interest of the American States to Emancipate all Their African Slaves,* he addressed the very kind of unconsciousness about the patriots claiming liberty for themselves while enslaving Africans that Pope's poem had cultivated. Hopkins writes that he hopes that congressmen will join the movement to ban the slave trade.[145]

That movement had begun as early as the Somerset case in 1772—a sudden reversal of a set of rulings that had established slaves were property everywhere in the British empire.[146] A year later, a Rhode Island court had ruled that a shipment of slaves was illegally captured in Africa, setting them free and ordering them

Figure 2.5 Portrait of Samuel Hopkins (1721–1803). Unknown Artist. Courtesy of the Congregational Library and Archives, Boston, Massachusetts.

[145] Samuel Hopkins, *A Dialogue Concerning the Slavery of the Africans, Showing it to be the Duty and Interest of the American States to Emancipate all their African Slaves* (Norwich: Spooner, 1776), front matter.

[146] George William Van Cleve, *A Slaveholders' Union: Slavery, Politics, and the Constitution in the Early American Republic* (Chicago: U Chicago P, 2010), 31–2.

returned to their homes there[147] In 1774, Rhode Island passed a "largely symbolic" slave-import ban "riddled with exceptions to protect the interests of its citizens, its slaveowners, and its traders," even providing that settlers from other colonies could bring their slaves to Rhode Island and that slaves imported for trans-shipment elsewhere were not free.[148] Further, it imposed fines on abolitionists who "brought slaves into the colony seeking to free them."[149] Later, during the Revolution itself, the new state passed a law banning the sale of Rhode Island slaves out of state.[150] By 1784, Rhode Island, like many other states, had passed a gradual emancipation Act saying that children born of slave parents after March 1 would be freed when they were eighteen (girls) and twenty-one (boys), though traders like John Brown continued to engage in the slave trade, as court cases from the 1790s attest.[151]

While there is no direct evidence that Hopkins drew his argument from books at the Redwood, the fact was that he was a reader there and that gradual emancipation was introduced during his lifetime. Brown's trial indicates that though many Rhode Islanders continued to ply the Atlantic on slave-trading routes, that business was becoming less and less acceptable to the general public and its leaders. The paradox of white patriots claiming liberty for themselves while enslaving Africans, in short, yields to a further paradox that the archive established by slavery would provide the ideological capital necessary to end that evil system. The literacy that the Redwood encouraged, accordingly, no doubt played a major role in the movement for emancipation that would overtake America in the nineteenth century.

As this book has been arguing, anti-slavery and the Revolution were therefore intimately connected facets of early American civic engagement. The beginning of Rhode Island anti-imperial agitation with protests against the Sugar Act of 1764 was built around commerce in a slave-cultivated product, leading to challenges to the existing transatlantic constitutional relationship between Britain and the colonies. As discussed in Chapter 1, the Declaratory Act of 1766 was Britain's major constitutional innovation bearing on Parliament's right to make laws and levy taxes on early Americans, meaning that in the adjudication of appealed Rhode Island legal cases, "crown and Parliament had become less willing to defer to colonial practice."[152] Incidents like protests against that and other acts, highlighted particularly by the patriot burning of the *Gaspee* in 1772, helped lead to "the collapse of the Transatlantic Constitution" and the arrangement by which colonial laws were legal as long as they were not "repugnant" to British law.[153] After Parliament passed the Coercive Acts in 1774 to protest the Boston Tea Party, "Rhode Island towns responded with resolves proclaiming that Parliament's ability to make laws for the colonies was 'inconsistent with the natural, constitutional and charter rights and privileges' of the colony."[154] By June 1774 the last Rhode Island legal appeal to the British Privy Council was decided in such language that it was clear that "the tension-laced respect for dual authority that had characterized the colonial period was no more."

---

[147] Van Cleve, 28.   [148] Van Cleve, 39–40.   [149] Van Cleve, 91.
[150] Van Cleve, 18, 52, 57.
[151] "Slavery in the Rhode Island." *Slavery in the North* Website. Accessed December 23, 2015. <http://slavenorth.com/rhodeisland.htm>.
[152] Bilder, 181.   [153] Bilder, 183–5.   [154] Bilder, 184–5.

In June 1775, there was one last case of Rhode Island having a colonial legal decision reversed in a lower British court.[155] In 1776, "the colony crossed the king's name out of the charter" in what might be regarded as the logical culmination of the reading of British law and political thought in places like the Redwood.[156] The cultural history of what was read and written in colonial America, accordingly, is also one encompassing this developing form and practice of civic engagement.

The painting of Redwood, the founder of the library, holding a copy of Pope's *Essay on Man*—a portrait hanging today in the boardroom of the very library that he helped to build—brings into focus a larger history of British literature in Rhode Island and the rest of the early American colonies. This archive, many of the books of which are still with us today, was obviously started with slavery capital, but has grown through the age of abolition and emancipation to include as proprietors men and women of all races, ethnicities, and walks of life. It is owing to the permanence of the book as a physical object, perhaps, that the library can, over time, graduate from slavery towards being an artifact that bears few traces of the pain of its origins. The Redwood's contribution to the cultural history of America, Britain, and the Atlantic is therefore substantial, rooted as it is in an equivocal attitude towards slavery that was nonetheless overcome.

As we turn our attention to the New York Society Library, however, we must be mindful of just how limited abolition and gradual emancipation were in the period after the Revolution. In many cases, slavery actually accelerated and got worse as the new nation sought to redevelop its economy after war. As Joanne Pope Melish has contended, "gradual emancipation statutes did not legislate slavery out of existence," the federal census of 1840 listed slaves in all of the New England states, and it was not until 1843 that Rhode Island passed a law specifically banning slavery.[157] The gradual emancipation statutes were racist in assuming that freed blacks would somehow disappear and not be integrated. Because there was a fear that former slaves would abuse their liberty, these laws were provisional on the "good behavior" of the freed persons, indicating that white paternalist attitudes were sustained.[158] As Melish has summarized:

> In all these ways, whites evaded the emerging necessity of creating a new set of relations with free people of color and, instead, transferred to them their old assumptions about slaves as publicly available commodities in permanent need of direction and control. The effect was to undermine any possibility of a shared entitlement between people of color and whites to real freedom and its fruits which might otherwise have taken root as slavery withered. Given whites' assumptions of entitlement to the labor of people of color and to blacks' acceptance of whites' authority, the material effects of these practices in turn confirmed the assumptions on which they rested.[159]

In short, abolition laws on the books actually gave way to racism; most abolitionists would maintain racial inequality despite wanting to end slavery, especially as they

---

[155] Bilder, 185.   [156] Bilder, 185.
[157] Joanne Pope Melish, *Disowning Slavery: Gradual Emancipation and "Race" in New England, 1780–1860* (Ithaca: Cornell UP, 1998), 76.
[158] Melish, 79, 63–4, 94.   [159] Melish, 107.

considered how to constitute who was entitled to citizenship during the Early Republic period.[160]

The Rhode Island example is therefore significant to my reading of how the New York Society Library was a home for both profiteers from slavery (the majority), and a minority of readers who were interested in anti-slavery. As I shall explain, this negotiation of pro- and anti-slavery sentiment may be taken as a central axis around which American cultural history turns, and the fact that many of the library's circulation records for the Early Republic period remain intact establishes that books on both sides were making it into the hands of elite readers. As New York became the financial and commercial center of the new nation, however, there is much evidence of its sustained involvement in the slave trade, even after it was banned by act of Congress in 1807. The wealth from commerce related to that trade, as in Salem and Newport, established the basis for cultural philanthropy towards colleges and libraries in the city, indicating that the cultural history of New York is as difficult to disentangle from slavery and the book trade as it is in the study of all the colonies that became states. One measure of this history is how the library's copy of Daniel Defoe's *Robinson Crusoe*, an adventure embracing slavery as a means to wealth, was interpreted and by whom, a task in which not only the library's new *City Readers* database, but also the evidence of the businesses of the library's readers, is instrumental.

[160] Melish, 3, 5–6.

3

They Were Prodigals and Enslavers
Patriarchy and the Reading of *Robinson Crusoe*
at the New York Society Library

The history of the New York Society Library makes plain not only that slavery persisted, and indeed accelerated, after the Revolution and into the Early Republic period, but also that this New York civic institution, as with the other libraries, continued to fund reading of both pro-slavery and early abolitionist books via the slavery enterprises of its proprietors. Founded in 1754, the library counted not only slave traders among its members, but also farmers, lawyers, printers, and men from other walks of life who were all, in one way or another, connected to the Atlantic slavery economy. Some of them were in correspondence with others like them in other port cities that had libraries, and many spent at least part of their lives in the Southern colonies and West Indies engaged in the business of the trade. People with anti-slavery opinions, such as Aaron Burr, Alexander Hamilton, and John Jay, became members of the library after the War of Independence, but they were still a small minority of the proprietors, and did not always push so much for general emancipation as manumission for individuals. Though anti-slavery legislation began to be passed in New York in the late 1790s, albeit later than all the other states in the North besides New Jersey, some laws, such as one permitting slaveholders to sell their slaves to the South if they were unruly, actually enhanced slaveholders' power. As New York's dominance as the center of American commerce grew into the nineteenth century, the city's merchants also came to own many ships trading from Africa to points south until at least 1860, despite having officially banned slave trading in 1788. If we accept even a qualified version of Virginia Harrington's conclusion that all merchants in New York were essentially West India merchants, it must be said that such men made up the vast majority of proprietors of the library.[1]

This chapter contends that the reading of Daniel Defoe's *Robinson Crusoe* at the library, evident in the impressive recent *City Readers* database of its circulation records, demonstrates that it was mostly appreciated as a pro-slavery work, though four of its forty-four readers from 1789 to 1805, according to borrowing records, clearly had anti-slavery opinions (see Figure 3.1). *Robinson Crusoe* is arguably the

---

[1] Virginia Harrington, *The New York Merchant on the Eve of the Revolution* (NY: Columbia UP, 1935), 63.

Figure 3.1 Michael Vandergucht.
Daniel Defoe (1660–1731), 1706.
© National Portrait Gallery, London.

novel in the English literary canon that most promotes the idea of economic man in the Atlantic marketplace—the "possessive individual" who was so much a part of the imaginations and consumer habits of the nation's founders.[2] Crusoe is a man who takes risks on the ocean, even to the extent of accumulating enough wealth from slave trading to own his own plantation in Brazil. Sometimes he is punished when losing in these risks, such as getting shipwrecked on a Caribbean island for many years. He views this shipwreck and isolation on the island as the result of his sin of disobeying his father—a sin of the prodigal son rebelling against the patriarch and his advice. As I shall explain, however, the critical reception of the novel explains this sin as very much bound up with slavery inasmuch as engaging in the trade was his motive for leaving home. This departure is actually in line with some Protestant theological views of Defoe's era, which aligned ethics with capitalism and which dictated that avoiding risk in business, as Crusoe's father recommended, was sinful. In this view, if taking the risks that Robinson did was actually virtuous in relying on God's providence, not the sin of the prodigal, then filial disobedience

---

[2] Ian Watt, *The Rise of the Novel: Studies in Defoe, Richardson and Fielding* (Berkeley: U California P, 1957), 170, 174; Ramesh Mallipeddi, *Spectacular Suffering: Witnessing Slavery in the Eighteenth-Century Atlantic* (Charlottesville: U Virginia P, 2016), 204–5.

was crucial to Crusoe's capitalism and its religious endorsement.[3] This move, accordingly, is explicitly anti-patriarchal, a fact that is compelling in light of recent postcolonial criticism that casts Robinson as the patriarch, not only presiding over slaves on his ships and Brazilian plantation, but also over his slave Friday and others on his island. Crusoe might be seen, then, as an anti-patriarchal son in the process of replacing the patriarch with himself, with his slave moving into the role of the son.

It is in Crusoe's process of making this maneuver, I contend, that we can see how the novel choreographs the similar move that, as Jay Fliegelman explains, American founders were making in their revolution. They were rebelling against a patriarchal Britain, embodied symbolically in the king, to preserve slavery (as Blackburn and Horne contend), replacing him with themselves as the patriarchal tyrants presiding over a slave nation-state. British literature, in this view, can be seen to be influencing the imaginations of early Americans, many of whom saw themselves as entrepreneurs in the Atlantic economy like Crusoe, who saw no problem with slavery as long as it was profitable. Crusoe's behavior, in short, was taken as a model for their own.[4] Indeed, the title of most American editions of the novel through 1789, *The Wonderful Life, and Surprizing Adventures of that Renowned Hero, Robinson Crusoe*, suggests that he, as a "hero" with a "wonderful life," was intended to be their role model.

The vast majority of the Society Library readers of the novel were merchants, some more directly tied to slavery than others. The *City Readers* database helps us cross-reference their reading tastes with their professions, and, perhaps, their views towards slavery and abolition. Though a handful of readers of *Robinson Crusoe* were also borrowing contemporary anti-slavery texts like James Lavallée and Phillis Wheatley's *The Negro Equalled by Few Europeans* and Olaudah Equiano's *Interesting Narrative*, most were not, indicating they were more interested in Crusoe's economic message than in abolition. In essence, these merchants were reading *Robinson Crusoe* as a pro-slavery narrative confirming their own pre-existing views of the virtues of, and opportunities within, the Atlantic slavery economy, seeing the novel's hero as a model for their own possessive individualist lives. Crusoe's filial disobedience, for these readers, might be seen to have launched and authorized slave capitalism, and his replacement of the patriarch, and of sons with slaves, could be received in the Early Republic context as the consolidation of control of that capitalism.

This chapter will make this argument by first examining the text of *Robinson Crusoe* and how scholars have explained its prodigal and slavery motifs. Here it will focus on the 1719 criticism of the novel by Charles Gildon, the first to consider the patriarchal and oedipal theme of the novel together with slavery, the latter of which he views as the sin at the root of Crusoe's exile. In doing so, it will connect these themes with the process of the early American appropriation of the place of the

---

[3] Dwight Codr, *Raving at Usurers: Anti-Finance and the Ethics of Uncertainty in England, 1690–1750* (Charlottesville: U Virginia P, 2016), 132, 134.

[4] J. Paul Hunter, *Before Novels: The Cultural Contexts of Eighteenth-Century Fiction* (NY: Norton, 1992), 327, 42; Deidre Lynch, *The Economy of Character: Novels, Market Culture, and the Business of Inner Meaning* (Chicago: U Chicago P, 1998), 126.

patriarch, focusing on George Washington's elevation as the "father" of the country and American editions of *Robinson Crusoe* that stressed filial obedience as an aspect of this appropriation. Next, it will discuss the founding and early years of the library, and, as I have done in other chapters, cross-reference library proprietors' names with those who we know were involved in the trade in slaves and slave-produced commodities. Here, I will read the republican orientation of many of these men as complicit with slavery inasmuch as the individual property that they saw at the root of the ideal civic republican was, in part, property in slaves. Third, I will explain the continuity and acceleration of slavery in New York in the Early Republic period and how the members of the re-founded post-war Society Library were involved in it. This slavery history will contextualize my cultural history of the library's circulation records pertaining not only to the readers of *Robinson Crusoe*, but also to the other books that were reading. It will also summarize the persistence of slavery despite historical evidence of anti-slavery activity. Finally, the chapter will conclude by showing that the Society Library, like so many others in this book, was an incubator of both pro-slavery and anti-slavery political thought, as manifest through mapping of proprietors' reading patterns.

The library was therefore a central civic institution for the mediation of reading in colonial and Early Republic New York, and the civic engagement of its mainly pro-slavery proprietors revolved not only around their patriot and loyalist activities, but also around the other civic institutions that they launched in this period. Organizations like King's College (Columbia University), the Manufacturer's Society, the Chamber of Commerce, the Society of the Hospital of New York, and the Marine Society were patronized by library members. Paradoxically, given New Yorkers' investments in slavery, so was the Manumission Society, the main anti-slavery organization in the city. That New York civic life sprung from the Atlantic slavery economy cannot be doubted, as many of the people involved in these organizations were also merchants and men of other, related professions. The mediation of reading that the library performed, accordingly, was providing an interpretive community and reading network suiting local needs, which meant that the political and civic action motivated by their members' reading of imported books was very different than what it would be in Britain itself. The cultural history of New York may be said to have evolved from such organizations as the library and the college as those were the main locations where imported cultural products were read, interpreted for New York purposes, and put to use in civic activity.

I

Crusoe's theory that his prodigal disobedience to his father was the cause of his woe is located about a third of the way into the narrative, in an island diary entry of June 27, 1660, after he awoke from a nightmare in which he is visited by an angel. He lives in terror after the angel says, "'Seeing all these things have not brought thee to repentance, now thou shalt die'; at which words, I thought he lifted up the spear that was in his hand, to kill me."[5] Crusoe's reflection on what sins these might be that made him a "Wretch" leads him to reconsider his father's advice:

> In this interval, the good advice of my father came to my mind, and presently his prediction which I mentioned at the beginning of this story, viz. that if I did take this foolish step, God would not bless me, and I would have leisure hereafter to reflect upon having neglected His counsel, when there might be none to assist in my recovery. "Now," said I aloud, "my dear father's words are come to pass: God's justice has overtaken me, and I have none to help or hear me: I rejected the voice of Providence, which had mercifully put me in a posture or station of life wherein I might have been happy and easy; but I would neither see it my self, or learn to know the blessing of it from my parents; I left them to mourn over my folly, and now I am left to mourn under the consequences of it; I refused their help and assistance who wou'd have lifted me into the world, and wou'd have made every thing easy to me, and now I have difficulties to struggle with, too great even for nature itself to support, and no assistance, no help, no comfort, no advice." Then I cried out, "Lord, be my help, for I am in great distress."[6]

Crusoe laments that he has rejected the "middle station" of life that his father had offered, which might have been available to him at home in England if he had heeded his parents' warnings and not gone to sea as a young man.[7] This religious causation, it appears, was what Defoe wanted to stress in moralizing Crusoe's situation. The elaborate paraphernalia of Puritan, individual salvation through independent Bible reading and other attitudes—borrowed from familiar stories like John Bunyan's *Pilgrim's Progress*—decorates the rest of the narrative.

Crusoe's providential interpretation of why he has fallen into his situation has animated Defoe criticism for decades, receiving its most thorough American contextualization in Jay Fliegelman's *Prodigals and Pilgrims: The American Revolution Against Patriarchal Authority*.[8] Contrary to Crusoe's own belief in his sinful prodigality, "Defoe's novel offered nothing less than a theologically and hence politically acceptable model for precisely such disobedience."[9] This aspect of the novel helps explain its appeal to American patriots contemplating their own filial disobedience to King George. In fact, the prodigal theme of the novel might be seen as a template for the American Revolution's sacrifice of the colonies' relationship with England, as Jay Fliegelman contends.[10] As much as Americans tried to replicate the English countryside life in their building, gardening, and book collecting—acts dependent upon imports—separation was more fortunate than sinful for them. Indeed, as Michael McKeon writes, Defoe's life might have been a model for them, since "Despite his trenchant attacks on the corruptions of lineage and aristocratic honor, Defoe was obsessed with the illusion of his own gentility,"

[5] Daniel Defoe, *The Life and Adventures of Robinson Crusoe*. Ed. Angus Ross (London: Penguin, 1965), 103.

[6] Defoe, 105–7.   [7] Defoe, 28.

[8] George A. Starr, *Defoe and Spiritual Autobiography* (Princeton: Princeton UP, 1965); J. Paul Hunter, *The Reluctant Pilgrim: Defoe's Emblematic Method and Quest for Form in Robinson Crusoe* (Baltimore: Johns Hopkins UP, 1966), 19, 48.

[9] Jay Fliegelman, *Prodigals and Pilgrims: The American Revolution Against Patriarchal Authority 1750–1800* (Cambridge: Cambridge UP, 1982), 67.

[10] Fliegelman, 77.

"inflated his ancestry," and used his pen to "aristocratize his name from Foe to De Foe."[11] "The American Revolution Against Patriarchal Authority," to use Fliegelman's title, therefore may have been about patriots putting themselves in the position of the patriarch. Further, as Roxann Wheeler has explained, slavery over Africans may have been how they achieved the "patriarchal model" seen in Crusoe's mastery over slaves and the island.[12]

Defoe might well have patterned this kind of oedipal complex for early Americans in that he speaks towards migrants from a home country who nonetheless ape its bourgeois pretensions and possessive individualism, behavior that "internalizes and reproduces the antinomies of bourgeois subjectivity, subordinating the political to the personal, the collective to the individual, the public to the private."[13] Nonetheless, we must regard the religious and psychological parable of the prodigal son in the novel as a product of Crusoe's narration and imperfect memory, and the sin of disobedience as not as egregious as the economic and humanitarian sins embodied in Crusoe's actions.[14] Crusoe's own explanation of the source of his troubles, accordingly, cannot be trusted. As Dwight Codr has contended, "there has been a tendency to take Crusoe at his word, to read the novel straight, to discount its ironies, and to mark his act of leaving as he himself marks it: as his 'Original Sin.'"[15] We should therefore treat Crusoe as an unreliable character speaking in a work of fiction who may not be aware of the true causes of his difficulties.

In short, we must regard Crusoe's prodigality also as economic, and therefore tied to the Atlantic slavery economy.[16] "Crusoe pursues his economic self-interest with steady, unwavering determination," writes Ramesh Mallipeddi, and he demonstrates a "privatized, hermetic possessive individualism."[17] In this more recent view, Fliegelman's prodigal son and fortunate fall thesis becomes problematic, as Crusoe's choice to leave his father's home is not necessarily "a fall or sin of some kind."[18] While there has been a critical tradition focused on slavery as the more significant sin than prodigality, "those who have read Crusoe as exposing the criminality at the heart of international trade and slavery have a great deal in common with those who brand his choice to leave England as his 'Original Sin.'"[19] Indeed, Crusoe's prodigality is bound up with slavery even if we regard him as not only enslaving others, but as having ended up in a form of enslavement himself on the island.[20]

[11] Michael McKeon, *The Origins of the English Novel 1600–1740* (Baltimore: Johns Hopkins UP, 1987), 326.

[12] Roxann Wheeler, "Powerful Affections: Slaves, Servants, and Labours of Love in Defoe's Writing." *Defoe's Footprints: Essays in Honour of Maximillian E. Novak*. Eds Robert M. Maniquis and Carl Fisher (Toronto: U Toronto P, 2009), 127–8.

[13] Mallipeddi, 201.   [14] McKeon, 332, 320.   [15] Codr, 143–4, 138.

[16] Watt, 65; Angus Ross, "Introduction." *The Life and Adventures of Robinson Crusoe*. Daniel Defoe (London: Penguin, 1965).

[17] Mallipeddi, 204–5.   [18] Codr, 131.

[19] Codr, 119. For previous works in this tradition of the slavery interpretation of the novel, see John Robert Moore, *Daniel Defoe: Citizen of the World* (Chicago: U Chicago P, 1958), 289, 290; Peter Earle, *The World of Daniel Defoe* (NY: Athenaeum, 1977), 69, 131, 134; Roxann Wheeler, "'My Savage, My Man': Racial Multiplicity in *Robinson Crusoe*." *ELH* 62.4 (Winter 1995): 821–61.

[20] Maximillian E. Novak, *Realism, Myth, and History in Defoe's Fiction* (Lincoln: U Nebraska P, 1983), 27; Gary Gautier, "Slavery and the Fashioning of Race in 'Oroonoko,' 'Robinson Crusoe,' and Equiano's

Most postcolonial critics, however, have focused their concerns about the slavery problem in the novel on Crusoe's enslaving of Friday—a focus in line with Fliegelman's theory of patriarchy in the novel.[21] On the one hand, "Crusoe's struggle, originating in the private sphere of the bourgeois family, is essentially oedipal," reflecting his desire not only to disobey the father, but to replace him.[22] On the other, this replacement requires his parental tyranny over another, in this case a slave. Wheeler claims that partly through Christianizing Friday, Crusoe's "patriarchal labour contract" creates what I have described in Chapter 2 as Alexander Pope's "chain of obligation from master to head slave."[23] Indeed, as Dan Carey has contended, a white enslaver like Crusoe living in America is engaged in "a patriarchal system of rule, with Crusoe substituting himself for Friday's actual father...no longer do they appear in the guise of master and slave but in a series of structurally related ways as father and son."[24] It is in this way that the novel choreographs the actions of slave-financed patriots, who were replacing the patriarchs with their own patriarchy over African "sons."

These critics who have linked prodigality, patriarchy, and slavery are not being anachronistic in doing so, as Charles Gildon, a friend of Aphra Behn's who witnessed her composing *Oroonoko* and who was the editor of her anthology *All the Histories and Novels Written By the Late Ingenious Mrs. Behn* (1698), anticipated these concerns.[25] He had an advanced understanding of the ethical problems presented by slavery, and he thought Defoe was backsliding into an attitude that books like Behn's had already sought to overcome by constructing the idea of a "royal slave" decades earlier. As George Boulokos observes, "Behn's hero lives in a lavish court, like any hero of a romance, although the trappings are distinctly oriental; Defoe's

---

'Life.'" *The Eighteenth-Century* 42.2 (Summer 2001): 166–7; Dennis Todd, *Defoe's America* (Cambridge: Cambridge UP, 2010), 83.

[21] Srinivas Aravamudan, *Tropicopolitans: Colonialism and Agency, 1688–1804* (Durham: Duke UP, 1999); Brett C. McInelly, "Expanding Empires, Expanding Selves: Colonialism, the Novel, and Robinson Crusoe." *Studies in the Novel* 35.1 (2003): 1–21; Peter Hulme, *Colonial Encounters: Europe and the Native Caribbean, 1492–1797* (London: Methuen, 1986); Aparna Dharwadker, "Nation, Race, and the Ideology of Commerce in Defoe," *The Eighteenth Century: Theory and Interpretation* 39.1 (1998): 63–84; Rajani Sudan, *Fair Exotics: Xenophobic Subjects in English Literature, 1720–1850* (Philadelphia: U Pennsylvania P, 2002), 1–7; Hans Turley, "Protestant Evangelicalism, British Imperialism, and Crusonian Identity." *A New Imperial History: Culture, Identity, and Modernity in Britain and the Empire, 1660–1840.* Ed. Kathleen Wilson (Cambridge: Cambridge UP, 2004): 176–93; Edward Said, *Culture and Imperialism* (NY: Knopf, 1993), 7; Syed Manzurul Islam, *The Ethics of Travel: From Marco Polo to Kafka* (Manchester: Manchester UP, 1996), 3; Bill Overton, "Countering Crusoe: Two Colonial Narratives." *Critical Survey* 4.3 (1992): 302–3; Hugh Ridley, *Images of Imperial Rule* (London: Croom Helm, 1983), 4; Patrick Brantlinger, *Crusoe's Footprints: Cultural Studies in Britain and America* (London: Routledge, 1990), 1–3; Helen Tiffin, "Postcolonial Literature and Counter-Discourse." *The Post-Colonial Studies Reader.* 2nd edition. Eds Bill Ashcroft, Gareth Griffith, and Helen Tiffin (NY: Routledge, 2006), 99-101; Andrew Fleck. "Crusoe's Shadow: Christianity, Colonization and the Other." *Historicizing Christian Encounters with the Other.* Ed. John C. Hawley (Basingstoke: Macmillan, 1998), 74.

[22] Mallipeddi, 205.   [23] Wheeler, "Powerful," 138.

[24] Dan Carey, "Reading Contrapuntally: Robinson Crusoe, Slavery, and Postcolonial Theory." *The Postcolonial Enlightenment.* Eds Dan Carey and Lynn Festa (Oxford: Oxford UP, 2009), 123, 128.

[25] Paul Dottin, "The Life of Charles Gildon." *Robinson Crusoe Examin'd and Criticis'd.* Ed. Paul Dottin (London: Dent, 1923), 7, 11.

Africans by contrast are nameless, naked savages in a bleak, empty landscape."[26] Gildon's critique of Defoe on those grounds came in *An Epistle to D......D' F..e, the Reputed Author of Robinson Crusoe* (1719), in which he connects prodigality, patriarchy, and slavery:

> I know you will reply, that it was his Disobedience to his Parents, for which he was punish'd in all the Misfortunes he met with, and that you frequently remind us of the Conviction of his Conscience in this Particular thro' the whole Course of his Life. I would by no Means be thought to encourage Disobedience to Parents; but the honouring our Father and Mother does not include a Duty of blindly submitting to all their Commands, whether good or bad, rational or irrational, to the entire excluding of all Manner of free Agency from the Children, which would in effect be to make the Children of Freemen absolute Slaves, and give the Parent a Power even beyond that of a Sovereign, to whom both Parents and Children are subject. Tho' the Authority therefore of Parents be great, it cannot extend to the Suppression of our Obedience to Reason, Law and Religion; and when a Child obeys these, tho' contrary to his Parents Command, he is not to be esteem'd disobedient or culpable.[27]

For Gildon, parental tyranny and sovereign tyranny are nearly equated. When applied to the American context in which Anglo-American patriots were claiming to be "slaves" of Britain, this equation amounts to a critique of patriarchy. *Robinson Crusoe*, as Fliegelman signaled, might have helped motivate "the revolution against patriarchal authority."

Yet Gildon goes on to discuss African slavery as something that the rebellious son who has gone to sea has engaged in, and as the providential cause of his shipwreck. He discusses Crusoe's first "prosperous" voyage to the Guinea coast, his second trip there in which he is captured and sold into slavery, and then his trip from Brazil to Africa:

> Well then, we are now to suppose *Robinson Crusoe* and *Xury* got as far almost as *Cape de Verd*, when a *Portuguese* Ship takes them up and carries them to *Brasil*; where, with the Money he had rais'd by the Sale of his *Boat*, his *Skins*, and his *Boy*, he settles himself as a Planter, and accordingly turns Papist in Thankfulness to Heaven for his great Deliverance; and, indeed, he always retains some Spice of the Superstition of that Religion, in that vain Faith, which he not only himself puts in *secret Hints*, as he calls them, but earnestly recommends to all others. Well, having fix'd his Plantation, he sets out upon new Adventures, as Supercargo to a *Portuguese* Ship, bound to the Coast of *Guinea* to buy Slaves; and tho' he afterwards proves so scrupulous about falling upon the Cannibals or Man-Eaters, yet he neither then nor afterwards found any check of Conscience in that infamous Trade of buying and selling of Men for Slaves; else one would have expected him to have attributed his *Shipwreck* to this very Cause.[28]

---

[26] George Boulokos, *The Grateful Slave: The Emergence of Race in Eighteenth-Century British and American Culture* (Cambridge: Cambridge UP, 2008), 39–40.

[27] Charles Gildon, *An Epistle to D......D'F..e, the Reputed Author of Robinson Crusoe. Robinson Crusoe Examin'd and Criticis'd*. Ed. Paul Dottin (London: Dent, 1923), 84–5.

[28] Gildon, 93–4.

Gildon, in short, provides a narrative arc actually performed and worked out by the American rebels against patriarchal authority, one in which the sons, in turn, enslave other people of a different race. What makes the New York reading of *Robinson Crusoe* so interesting is this play between the reader as a slaveholder and a rebel, once again underscoring Morgan's argument that the paradox of the Revolution was whites claiming to be slaves of Britain while enslaving others.

Gildon thus anticipates Fliegelman's reading of "the familial rhetoric" of the War of Independence that held that "For Britain to deny her child colonies 'that equal and independent station' was to confess itself, in the popular phrase of the period, 'an unnatural and tyrannical parent.'"[29] Yet that parent is replaced by the Early Republic's most prominent slaveholder: "Washington is the 'father figure' who serves to bring the new nation together. His is the 'sacred story of the divine man and his heroic friends who had in a mighty act of power effected the foundation of the republic' thus making him 'a *theios aner* in the pattern of a charismatic founder.'"[30] He and other founders are then mythologized as benevolent paternalists, not rebellious sons of Britain, in an effort to ensure "'the permanent loyalty of future generations,' and forestall subsequent generational revolutionary conflict."[31] Far from being a fiction that creates "a new understanding of parental responsibility and filial freedom," however, a novel like *Robinson Crusoe* actually anticipates the process of replacing the father with the son, and the son with the slave.[32]

Indeed, some American editions of the novel that altered the prodigal theme in favor of more filial obedience were actually being reprinted by British loyalists. Hugh Gaine, for example, published a New York abridgment of the novel in 1774. In this edition, Crusoe's prodigality is under-emphasized and the filial obedience of characters like Friday and Will Atkins from *The Farther Adventures of Robinson Crusoe* is instead brought forward. Though Crusoe, in the first pages, acknowledges the "rash and disobedient step" he had taken in first leaving his parents' house for the sea, Gaine omitted the angelic visitation and reflection on his prodigality in the 1660 diary entry.[33] Instead, he showed how Friday's joy at seeing his father when returning to the island reflects that the natives "had no need of the fifth commandment" to honor thy father, unlike Europeans like Crusoe, and how Atkins regrets his "bad behavior" that broke his father's heart.[34] Indeed, Atkins's prodigality is equated to oedipal murder: "but like a beast, I despised all instruction. I murdered my poor father; for my bad behavior broke his heart."[35] Gaine therefore chose a theme of reconciling with the father, one entirely appropriate for a loyalist trying to stress America's need to make peace with Britain before war breaks out.

Most American editions of the novel published after the war continued this theme of filial obedience and reconciliation, though by that time, probably for the purpose of constructing obedience to an American patriarchy. The 1784 Boston Coveely abridgment, for example, also omits the angelic visitation and prodigal

[29] Fliegelman, 4.   [30] Fliegelman, 199.
[31] Fliegelman, 199.   [32] Fliegelman, 4.
[33] Hugh Gaine, ed., *The Wonderful Life, and Surprizing Adventures of that Renowned Hero, Robinson Crusoe. By Daniel Defoe* (NY: Gaine, 1774), 6.
[34] Gaine, 116, 128–9.   [35] Gaine, 128–9.

reflection episode, though the novel, as if to emphasize the cost of filial freedom, does close with a short statement of Crusoe's repentance: "I really believe myself the most miserable object living, and heartily I repent giving way to the restless disposition which made me leave my parents, as from that hour I date all the subsequent misfortunes of my life."[36] Similarly, the 1786 and 1789 Worcester Thomas abridgments condemn Crusoe's oedipal disobedience; his father wants him to "obey the advice of a father," Friday's sight of his father is celebrated, and Crusoe considers himself "entirely the author of their [his parents] deaths" due to his disobedience.[37] In fact, appended to the back of the edition are stories of filial obedience and disobedience in which a boy is beaten by his father to remind him "that it was his duty and his interest to take his parents advice."[38] Two 1787 Philadelphia editions also omit the angelic visitation and prodigal reflection scene, though they do explain Crusoe's regrets about his disobedience.[39] The 1789 Wait edition, published in Portland, Maine, omits the angelic episode, but Crusoe reflects elsewhere in this edition that "the justice of God followed me, and that severe punishment was justly owing to my disobedience and wicked life."[40] Even a Newburyport, Massachusetts adaptation of 1790 that has a female Robinson Crusoe—*The Female American*—emphasizes her filial piety.[41] In short, filial freedom is shown to be treacherous in these American editions, further underscoring the process by which patriarchy is deconstructed by Crusoe and reconstructed for himself, casting the novel as a moral fable for the new slave nation-state.

Though we do not know which edition of *Crusoe* was stocked by the New York Society Library by the time the 1789 catalog in which it appeared was printed, the evidence from these American editions suggests that this filial obedience theme was valued by at least some readers in the Early Republic period. Regardless, it is clear that slavery is central to both the novel and the reading context of the founding of the Republic, and as I shall explain, the latter was particularly evident among the proprietors of this library. New York's involvement in the trade in slaves and slave-produced commodities, evident in the colonial period, did not end in the late eighteenth century, but continued until well into the nineteenth. The history of the founding—and re-founding—of the library bears out this fact, and the reading network surrounding the library's copy of *Robinson Crusoe* indicates that most of its readers were involved in the Atlantic slavery economy. The New York reception of the novel, accordingly, may be analyzed by reference to the library's circulation

---

[36] N. Coveely, ed., *The Wonderful Life, and Surprizing Adventures of that Renowned Hero, Robinson Crusoe. By Daniel Defoe* (Boston: Coveely, 1784), 32.

[37] Isaiah Thomas, ed., *Travels of Robinson Crusoe. By Daniel Defoe* (Worcester: Thomas, 1786 & 1799), 6, 21, 23.

[38] Thomas, 26, 27.

[39] Charles Cist, ed., *The Wonderful Life, and Surprizing Adventures of that Renowned Hero, Robinson Crusoe* (Philadelphia: Cist, 1787); Peter Stewart, ed., *The Most Surprising Adventures, and Wonderful Life of Robinson Crusoe, of York, Mariner* (Philadelphia: Stewart, 1789).

[40] Thomas Wait, ed., *The Most Surprising Adventures, and Wonderful Life of Robinson Crusoe, of York, Mariner* (Portland: Wait, 1789), 35.

[41] Tremaine McDowell, "An American Robinson Crusoe." *American Literature* 1.3 (Nov. 1929): 308.

records, which tell the tale of how the patriarchal theme of the prodigal and the enslaver may have appealed to early Americans.

II

The New York Society Library entered the city's book trade at a crucial stage in its development, and was undoubtedly founded and subscribed to by men profiting from the Atlantic slavery economy. As explained in the Introduction to this book, Thomas Bray, founder of England's Society for the Propagation of the Gospel in Foreign Parts (SPG), sought to bring libraries to each English colony in America for the moral development of ministers and laymen. It should be noted that Bray's books were already linked to slavery at the beginning of the eighteenth century because the SPG owned 300 slaves that helped pay for them.[42] Bray initiated New York's first library in 1698 with a shipment of 220 volumes that were stored in Trinity Church, and these were added to by donations from the bishop of London and other religious organizations.[43] Other people wanted a non-parochial library and made contributions to a "City Library" and a "Corporation Library," the books of which were eventually incorporated into the Society Library. There was also a "Union Library Society" founded in 1771 that kept its books in the same room in City Hall as the Society Library did.[44] The King's College Library had no housing of its own until 1760, so students used the Society Library.[45] There were also booksellers that had commercial circulating libraries, such as William Bradford, John Peter Zenger, James Parker, Hugh Gaine, James Rivington, Garret Noel, and Samuel Loudon. Printer-booksellers like Gaine and Parker would become subscribers to the library, with Gaine printing its catalogs for several decades.[46] To be sure, many individuals had their own private libraries, some of them funded by slavery. Revd John Miller, Governor Hunter, Governor Burnet, Governor Montgomery (who had 1,400 volumes), Col. Lewis Morris, Robert Elliston, James De Lancey, William Smith, James Alexander, Cadwallader Colden, Joseph Murray, David Clarkson, and others had substantial household collections.[47] Some of these individuals would become involved in the Society Library and make donations to it, and while many of the more prosperous donors derived their wealth from the Atlantic slavery economy, it is clear that men of all professions were socially networked with the library and that economy.

The New York Society Library, like the others mentioned in this book, sprang from a club for improvement. This club—the Society for the Promotion of Useful Knowledge—was founded in 1748 by three lawyers: William Livingston, John Morin

[42] Tom Glynn, *Reading Publics: New York City's Public Libraries, 1754–1911* (NY: Fordham UP, 2015), 19; Todd, 79.

[43] Glynn, 19; Austin Baxter Keep, *History of the New York Society Library. With an Introductory Chapter on Libraries in Colonial New York, 1698–1776* (NY: De Vinne P, 1908), 19–20, 33.

[44] Keep, 6–7, 64–79, 81.   [45] Keep, 93.

[46] Keep, 101–2, 104, 108–10.   [47] Keep, 122.

Scott, and William Smith Jr.[48] This "triumvirate" published a newspaper called the *Independent Reflector*, which promoted the dissenting, republican Whig ideals of the "popular party" of which they were a part (a landed interest) against the party of the De Lanceys, a mainly Anglican interest backed by merchants.[49] Their immediate political aim in founding the library was "to help counteract the Anglican influence" that was threatened by the establishment of King's College (Columbia University) in the same year, an institution that was perceived to be "an Anglican plot to subvert the city's intellectual as well as its religious liberty."[50] Accordingly, meetings to elect trustees of the library in the first few years after its founding were "rancorous" until the college formed its own library in 1758.[51] In reality, however, Livingston was one of three non-Anglicans on the college's ten-person board of trustees, and the board of the library would remain evenly split during the colonial period.[52]

Six individuals, including the triumvirate, met in March 1754 to establish the library: Philip Livingston, William Alexander, Robert R. Livingston, William Livingston, John Morin Scott, and William Smith Jr (see Figure 3.2).[53] Tom Glynn has most succinctly described the original formation of the society over the course of that spring, so I quote him at length here:

> Within a month they had collected nearly £600 and written a constitution, the "Articles of the Subscription Roll of the New York Library." Modeled after the Library Company of Philadelphia, which Benjamin Franklin in his autobiography called "the mother of all subscription libraries," the New York Society Library was set up as a private corporation in which members of the public could purchase shares or "rights." Shareholders paid 5 pounds initially for a share and an annual "subscription" of ten shillings to maintain their borrowing privileges. The subscribers or shareholders elected a twelve-member Board of Trustees annually that was empowered to hire a librarian, buy books, secure a room in which to house them, and draw up regulations for the use of the collection. Members could repeal decisions of the board by a majority vote at the annual meeting.[54]

Scott was appointed the first librarian of the society, but was soon replaced by Benjamin Hildreth, who served until 1765; Thomas Jackson, who served until 1773; James Wilmot, who served until 1774; and George Murray, the last librarian before the war.[55] The library received a royal charter in 1772, which after the Revolution was validated by the New York state legislature. This charter is significant beyond just documenting the library's foundation because it contains one woman's name, "'Anne Waddell, widow,' a lady of unusual ability and force of character who carried on the large shipping interest of her husband, one of the original supporters of the Library."[56] Initial regulations included that members would have the right to

---

[48] Glynn, 22–3.   [49] Glynn, 22–3.   [50] Glynn, 23.   [51] Glynn, 25.
[52] Glynn, 23, 25.   [53] Keep, 130–1.   [54] Glynn, 24.
[55] Keep, 164–5, 173, 187, 192.
[56] Glynn, 28–9; Keep, 181; Arnold Whitridge, "The New York Society Library: A Comparison." *Redwood Papers: A Bicentennial Collection*. Eds Lorraine Dexter and Alan Pryce-Jones (Newport: Redwood Library and Athenaeum, 1976), 114.

PHILIP LIVINGSTON.

Engraved by J.B.Longacre from an Original Painting
in the Possession of J.T.Jones Esq. of New York.

Figure 3.2 James Barton Longacre (1794–1869). *Philip Livingston* (1716–78), c. 1765. Stipple Engraving. Emmet Collection of Manuscripts, From The New York Public Library. http://digitalcollections.nypl.org/items/

take out one book at a time, leaving a deposit in cash that was at least one third more than the value of the book; that the length of the loan would be determined by the size of the volume; that there would be penalties for volumes that were returned late; that a majority of members may amend the regulations; that the trustees should be elected by ballot and could appoint a treasurer; that individual shares ("rights") could be bequeathed, inherited, or alienated; and that each shareholder could have only one vote.[57] Later regulations were established that provided for a one month borrowing period and a fine for overdue books of one shilling a day, and that shareholders should leave deposits for taking out a book consisting of four shillings for a folio, two shillings for a quarto, and one shilling for an octavo or smaller volume.[58] Non-shareholders had to deposit one-third more than the value of a book to take one out for a month period, with charges ranging from one shilling for folios to three pence for duodecimos. Books could be borrowed by members and non-members from the library's location in City Hall only on Tuesdays and Fridays from ten to twelve.[59]

Livingston was active in selecting the library's earliest books.[60] To that end, each subscriber prepared a catalog of books for the inaugural meeting of the board on May 7, 1754, and the trustees made selections from those lists.[61] These selections were forwarded, with £300, to the library's purchasing agent in London, Moses Franks.[62] The collection arrived in New York on October 14, 1754, and consisted of 250 titles in 650 volumes—a list of which was published a week later in the library's first catalog.[63] This shipment contained ancient classics, Elizabethan writers, essayists of Queen Anne's age, historical works, memoirs, diplomatic correspondence, party pamphlets, philosophical and scientific brochures, "State Tryals" and "Debates in Parliament," books of travel, devotional and theological works, and treatises in mathematics and natural sciences, music, oratory, and logic.[64] The second and earliest surviving catalog of 1758 lists 335 titles in 859 volumes, and has a list of the 118 original subscribers to the library in an appendix.[65] The 1773 catalog, the final one published before the outbreak of war, contained 1,291 volumes.[66]

There were few literary works stocked in the library's earliest years (*Don Quixote* was the only novel), though there was "an extensive selection of poetry and other literature, broadly speaking, of an improving nature. The library had a complete run of *The Spectator* as well as issues of its many successors and imitators, including the *Guardian* and the *Rambler*."[67] As we have seen with the other libraries, however, acquisitions of literary genres accelerated in the 1760s and 1770s. The minutes of the March 9, 1764 board of trustees meeting, for example, show that the trustees drew up a list of new books to order that contained many literary works:

Swift's Works latest & best Edition with Cutts; Lady Mary Worthly [*sic*] Montague's Letters or Travels; Elements of Criticism by Lord Keams [*sic*]; Broughton's History of All Religions; All the Volumes of Warburton's divine Legation of Moses, succeeding the fourth Volume if any; Commons Debates, 1667–1694; Montaign's [*sic*] Essays; St. Evremont [*sic*]; Dodly's [*sic*] Collection of Poems; Reflections on the Rise and fall of Ancient Republicks adapted to the present state of G Britain by E. Worthly [*sic*] Montague Esq.; The Present State of Europe by John Campbell Esq.; The Duke of Sully's Memoirs; Kempfer's History of Japan; Levy's Roman History in English, the best Edition; An Account of the European Settlements in America & c.; The Works of Daniel Defoe; Clarendon's History of His own Life; The Adventurer; The Connoiseur

---

[57] Keep, 136.   [58] Keep, 156; Whitridge, 115.   [59] Keep, 157; Whitridge, 115.
[60] Glynn, 25.   [61] Glynn, 25.   [62] Keep, 154–5.   [63] Glynn, 25.
[64] Keep, 153.   [65] Glynn, 25, 28.   [66] Keep, 187.   [67] Glynn, 27.

[*sic*]; Hume's Political Discoveries; The Voyages from Asia to America for Compleating the Discoveries of the North West Coast of America translated from the High Dutch of S. Muller by Thomas Jeffery's with the Maps; All Sheridan's Works; Fuller's Gymnastic Exercises; Montesqui's [*sic*] Persian Letters.—All Lettered on the Backs.[68]

A volume of Shakespeare's works and the *Adventurer* were reported missing in the *NY Gazette* of September 19, 1765, suggesting that they circulated well, and works on aesthetics and sensibility like Smith's *Theory of Moral Sentiments* and Gerard and Burke's treatises on taste were reported as received by the library in 1771.[69] Further, there is evidence that subscribers donated literary titles such as Addison's *Works*, a five-volume lives of the poets, a seven-volume edition of Richardson's *Sir Charles Grandison*, an eight-volume Shakespeare, Waller's poems, and Montague's letters.[70]

Works of political thought were as evident at the Society Library as they were in Salem and at the Redwood. Many of these would be identified today as classics or histories, though they contained ideas of government, and there were more modern works of political theory. As Glynn writes, "In 1758, Society subscribers could borrow a wide range of works that [Bernard] Bailyn identifies as part of the intellectual foundation of the American Revolution."[71] The Society Library might therefore be understood as an incubator of political ideas of liberty and virtuous, representative government for early Americans. As we have seen in Chapters 1 and 2, however, the dissemination of these ideas was limited by problems of access and the wealth creation that enabled their reading. As with the libraries of Salem and Newport, the costs associated with membership in the library made it inaccessible to many, though it was less expensive than the Charleston Library Society.[72] As with the other early American proprietary subscription libraries, the wealth that made one's library proprietorship profitable was likely derived from the trade in slaves and related enterprises.

Indeed, New York had been involved in slavery from the early seventeenth century, as the Dutch had imported slaves to New York beginning in 1626.[73] In 1648, the Dutch West India Company decided to allow the colony of New Netherland to trade agricultural products for slaves with Angola.[74] Though this endeavor was unsuccessful, slaves helped New Netherland become an agricultural colony (not just a fur trade one), building forts and feeding the troops as well.[75] With the 1664 English take-over of New York, the Duke of York, who with others held a controlling interest in the Royal African Company, ordered his "representatives in New York—governors, councilors, and customs officials ... to promote the importation of slaves by every possible means."[76] From 1701 to 1726, 1,570 slaves were imported from the West Indies and 802 from Africa, though at least forty more were brought in illegally by one smuggler, and another 150 were smuggled-in in 1726.[77] In 1698 there were 2,170 slaves in the colony, growing to over 9,000 adult slaves by 1746—"the largest slave force in any English colony north of Maryland,"

[68] Keep, 171–2.   [69] Keep, 173–5.   [70] Keep, 191–2.
[71] Glynn, 27–8.   [72] Glynn, 28.
[73] Edgar J. McManus, *A History of Negro Slavery in New York* (Syracuse: Syracuse UP, 1970), 4.
[74] McManus, 5.   [75] McManus, 7–8.   [76] McManus, 23.   [77] McManus, 24–5.

as Edgar McManus has calculated. Slaves accounted for more than thirty-five percent of immigrants coming to New York from 1732 to 1754.[78] "The slave trade fast became one of the cornerstones of New York's commercial prosperity in the eighteenth century," writes McManus, so it is not surprising that the city's leading citizens were involved:

> No social stigma attached to slave trading in the eighteenth century. Some of New York's leading importers, such as Gabriel Ludlow, Philip Livingston, and Nicholas De Ronde, were men of unimpeachable social standing. Likewise, many respectable commission merchants, factors, and general agents engaged in the trade on a part-time basis without damage to their reputations. Indeed, the entire business community was deeply involved, for the profits of the importers seeped down to the insurers, lawyers, clerks, and scriveners who handled the paperwork of the trade. New York City's vendue houses obtained a considerable share of their income from slave transactions. Slave auctions were held weekly, and sometimes daily, at the Merchant's Coffee House, the Fly Market, Proctor's Vendue House, and the Meal Market. All the commission houses profited from the trade to some extent, and some—like the Meal Market—were almost exclusively markets for the sale or hire of slaves.[79]

After 1750, when the Asiento was revoked, the New York slave trade accelerated, and due to the large numbers of slaves imported, prices for them dropped, leading to more direct importations from Africa rather than from the West Indies.[80] This was particularly the case for the following twenty years—the boom time in the slave trade in the North American colonies. "In all, a hundred New York merchants and captains shared in the ownership of vessels carrying more than seven slaves per entrance," James Lydon writes, "The mercantile community was thus quite broadly concerned in the traffic."[81] Though there was a lapse in the trade during the War of Independence, it returned and even accelerated in the post-war period.

The slave trade was connected to the New York book trade, of which the Society Library was a part, even if we go by newspaper printing alone, as newspapers depended on advertisements for slaves and rented their offices for slave transactions.[82] The frequency of these advertisements indicates that the New York market for slaves "was very broadly based."[83] Other businessmen besides printers profited from slavery, with one dry goods merchant having raised capital for his business by first working as a slave broker. Professionals like lawyers and scriveners also profited by arranging slave sale contracts and keeping lists of slaves for sale.[84] Imported slaves were also taxed, which led to much smuggling, including by library member John Watts.[85]

Indeed, in 1754 "the majority of the eighty-three subscribers to the New York Society Library . . . were traders" involved, to some extent, in slavery; Virginia Harrington places that number at fifty-seven.[86] The remaining library proprietors,

---

[78] McManus, 25.   [79] McManus, 26–7.   [80] McManus, 29.

[81] James G. Lydon, "New York and the Slave Trade, 1700–1774." *William and Mary Quarterly* 35.2 (Apr. 1978): 390.

[82] McManus, 31.   [83] McManus, 31.   [84] McManus, 31–2.

[85] McManus, 38–9.

[86] Craig Steven Wilder, *Ebony and Ivy: Race, Slavery, and the Troubled History of America's Universities* (NY: Bloomsbury P, 2013), 48; Virginia D. Harrington, "The Place of the Merchant in New York Life." *New York History* 13.4 (Oct. 1932): 376.

however, also benefited from the slavery economy; whether their wealth derived from land or shipping, no distinction should be made between landholding elites like those represented by the "triumvirate" and merchants. As Harrington wrote, "for the most part, socially, economically and politically the landholders, lawyers and merchants formed a single, privileged, important ruling class...Indeed, generations of intermarriage had welded these first groups into a large, inter-related clan whose interests could not be far separated."[87] By the middle of the eighteenth century, "The great landlords of colonial New York had transitioned into a more diverse range of investments, including shipping and insurance."[88] The Livingston family had been trading in slaves since at least 1690, and library founders William and Philip had been sent to Yale "to prepare them to manage the web of commercial sites and relationships in the Mid-Atlantic, New England, the West Indies, Europe, and Africa that formed Livingston Manor."[89] Philip, like many of his class, was a "comprehensive genius" who united in himself "the landlord, the merchant and the lawyer"; he shared in "four vessels, 219 slaves" in this period.[90] Some members of this family were sent to Antigua and Jamaica to further the family trade and to network. The Cruger clan, with members like John (mayor of New York, 1739–44), John Jr (mayor of New York, 1757–66), Henry, Tileman, and Nicholas did the same.[91] Many families were involved; "Gedney Clarke Jr. was in Barbados, William Lloyd operated in Jamaica, DePeyster and Duyckinck houses opened in Curacao, and David Beekman kept and plantation and merchant house in St. Croix."[92] John Walter partnered with Arnot Schuyler in hiring Captain Jasper Farmar for a slaving mission to Angola in 1730, and hired him again in partnership with John, Peter, and Adoniah Schuyler in 1732.[93] In the summer of 1741, the year of the great slave revolt in New York, "at least twenty slaving vessels docked in New York" including ones owned by Philip Livingston, Philip Van Cortlandt, Stephen Bayard, David Gomez, Peter Van Brugh Livingston, and Mordecai Nunez."[94] In 1742, ships from the West Indies owned by Robert Livingston Jr, Philip Livingston, the Cuylers, and the Crugers led New York trade, reflecting "the activity of the family networks that undergirded the Atlantic system and the city's integration into and dependence upon a dangerous and brutal trade."[95] In 1754, the year of the library's founding, and in succeeding years, the major New York slave traders, some of whom were trustees of King's College, were Nathaniel Marston, Philip Livingston, John Livingston, David Clarkson, and Matthew Clarkson.[96]

The other three of the six founders of the library—William Alexander, John Morin Scott, and William Smith Jr—were also connected to slavery. Alexander was Philip Livingston's son-in-law and a merchant, military supply contractor, and later a member of the governor's councils of New Jersey and New York and a major general in the patriots' continental army.[97] Because the legal processing of slave transactions was part of the trade, the attorneys Scott and Smith were of course complicit.

[87] Harrington, "The Place," 366.   [88] Wilder, 48.   [89] Wilder, 52.
[90] Harrington, "The Place," 368; Lydon, 390.   [91] Wilder, 52–3.   [92] Wilder, 53.
[93] Wilder, 53–4.   [94] Wilder, 58.   [95] Wilder, 60.
[96] Wilder, 68.   [97] Wilder, 69; Keep, 135.

The same can be said of the library's first trustees, Robert Livingston, William Livingston, William Alexander, Smith, James De Lancey, Joseph Murray, John Chambers, Henry Barclay, James Alexander, John Watts, William Walton, and Benjamin Nicoll.[98] De Lancey was a slaveholding lawyer who benefited from the trade, partly through his brother Oliver's relationship to the prominent slave trader John Watts. He helped further the cause of New York's commerce in his roles as chief justice of the colony's supreme court and lieutenant governor. Murray, Chambers, and Nicoll, also lawyers, joined with other non-merchants like De Lancey to form "powerful relationships to increase and maintain their own political and economic status in New York. And this elite group's very existence was connected to the institution of slavery."[99] Barclay was a crucial member of the board because he was the rector of Trinity Church, which donated the land that formed King's College. He was also the most educated member, having been awarded an honorary doctorate from Oxford, and he was well networked to the extent that his son married into the De Lancey family.[100] James Alexander was William's father and also a lawyer allied to New York merchants through his marriage to Mary Sprat DePeyster.[101] Watts was a major slave trader in business with people like Farmar.[102] Walton "Inherited and acquired great wealth" and was active in the West Indies trade; he "shared in six vessels that imported 240 blacks."[103]

There were only ten new trustees elected 1758–76, Walter Rutherford, Samuel Verplanck, John Bard, Samuel Bard, John Jones, Whitehead Hicks, John Tabor Kempe, Samuel Jones, Peter Van Schaak, and Robert R. Livingston Jr (Chancellor Livingston). Rutherford and Verplanck were "merchants of high repute," the former a dry goods trader notable for supporting the non-importation movement and the latter the scion of an old Dutch landowning family that had diversified into trade—he was a "Wall Street importer."[104] Bard, a New York surgeon, "secured his family's economic position by investing in land and slaves," with which he paid for his son Samuel's education as a doctor of medicine in Europe.[105] Jones was also a physician, and, as a professor at the slavery-financed King's College, was complicit in slavery.[106] Hicks was one of the many lawyers benefiting from the slave trade and he served as mayor from 1766 to 1776, as was Kempe, who became Attorney General and one of the wealthiest men in the colony, and Jones, who became comptroller.[107] Van Schaak, also a lawyer, was descended from an old Albany landed family, and Livingston, a lawyer who, though descended from major slaveholders, was a founding member of the New York Manumission Society.[108]

In short, New York Society Library subscribers were as active in the slave trade as the members of the Salem Social Library and Redwood Library, which was as ironic

---

[98] Keep, 140–5.

[99] Tyler Zimmet, "Joseph Murray, Edward Antill, and New York City's Interlocking Elite." Columbia University and Slavery Website. Accessed July 10, 2017. <https://columbiaandslavery.columbia.edu/content/joseph-murray-edward-antill-and-new-york-citys-interlocking-elite>.

[100] Wilder, 68.   [101] Wilder, 69.   [102] Wilder, 67, 74, 132, 158; Lydon, 389.

[103] Keep, 143, 144; Cathy Matson, *Merchants and Empire: Trading in Colonial New York* (Baltimore: Johns Hopkins UP, 1998); Lydon, 390.

[104] Keep, 195; Matson 431 n. 105; Wilder, 48.   [105] Wilder, 228–9.   [106] Keep, 196.

[107] Keep, 196.   [108] Wilder, 53, 75; McManus, 168.

for them as it was for their peers in Massachusetts and Rhode Island considering that they were contemplating the liberties associated with the republican tradition in British political thought. As Glynn has written,

> The republican founders of the Library believed in the division of civil and religious authority, in the separation of church and state, and in the power of rationalism to dispel myth and dogma. They sought, to varying degrees, to break the bonds of hierarchy that tied individuals in a monarchical society so that they were judged on personal merit rather than the accident of birth. Above all, the founders sought to promote and safeguard the commonweal. They valued a public good that transcended selfish, private interests and believed that the Society Library served the public good by educating and refining a republican citizenry.[109]

Yet, from the enslaved African's perspective, what could be more of a "selfish, private interest" than accumulating wealth through the ownership and trade of other human beings? Further, what could be more hierarchical? As Leslie Harris has written,

> The ideology of republicanism that emerged from the Revolutionary War depicted a society whose success depended on a virtuous, self-sufficient, independent citizenry that was not beholden to any social group or individual. Slaves, as the property of masters, were symbolically and literally the inverse of the ideal republican citizen. Although the new nation celebrated colonists who resisted "enslavement" to England as revolutionary patriots, African Americans who sought their freedom by siding with the occupying British during the war were considered traitors. Whites viewed even those slaves and free blacks who assisted the colonists during the Revolutionary War as unable to throw off the degradation of their enslavement.[110]

As in the case of the Salem Social Library and the Redwood, this paradoxical articulation of republican virtue and liberty by those who tyrannized over other people was, in part, a product of the books they were reading. Yet these books could also support the growing enthusiasm for liberation; "The political ideology of the Revolution, with its emphasis on the American colonies' enslavement to Britain, provided a secular language with which to critique the holding of blacks as slaves."[111] Accordingly, this particular idea of citizenship changed as liberal democratic ideas of equality and individualism emerged, and republicanism became more exclusive and disconnected from the reality that most people were living.[112]

The occupation of New York and the Society Library by the British in 1776—an event that meant much looting of the books by troops—not only ended library operations until after the war; it also led to increased freedoms for blacks living under British occupation, and "the city became a center for blacks from all colonies seeking freedom."[113] After the war, many black loyalists travelled to places like Nova Scotia, England, or through those two places to Sierra Leone.[114] For those blacks who remained in New York, however, life would be more difficult. Though

---

[109] Glynn, 17.
[110] Leslie M. Harris, *In the Shadow of Slavery: African-Americans in New York City, 1626–1863* (Chicago: U Chicago P, 2003), 49.
[111] Harris, 48.   [112] Glynn, 18.
[113] Whitridge, 116, Harris, 55.   [114] Harris, 55.

an anti-slavery organization like the Manumission Society was founded in 1785, New York was an outlier among the Northern colonies in this period in not legislating for abolition: "the continued need for slave labor in the city and in the rural Hudson Valley through the 1780s led whites to resist including general abolition in their state constitution or in legislative action," and they even strengthened their slave codes in 1784 and 1788.[115] Indeed, even by the time the library's directors held their first post-war meeting on December 20, 1788, their first since 1774, the "Manumission Society members' hesitancy to free their own slaves" and "the reluctance of New Yorkers to legislate emancipation in the 1780s and 1790s" indicate that little had changed since pre-revolutionary times.[116] That the surviving circulation records of the library stem from this moment is significant to our understanding of how the reading of a text like *Robinson Crusoe* could serve as a blueprint for how the patriots replaced one imperialist patriarchal tyranny with their own republican one in the Early Republic period.

III

As the Society Library began afresh in 1788, a number of initiatives were launched to rebuild its membership and collection of books, as well as to find a building other than the city hall office that had been used up until that point. By the time Gaine published the new catalog in 1789, there were more than 3,100 volumes in the library's possession, almost all of which were new acquisitions, though they had advertised for the return of the library's lost books in 1784; one member much later wrote that "the present library has been purchased since 1784."[117] A list of the 239 shareholders was published in 1789, containing many predictable names of long-standing pre-Revolution members and some new ones; ten members of the Livingston family held shares, as did newcomers like Aaron Burr, Alexander Hamilton, George Clinton (governor), John Jay, General Steuben, and Rufus King (see Figure 3.3).[118] Others included Theophylact Bache, a merchant, Mayor Duane, John Sloss Hobart (the jurist), Nicholas Fish, Carey Ludlow, Samuel Louden (a printer and editor), James McEvers (the stamp collector of pre-revolutionary days), James Roosevelt (representative of the Rhinelander family), William Seton (long identified with the Bank of New York), Isaac Stoutenburgh (a name found throughout the colonial period from the earliest Dutch days), the Van Cortlandts and Van Hornes, Col. Marinus Willett, and Recorder John Watts.[119]

Without going into great detail about these men's professions, it is clear that New York's economy had changed little; indeed the "sharp rise in the volume of trade" led to a "business revolution" in the city, and "The dominant feature of the economically buoyant 1790s was, rather, a renewed interest in the institution of slavery."[120]

---

[115] Harris, 56, 62.   [116] Keep, 190, 192; Harris, 62.   [117] Keep, 212–13, 201–3.
[118] Keep, 213; Whitridge, 116–17.   [119] Keep, 212–13.
[120] Shane White, *Somewhat More Independent: The End of Slavery in New York City, 1770–1810* (Athens: U Georgia P, 1991), 24, 30.

Figure 3.3 *Alexander Hamilton* (1757–1804). By James Sharples, c. 1796. Pastel on Paper. National Portrait Gallery, Smithsonian Institution.

So, as with the subscribers before the war, even the non-merchants in the Society Library were complicit with the continuing trade in slaves and their products. Even after the African slave trade was banned by Congress in 1807, there is evidence that New York-based and owned vessels continued to trade, albeit illicitly, from the African coast to Brazil and other Atlantic destinations through the 1860s.[121] Nonetheless, abolitionist sentiment was gaining ground even among slaveholders. Indeed, Burr, Jay, and Hamilton were members of both the library and the Manumission Society, as were James Duane, Chancellor Livingston, and John Murray Jr.[122] Clearly, as we have seen with some of the other libraries in this book, there were both slavery profiteers and anti-slavery advocates among the elite members of the Society Library as it resumed business in the late 1780s. Together, they were able to raise 883 pounds, 3 shillings, seven pence, and a halfpenny to put a

---

[121] Anne Farrow, Joel Lang, and Jennifer Frank, *Complicity: How the North Promoted, Prolonged, and Profited from Slavery* (Hartford: Hartford Courant Co., 2005), 121–33.
[122] New York Society Library, *The Charter, Bye-laws, and Names of the Members of the New-York Society Library. With a Catalogue of the Books Belonging to Said Library* (NY: Gaine, 1789), 77–80; Harris, 56; McManus, 168.

new library building on Nassau Street, which opened for business June 2, 1795.[123] Examining how *Robinson Crusoe* was read after this re-founding of the Society Library helps us understand the impact of the novel on a particular elite interpretive community. It also, however, informs us of how the other tastes of its readers indicate that it was taken as a pro-slavery novel even as some were actively reading anti-slavery works in a context of both increased abolitionist legal activity and expanded slave trading and ownership.

Establishing the reading network around *Robinson Crusoe* from 1789 to 1805 using the *City Readers* database reveals that forty-four people read at least one volume of the novel for a total of fifty-four borrowings.[124] The database has determined that seven (the majority) of these readers were merchants, one was in manufacturing, one was in education and scholarship, one was in arts and letters, one was in the military, two were in religion, one was in medicine, one was in law, two were in politics, government, and public service, and the occupations of two are unknown. This database cannot be entirely accurate, however, as it has only identified nineteen names. A short biographical sketch of at least some these borrowers and of the missing twenty-five may help us to understand at least the distribution of taste for *Robinson Crusoe*, if not how the book was being received. Evidence about these twenty-five unknowns that I have found from newspapers overturns the database's explanation of the distribution of the novel's readership. It establishes that the distribution of professions is more likely twenty-six merchants, one abolitionist, one professor, one apothecary, two or three politicians, and more than ten unknowns, suggesting the very tight connection between New York West India trade merchant wealth and library proprietorship.

Secondary sources and early American newspapers tell us that there were some members of the library that were not involved in Atlantic commerce. For example, John Keese, the first recorded reader of *Crusoe* in the reconstituted Society Library on November 30, 1789, is listed as Secretary of the Society Promoting the Manumission of Slaves in the *New York Daily Gazette* of February 19, 1789. A few months later, he is described as the Secretary of the Governors of the Society of the Hospital in the City of New York. However, he may have been like many hypocritical members of the Manumission Society, as in the *New York Packet* of November 12, 1789, and continuing for several weeks, he took out an advertisement for an escaped slave of his, "a MULATTO MAN, named Sam, aged about 20 years."[125] John Christopher Kunze, "Professor of the Orient. Languages of Columbia College," did not seem to have been directly involved in slavery.[126] Similarly, Henry Van Solingen, who may have been related to Bogardus van Solingen, who routinely

---

[123] Whitridge, 116.

[124] *City Readers*, New York Society Library. <http://cityreaders.nysoclib.org/Detail/objects/2618>. Accessed September 20, 2017.

[125] *America's Historical Newspapers*. Accessed July 1, 2015. <http://infoweb.newsbank.com.libproxy. unh.edu/>. All newspaper articles in this database will be documented in the following footnotes by newspaper name and date of publication. *New York Daily Gazette* 2/19/1789, 5/16/1789; *New York Packet* 11/12/1789, 11/19/1789, 12/1/1789, 12/5/1789.

[126] *New York Daily Gazette* 2/22/1799.

traded to the Spanish and French islands in the 1760s, was a surgeon and apothecary with very little connection to Atlantic trade.[127] Cornelius Van Allen seems to have been a career politician and civil servant; an editorial complained that he had bought property in the fourth ward "for the sole and avowed purpose of procuring qualifications to vote." He was later appointed auctioneer for the city and county of New York.[128] Little is known about John Sullivan, though he is mentioned in an article as one of many freeholders endorsing Robert Yates for governor, as was James Robinson.[129] Peter Ogilvie was a probate court judge who had retired by the time he borrowed Defoe's novel.[130] Many names of borrowers—Francis Harison, Catherine Hill, Gillian Cornell, Augustus Bailey, Robert McMennony, Philip Fisher, Christian Nestel, David Wolfe, Joshua Whitcomb, and Israel Haveland—leave no record in the New York newspapers of 1789–1805.[131] This absence from the record, however, indicates that they were probably not merchants, as if they were, they would have been mentioned in advertisements, shipping news, reports on associations they belonged to, and so forth.

For those who were merchants, however, there is much information, and given the interconnected commerce at the time, the term "West India men"—those profiting from the trade to the islands—"included practically all the merchants of New York."[132] John Blagge is mentioned as a member of the Chamber of Commerce, listed as "John Blagge, merchant" in an article. He was also the owner of the sloop *Merry Andrew* and a packet boat to Boston, and can be seen advertising Madeira wine, "Havannah, white sugar in boxes," and other goods.[133] Robert Hunter was an "East India and European Dry Goods" merchant. Peter Schermerhorn was heir to a family business in trade with South Carolina, owning a wharf in New York City. His family had established a packet service to Charleston in 1728, and, like the Lyons family of Newport, usually had a member of the family established there to help enable exchange.[134] Samuel Ward and his brothers sold "Jamaica Pimento," ten hogsheads of New England rum, rice, coffee, and other West India goods; they even, at one point, advertised the sale of one of their ships.[135] Dominick Lynch was an Irish Catholic merchant who had immigrated to New York in 1785 after going into partnership with Thomas Stoughton, whom he had met when both were on trading missions from their countries of origin to Bruges. Though his firm went under, he lived as a retired merchant, investing in land and manufacturing, and he was a member of the New York Manufacturing Society.[136]

[127] Matson, 280; *New York Packet* 5/25/1790.

[128] *New York Herald* 1/16/1802, 3/16/1803.

[129] *Greenleaf's New York Journal* 4/15/1795; *New York Daily Gazette* 2/12/1789.

[130] *New York Packet* 1/2/1789.   [131] *Greenleaf's New York Journal* 9/8/1798.

[132] Harrington, *New York*, 63.

[133] *New York Daily Gazette* 11/7/1789, *New York Journal and Patriotic Register* 2/4/1790, *New York Daily Gazette* 4/1/1790, *New York Daily Gazette* 4/14/1790, *New York Daily Gazette* 4/14/1790, *New York Daily Advertiser* 6/4/1790, *New York Daily Advertiser* 11/5/1790.

[134] Harrington, *New York*, 210, Philip L. White, *The Beekmans of New York in Politics and Commerce, 1647–1877* (NY: New York Historical Society, 1956), 301.

[135] *Daily Advertiser* 10/29/1789, 11/3/1789, 8/24/1790, *New York Journal* 12/28/1791.

[136] Thomas Meehan, "Some Pioneer Catholic Laymen in New York." *United States Catholic Historical Society Records and Studies* 4.1–2 (Oct. 1906): 285–90; *New York Daily Advertiser* 3/17/1789.

There were many other merchants, particularly identifying themselves as part of the dry goods trade. Abraham Bussing "was a dry goods merchant, who, with thirty-six other citizens, assisted in raising funds with which to erect one of the earliest public school houses in New York City."[137] Other dry goods merchants included John Hone, James Boyd, William Wilson, and Thomas Cadle.[138] Manuel Myers was a merchant who had arrived in New York in the early 1750s and was prominent enough to become President of the city's synagogue.[139] Andrew Mitchell sold imported Madeira wine, Samuel Doughty imported staves and shingles from North Carolina, and "William Bowne, merchant" received twenty hogsheads of rum from Jamaica; the latter was also part owner of the ship *Fanny*.[140] George Barnewall was more clearly than most a West India merchant, as in some correspondence with James Madison he complains of one of his ships' crews being captured on a trading mission to Hispaniola.[141] Henry Ten Brook (Broeck) is listed as a merchant who punished illegal peddlers, and he helped take in subscriptions at the founding of the Manufacturing Society and was elected an alderman.[142] Catering to those with tastes for the exotic, Joseph Williams imported a cargo of tallow, tiger skins, otter skins, elephants' teeth and horns, sheep skins, and ostrich feathers from Montevideo.[143] Philip Rhinelander Jr, scion of the great sugar merchant family, advertised a ship for sale named the *Manhattan* in 1805.[144] Thomas Storm seems to have been a grocer of some type, as he advertised "White Mulberry Trees" and 200 barrels of beef "in good shipping order" for whomever would like to export them.[145] Charles Camman, "an eminent merchant of this city," imported gin, steel, dry goods, glassware, and iron ware from Amsterdam.[146]

No enumeration of New York commercial men would be complete without members in finance and insurance. Hamilton Stewart advertises himself as a "Money Broker" or currency exchange banker in the late 1780s and early 1790s, later becoming mainly a landlord.[147] James Saidler had his own firm specializing in marine insurance, and also advertised himself as having a "VENDUE, COMMISSION, and INSURANCE" business.[148] Sidney Phoenix, a graduate of Columbia whose

---

[137] "John Stuyvesant Bussing." *The National Cyclopedia of American Biography*, Vol. 17 (NY: White, 1920), 170.

[138] *New York Daily Gazette* 12/27/1999; *American Citizen* 9/28/1802; *New York Daily Advertiser* 3/18/1789, *New York Daily Gazette* 5/9/1789, *New York Gazette* 4/21/1801; *New York Gazette* 9/22/1801, 3/29/1802.

[139] Jacob Rader Marcus, "Light on Early Connecticut Jewry." *American Jewish History: The Colonial and Early National Periods, 1654–1840*. Ed. Jeffrey S. Gurock (NY: Routledge, 1998), 169–18, 198–9.

[140] *New York Daily Gazette* 3/13/1801; *New York Daily Gazette* 3/19/1802, 8/2/1802; *New York Price-Current* 10/4/1800, *New York Gazette* 5/8/1802.

[141] Madison, Accessed June 16, 2018. <https://founders.archives.gov/documents/Madison/02-08-02-0021>.

[142] *New York Daily Gazette* 12/27/1791, 2/20/1789, *Greenleaf's New York Journal* 12/4/1794.

[143] *New-York Price-Current* 6/13/2001.   [144] *New York Gazette* 8/24/1805.

[145] *New York Packet* 11/10/1791, *New York Daily Gazette* 3/1/1798.

[146] *New York Herald* 12/7/1805, *New-York Price-Current* 11/1/1800, 4/4/1801, 4/18/1802.

[147] *New York Daily Gazette* 8/4/1789, 3/23/1798.

[148] Jules Goebel, Jr, ed., *The Law Practice of Alexander Hamilton: Documents and Commentary*. Vol. 2 (NY: Columbia UP, 1969). 403, *New York Daily Advertiser* 9/21/1801.

commencement oration was entitled "On Poetry," was secretary of the New York Insurance office.[149]

Even smaller shopkeepers and tradesmen in New York were not exempt from complicity in the Atlantic slavery economy. Indeed, these two professions were gateways into the larger merchant world of slavery. "Many ambitious retailers, attracted by potential profits far exceeding those to be made running a shop, gambled and set up as merchants," writes Shane White, and "Four out of every ten of the merchant slaveowners in 1800... had started out as retailers."[150] David Wolfe had been in the New York City militia during the revolutionary war as a quartermaster, later going into business in hardware.[151] Bernard Judah, likely the scion of a bibliophile merchant family that included Samuel and Hillel Judah, sold "Glauber salts," "DRUGS and MEDICINES," and even a set of imported printers' type on Broadway.[152] Edward Watkeys was a tallow chandler on Nassau Street, and John Stoutenburgh, scion of a candlemaker who had helped found the United Company of Spermaceti Candlers in 1773, was a starch and hair powder manufacturer and part owner of the ships *Experiment* and *Melpomene*, which brought in cargoes from Philadelphia and Amsterdam.[153]

Most of these men were affiliated with the New York Chamber of Commerce, which had been founded with specifically patriotic aims in the 1760s when merchants banded together to boycott British imports in the hope that Parliament's tax measures would be reversed.[154] Though loyalists dominated the Chamber during the British occupation in the late 1770s, in 1784 the Chamber was re-chartered in a manner that linked merchants to patriotism. Minutes of the Chamber from 1784 complained of "the Arbitrary and Tyrannical conduct of Great Britain towards the late Colonies" that compelled colonists "to have recourse to Arms for the Defence of their Liberty and Property."[155] They sought to reverse the fact that the "Chamber" had "been Manifestly directed to Aid the British" during the war.[156] In short, New York's commercial men, largely bound up with the West Indies trade, were, like Rhode Islanders, articulating their liberty even as they profited from the enslavement of others.

---

[149] *New York Daily Advertiser* 5/8/1795, *The American Minerva* 5/6/1795, *New York Daily Advertiser* 7/9/1800, 7/25/1800.

[150] White, *Somewhat*, 35.

[151] Evert A. Ducykinck, *A Memorial of John David Wolfe* (NY: New York Historical Society, 1872), 4–5.

[152] Matson, 181; White, *Beekmans*, 471; *Finlay's American Naval and Commercial Register* 4/29/1996; *New York Daily Advertiser* 7/5/1796, 10/6/1795.

[153] Matson, 262, *New York Daily Gazette* 4/13/1805; *New York Journal* 1/22/1789, *New York Daily Gazette* 12/6/1802, *New York Daily Gazette* 1/15/1805.

[154] Sean Moore, "The Irish Contribution to the Ideological Origins of the American Revolution: Non-importation and the Reception of Jonathan Swift's Irish Satires in Early America." *Early American Literature* 52.2 (Spring 2017): 335–6.

[155] Joseph Bucklin Bishop, *The Chamber of Commerce of the State of New York, 1768–1918* (NY: Scribner's, 1918), 39.

[156] Bishop, 40.

For them, then, *Robinson Crusoe* was reflective of the action of overcoming one patriarchy only to assume the role of patriarch over African slaves that they, like Crusoe, were infantilizing. Though the novel must have been read and interpreted in various ways by the members of the library, its general theme of rebellion against the father and domination over the "primitive" or "savage" mirrors what readers in the Early Republic had done and were in the process of consolidating. Particularly for New York merchant patriots, the securing of the continuity of slavery had required such a rebellion and consolidation of power.

The other books that *Robinson Crusoe's* Society Library consumers checked out—or did not check out—bear out this development, though the abolitionists among them had diverging tastes. John Keese, the Manumission Society secretary and clearly a more cosmopolitan person than most, was reading travel narratives, such as Cook's voyages to the South Pole and around the world and Aubry de la Mottraye's *Travels Through Europe, Asia, and into Part of Africa*. Though he also was reading much literature of the kind that we have seen in Chapters 1 and 2, his record is evidence of something further—an interest in orientalist tales like Lady Mary Montagu's *Turkish Letters,* Edward Button's *Persian Letters*, Robert Bage's *The Fair Syrian*, James Fraser's *The History of Nadir Shah, formerly called Kuli Khan*, and *The Arabian Nights*. Of particular interest is his reading, two months after checking out *Crusoe*, of two volumes of the French Royal Academy member François-Jean de Chastellux's *Travels in North America*, a book offensive enough concerning race that a French abolitionist, Jacques Pierre Brissot de Warville, published a book refuting it in 1788. Keese was also enlightened enough to be checking out, on numerous occasions, James Lavallée and Phillis Wheatley's *The Negro Equalled by Few Europeans*.[157]

Men of similar dispositions to Keese were reading much of the same material. Kunze, the professor, read many travels, including to the Pacific, the Lavallée/Wheatley book, François le Vaillant's *Travels into the Interior Parts of Africa*, and the "Negro Plot," an unidentifiable book that most likely was an account of the New York slave conspiracy of 1741. His borrowing record indicates that like many on the Eastern seaboard, he also had a fascination with Charles Johnstone's *Chrysal, or, the Adventures of a Guinea*.[158] Van Solingen had little taste for literature, mostly reading medical and travel books including Mungo Park's *Travels into the Interior Districts of Africa* and Bryan Edwards' *The History, Civil and Commercial, of the British Colonies in the West Indies*.[159] Van Allen worked his way, volume by volume, through histories of the Near and Middle East, Rome, and England as well as Samuel Johnson's *Works of the English Poets*, many novels by Tobias Smollet, and several volumes of the *Works* of Jonathan Swift.[160] Ogilvie, the retired judge, read literature

---

[157] *City Readers*, New York Society Library. Accessed September 20, 2017. <http://cityreaders. nysoclib.org/Detail/entities/593>.

[158] <http://cityreaders.nysoclib.org/Detail/entities/632>.

[159] <http://cityreaders.nysoclib.org/Detail/entities/1241>.

[160] <http://cityreaders.nysoclib.org/Detail/entities/1219>.

prolifically, borrowing volumes of Fielding's *Works*, Cervantes's *Don Quixote*, Henry Brooke's *The Fool of Quality*, Goldsmith's *The Vicar of Wakefield*, and Richardson's *Pamela, Clarissa*, and *Sir Charles Grandison* in sequential volumes. Such a borrowing pattern is indicative of actual reading. He also read Gibbon's and Ferguson's histories of Rome, and, of particular interest to this chapter, he read Christian Frederick Damberger's *Travels Through the Interior of Africa* and Michel Adanson's *A Voyage to Senegal, the Isle of Goreé, and the River Gambia*.[161]

Without enumerating the circulation records of every merchant reader of *Crusoe*, a few of them seem representative of the rest. Schermerhorn was reading a mixture of fiction and non-fiction, checking out novels like Smollett's *Roderick Random* and *Peregrine Pickle*, Fanny Burney's *Evelina* and *Cecilia*, *Chrysal*, and the *Tatler*, in addition to works related to his trade like Cook's voyages, Anson's voyages, and Griffith Hughes's *The Natural History of Barbados*. Barnewell read Mungo Park on Africa, de Warville on America, and some of the English literature that others mentioned here were reading like Charlotte Turner Smith's novels and *Chrysal*. But his literary taste tended towards continental literature in translation as well as romances and the Gothic. Books like Mouhy's *The Fortunate Country Maid*, Anne Fuller's *The Convent*, Ann Radcliffe's *The Italian*, *The Mysteries of Udolfo*, and the *Romance of the Forest*, Fenelon's *Telemachus*, Le Sage's *Gil Blas*, Edward Du Bois's *The Fairy of Misfortune; or the Loves of Octar and Zulima, an Eastern Tale*, and many other foreign or foreign-themed books were frequently in his possession.[162] William's tastes, perhaps resembling his exotic imports, were also for such continental romantic tales.[163] Rhinelander also read romances, such as Stéphanie Félicité's *Tales of the Castle* and Elizabeth Gunning's *The Gipsy Countess*, but like many such men at other libraries, he was mainly interested in travels like Vaillant's Africa book, Johan Splinter Stavorinos' *Voyages to the East Indies*, essays on astronomy and geography, and other business-related non-fiction.[164] Camman had a remarkably well-rounded curriculum, reading the *Transactions of the American Philosophical Society*, a multi-volume work on the arts, multiple volumes of *The Wonderful Adventurer, or Rajah Kisna, an Indian Tale*, and the novels of Brooke, Félicité, William Godwin, and many others.[165] Phoenix, the poetic insurance broker, checked out no poetry, but he did take out novels like *Chrysal*, *Don Quixote*, and Smith's *Desmond* as well as the works of Swift and Johnson. Perhaps reflecting his business, he borrowed mostly travels and histories, though an abolitionist spirit might be evident in the fact that he probably read *The Negro Equaled by Few Europeans*, Vaillant's African travels, and Olaudah Equiano's *Interesting Narrative*.[166]

[161] <http://cityreaders.nysoclib.org/Detail/entities/865>.
[162] <http://cityreaders.nysoclib.org/Detail/entities/1038>.
[163] <http://cityreaders.nysoclib.org/Detail/entities/1330>.
[164] <http://cityreaders.nysoclib.org/Detail/entities/955>.
[165] <http://cityreaders.nysoclib.org/Detail/entities/179>.
[166] <http://cityreaders.nysoclib.org/Detail/entities/900>.

The New York Society Library reading network around *Robinson Crusoe*, in short, was remarkably consistent across professions, though undoubtedly with some variations such as whether the reader had more or less of an abolitionist leaning. The overwhelming interest in voyages and travels, whether read by men seeking to further their oceanic trade or by those who may have been interested in places like Africa for anti-slavery purposes, is an unsurprising contextualization of the reception environment for Defoe's novel. *Crusoe*, above all, is a seafaring story and adventure complete with shipwreck. It might to be said to incorporate all of the genres that these men were reading with an economic interest—slavery—that was motivating his travel in the first place. Perhaps Society Library members regarded themselves as Robinson Crusoe, or wanted readers in their household to do so. Regardless, Crusoe was the prototype of the economic man in the Atlantic economy, and as most of these men were the same, he was a fictional role model for their own lives. They themselves had cast off the parental tyranny of Britain, perhaps with some regret, only to preside as patriarchs over their own slave empire. That anti-slavery advocates found a space to express themselves within this empire is what seems most surprising.

The Society Library reading networks surrounding some of the more unequivocally anti-slavery books (as opposed to Africa travel books), however, indicate that we should not necessarily be surprised by the presence of abolitionists in the library. Indeed, the reading networks around anti-slavery texts are indicative of what I described in Chapter 1—the discrepancy between countercultural texts and the hegemonic economy and culture in which they arise. For example, Lavallée and Wheatley's *The Negro Equalled by Few Europeans* was borrowed 144 times between 1791 and 1800, though only Keese, Phoenix, Kunze, and Hunter were among the *Robinson Crusoe* readers who checked it out, a fact that only further enhances my case that the dominant reading of *Crusoe* was pro-slavery.[167] Books by the French abolitionist de Warville were borrowed only twenty-one times from 1789 to 1805.[168] Equiano's slave narrative was borrowed ten times in this period, though Phoenix was the only one who took out it, de Warville, and *Crusoe*.[169]

The relative popularity of such books can be explained, I argue, by the growing anti-slavery sentiment in the city and state. Private emancipation of slaves had been legal since 1712, and there were efforts to enact tariffs on slave imports, though these were more for the suppression of slave insurrections than for abolition.[170] In the 1760s and 1770s newspaper articles had denounced slavery and reprinted attacks on it that had originally been written by English anti-slavery advocates, and by the 1780s newspapers were taking an "increasingly militant anti-slavery line."[171] Manumissions of slaves increased after 1774, partly because the New York Quaker

---

[167] <http://cityreaders.nysoclib.org/Detail/objects/3058>.
[168] <http://cityreaders.nysoclib.org/Detail/objects/1418>; <http://cityreaders.nysoclib.org/Detail/objects/1342>.
[169] <http://cityreaders.nysoclib.org/Detail/objects/3003>.   [170] McManus, 142, 151.
[171] McManus, 152, 168.

Yearly Meeting of that year established sanctions for those who bought and sold slaves, and the 1778 meeting ejected slaveholders from the congregation; by 1787 all New York Quaker congregations had "completely divested themselves of their slaves."[172] Partly due to the efforts of the newly established Manumission Society, a law was passed in 1785 against the slave trade that imposed a fine of £100 for those who imported slaves into New York. In 1788, New York completely banned the trade.[173] There were also African Free schools for boys and girls opened in 1787 and 1793.[174] In 1799 a gradual emancipation law was introduced that freed all children born to a slave woman after July 4, 1799 at the age of twenty-eight for men and twenty-five for women.[175] In 1809 the state recognized slave marriages and the right of slaves to own property and transfer it by will, in 1813 slaves were allowed to bear witness in courts against whites and acquired the right to a trial by jury, and in 1817 a law was passed that slaves born before July 4, 1799 were to be free as of July 4, 1827.[176]

The discourse that newspapers and these laws generated no doubt helped produce a readership for anti-slavery texts in the Society Library, though laws like the one of 1792 that permitted slaveholders to export unruly slaves out of state clearly undermined that spirit.[177] In fact, there was a 22 percent increase in the number of enslaved blacks in New York from 1790 to 1800, and a 33 percent increase in the number of slaveholders, contributing to a "paucity of manumissions" despite the best efforts of the Manumission Society.[178] The rise of the merchant class was partly to blame, as merchants, not artisans as previously, had become the most important group of slaveholders in the city by 1800.[179] The liberal discourse on abolition and the economic facts of the persistence, indeed expansion, of slavery in the Early Republic were at odds. *Robinson Crusoe*, it seems, was even more relevant from 1789 through the early nineteenth century in New York than it may have been before the War of Independence.

IV

The particular "Crusoe effect" that this novel had on the New York slave capitalists that I have been describing is, of course, not the only possible interpretation of its reception in all places. The Early Republic context of its reading in an elite archive, however, is highly suggestive of the possibility that Society Library proprietors recognized themselves in the character of Robinson Crusoe. This interpretation intervenes in a long-standing dispute between critics like Ian Watt and Mallipeddi, who argue that the novel is a celebration of the "economic man," and others like Max Novak and John Richetti who claim that the novel is actually a critique of possessive individualism. Summarizing his position, Novak writes that "everything in

[172] McManus, 152; Harris, 50–1.   [173] McManus, 166.   [174] Harris, 64.
[175] McManus, 174.   [176] McManus, 178.   [177] Harris, 70.
[178] White, *Somewhat*, 27–8.   [179] White, *Somewhat*, 34.

Robinson Crusoe…constitutes an attack upon economic individualism."[180] Richetti has been even more strident, saying that "the pressure of wayward individualism upon society and tradition is perhaps the most urgent moral theme of the period."[181] Novels like Defoe's "are about the limitations (and the moral dangers of) individualism and feature characters who often yearn for a meaning or purpose which is more than merely personal or selfish."[182] These arguments on all sides, however, have been made without much reference to documented evidence of the novel's reception, and how its readers' tastes in other books say something about how they might have interpreted it. This analysis of the Society Library circulation records, though it regards the novel as a model for merchants who embraced its choreography of the replacement of the father by the enslaver, may contribute to this conversation in a manner that will promote further efforts to use actual archives to document how *Robinson Crusoe* was read.

If we regard New York as the primary beneficiary of the "business revolution" of the late eighteenth and early nineteenth centuries, it is because its merchants were not only engaged in slavery as they had been before, but expanding upon it. The wealth that they accrued through this involvement went into the philanthropy endowing schools, hospitals, and the Society Library itself, once again indicating that as with the other institutions explored in this book, the library was performing an important civic function. The community formed among the proprietors of the library was also an interpretive one, and though there were often diverging tastes in books, as the case of pro-slavery versus anti-slavery reading attests, the preponderance of the evidence indicates that the meaning put into books by this community suited local needs. The civic engagement of these proprietors before, during, and after the War of Independence may have differed in terms of patriot, loyalist, or ambivalent opinion, but reading at the library helped put imported books into service regarding matters of the status of the colony and early state. The cultural history of the city might therefore be understood as springing from how reading at a civic institution created a sense of place, interest, and community for those employing books and putting them into use for local, state, and national civic purposes.

The New York Society Library was therefore connected with the other libraries in that it helped build a colonial elite whose reading helped cultivate the leadership of the American colonies and, later, United States. As with Salem and Newport, the wealth behind this civic life was not primarily based on the use of slaves in New York itself. Rather, New Yorkers' global shipping businesses, banking, insurance, and investments in slavery-intensive plantations in points south, often managed by their family members in those places, led them to profit while removed from the terror and violence of those plantations. This was not the case in South Carolina, where another distinguished library—the Charleston Library Society—brought

---

[180] Maximillian Novak, "Robinson Crusoe's Original Sin." *SEL* 1.3 (1961): 24.

[181] John Richetti, *Philosophical Writing: Locke, Berkeley, Hume* (Cambridge: Harvard UP, 1983), 29.

[182] John Richetti, "Introduction." *Cambridge Companion to the Eighteenth-Century Novel*. Ed. John Richetti (Cambridge: Cambridge UP, 1996), 8.

merchants engaged in slavery and the production and trade of slave-produced commodities into close proximity to this violence. How Charlestonians managed their pursuit of imported literary refinement through the library, in this plantation context, is a problem that sets them somewhat apart from the residents of Salem, Newport, New York, and Philadelphia, and closer to the Virginians with whom this book began.

4

Slaves as Securitized Assets

Chrysal, or, the Adventures of a Guinea, Paper Money, and the Charleston Library Society

Slaveholders in South Carolina, "by very far the richest in North America," could be expected to collect people, books, and currency.[1] Those things, in tales of personification known as "it-narratives," attest to the fact that objects—and objectified people—sometimes can also collect strings of owners as they change hands. An "it-narrative" was a genre prevalent in the eighteenth century that had a thing like a coin, pet, stagecoach, or other non-human item as its central character, whose first-person narration about its adventures and owners served as a means of satirizing various types of people and the period's vices. The borrowing of a book about an English coin, Charles Johnstone's *Chrysal, or, the Adventures of a Guinea*, at the Charleston Library Society indicates that such "fictions of social circulation" were not only disseminated in Britain, but as objects in the very kind of international transactions they describe themselves, "circulated" to the colonies.[2] *Chrysal* was available and frequently borrowed in just about every library mentioned in this volume, but it takes on new importance when considered in the Charleston context not only because the city, like others, was a hub of transatlantic trade, but also because of its unique monetary system. The British colonies in North America had been experimenting with colonial paper money since the 1690s, and South Carolina, too, had its own scrip. The difference with South Carolina is how the currency was collateralized; colonies like Massachusetts initially made it redeemable for silver, and others issued it on the security of real estate or a "land bank." South Carolina's currency, though, was slave-backed paper money, even when slaves were regarded as part of real estate. This made slaves' bodies the gold standard—the assets—for which paper securities were ultimately redeemable. Put another way, people served as collateral for the public sector equivalent of what we would today call a "mortgage-backed security"—a term highly appropriate in that slaves were initially considered real estate, not chattels, in local property law for part of the eighteenth century.

---

[1] James Raven, *London Booksellers and American Customers: Transatlantic Literary Community and the Charleston Library Society, 1748–1811* (Columbia: U South Carolina P, 2002), 23.

[2] Deidre Lynch, *The Economy of Character: Novels, Market Culture, and the Business of Inner Meaning* (Chicago: U Chicago P, 1998), 80–119.

The paper money of South Carolina, partly because it was a "colony of a colony" (it was settled from the earlier plantation of Barbados), was therefore part of a species of land-banking in which people were very much part of a deceased person's landed estate, if not the most valuable part of it.[3] The government could "bank" such human assets in the treasury because they could be used in payment of taxes, and thus the government had material collateral from which to issue paper promises upon these assets. The South Carolina case thus makes visible that the value of an abstract object like a piece of currency or a book is not only created by provenance—transitions in the ownership of the object by circulation and whom the object could be said to "own." It is also created by the real people who create value though their labor and for which it stands as a mere representative. Indeed, the eighteenth-century monetary theorist and Rhode Island slaveholder George Berkeley was to ask, in recommending a paper currency for Ireland, "Whether Power to command the Industry of others be not real Wealth? And whether Money be not in Truth, Tickets or Tokens for conveying and recording such Power, and whether it be of great Consequence what Materials the Tickets are made of?"[4] Slave labor—"the industry of others"—in short, was the asset that paper moneys like that of South Carolina commanded, as Berkeley may have realized from his experience dealing in Rhode Island scrip.

This monetary system was appropriate to South Carolina, as it had the highest slave population in the colonies, partly due to the heavy work needed on large-scale agricultural plantations, but also because it was the most important port for the entry of imported slaves into mainland North America. Forty percent of slaves destined for the North American colonies entered through South Carolina between 1700 and 1775, to the extent that they outnumbered whites two to one in the colony by 1740, showing how crucial they were to the economy and the cultural life built upon it.[5] Labor-intensive cash crops like rice and indigo, exported throughout the Atlantic but especially for credit with London banks and mercantile houses, required slave labor; many Carolinians therefore reaped profits from the sale of slaves to planters, the labor on their plantations, and commerce in plantation products.[6] African slaves were thus the primary assets driving regional economic growth, so it is not surprising that they would serve as the "real" property securing the more abstract property of paper currency.

The development of paper currency throughout the colonies was generally a case of paper with "nominal" value becoming redeemable for something of "intrinsic value"—a standard, largely developed through the mechanism of fetishization. These standards were, needless to say, arbitrary and ideological, given what we

---

[3] Peter H. Wood, *Black Majority: Negroes in Colonial South Carolina from 1670 to the Stono Rebellion* (NY: Knopf, 1974), 34.

[4] George Berkeley, *The Querist, Containing Several Queries, Proposed to the Consideration of the Public* (Dublin: Reilly, 1725 & 1735), 9.

[5] Wood, xiv.

[6] Edward Pearson, "'Planters Full of Money': The Self-Fashioning of South Carolina's Plantation Society." *Money Trade and Power: The Evolution of South Carolina's Plantation Society.* Ed. Jack P. Greene, Rosemary Brana-Shute, and Randy J. Sparks (Columbia: U South Carolina P, 2001), 302.

know of changes in them both within the period and since. But their "reality" was one in being with their ideology inasmuch as both were products of the same processes of fetish-formation. In Barbados, African slaves were the fetish upon which paper currency was based and for which it was ultimately redeemable; they were therefore the sublimated unconscious identity of the colonial community and the basis for its value and legal traditions. Land and the slaves upon it were at a later time the measure of "intrinsic" value in South Carolina. In Massachusetts, silver and gold coin—either from Britain or Spanish, French, or Portuguese America— remained the standard for the redemption of paper currency, supplying a "real" to the "imaginary" promises on paper. These fetishistically misrecognized standards of intrinsic value were the legally established ones that theoretically secured the redeemability of paper currency. Customs, however, often dictated that other commodities would govern value and money at different periods and in different circumstances in each of these colonies, and a blend of fetishized commodities often secured confidence in credit.

The importance of the evidence of the reading of *Chrysal* in the Charleston Library Society in this context of the South Carolina currency and economy is that the conditions in Charleston, more so than in the other colonial cities, highlight how the civic engagement that early Americans were imagining and performing was based on property in slaves. The advantages of a postcolonial literary history of the culture of paper credit in South Carolina like this chapter performs, accordingly, are not only that this methodology accounts for how money shaped "interpretive communities" and value distinct from that of the mother country. Nor is this approach limited to how currency and these communities formed ideologies that expressed the identity of colonial subjects and framed regional legal norms leading to proto-national constitutional imaginings. Most importantly, this study of slave-backed money is a challenge to the field of the History of British Political Thought and the doctrine of civic republicanism. This doctrine embraced the constitution of the civic virtue of the republican citizen through property ownership, which the Robbins/Pocock/Bailyn thesis has posited as central to the formation of the early United States, its political ideology, and its legal framework. This thesis is critiqued in this chapter on the basis of the laws of money and property in South Carolina. Because property in land in South Carolina necessarily meant property in people, it could be said that the ideal American republican subject drew his agency for his civic engagement from the intrinsic value of his slaves. The cultural-historical problems of the particular case of the Charleston Library Society as a civic organization for the mediation of the reading of a particular imagined community and reading network therefore help make obvious how these are problems for all of the libraries discussed in this book. Slavery was that which connected these libraries economically, the remarkable similarity in the books they imported linked them intellectually, and the legal, political, and civic challenges their members encountered in the 1760s and 1770s bonded them ideologically. The early American proprietary subscription libraries were therefore crucial not only to the ideological origins of the Revolution, but also to slavery as the economic basis for revolutionary civic engagement and mobilization for action.

Even as slavery can be seen as the basis for both eighteenth-century economics and reading, however, there is a greater paradox in that the figure of the African slave is legally constructed as an embodied asset containing more intrinsic civic virtue than the white republican slaveholders claimed to have. Granting the slave intrinsic value through the process of fetishization as money paradoxically grants the slave tremendous centrality to the economy and polity. The slave has therefore a degree of agency over his or her owner in the same way as pieces of money (as scholars of the "it-narrative" have argued) come to control similar people to those composing a planter elite. The slave then can be seen as having a greater claim of ownership of the cultural history of South Carolina, or the other states for that matter, than the readers who subscribed to these libraries.

Books, like slaves and currency, were things that could and did have "it-narratives" written about them. As much as they were objects owned by Carolinians, they were also subjects of the colonial imagined community that they were creating. Books had become an addiction shaping Carolinians' behaviors, consumer habits, and outlook on social class and imperial belonging—"things" that seemed to have an agency and personality of their own that, as I have argued in Chapters 1 to 3, helped Americans model their own identities. As Isabelle Lehuu has written of the Library Society, "it is as if library books represented an important thread in the social fabric and helped cement the social elite of the seaport city in spite of differences of occupation, wealth or politics."[7] These books were crucial to the self-fashioning of Charlestonians and "the ways in which this elite articulated its power in cultural terms on a daily basis, and the ways in which it fashioned a distinct identity through the deployment of taste and genteel behavior."[8] As we have seen with the other libraries mentioned in this study, taste and prestige were part of the draw of belonging to this Society: "the Library Society became associated with the refined tastes and sensibilities of the metropole rather than with the 'wolfish and brutish' nature that many elite Carolinians believed signified the New World."[9] Books signified both valuable "things" and the "persons" that Charlestonians wanted to be.

This chapter will explore the tangled relationship between money, slavery, books, and the library by first examining *Chrysal*, other it-narratives like it as described by critics, the history of innovations in South Carolina paper currency, and the development of the laws and the pamphlet arguments around that money. Here, I will contend that slavery challenged the period's distinction between "thing" and "person," with the sentimental movement in literature helping to shape the abolitionist claim that Africans were people, not objects. I will also argue that the kind of fetishization constituting both the "it" of the it-narrative and the "person" of the slave laid the foundation for the mortgaging and financialization of slaves that many historians have recently documented as characteristic of the antebellum nineteenth century. Next, I will explain the history of the South Carolina book

[7] Isabelle Lehuu, "Reconstructing Reading Vogues in the Old South: Borrowings from the Charleston Library Society, 1811–1817." *The History of Reading, Volume 1: International Perspectives, c.1500–1900*. Eds Shafquat Towheed and W. R. Owens (London: Palgrave Macmillan, 2011), 79.

[8] Pearson, 300.   [9] Pearson, 306–7.

trade and the Charleston Library by using the papers of Eliza Lucas Pinckney to demonstrate the relationship between how a plantation owner did business and his or her acquisition of metropolitan education and cultural capital. Third, I will examine what we know of the history of reading in South Carolina, not only by reference to Pinckney's reading, particularly her reaction to Samuel Richardson's *Pamela*, but also for what the library's circulation records of 1811–14 can tell us about the reading of *Chrysal* there. Here, I will connect one of its readers, William Boyd, to his illicit trade to the Spanish Florida port of Amelia in the period immediately following Congress's ban on Americans engaging in the slave trade. I will conclude by contending that the epistemology of the slave backing to paper value is also manifest in the book trade. I will explain that the slave author, or emancipated writer, became a brand identity in the book marketplace signifying the intrinsic value behind the writing on paper that he created.

I

It-narratives were as popular in colonial America as they were in Great Britain, *Chrysal* being only one of many that circulated in libraries, including four out of five examined in this book. Alain René Lesage's *The Devil Upon Two Sticks*, arguably the first of the genre, was borrowed 114 times at the New York Society Library between 1790 and 1805, at least twice at the Library Company in 1795 and 1806, and at least once in the Charleston Library Society (1811), with a sequel, *The Devil Upon Two Sticks in England*, also circulating. Susan Smythies' *The Stage-Coach: Containing the Character of Mr. Manly, and the History of His Fellow-Travellers*, was borrowed no less than twenty-three times in the Salem Social Library from 1764 to 1768, and a knock-off, *The Adventures of a Hackney Coach*, was taken out thirty-nine times at the New York Society Library between 1789 and 1805. *Chrysal* was checked out five times under "Chrysal" and another five under "Adventures of a Guinea" at the Salem Social Library from 1764 to 1768, 220 times at the New York Society Library 1789–1805, and at least twice in Charleston. As this book has been arguing, early Americans wanted both the latest British literary works and those bestsellers of the previous centuries, so it is not surprising that it-narratives were in demand at early American libraries.[10]

Chrysal engages with the question of Atlantic slavery throughout the novel as the coin-narrator makes transatlantic and pan-European travels. Its life begins in a mine in Peru, where its first, English mercantile owner, "Traffick," had been enslaved by the Spanish imperial government not only for piracy in the Caribbean, but also for previously stealing the inheritance of a captive English woman, Amelia, who the local Spanish authorities had come to love. After it is coined, it passes to

---

[10] City Readers, New York Society Library. Accessed September 20, 2017. <http://cityreaders.nysoclib. org/>; Circulation Receipt Books, Library Company of Philadelphia; Circulation Records, Charleston Library Society Records, MS 29, Charleston, South Carolina; "Charge Book, 1760–1768," MSS 56, Social Library Records, Phillips Library, Peabody Essex Museum, Salem, Massachusetts.

a second owner, an enslaved native of Peru, who gives the coin to a corrupt Jesuit priest, during confession. The Jesuit then converts the coin into a crucifix. It then is transformed into a doubloon in the possession of a corrupt English naval captain, who brings it to England, where it ends up in the hands of corrupt Admiralty officials, who send it to the Mint to be converted into a guinea. It is then deposited in the Bank of England, and is paid out in the form of a government pension to a corrupt English lord.[11] Without enumerating all of its travels, it variously then ends up in diplomatic hands in England, is trans-shipped to Germany through a Jew and a Dutch banker to pay a German prince for mercenaries hired for English warfare, to a Bulgarian king, to Vienna to be in the hands of one of the Jesuits from Peru, to Lisbon, to Brussels, and further.

In short, "the hundreds of pages in which Chrysal passes from hand to hand—through bribery, corruption, and prostitution—presents us with a vicious and perverse society"; the novel targets "the greed and luxury promoted by commerce and the superficial pretence to high rank that money disruptively facilitates."[12] Throughout, the people Chrysal encounters are shown to be a slave to him through their avarice, yet he is also portrayed as their slave, in Johnstone's vision one with no real agency of his own: the "inhuman characters" of novels like *Chrysal* "are devoid of volition. They do not find their own way between the various locations of the novels, but are passed from owner to owner."[13] Every time Chrysal moves on to a new owner a phrase like "he changes his service," "enters into a new service," or "quits his service" appears, which suggests that he is voluntarily choosing to whom he belongs, when it is clear that they choose where he goes.

At stake in *Chrysal* are the questions of how value is created and mediated, and how the agency of persons and things is constituted, problems that have preoccupied recent critics of the "it-narrative" and "thing theory." The dominant view has been that the Marxist focus on labor as the origin of value is a nineteenth-century concept, and that what eighteenth-century mercantilist theory emphasized was that the circulation of commodities and other objects is what creates value. As Wolfram Schmidgen has explained, "the most advanced analysis of economic processes in the seventeenth and early eighteenth centuries tended to locate the production of wealth not in the exploitation of human labor, but in the global circulation of goods."[14] As goods move across heterogeneous global spaces of particular economic and cultural norms in the way that a novel like *Robinson Crusoe* imagines, the differences that they encounter help turn them into fetish objects.[15] These travelling fetish objects "assume intentionality," though in mercantilism, this agency of the object

---

[11] Charles Johnstone, *Chrysal, or, the Adventures of a Guinea*. Ed. Kevin Bourque, Four Volumes in Two (Kansas City: Valancourt Books, 2011), 1: 19–74.

[12] Aileen Douglas, "Brittania's Rule and the It-Narrator." *Eighteenth-Century Fiction* 6.1 (Oct. 1993): 76; Nicholas Hudson, "Social Rank, 'The Rise of the Novel,' and Whig Histories of Eighteenth-Century Fiction." *Eighteenth-Century Fiction* 17.4 (2005): 587.

[13] Liz Bellamy, *Commerce, Morality and the Eighteenth-Century Novel* (Cambridge: Cambridge UP, 1998), 120.

[14] Wolfram Schmidgen, *Eighteenth-Century Fiction and the Law of Property* (Cambridge: Cambridge UP, 2002), 106–7.

[15] Schmidgen, 117.

is never fully actualized by the middle of the eighteenth century.[16] The sentimental literature and philosophy of the 1760s of the kind that I discussed in Chapter 1, however, begins to separate the object from its grounding in human use, the thing from the person. It is in this distancing that the circulatory theory of value ceases to be explanatory, and mobile, fetishized property like currency begins to assume its own agency.[17]

Consequently, monetary narratives like *Chrysal* begin to emerge as ways to explain this epistemological and evaluative transformation. These it-narratives, which help document the emergence of consumer culture, in Aileen Douglas's words, subordinate "the individual (and that individual's moral or immoral acts) to impersonal patterns of circulation."[18] That coins change hands so frequently helps map how exchange links people together into one society.[19] As Deidre Lynch writes, money, therefore, is "an appropriate vehicle for a narrative form organized to enable readers to collect the characters of experience by collecting characters" in a way that other narrative forms do not permit.[20] The plot featuring such exchanges in *Chrysal* is able to portray a great diversity of individuals in the community these exchanges create.[21] These narratives are able to achieve this unique way of mediating reality to readers because money itself has no personality and can assume that of its owner.[22] The money in them circulates in a manner that while revealing "the economic links that bind society," also exposes the "entirely illusory autonomy" of the humans and "the selfishness within modern society, while the condemnation of this system is implicit in the predominant satirical tone."[23] The problem money-centric narratives like *Chrysal* point to, in this line of criticism, is one of the existence of human agency in the face of the agency of the circulating "thing" that can essentially collect more people than a slave-trading human narrator like Robinson Crusoe can.

If Chrysal is a kind of slave, then, he is also one whose personification lends him agency in much the same way as an African slave was regarded as both a "thing" and a "person" by the enslavers of the time. "The period that jubilantly devoured tales narrated by talking objects," writes Lynn Festa, "was also a period in which persons were brutally and insistently seized upon as things in the form of slavery and the slave trade."[24] In such works as Olaudah Equiano's *Interesting Narrative*, discussed in Chapter 5, "there is even a perverse sense in which slave autobiographies are themselves tales told by (former) things, given the legal status of slave as chattel or *res*."[25] For this reason, the slave narrative separates the humanity of slaves from the objectivity of things, and is therefore considered a biography of a person, not an it-narrative.[26] Yet this separation in abolitionist writing had not yet taken place in South Carolina in this period.[27]

---

[16] Schmidgen, 121, 141.   [17] Schmidgen, 148–9.   [18] Douglas, 71.
[19] Douglas, 71.   [20] Lynch, 96.   [21] Bellamy, 126.   [22] Lynch, 98.
[23] Bellamy, 126, 128.
[24] Lynn Festa, *Sentimental Figures of Empire in Eighteenth-Century Britain and France* (Baltimore: Johns Hopkins UP, 2006), 112.
[25] Festa, 132.
[26] Markman Ellis, "Suffering Things: Lapdogs, Slaves, and Counter-Sensibility." *The Secret Life of Things: Animals, Objects, and It-Narratives in Eighteenth-Century England*. Ed. Mark Blackwell (Lewisburg: Bucknell UP, 2007), 96, 106.
[27] Ellis, 95.

Part of the reason for this lack of rethinking this equation of "slave" and "thing" in the South was that early eighteenth-century experiments with paper currency in South Carolina demonstrated how shifting notions of "real" value eventually settled on the body of the African slave as the agent supporting money's nominal value. This discourse on what constitutes "real" and "intrinsic" worth, as often as not juxtaposed against the "extrinsic" or nominal worth of "imaginary" paper money, follows a trajectory in late seventeenth-century to early eighteenth-century political economic thought in which labor theories of value give way to landed-property theories of value. This shift in economic thinking in this period is accomplished over the body of the African slave, who is initially legally recategorized from "chattel"—a laboring and mobile embodiment of value—to "real estate." As real estate, he or she is an immobile, and, at least according to real property ideologues, more permanent and immutable property before becoming mobile property again in 1740. This legal inscription of the African body as a fundamental "real" in both the chattel and real estate schemata took on a further significance when slaves were garnisheed by the colonial governments of Barbados and South Carolina as the security for the paper moneys they issued in 1702 and 1703, respectively (see Figure 4.1). This development paradoxically invested the slave with agency, for by continually locating the slave as the embodiment of the real, intrinsic, and material presence redeeming the nominal, extrinsic, and ideal absent forms of paper money and legal contracts, it granted the slave tremendous centrality.

The decision of Barbados and South Carolina to ground all transactions in the trade in human bodies, though following general British Atlantic labor theory of value principles, attempted to deliver substance to fetish, or more precisely, establish

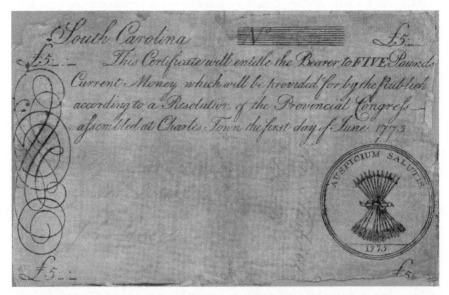

Figure 4.1 £5 South Carolina Paper Currency Note (1775). Reproduced from the original held by the Department of Special Collections of the University Libraries of Notre Dame.

one fetish as the preeminent standard for all fetishes—the flesh standard. Those subjects on the periphery of power in the seventeenth-century British Atlantic thus move into the center when questions of "intrinsic" value are considered. The colonial master, involved in a series of transactions throughout Barbados and South Carolina, the empire, and the wider Atlantic, increasingly found himself "extrinsically" contracted to within an inch of his being, and saw in the slave a primitive completeness—a completeness he could control. The fetish for the black body—the persistence of its commodity-function—provided the white ego with a temporary completeness that reaffirmed the fiction that the black subject represented a primitive intrinsic value unattainable by the divided white subject except through the fulfillment of desire in the commodity.[28] As Frantz Fanon asserts, "the Negro symbolizes the biological" to the white subject, and the black body becomes the location for the standardizing values as they are organized across inextricably linked economic, political, and unconscious territory.[29] Misrecognition, fetishization, and the attribution of intrinsic value to the slave are therefore connected.

This fetishization of African slaves as alienable, mobile properties changed in the 1680s, however, when their legal status was altered from that of "chattels" to "real estate," from mobile property to immobile property, with Barbados setting the legal code for what was to follow in South Carolina.[30] This shift in the legal discourse on Barbadian slavery was significant because ideologies of intrinsic value migrated with it away from the figure of the laboring African body and towards the soil as the ultimate security for contract and guarantee of value. With the epistemological eclipse of the labor theory of value to which Schmidgen alluded, the slave lost his or her preeminence as the standard fetish organizing other commodity-fetishes in the colony and became an "extrinsic" subject of the "intrinsically" constituted landed estate. This epistemological shift towards real property being the source of intrinsic value was part of a general trend in anglophone Atlantic thought, and was occasioned by a theory of subjectivity and citizenship that was attempting to restore virtue to public action by suggesting that land ownership integrated the political personality.

The reality of slavery, therefore, has a bearing on what the Robbins/Pocock/Bailyn thesis has explained to be a landed-class political ideal within an "ideology of real property." This ideology held that "land, whose stability—as opposed to the mobility of goods and money—set men free to be the rational political creatures which they were by nature."[31] This putatively organic means of substantiating individual authority—a means that granted "intrinsic value" to the subject through his land—was part of a republican trend in thinking in which a naturalized autobiographical sense of an autonomous, unified subjectivity was equated with the

---

[28] Frantz Fanon, *Black Skin White Masks*. Trans. Charles Lam Markmann (NY: Grove Press, 1967), 132.

[29] Fanon, 167.

[30] Edward McCrady, *The History of South Carolina Under the Proprietary Government 1670–1719* (NY: Macmillan, 1901), 359.

[31] J. G. A. Pocock, *Virtue, Commerce, and History: Essays on Political Thought and History, Chiefly in the Eighteenth Century* (Cambridge: Cambridge UP, 1985), 68, 61.

historiographical process of temporally transmitting legal titles to land.[32] Soil was taken as the substantive medium of continuous referral to the past and the natural rights and liberties it confers. It thereby served as proof of present "disinterested" virtue, the genealogical source of an authorizing rhetoric of identity, and the underwriting depository of the landed class's moral capital. Where modernity had brought about a subject derived negatively from his "extrinsic" contractual connection with the community and the state, this anti-modern ideology substituted a positively derived subject constituted by the "intrinsic" properties and proprietorship of the soil. Yet this was premised on property in slaves, in Carolina understood as part of real estate until 1740, being that which granted virtue in a republic. Property in slaves, whether as immobile property before 1740 or as mobile chattels after it, therefore appears to be part of the constitution of the virtuous republican citizen imagined by Pocock and others. Slaves were permanent assets whose labor freed that citizen to become civically engaged, and as such represented the central "real" value upon which imaginary, paper value was secured.

As I have argued elsewhere, the centrality of the slave as a fetishized asset securing paper currency thus came to serve as the material substrate for various forms of paper value, including financial documents, law, and literature, which were circulating throughout the Atlantic, a fact that the South Carolina example makes clear.[33] Slaves, as property, thereby underwrote Carolina institutions and culture, including abstract printed matter like mortgages, insurance policies, and books themselves. As the "real" assets behind paper, they effectively transubstantiated "circulating finance capital, print, and the social contract of the white settler public with their "other": the fixed, biologized, and racialized identity of people of restricted circulation and liberty."[34] If circulating objects like currency "create more of a community than subjects do," then the body of the slave secured how such an imagined community was being constructed in South Carolina.[35]

This securing of paper upon the body of the slave in the early eighteenth century was thus the legal foundation for the mortgaging of slaves, the writing of insurance policies on the basis of them, and the other financial innovations that many scholars have recently described as characteristic of both Southern and Northern finance in the nineteenth century.[36] Even before they had been the security for paper money, enslaved Africans had been used as money in bartering for other things, a role that

[32] Pocock, 97.

[33] Sean Moore, " 'Our Irish Copper-Farthen Dean': Swift's *Drapier's Letters*, the 'Forging' of a Modernist Anglo-Irish Literature, and the Atlantic World of Paper Credit." *Atlantic Studies* 2.1 (2005): 70.

[34] Moore, 71.   [35] Festa, 114.

[36] See Richard Kilbourne, Jr, *Debt, Investment, Slaves: Credit Relations in East Feliciana Parish, Louisiana, 1825–1885* (London: Pickering and Chatto, 1995); Joshua Rothman, Edward Baptist, and Gavin Wright, *Slavery and Economic Development* (Baton Rouge: Louisiana State UP, 2006); John Majewski, *Modernizing a Slave Economy: The Economic Vision of the Confederate Nation* (Chapel Hill, U North Carolina P, 2009); Bonnie Martin, "Slavery's Invisible Engine: Mortgaging Human Property." *The Journal of Southern History* 76.4 (Nov. 2010): 817–66; Sharon Ann Murphy, *Investing in Life: Insurance in Antebellum America* (Baltimore: Johns Hopkins UP, 2010); Sven Beckert, *Empire of Cotton: A Global History* (NY: Vintage Books, 2015); Calvin Schermerhorn, *The Business of Slavery and the Rise of American Capitalism, 1815–1860* (New Haven: Yale UP, 2015); Bonnie Martin, "Neighbor-to-Neighbor Capitalism: Local Credit Networks and the Mortgaging of Slaves." *Slavery's Capitalism:*

was the most basic foundation of their later securitization, including for Confederate currency. *An Essay on Currency, Written in August 1732* explained this origin in defending the issuing of a new South Carolina paper currency against people who thought barter was preferable to paper currency in a context where there was little circulating gold or silver. Bartering slaves for other goods had created a situation, the author wrote, where "the Country-Stores have left many Families, which had several Negroes, without scarce a Negro to help them."[37] In this writer's opinion, slaves themselves, accordingly, were best used as assets for which money could be redeemed rather than serving as money themselves.

As this chapter explains, slaves were therefore the material basis for the books, in their capacity as abstract value, which circulated in the Charleston Library Society. Indeed, there had been it-narratives about books, like the *History of a Bible* and "Adventures of a Quire of Paper" that had personified books as circulating characters accruing value. The talking Bible, for instance, regarded its restricted circulation by being put in a library as being in a "Jail for books."[38] The Charleston library, though it may not have been such a jail in that its books circulated, might well be regarded as a prison built on the captivity of people of restricted circulation who underwrote that book circulation. The library therefore might be regarded as akin to the "talking book" motif explored by Henry Louis Gates, in which the book of the white master is regarded as magical by the narrators of slave autobiographies. The master's book "is a book that perversely refuses to talk. It speaks to the literate white master who reads from it, but presents an obdurately silent face to the slave who addresses it."[39] Because the slave is an illiterate, fetishized object or thing instead of being a humanized person, he or she is not an interlocutor with the book. With the acquisition of literacy, as I shall explain in Chapter 5, the former slave claims agency and circulation as more than a primitive, non-circulating asset, but as a modern subject on the performative, written model.[40] The majority of South Carolinian whites' resistance to granting slaves this agency, however, indicates that they were not ready for books to talk to their slaves. The narrative of the Charleston Library Society's origins and development bears witness to the continued use of African slaves as the asset backing not only the library's books, but also all kinds of economic transactions in the South.

II

The Charleston Library Society presents what is arguably one of the best-documented cases of how transatlantic transactions like those mapped-out in *Chrysal* worked. Its history, however, not only encompasses the library itself, but also the Southern book trade of which it was a part. This trade was very much the junior partner of

---

A New History of American Economic Development. Ed. Sven Beckert and Seth Rockman (Philadelphia: U Pennsylvania P, 2016), 107–21.

[37] *An Essay on Currency* (Charlestown: Lewis Timothy, 1732), 4.   [38] Festa, 129.
[39] Festa, 138.   [40] Festa, 140–1.

those more developed ones in the North, though in the case of Williamsburg, Virginia, Annapolis, Maryland, and Charleston, it soon came to rival Northern cities in imports and printing. The leading printer-booksellers by the Revolution were William Park of Annapolis (and, later, Williamsburg), and Robert Wells in Charleston.[41] Lewis Timothy (also called Louis Timothée) had established himself as the first important printer in Charleston in 1734 after leaving work at the Library Company of Philadelphia, and his widow and son Peter took over the business to publish government documents and the *South Carolina Gazette*.[42] Wells arrived in Charleston in 1752, first as a dry goods merchant and then a proprietor of a stationery and book shop, eventually establishing a book bindery, a printing business, and a competing newspaper, the *South-Carolina Weekly Gazette*.[43] He was noted by Isaiah Thomas, the Massachusetts printer, as "having employed heavy-drinking Negro slaves as his pressmen."[44] Nicholas Langford opened a competing bookstore in about 1769, joining a genealogy of importing booksellers like the Timothys, Henry and Alexander Peronneau, Edward Wigg, Peter Horry, Robert Raper, Wells, and Charles Crouch.[45] There was a significant intra-colonial book trade, initiated at first by Timothy in his relationship with Benjamin Franklin, and in the career of William Aikman, who was trying to market to Annapolis, Charleston, and Williamsburg by 1773.[46] These merchants catered to South Carolinian whites made upwardly mobile and literate by slavery, and it was only natural that the library arose from such elites and the book trade serving them.

Charleston was "importing thousands more slaves than books" when the library was founded in 1748, needing them for the cultivation of cash crops like rice, indigo, cotton, tar, pitch, and turpentine.[47] The example of the plantation life of Eliza Lucas Pinckney indicates just how South Carolina's slavery economy worked. Pinckney's father, George Lucas, had purchased a slave plantation near Charleston in his efforts to become as well situated as a British gentleman. George Lucas owned a plantation in Antigua and three in South Carolina: a 600-acre estate, Wappoo, where his daughter lived; a 1,500-acre estate, Garden Hill; and 3,000 acres of rice lands.[48] He purchased these properties through mortgages with Richard Boddicott of Dunbar Mortgages in London, who would serve as his business agent in England, and the overseer of his estates in South Carolina was William Murray. Because her father was stationed in Antigua in military service, Lucas Pinckney managed the estates from Wappoo, which had at least twenty slaves working it.[49] When Eliza married Charles Pinckney in 1744, her father's three estates were sold to pay off their heavy mortgages, but she continued in plantation life with Charles's estates: his Belmont plantation on the Cooper River; his farms on the islands of Hilton

[41] Calhoun Winton, "The Southern Book Trade in the Eighteenth Century." *A History of the Book in America, Volume 1: The Colonial Book in the Atlantic World*. Eds Hugh Amory and David Hall (Chapel Hill: U North Carolina P, 2007), 224, 229.

[42] Winton, 233.   [43] Winton, 233.   [44] Raven, *London*, 41.

[45] Winton, 236; Raven, *London*, 28–33.   [46] Winton, 233, 239–40.

[47] Raven, *London*, 4, 19–20.

[48] Elise Pinckney, ed., *The Letterbook of Eliza Lucas Pinckney 1739–1762* (Columbia: U South Carolina P, 1997), xv–xvi.

[49] Pinckney, xvi.

Head; the 1,000-acre Auckland estate; Pinckney Plains; some marshland on the Cooper River; 500 acres on the Savannah River near Silver Bluffs; and 500 acres at Four Holes.[50]

Early in her time in South Carolina, Eliza Lucas Pinckney wrote of what hers and other plantations exported: "The staple comodity here is rice and the only thing they export to Europe. Beef, pork, and lumber they send to the West Indias."[51] In addition to rice, she and her father soon introduced indigo, over which the French Caribbean had a monopoly, as a cash crop as early as 1739, albeit only at first to cultivate and sell its seed: "Wrote my father today a very long letter on his plantation affairs, on the pains I had taken to bring the Indigo Ginger Cotton Lucerne and Casada to perfection & had greater hopes from the indigo than any other."[52] They hired a pair of brothers, the Cromwells, from the West Indies to help convert the indigo plant into dye in the middle of the 1740s after "several fruitless attempts to gett a negro from Montserat skilled in making Indigo."[53] Like many South Carolinians, George Lucas did not want to have to pay white men like the Cromwells for dye production, and sought to purchase French slaves to teach his own slaves how to do it. He wrote, "I shall however Continue to look out when any French negroes are to be Sold, will not your Laws keep refractory Servts. in order Cromwell is obliged by his Articles to teach two of my negroes the art of making Indigo, & if he perform then it will remidy the Evil of the want of purchase [of French slaves]."[54]

Indigo required labor-intensive growing, harvesting, and processing that was done by slave labor, and it produced the wealth needed to import British luxuries; it "soon established the kinds of credits in London banking houses that supported South Carolina in style during the decades before the Revolution."[55] The Lucas' main export crop, rice, was also labor intensive, especially to clean it for the market. George Lucas wrote to Charles Pinckney that in addition to lumber, he should ship "ruff rice also, which I think will prove more profitable in Shipping than Clean when the Freight is our own, Espotaly when it is Consider'd that the very great labour of Cleaning rice will be Saved from whence I look upon the greatest loss on Slaves to proceed."[56] The labor and time of slaves, Lucas is saying, would be best spent on other tasks if this shipment were to be overall profitable.

Slaves were considered important enough to the South Carolina economy that when the Spanish were encouraging slaves to escape to their garrison at St Augustine in 1749, the Governor of South Carolina declared that the failure to stop these escapes would "prove . . . destructive to the Province."[57] The fact was that slaves outnumbered

---

[50] Pinckney, xxii–xxiii.   [51] Pinckney, 40.

[52] Constance Schulz, ed., *The Papers of Eliza Lucas Pinckney and Harriott Pinckney Horry Digital Edition* (Charlottesville: University of Virginia Press, Rotunda, 2012). Accessed December 9, 2014. <http://rotunda.upress.virginia.edu/PinckneyHorry/ELP0869>.

[53] Schulz, <http://rotunda.upress.virginia.edu/PinckneyHorry/ELP0219>.

[54] Schulz, <http://rotunda.upress.virginia.edu/PinckneyHorry/ELP0209>.

[55] Pinckney, xix.

[56] Schulz, <http://rotunda.upress.virginia.edu/PinckneyHorry/ELP0209>.

[57] Pinckney, 57 n. 72.

whites two to one in the colony by 1740.[58] During the destructive years of the Revolutionary War, Eliza Lucas Pinckney complained that she had been "rob[b]ed and deserted by my Slaves" and that "the Crops made this year must be very small by the desertion of the Negroes in planting and hoeing time."[59] Though she could be regarded as a benevolent slave owner due to her efforts to educate some slave children, she was nonetheless a beneficiary of a slave system that afforded her imported commodities.[60]

The record of the commodities the Lucases and Pinckneys were importing from all around the Atlantic with the proceeds of their crops begins as early as 1741. Eliza records in her diary that she wrote a letter from Wappoo to her father in Antigua, and details the rice-for-imports pattern:

> Wrote to my Father acquainting him that I received a letter from Mr. Boddicott with a very aimable character of my brother George, he says he is a very fine Youth. Acknowledge the receipt of a piece of rich Yellow Lutstring consisting of 19 yards for my self, ditto of blue for my Mama, and thanked my father for them. Also for a piece of Holland and Cambrick received from London at the same time. Toll him we have had a moderate and healthy summer and preparing for the Kings birthday next day. Toll him shall send the rice by Bullard.[61]

The importation of textiles in exchange for Carolina crops is echoed in a letter from Eliza to her father in 1744: "We lately received a Trunk of silks from London for which we are very much obliged to you, they are very gentile: we received nither linning nor lace with them, nor one line from Mr. Boddicott, if there was any, I am afraid they are lost."[62] As Julie Flavell has written, "As quickly as Carolinians made money hewing rice swamps out of the semi-tropical wilderness, they exchanged it for a façade of something English and genteel," with textiles being some of the most prominent tasteful imports.[63]

After the Lucas plantations were sold, Eliza and Charles Pinckney continued to work with a London agent, George Morley, to facilitate their export/import business. In 1760, after Charles's death, Eliza records that she had sent a barrel of rice to her son's London schoolmaster as tuition payment, and has sent several bills of exchange to pay for other expenses in England.[64] In 1761, she wrote Morley that she received beer he had sent, and that she sent seeds to him in return:

> Since mine to you by Mr. Simpson in the Febr. Fleet, I received your favour by Ball of the 4th Nov., and the hogshead of beer in very good order except the straining cock which I sopose was lost on board—also Mrs. Kings letter by Mr. Rutledge, but he forgot your verbal message about the beer, so that I gave it over for lost till Ball arrived. I hope the box of seeds for Mr. King sent by Mr. Simpson in the man of war in Feb. is safe arrived.[65]

[58] Wood, xiv.   [59] Pinckney, xxiii–xxiv.
[60] Pinckney, 12, 34.   [61] Pinckney, 23.
[62] Schulz, <http://rotunda.upress.virginia.edu/PinckneyHorry/ELP0816>.
[63] Julie Flavell, *When London Was Capital of America* (New Haven: Yale UP, 2010), 10.
[64] Pinckney, 143–6.   [65] Pinckney, 163.

There can be no doubt that there were multiple such exchanges, especially when the Pinckney children were studying in England, and there are many letters enclosing bills of exchange for those expenses as well as paying debts for unspecified merchandise. The Pinckney family, together with the Manigaults of Charleston, were the "most conspicuous" of what some New Englanders considered to be "lordly and opulent planters."[66] Eliza and Charles Pinckney, who himself, together with other men of his family, were members of the library, are therefore examples of how South Carolinians did business in an economy that revolved around Atlantic slavery.

It should come as no surprise, then, that the originators of the Charleston Library Society derived their wealth from slavery. It was founded by seventeen men, including plantation owners like Thomas Middleton and Thomas Sacheverell, as well as the slave traders Samuel and Morton Brailsford.[67] Two more men joined before they signed the articles of agreement on establishing the library, making for eight other merchants, as well as two lawyers, a physician, the printer Peter Timothy, a wig maker, and a schoolmaster.[68] The father of two of these men, the Wraggs, "had broken the monopoly of the Royal African Company to bring in record numbers of Negroes in the 1730s," and "the earliest recorded library member who was a sea captain, Peter Bostock, was master of a slaving ship."[69] All, however, could be said to be benefiting from the slavery economy regardless of profession in the same way they did in the other cities discussed in this book. The library's "founders and early members included most of the leading slave importers of the century and others whose ethical perspectives now appear contorted and bounded by self-interest."[70] By 1770, vice-president of the Society Henry Laurens was "one of the wealthiest men in North America and the owner of at least eight plantations."[71] He had "consigned cargoes of men, women and children from Africa's west coast to his business associates in England and America. He had dispatched scores of male slaves to his remote plantations on the colonial frontier. He had sent dozen of enslaved women after them."[72] The library counted two-thirds of the leaders of the legislative assembly—similar men—as members.[73] The library, as both a space of reading and a social network, was therefore, like the other libraries, a slavery-financed forum for the cultivation of polite, Enlightenment society, or a "locus for the expression of social and political community, most obviously in its promotion of notions of civility."[74] The £50 cost of a share in the library was the highest in the colonies; indeed, when the fee of five shillings per week was added to it, each member was required to accumulate library stock to the value of £200, with a further weekly payment after reaching that amount of 2 shillings and sixpence.[75] This highest share value of any North American proprietary subscription library reflected Charleston's standing as the city made wealthiest by slavery. Ownership of a share was not simply about access to books, but "an affirmation of distinction achieved" that lent prestige and a social network to a proprietor.[76]

---

[66] Raven, *London*, 23; Pearson, 301.   [67] Raven, *London*, 37.
[68] Raven, *London*, 343.   [69] Raven, *London*, 39.   [70] Raven, *London*, 45.
[71] Raven, *London*, 67.   [72] Julie Flavell, 7.   [73] Raven, *London*, 67.
[74] Raven, *London*, 14.   [75] Raven, *London*, 72.   [76] Raven, *London*, 67.

The rules and fines of the library were the most stringent in North America. "Only a single pamphlet or book could be borrowed on each occasion," and "loans were limited to four days for pamphlets, twelve days for duodecimos and octavos, sixteen days for quartos, and twenty-four days for folios."[77] Overdue books were fined five shillings for every twelve hours overdue, though members in the country could obtain longer leases.[78] All members were required to serve as an officer of the library at least once every seven years, and were fined for trying to escape these responsibilities and the meetings associated with them. They were also barred from voting or attending meetings if they were more than six months behind in their fees and fines.[79]

The Library Society did not employ Charleston's growing number of local retailers to obtain its books, but rather dealt directly with London wholesalers, a fact that has been taken as "a signal affirmation of their determination to maintain direct contact with the literary and political center" in order to obtain political, social, cultural, and real capital.[80] Over the course of the second half of the eighteenth century, the Society's board hired and fired notable London booksellers like William Strahan, John and James Rivington, Thomas Durham, David Wilson, James Dodsley, James Fletcher, William Nicoll, and John Stockdale.[81] The board employed, as agents and payment guarantors, familiar London merchants of the "Carolina Walk" on the Royal Exchange and "Carolina Coffee House" such as Sarah Nichleson, who had partnered with her brothers Richard and Thomas Shubrick, and who were "involved in the 1740s in slave consignments."[82] The business end of obtaining the books for the library therefore made use of the pre-existing Charleston–London slave-trading infrastructure.

The books that the library ordered were similar to those available at the Salem, Newport, New York, and Philadelphia libraries. As with the Redwood Library, it did not contain much fiction in its early years.[83] James Raven has summarized what British literary titles the library held and did not hold, noting that even though the majority of the collection consisted of non-fiction,

> Exceptions, already part of the foundation collection by 1750, included Sarah Scott's *History of Cornelia* and Marie Antoinette Fagnan's *Kanor*. These had both been published that year and had therefore quite possible been sent over unsolicited by the bookseller as examples of current light reading. Less surprising inclusions in the 1750 *Catalogue* were Henry Fielding's *Joseph Andrews* and *Tom Jones*, but again, both were then very topical, having been published in 1749 and 1750, respectively, and the *Catalogue* contains no Richardson, Haywood, or other popular novelists of the 1740s. Gay's *Fables* and *Poems* were at least present. Later, Charles Johnstone's *Chrysal or the Adventures of a Guinea* and Hawkesworth's *Adventurer* were ordered in 1771, both of which were not only popular and favorably reviewed in Britain, but appealed to the

---

[77] James Raven, "Social Libraries and Library Societies in Eighteenth-Century North America." *Institutions of Reading: the Social Life of Libraries in the United States*. Ed. Thomas Augst and Kenneth Carpenter (Amherst: U Massachusetts P, 2007), 24–52, 26.

[78] Raven, "Social Libraries," 27.   [79] Raven, "Social Libraries," 27.

[80] Raven, *London*, 85.   [81] Raven, *London*, 87–8.   [82] Raven, *London*, 126.

[83] Raven, *London*, 198.

serious male reader. Johnstone's novel also included some American episodes, although if that had been the basis for the choice, one might so expect the Charleston library to have ordered Defoe's *Moll Flanders* or Charlotte Lennox's *Harriet Stuart*. The 1770s Catalogue lists some additions since 1750, including Fielding's *Amelia*, Sterne's *Tristram Shandy*, Smollett's *Roderick Random* and *Ferdinand Count Fathom*, Dodsley's *Collection of Poems*, and Gay's *Beggar's Opera*. Shakespeare's *Works*, surprising absent from the 1750 Catalogue, were later ordered only in a duodecimo edition in the pre-1778 collection. By contrast, the 1750 holdings did include the works of Chaucer, and of Spenser (and later Spenser's *Faerie Queene* separately), and a 1738 two-volume edition of Milton's prose works (and, separately, his *Paradise Lost* and *Paradise Regained*).[84]

The library also contained works by George Farquahar, Samuel Johnson, Giovanni Marana (author of the popular *Turkish Spy*), Jonathan Swift, James Thomson, and Edward Young.[85] The category of "literature" "amounted to 10 percent of the total [holdings] by title in 1770 but 23 percent by 1811."[86] Magazines like the *Gentleman's Magazine* and the *London Magazine* kept Charlestonians apprised of the latest London fashions in books, and Addison and Steele's *Spectator* was as popular there as in the other cities.

Political thought, represented in works of history, law, and philosophy, was also central to the library's collections, in part due to the conflict with Britain: "The library requested a cluster of fundamental legal texts, and it did so in the midst of colonial conflict over the Townshend duties and other complaints against Parliament."[87] The library's "reading list on Englishmen's rights" included a three-volume 1751 folio edition of Locke's *Works* and an octavo edition of his *Two Treatises of Government*.[88] It stocked much seventeenth-century political theory by James Harrington, John Milton, Algernon Sidney, and others, and was quite current in ordering Blackstone's *Commentaries on the Laws of England*.[89] Histories of England and Rome were numerous.[90]

In short, the Charleston Library Society was much like the other libraries described in this book, but richer due to being more directly connected with the trade in slaves and slave-produced commodities, particularly those made in South Carolina. Its members were as engaged with metropolitan literary taste as their neighbors to the North, if not more so, and as tensions with Parliament increased, they were equally as interested in establishing a political, legal, and philosophical basis for resistance. Charleston was the hub in the North American slave trade because it, unlike Rhode Island, actually received imported slaves on a large-scale basis and employed them in agricultural labor, adding to the value of the local economy in a way that Northern port cities could not. South Carolina families could better afford to send their children to England for secondary, college, and legal education due to this slave wealth to the extent that there were "more members of the Middle Temple from South Carolina than from any other colony in the eighteenth century."[91] The library helped make that level of education possible, and

[84] Raven, *London*, 198–9. [85] Raven, *London*, 357–74. [86] Raven, *London*, 184.
[87] Raven, *London*, 156. [88] Raven, *London*, 156. [89] Raven, *London*, 157, 159.
[90] Raven, *London*, 161–2. [91] Raven, *London*, 160.

its collection would go on to aid students at the fledgling College of Charleston, chartered in 1785. Understanding how the library contributed to the literacy of South Carolinians requires an assessment of reading patterns in the colony, and at the library in particular. Making such an assessment makes possible an examination of the relationship between slavery and money that works like *Chrysal* were establishing.

III

Documenting the reading trends, patterns, and tastes of Charleston Library Society proprietors requires not only citations from primary sources like diaries, letters, and circulation ledgers of South Carolinians, but also attention to secondary work by scholars who have explored some of those primary sources in their colonial contexts. It is through these contexts, particularly in that of the library as a reading network, that evidence of the reading of *Chrysal* by William Boyd, an owner of ships probably carrying African slaves, might hold clues to its interpretation, or at least to the motives for it being checked out. A book like this—one about the people behind the circulation of a piece of money—might therefore itself exist as the paper expression of the slaves as the assets backing its dissemination, or as what Berkeley deemed a "ticket" to the "industry of others."[92] The papers of Pinckney and the library's circulation ledgers, together with documentation of their mining by other scholars such as Raven, Kevin Hayes, and Isabelle Lehuu, help make the case that South Carolinians were up to date on the latest fashions in British litera-ture as well as other genres. Pinckney's reading of Richardson's *Pamela*, in particu-lar, engages with the central character's possessive individualism in a manner that tells us much about attitudes towards social propriety on plantations like Pinckney's. These attitudes were as much a product of British cultural importation as they were about maintaining distinct barriers between whites and slaves. Indeed, they presided "over a society built upon slavery," and "used the luxuries with which they sur-rounded themselves to define themselves as rulers over their own dominion" and to create such distinctions, with books both representing such luxury and contain-ing lessons on how to maintain such social barriers.[93] The history of the Carolina book trade, and the libraries formed from it, therefore helps teach us lessons about how Charlestonians perceived the social value of books like *Pamela* and *Chrysal*, which though very different, have left traces of their reading in the period.

The private, household libraries of many South Carolinians exemplify the colo-ny's tastes. As Richard Beale Davis observed, "there was no cultural lag in the South in the matter of reading current political philosophy and employing it in argument, as there was no cultural lag in other artistic and intellectual areas."[94] Many planters "owned private libraries," one, Major Alexander Garden, leaving fourteen slaves and a personal library of 480 books when he died in the early nineteenth century.[95] Religious and theological titles were the largest genres in these personal collections,

---

[92] Berkeley, 9.   [93] Pearson, 301.   [94] Quoted in Raven, *London*, 152.
[95] Lehuu, 68.

educational and occupational titles on topics like husbandry and medicine came second, "recreational reading" like novels and arts came third, and historical, political, and philosophical books came fourth.[96] The single most popular title was the *Spectator*, which was in twenty-seven collections.[97] Legal books like Sir Geoffrey Gilbert's *Law of Evidence*, Thomas Simpson's *Annuities and Reversions*, Emmerich de Vattel's *Droit de Gens*, *Journals* of the House of Lords, *Statutes at Large*, the *State Trials*, *Biographia Brittanica*, Richard Burns's *Justice of the Peace* and *Parish Officer*, Michael Dalton, Joseph Shaw, and William Nelson's books on the same subject, and Charles Malloy's *De Jure Martimo e Navali* were in many of these libraries.[98] Law books by Beccaria, Fortescue, Coke, and de Vattel were common in estate inventories, as were Wood's *Institutes of the Laws of England* and Blackstone's *Commentaries*.[99] Works of political philosophy like Montesquieu's *Spirit of the Laws*, Grotius' *The Rights of War and Peace*, and Puffendorf's *The Law of Nature and Nations* were also common in household collections.[100]

The library and reading of Eliza Lucas Pinckney may be taken as an example of how South Carolinians were up on the latest London tastes in books, and her papers give several examples of her reading habits, particularly regarding one of the most important and popular novels of the century, Samuel Richardson's *Pamela*. Early in her time in South Carolina, Pinckney writes that her father gave her his books, but we do not learn where he got them; "I have a little Library well furnished (for my papa has left me most of his books) in which I spend part of my time."[101] In addition to her reading of *Pamela*, Locke's *Essay on Human Understanding*, and Locke on education, we find that before she married Charles Pinckney, she borrowed his copies of Virgil, Plutarch, Malebranche, the *Life of Prince Eugene of Savoy*, and the poem "Docr. Parnels Hermit."[102] Later, while living in England, she writes that she has read Richard Glover's play *Boadicea* and Richardson's *The History of Sir Charles Grandison*.[103] Much later in life, in 1775, Elizabeth Chalmers Huger sent her Thomas Leland's novel *Longsword, Earl of Salisbury, an Historical Romance* and Charlotte Lennox's *The Female Quixote*.[104] Such gift exchanges of books were common in the British Atlantic, and in addition to the gifting itself, there was an "element of intellectual exchange involved in book swapping or lending" in America as in Britain.[105] Eliza's husband Charles had apparently amassed a large library, presumably used by Eliza, by the time of his death in 1758. His will provided for his law books to be given to his nephew Charles Pinckney, who was studying in England, and, in a line showing how books and slaves were comparable assets, to his son he bequeaths several "slaves with all their future Issue and increase" and "all the rest of my Library." He specifies that this library "shall be sold and the money arising thereby put out at Interest for his use till he is twenty years of age and then to be laid out in books for his use."[106] These books must have been acquired

---

[96] Raven, *London*, 152.   [97] Raven, *London*, 153.   [98] Raven, *London*, 155–6.
[99] Raven, *London*, 158–9.   [100] Raven, *London*, 156, 159.
[101] Pinckney, 7.   [102] Pinckney, 33, 35–6, 65, 66.   [103] Pinckney, 82.
[104] Schulz, <http://rotunda.upress.virginia.edu/PinckneyHorry/ELP0316>.
[105] Abigail Williams, *The Social Life of Books: Reading Together in the Eighteenth-Century Home* (New Haven: Yale UP, 2017), 124.
[106] Schulz, <http://rotunda.upress.virginia.edu/PinckneyHorry/ELP0199>.

by importing booksellers in Charleston, by order through the Lucas-Pinckneys' agents in London, or directly from London booksellers while they were living in England. The only direct order of reading material from her London agent, George Morley, that I have found is a 1761 letter from Pinckney, writing from her Belmont plantation, thanking Morley for magazines—a popular item in the colonies, the book reviews in which helped early American consumers know what books to purchase.[107]

Eliza Lucas Pinckney's plantation scene of reading contextualizes the evidence uncovered by Hayes, who uses Pinckney's letters to provide proof of what books were on a colonial woman's bookshelf and, on the basis of that, to ascertain what books were selling in early America. She was particularly interested in Samuel Richardson's *Pamela*, an epistolary novel popular on both sides of the Atlantic to the extent that Benjamin Franklin reprinted an American edition in 1742 (see Figure 4.2). *Pamela*, the story of the seduction of a maid in an English gentleman's household, combined a Protestant dissenter ethic of chastity with a material reward for that ethic in the form of the social mobility and wealth gained by a profitable marriage to a member of the gentry. In Richardson's gradual unveiling of the process of acquiring this mobility through the revelations in Pamela's letters, a private subject

Figure 4.2 Joseph Highmore. *Samuel Richardson* (1689–1761), 1750. © National Portrait Gallery, London.

---

[107] Pinckney, 171.

attempting to immunize itself from the rapaciousness of a wealthy public man (Mr. B, a landowner and local magistrate) emerges as the person of character who can redeem the moral failings of the public caste. Pamela's restrained possessive individualism, figured in her desire to control her property (her letters and her body) against confiscation by the public man, is constituted as a counterpoint to the excessive possessive individualism of the gentry, depicted in Mr. B's desires, whether we consider them sexual or economic. At the same time, Pamela is modeling a different way of going about unlimited accumulation: engaging in the polite forms of seduction—manifest as much in her epistolary manner as in her bodily resistance to Mr. B—necessary to become mistress of a public man's estate. She is, in essence, shown to be a more enlightened and refined acquisitor, a person of taste—a reader and writer produced by the Enlightenment book market. She knows how to use her moral capital to represent herself properly both in her writing and in her behavior to gain social, cultural, and material capital. The letters of Pinckney and other Americans, I contend, indicate that Pamela was read as a possessive individualist by some colonial readers, though not always favorably.

The responses of Pinckney and other readers of *Pamela* in other colonies like Connecticut's John Trumbull show both admiration and critique of various aspects of Pamela's possessive individualism. Pinckney positions herself as an admirer of Pamela's moral virtue, but as a critic of her manner of self-representation: "I must think her very defective and even blush for her while she allows her self that disgusting liberty of praising her self, or what is very like it, repeating all the fine speeches made to her by others when a person distinguishd for modesty in every other respect should have chose rather to conceal them or at least to let them come from some other hand."[108] Pamela, to Pinckney, in an ill-mannered act of self-branding, is commodifying herself as a virtuous brand of female character by reporting outside, extrinsic opinions of her moral capital, rather than more modestly assessing her intrinsic value. This act of mirroring is also satirized by Trumbull, who comments upon how the archetypical American female " 'Believes herself a young Pamela |. . . Before her glass, with smiling grace | She views the wonders of her face; | There stands in admiration moveless | And hopes a Grandison, or Lovelace.' "[109] Both Pinckney and Trumbull are evincing a consciousness of how novels were creating models of subjectivity and behavior.[110] Yet both were also skeptical of this phenomenon as a vulgar and uncritical reception of fictional persons, who tend to be more idealized types rather than more fully rounded and complex individuals. In that sense, Pinckney and Trumbull might be regarded as upper-class critics of Pamela's social mobility.

Yet Eliza Lucas Pinckney finds error with the author, Richardson, for Pamela's self-regard, and recommends a solution. She writes that Richardson should have shown Pamela growing out of her youthful naive mirroring through others by

---

[108] Schulz, <http://rotunda.upress.virginia.edu/PinckneyHorry/elp-details.xqy?letter=/Pinckney Horry/ELP0121.xml&qs=I%20must%20think%20her%20very%20defective>.
[109] Kevin Hayes, *A Colonial Woman's Bookshelf* (Knoxville: U Tennessee P, 1996), 114.
[110] Lynch, 126.

showing other correspondents articulating her merits rather than herself repeating them in her own letters. In short, after her marriage she should have become more fully rounded rather than static, "'after she had the advantage of Mr. B's conversation and others of sence and distinction.'"[111] Pinckney articulates both taste and social caste as being crucial for producing critical self-awareness and a more refined self-possession. Distinction—the judgment of taste—is here constituted by Pinckney as a very English ability to engage in polite literary criticism, though she, in a self-deprecating way characteristic of what she thinks Pamela should perform, says that "'I have nither capacity or inclination for Chritisism.'"[112]

Nonetheless, Pinckney does indeed exercise criticism and internalizes it in her own writing; Pinckney, who "remains an enigma partly because of her reluctance to write letters," may have been influenced by Pamela's anxiety about her letters.[113] Pinckney's surviving letterbook, however, suggests that she was concerned for practicing politeness in written expression and reflects that "the most careful portrait of Mrs. Pinckney was, of course, drawn by herself" in her careful communications.[114] As Hayes has written, she was acutely conscious of how a young woman should present herself in writing, as she was clearly a critic of Pamela's epistolary style for what it said about her.[115] At the same time, she was conscious of the proper propriety of reading and responding to writing, which she commends in Pamela's reading of Locke: "Pamela's reading . . . set a standard of behavior which allowed eighteenth-century women to discuss their own reading more freely, without censure," writes Kevin Hayes, and Pinckney adopted this aspect of Pamela's behavior.[116] In this sense, Pinckney is an example of how the individuals modeled in novels, much like Robinson Crusoe in Chapter 3, become subjects of fascination and empathy for readers.[117] While some aspects of Pamela's individualism were repugnant to Pinckney, it is clear that she, to some extent, modeled her writing and behavior on both the positive aspects of Pamela's style and the caution that her flaws generated. Pinckney, therefore, might be regarded, in part, as the product of *Pamela*, with the title character's social circulation holding clues to how the unmarried Eliza Lucas might herself circulate.

The upper-class readings of Pamela by Pinckney and Trumbull—their derisive view of her self-regard and the way that young American women were mirroring their behavior and expectations on Richardson's heroine—are in many ways a class suspicion of the social mobility promised in Pamela's marriage to Mr. B. Particularly for the mistress of a slave estate like Pinckney, the prospect of a servant or slave rising to marry the master of a plantation would be distressing. While Pinckney acknowledges that a servant girl could improve her manners and self-representation through exposure to a man of a superior class like Mr. B, there is nonetheless an

---

[111] Schulz, <http://rotunda.upress.virginia.edu/PinckneyHorry/elp-details.xqy?letter=/Pinckney Horry/ELP0121.xml&qs=I%20must%20think%20her%20very%20defective>.

[112] Schulz, <http://rotunda.upress.virginia.edu/PinckneyHorry/elp-details.xqy?letter=/Pinckney Horry/ELP0121.xml&qs=I%20must%20think%20her%20very%20defective>.

[113] Pinckney, xvi.   [114] Pinckney, xi, xxvi.   [115] Hayes, 105.   [116] Hayes, 107.

[117] J. Paul Hunter, *Before Novels: The Cultural Contexts of Eighteenth-Century Fiction* (NY: Norton, 1992), 41–2.

elitist tone in Pinckney's condemnation of Pamela's "disgusting liberty of praising herself" that can be read as a mistress worried that a servant might think herself too important. It is as if American readers like Pinckney regarded themselves as something other than people engaged in advantageous marriages and enterprises like slavery that were providing them with the means of acquiring the trappings of fashionable British ladies and gentlemen.

In short, we should be mindful that Pamela's letters are a possession—literally a book—that Americans were regarding as a consumer commodity upon which to exercise an abstract commodity, education (often also acquired from abroad in England, like that of some of the Pinckney family), through polite criticism. Just as Mr. B craves interception and ownership of Pamela's letters in order to impose the authenticity of his counter-narrative upon them and his control over her, sophisticated American readers stood in judgment of the servant girl whose materialist cravings, masked by her conduct, are rewarded. Pinckney and Mr. B are both masters of manor houses, the first of an American plantation owner, and the second of a fictional English estate. That both seek to be master of letters, each in her or his own way, links reading and criticism to the mastery of people, a reality particularly rarified on Pinckney's slave plantation—an economic engine for the acquisition and consumption of British books. Slavery, as Gikandi has written, was fueling the culture of taste in which people like Pinckney and the fictional Mr. B were participating, and the novel was one medium and genre through which the arts spread the ideology legitimizing that economic base. Nonetheless, Pinckney's reading is an example of how South Carolinians were very much engaged with the problems posed by the literature that they were reading. They did indeed exercise the faculty of literary criticism, not only assessing novels, but also how novels related to real human behavior. They were, in part, modeling their propriety and distinction on the characters they were reading about.

The personal collections of Pinckney and other Carolinians were no doubt financed by slavery, though institutional libraries, in some cases, were funded from other sources. Bray, as he had in other colonies, had established a Society for the Propagation of the Gospel library in South Carolina in the early eighteenth century containing "83 nonreligious works among the 225 titles."[118] These included "42 histories, voyages, and travels, followed by 15 works of physiology, anatomy, surgery, and medicine, 6 mathematics, 6 grammars, and 2 volumes of poetry."[119] A statehouse library was established when that building opened in 1756. It contained works such as Camden's *Britannia*, the *Journals* of the House of Commons, Trott's South Carolina *Laws*, and six volumes of the *Statutes at Large*. But when the state house moved to Columbia, the Library Society "provided the only such collected resource" of law books remaining in Charleston.[120] The collection of the College of Charleston, of course, would come to supplement the Library Society's holdings in town, as did the Literary and Philosophical Society, founded in 1813.[121]

---

[118] Raven, *London*, 153.   [119] Raven, *London*, 153.   [120] Raven, *London*, 158.
[121] Raven, *London*, 86, 45, 77, 65.

Circulation ledgers for the Library Society may tell us something about borrowing patterns, though they only survive for the period 1811–17. Nonetheless, the evidence of the borrowing of popular eighteenth-century titles from these records, ranging from Samuel Richardson's novels to Henry Brooke's *The Fool of Quality* and to works by women novelists like Frances Burney, suggests durable interest in them at the library throughout the late eighteenth century. These titles were still read in the early nineteenth century, though the most popular novels to borrow in the period covered by the ledgers "were gothic novels and historical romances, the majority of which were written by British women novelists."[122] Irish authors like Charles Maturin and Maria Edgeworth seemed to have "lasting popularity," if these records can be trusted.[123] Though periodicals were the most popular type of book to borrow, novels and history books were the second most frequently borrowed. Indeed, novels would get their own column in the ledgers in 1816.[124]

As Isabelle Lehuu has explained, the library stocked 4,500 volumes by 1808, and 8,000 volumes by 1813, with active users rising to 283 by 1818.[125] These included sixty-four planters, eighty-six merchants, eighty-three professionals (including thirty-seven lawyers), and ten widows, indicating that as with the New York Society Library, membership revolved around the profits generated by Atlantic trade. There were 41,973 library transactions between July 24, 1811 and February 28, 1817, consisting of 3,033 titles of books and periodicals.[126] Given this number of transactions, it is difficult to come up with a comprehensive listing of all who borrowed a given book, or what other books a proprietor was checking out over a period. Accordingly, anecdote has been Lehuu's preferred method of explaining the frequency of the circulation of a single title, or the borrowing patterns of a handful of individuals, and it will be mine in focusing on one transaction involving *Chrysal*.

The ledgers reveal that on May 8, 1812, William Boyd borrowed *Chrysal* which, though not listed in the 1806 catalog of the library, was entered as "Adventures of a Guinea" in an octavo four-volume format in the 1811 catalog. In a pattern that indicates sequential reading of volumes of the novel, "1," "2," and "3" are methodically crossed out. As in entries from other libraries where paper was expensive and economy in writing was at a premium, this one entry apparently was used to account for those three volumes being checked out over the course of several dates, and it is probable that Boyd read at least the first two volumes.[127]

There are several Charleston newspaper articles mentioning a William Boyd that indicate that he fits the profile of a Library Society member, which makes his biography significant to the reading of the novel. The *City Gazette* of February 15, 1810 lists him under "Ship News" as the owner of the schooners *President* and *George*, both of which had cleared the Port of Charleston and were headed to the port of Amelia in Florida.[128] Other articles indicate that he was civically active on

---

[122] Lehuu, 74.   [123] Lehuu, 78.   [124] Lehuu, 68–9, 72.
[125] Lehuu, 67.   [126] Lehuu, 65.
[127] Circulation Records, Charleston Library Society Records, MS 29, Charleston, South Carolina.
[128] This citation and all following citations of early American newspapers come from the *America's Historical Newspapers* database and will be cited in-text by date unless a footnote is provided.

the model of a member, being elected to the Board of Directors of Union Bank, the board of the South Carolina Insurance Company, and a commissioner of a lottery to build a bridge.[129] Accordingly, we can be reasonably sure that this man was the borrower of *Chrysal*.

The case that he, as a shipowner, was involved in the trade in slaves and/or slave-produced commodities is enhanced when we consider the destination of his vessels. Amelia is an island on Florida's Atlantic coast that has a large and sheltered harbor. It had changed hands several times before this period, notably in 1783, when Britain ceded the island to Spain, resulting in a massive exodus of English settlers (who were mainly loyalists). It had become a foreign, Spanish-controlled haven of illegal commerce and smuggling during the embargo signed into law by President Jefferson on December 22, 1807 to sanction Britain and France for raiding US commerce during the Napoleonic Wars. The embargo was ultimately revoked on March 1, 1809.[130]

Given that newspaper articles about Boyd's ships date from after 1809, it is probable that he was using Amelia not to avoid Jefferson's embargo, but to circumvent the Act Prohibiting Importation of Slaves of 1807, which took effect in 1808. Despite the ban, many slaves were illegally imported after 1808, largely through Spanish Florida ports like Amelia. Given this history, it is highly likely that Boyd was plying the relatively short route between Charleston and Amelia in such a trade, or if not, he was using Amelia to deal in other goods that were the proceeds of slave labor. Slavery was the key to Charleston prosperity, so it is not surprising that it was at the root of Boyd's wealth and his civic engagement.[131]

Consequently, it should not come as a surprise that a novel like *Chrysal*, with its transactional life of the narrator and its documentation of transatlantic, even global, travels, would have appealed to Boyd. Its themes of secrecy, diplomacy, and duplicity would also likely have characterized Boyd's dealings on Amelia, and it is clear that he was reading it enough to go through two or three of its four volumes. He may have been collecting slaves and currency through these illicit transactions, but it is clear that many people and coins, much like Chrysal, passed through his hands on their way to other owners, indicating that he was as much an experience of theirs—an exposure to his tyranny—as they were of his proprietorship.

Carolina reading, and that of Library Society members in particular, therefore provides us clues to how the sociology of the texts mentioned here were helping to create both cultural and social capital for their readers in the context of a slavery economy. Where *Pamela* helped readers like Pinckney imagine how to make themselves people of propriety on the English model—a phenomenon of reception not without its implications for creating barriers between the planter class and the slaves—*Chrysal* in fact modeled that economic relationship in a novel that takes economics as its central theme. The Carolina monetary system's status as one that

---

[129] *City Gazette* 4/4/1810; *Carolina Gazette* 7/6/1810; *City Gazette* 10/31/1810.

[130] Rob Hicks, *Amelia Island* (Charleston: Arcadia Publishing, 2014), ix.

[131] W. E. Burghardt Du Bois, *The Suppression of the African Slave-Trade to the United States of America, 1638–1870* (NY: Longmans, 1904), 94–117.

historically had placed slaves as the assets behind circulating paper currency thereby makes it a highly appropriate one for understanding how paper texts like *Chrysal* themselves circulated on the basis of African slaves and the wealth that their labor created. Slaves may have served as objects of ownership, and therefore as status for whites, but that they circulated from owner to owner in the creation of such cultural capital and distinction also made them the producers, and therefore the just owners of, not just the assets behind, abstract Carolina culture.

IV

Examining how the standing of the slave disrupted the eighteenth century's distinction between "thing" and "person" through the reading of an it-narrative like *Chrysal* and other imported cultural capital in the Library Society helps explain how elite white Carolinians were constructing their standing as "humans" against slaves and others they regarded as "things." Books, and the literacy that enabled their use, helped create their class—or more accurately, caste—distinction from non-members of the library. Their "hold over the low country's social order rested as much on their economic strength as it did on their ability to project power through their public performance of refinement and gentility," and the library was the central space for the assertion of this power.[132] Even the money that they created for themselves was based on the intrinsic value of property in slaves, and that property was at the root of their participation in civic life in the colonial and Early Republic periods. The eighteenth-century British political thought on republicanism, as the Carolina case makes clear, might therefore be understood as appropriated in America to establish property in slavery as the basis of the Republic and for citizenship. Political theory as an aspect of American cultural history therefore can claim slavery as one of its points of origin, whether we regard it as the source of the capital to create books and reading, or as the very issue, as Chapter 1 made clear, motivating political thinking about rights and liberties.

Consequently, the distinction between "books" and "people" was not as strong for Charlestonians as the distinction between "slave" and "the human": "If the commodity proclaims the autonomy of things from persons, tales told by things remind us of the intimate connections between the two . . . the boundaries between persons and things become increasingly precarious" in them.[133] Personified books, as much as personified coins, circulated in the Atlantic, and as I have been arguing, helped model identities for their readers. These were highly reified metropolitan identities in America at that, as in both Britain and America blackness represented the opposite of civilization and taste.[134] The Charleston Library Society, despite its need for these tokens of sophistication, was as much a "Jail for books" as South Carolina was a prison for the majority of its population.

The concept of the book as such a prisoner or slave was anticipated in *Chrysal*. One of its characters, an author and Ph.D., is regarded as a debt-slave for paper supplied

---

[132] Pearson, 300.   [133] Festa, 114, 123.   [134] Gikandi, 5–6.

by the booksellers for whom he is working, Mr. *Vellum* and Mr. *Pamphlet*.[135] Though he is not an African chattel slave, he is, as in the case of the slave-backed paper currency, fetishized as the "real" asset behind that paper and the writing he is producing that will pay his debt. As I shall argue, constructing the author as that asset behind the book is a strategy that Olaudah Equiano, the subject of Chapter 5, appropriated in the promotion of his abolitionist book. The slave author, accordingly, brought value back to his paper—transubstantiated it—and the result was a transatlantic bestseller, the *Interesting Narrative*. Abolitionist literature therefore begins to take the central space in the constitution of an Anglo-American cultural history that embraced greater and greater personal and political freedoms. The slave narrative stood as the premier genre documenting the triumph of the human and the justness of a society in which the former slave has liberties. The slave narrative is a genre, accordingly, that proclaims the success of the experiments in civic engagement during the Revolution that had made abolition thinkable, even as the conditions of geographical spaces like South Carolina made it unconscionable there.

---

[135] Johnstone, 108–12.

5

"See Benezet's Account of Africa Throughout"
The Genres of Equiano's *Interesting Narrative* and
the Library Company of Philadelphia

> Thus all Art is propaganda and ever must be, despite the wailing of the purists.
> I stand in utter shamelessness and say that whatever art I have for writing has
> been used always for propaganda for gaining the right of black folk to love
> and enjoy. I do not care a damn for any art that is not used for propaganda.
> But I do care when propaganda is confined to one side while the other is
> stripped and silent.
>
> W. E. B. Dubois, "Criteria for Negro Art"

The Library Company of Philadelphia is exceptional among the early American libraries in that its earliest proprietors not only consisted of individuals involved in slavery and related enterprises, but also included abolitionists like Anthony Benezet from its earliest days. It is also exceptional in that the Junto, the quasi-masonic club that founded the library in 1731, explicitly intended it to be a civic institution for the improvement of trade as well as of knowledge; its members were frank in establishing the library as a social network of businessmen as much as a place for books and learning. This dual role is borne out by evidence that shareholders were engaged in extensive business dealings with each other, particularly in the West Indies trade in slaves and their products, and by the fact that the library, by absorbing other institutions over the course of the century, was inexorably becoming the center of reading for the city.

The fact that Philadelphia was the most abolitionist of any Atlantic city is owing in no small part to Quakerism, as well as to the Company's members and books, despite the fact that the library was created by slave capitalism. The civic engagement of this library's proprietors—more so than those of the other libraries discussed in this book—was not only oriented towards the Revolution, but also towards abolition as an expression of the city's Enlightened cosmopolitanism. The city was so prominent in the anti-slavery movement that Benezet's writings influenced those of British abolitionists, including Olaudah Equiano, whose *Interesting Narrative* of his life as a slave and free man was among the most popular American reprints of British books in the 1790s. Equiano was so dependent on Benezet's texts, themselves the product of the latter's reading at the library, that he would footnote Benezet early in the *Narrative*, writing, "See Benezet's account of Africa throughout" the book.[1] British writing, itself the impetus for Benezet's, in turn informed American writing on equality, to the extent, as Maurice Jackson and J. R. Oldfield have established, that there was clearly two-way traffic between Pennsylvania and British anti-slavery writers.[2] This traffic in writing was, necessarily, also an exchange of reading, and the Library Company soon came to stock an array of books on abolition, as well as on commercial exchange with areas dominated by the slave trade and plantations. In short, its shelves held almost every title one would need to write a comprehensive account of the Atlantic economic system and its injustices, making it a unique archive of the role of abolition in the cultural history not only of the United States, but of the broader Atlantic region.

The Company's provisioning of books, accordingly, was requisite to the creation of abolition as an Atlantic-wide print media event that took place over several decades, as readers were experiencing the movement largely through the virtualizing medium of writing. For example, Benezet, particularly in works like *Some Historical Account of Guinea* that created a sympathetic portrait of West African civilization for abolitionist purposes, was making use of travel narratives the library stocked because he had never been to Africa himself. His use of that research is significant because the British Equiano, who, we have learned from Vincent Carretta, may not have been born in Africa, was footnoting the American Benezet to explain the virtues of his innocent childhood village.[3] If we take Equiano's book as the most significant slave narrative to ever have been written up until that point in history, Benezet's influence is paramount in our understanding of the problem of whether the *Narrative* is non-fiction, creative work, or some blend of both. That is to say, Equiano may have been experiencing Africa textually, rather than physically, at three removes: (1) Africa as an actual geographical place; (2) Africa as discussed by the travel writers Benezet was citing; and (3) Africa as discussed by Benezet. Equiano's account, even though it may have been influenced by his possible serving as a crew member on a slaving trip to Africa and his involvement in the settling of Sierra Leone by free blacks, is something that he himself acknowledged to be a fourth layer superimposed upon an original explained by European travelers and Benezet himself.[4] Indeed, he was enough of an admirer of Benezet that he travelled to Philadelphia in 1785 and visited an African free-school that Benezet had helped found.[5]

Equiano's *Narrative*, in this view, may have been so successful in sales and in furthering the abolitionist cause because it showed his skill in working with texts that he had read about Africa and the Atlantic system (see Figure 5.1). Compressed into its dominant genre of the slave narrative are several other genres that would have been available to him via the Atlantic book market and institutions of reading

---

[1] Olaudah Equiano, *The Interesting Narrative and Other Writings*. Ed. Vincent Carretta (New York: Penguin, 1995), 39 n. 62.
[2] Maurice Jackson, *Let this Voice be Heard: Anthony Benezet, Father of Atlantic Abolitionism* (Philadelphia: U Pennsylvania P, 2009); J. R. Oldfield, *Transatlantic Abolitionism in the Age of Revolution: An International History of Anti-slavery, c.1787–1820* (Cambridge: Cambridge UP, 2013).
[3] Vincent Carretta, *Equiano the African* (Athens: U Georgia P, 2005), xiv–xv.
[4] Carretta, *Equiano*, 30–1, 34, 223–9.   [5] Carretta, *Equiano*, 224.

Figure 5.1 Frontispiece of *Interesting Narrative* (1789), by Olaudah Equiano (1749–97). Stipple Engraving by Daniel Orme, after W. Denton. © National Portrait Gallery, London.

like the Library Company. In a virtual sense, the types of writing circulating in that market constituted a matrix of characters and storylines that he had to negotiate in claiming his space in that matrix as a modern subject, with authorship being the sign of mastery of that virtual world. The ethnic author, in this instance, might be seen not only as one claiming self-possession by taking hold of the narrative of his subjectivity, or as one who "overcomes dispossession by becoming a possessive individual."[6] He also may be seen as one whose self-fashioning through autobiography is achieved by being a very sophisticated reader of the texts composing that matrix—a reader/writer to whom that textual system was visible and highly reified due to his subjected status. As Lynn Festa has written, "autobiography describes and enacts the slave's move from the status of chattel to that of person through his written mastery over the self."[7] The *Narrative*, accordingly, could be described as a special kind of intervention into the Atlantic book market that helped put that matrix into place, reflecting the author's mastery of the market and liberated self through that mastery. Equiano "sought to master and appropriate the culture of

[6] Ramesh Mallipeddi, *Spectacular Suffering: Witnessing Slavery in the Eighteenth-Century British Atlantic* (Charlottesville: U Virginia P, 2016), 183.
[7] Lynn Festa, *Sentimental Figures of Empire in Eighteenth-Century Britain and France* (Baltimore: Johns Hopkins UP, 2006), 143.

taste itself," not only creating a place for himself in the literary world by doing so, but also altering that matrix of tastefulness in a way that made room for abolitionism as a tasteful attitude.[8]

This chapter will explain how the Philadelphia book market could both make available the texts that made their way to Equiano through Benezet and be considered a promising enough venue for a Philadelphia bookseller to have the confidence to buy 100 copies of the *Narrative* with the view of selling them to Philadelphians. First, it will close-read the *Narrative* for its formal problem of genre, discussing the types of writing that are employed in it that compose Equiano's self-fashioning to readers accustomed to those genres' conventions. Next, it will discuss the history of the Library Company by reference to what we know of Philadelphia printing and bookselling in the period. Third, it will interpret archival evidence of Company shareholders' involvement in slavery and related enterprises, and their business dealings with each other, in order to establish the fact that the library was a slavery-produced institution. Fourth, it will explore the history of Philadelphia Quaker abolitionism and anti-slavery writing, citing what we know of Philadelphia reading, the composition of Benezet's texts, and the Library Company's book collection to illustrate the dominant genres in which abolitionists were working, a task that also features the first-ever reading of the Company's borrowing records.

This chapter will use these observations to conclude that though there is no evidence that the Company's copy of *The Interesting Narrative* was borrowed in the late eighteenth or early nineteenth century, the potential sales of the New York reprint of it in this most abolitionist of American cities indicate a readership with an appetite for it. This appetite was being shaped by the availability of other abolitionist writing in the library as well as multiple other genres and titles that were shaping readers' tastes and horizons of expectations for those genres. Yet the library was also creating "Equiano" through Benezet's reading there, indicating that the freed British slave was as much a Philadelphia creation as a British one, a fact that only further enhances our appreciation of the two-way traffic in Philadelphia and British abolitionism.

I

A central research problem in the study of *The Interesting Narrative* is the question of genre in what seems to be mostly an autobiography or memoir. As Carretta remarked in his edition of this work, "Spiritual autobiography, captivity narrative, travel book, adventure tale, narrative of slavery, economic treatise, and apologia, among other things, Equiano's *Narrative* was generally well received."[9] Some of this tentativeness on deciding on the genre may be due to how Equiano "reclaims his voice by masking and disguising it" within those issuing from genres more

---

[8] Simon Gikandi, *Slavery and the Culture of Taste* (Princeton: Princeton UP, 2011), xv.
[9] Equiano, xxv.

authorized than the slave narrative in order to make his story more appealing to a white audience.[10] At its most basic level, however, the problem of genre is one of reading habits and tastes—both Equiano's and those of his audiences; he may have been situating himself "at the culmination of a national culture, reworking a range of English literary figures, including Milton, Bunyan, Defoe, and Cowper."[11] Indeed, Equiano's *Narrative* probably bears the strongest relation to Defoe's *Crusoe*, which has long been "the acknowledged generic precursor" of it.[12] The narrative of the life of a former slave, accordingly, was being made more appealing by a storytelling technique that was making use of the formal strategies and content of genres that had come before and around it. Equiano "imagined the act of reading as the key to understanding 'how all things had a beginning'" to the extent that he was surprised that a book did not speak back to him when he was initially exposed to one as a pre-literate person.[13] His writing, accordingly, drew on his reading of such genres as he self-fashioned his identity in his autobiography.

At stake in these narrative choices, said also to be life choices and experiences, is a "Britishness" of authorial identity of a particularly Protestant and capitalist kind. Indeed, in places the *Narrative* reads like Equiano is inserting his authorial identity into all the categories necessary to qualify himself as a "whitened" British subject. As Festa writes, he is attempting to be "a particular model of the human: the proprietary possessive individual, the representative African, the mimic Englishman, the convertible religious self, the juridical subject, the reflexive narrator."[14] He explains his conversion to Protestantism, his commercial development from small-time trader between West Indian islands to one who works on a slave ship, his combat service in the British navy, and his hewing to other components of the patriotic Briton. His goal is to come across as a "manumitted black British entrepreneur"—to be "both capitalist agent of his own liberation . . . and racial victim of swindling trade"—exactly the kind of individual reader who had the power to either eschew or participate in the Atlantic slave economy.[15] Equiano traded slaves to achieve his own emancipation in a manner consistent with the appearance of the Protestant capitalists he was trying to persuade to be abolitionists; "the commercial ideology of Equiano's African ventures resembles the earlier form that we have already encountered, that of Defoe's progressive Protestant mercantilism."[16] Participating in what Philip Gould has called the "commercial jeremiad" of anti-slavery advocates, "the *Interesting Narrative* juxtaposes the virtue of Equiano's commercial identity with the barbarity of the African slave trade" in order to preserve the idea of a Christian, moral commerce that could be contrasted with an immoral, unchristian commerce in slaves.[17] In order to persuade those who held economic power to end

[10] Wilfred D. Samuels, "Disguised Voice in *The Interesting Narrative of Olaudah Equiano, or Gustavus Vassa, the African*." *Black American Literature Forum* 19.2 (Summer 1985): 69.

[11] Srinivas Aravamudan, *Tropicopolitans: Colonialism and Agency, 1688–1804* (Durham: Duke UP, 1999), 235.

[12] Mallipeddi, 180.   [13] Gikandi, 86.   [14] Festa, 134.

[15] Aravamudan, 237; Philip Gould, *Barbaric Traffic: Commerce and Anti-slavery in the Eighteenth-Century Atlantic World* (Cambridge: Harvard UP, 2003), 136.

[16] Gould, 134, 137; Aravamudan, 237.   [17] Gould, 133, 15.

slavery, he had to appeal to the "sentimentalization of commercial exchange" that was transforming the morality of the market as the Protestant ethic and spirit of capitalism turned more towards secular Enlightenment.[18] The challenge for abolitionists like Equiano was to harness this sentimental construction of capitalism—a construction matched by the sentimentality movement in contemporary philosophy and literature—to publicize their cause, and that challenge was largely one of the choices of genres in the publishing marketplace.

The publishing history of Equiano's book helps explain its appeal and how this publicity was achieved. It was first published in London in 1789 in two volumes "in the small duodecimo format, like a typical memoir or novel"; its format size, in other words, may have been a hint as to the desired market niche for it as potentially one of those genres.[19] A second edition emerged that year, and a third in 1790. In 1791 a Dublin edition was published, and in 1792 a fifth edition came out in Edinburgh. There were two more London editions in 1793, an eighth edition in Norwich in 1794, and a ninth edition in London in 1794. It was also translated into Dutch, German, and Russian in those years.[20] It was published by subscription, meaning that Equiano had a number of prominent people agree to pay for a copy up front, and he retained copyright to all editions published in his lifetime rather than selling his copyright to a bookseller. There was only one edition published in America before 1837, the 1791 New York edition by the bookseller William Durell, who, as one who was not noted to publish abolitionist literature, likely did so for profit.[21]

This New York edition is notable in that it was "the only new English literary work reprinted in America in 1791," indeed in the entire 1789–91 period.[22] Like its British and Irish counterparts, it too was published by subscription, but its subscription list "was different in that American subscribers were primarily artisans, not aristocrats."[23] The only notable names on the list were two abolitionist Quaker merchants, Melancton Smith and John Murray, a fact that is significant because "most New York merchants were slave owners during the period" and because Smith and Murray were board members of the New York Manumission Society and New York African Free-Schools.[24] According to Akiyo Ito, the *New York Directory, and Register, for the Year 1790* reveals "that many of the New York subscribers were...bakers, grocers, cartmen, cabinet makers, carpenters, tailors, watchmakers, blacksmiths, shoemakers, tanners, masons, hatters, perfumers, and so on."[25] That many of these artisans owned slaves and feared competition from the cheap labor of freed slaves makes one wonder about their commitment to the abolitionist

---

[18] Gould, 25.

[19] James Green, "The Publishing History of Olaudah Equiano's Interesting Narrative." *Slavery and Abolition* 16.3 (1995): 363.

[20] Green, "Publishing," 363.   [21] Green, "Publishing," 369.

[22] Green, "Publishing," 368.

[23] Akiyo Ito, "Olaudah Equiano and the New York Artisans: The First American Edition of *The Interesting Life of Olaudah Equiano, or Gustavus Vassa, the African.*" *Early American Literature* 32.1 (1997): 83.

[24] Ito, 86.   [25] Ito, 88–9.

theme of the work.[26] Ito, however, explains this by saying that "The book may have attracted the artisan reader, then, for its information and not for its anti-slavery message, but there is another possibility. It may have appealed to his sense of pride in what he believed an egalitarian society."[27] Perhaps one could like the work's emphasis on self-improvement through artisan-like entrepreneurship without fully embracing the anti-slavery cause.

The question of the book's genre, again, might also have been why it appealed to a mostly artisan audience. In New York in 1789, types of books being sold ranged from schoolbooks, to books of travel, to histories, to many more. As Ito argues, "Placing the *Narrative* among these books, then, we might consider it in the genre of geography book or instruction. It informs the reader about various places— Africa, West Indies, America, Europe—and about traveling. It teaches the reader about sailing and even about survival."[28] These practical elements of the book, more than its abolitionist message, perhaps, might also be one explanation as to why artisans were the majority of the book's purchasers.

This New York edition, however, is significant to Philadelphia reading because the largest single consignment of the book was purchased by the Philadelphia bookseller Thomas Dobson, who is listed in the subscribers' list for 100 copies, almost 30 percent of the entire number of copies on that list.[29] It is strange that the American edition was published in New York instead of Philadelphia: "Philadelphia was the most likely market for the book; indeed since virtually every other American anti-slavery imprint up to that date had come from the Philadelphia presses, one could even wonder why Equiano's narrative was not published there instead of New York."[30] It is possible that Philadelphia abolitionists did not want to pirate the work of a former slave who was profiting from the sales of the *Narrative*, as "Durell did not even choose one of the Quaker booksellers to take this role, but rather the bookseller with the largest retail shop."[31] As in New York, in Philadelphia there were few noted abolitionists who subscribed: "Of the 31 delegates to the 1794 convention of state abolition societies, only one was a subscriber, Rev. William Rogers, Professor of English in the College of Philadelphia."[32] All the same, the fact that Dobson could project that he could sell 100 copies indicates a Philadelphia audience for this book that was drawn to its abolitionist sentiment—an audience in a city where the Library Company was the most central space of reading.

As I have been arguing, if *The Interesting Narrative* is a pastiche of genres and canonical authorial voices, it is because it is crafted in a way to appeal to particular kinds of readers who were being marketed particular kinds of texts, including sentimental ones that celebrated commerce as virtuous exchange between free individuals. The *Narrative*'s genre problem, in short, is the result of the categories of the transatlantic book market—categories or genres that early American libraries were purchasing and disseminating. The Library Company was no different, and

---

[26] Ito, 91, 88–9.   [27] Ito, 91.   [28] Ito, 90.
[29] Green, "Publishing," 370.   [30] Green, "Publishing," 370.
[31] Green, "Publishing," 370.   [32] Green, "Publishing," 369.

the evidence of its collection and borrowing from it, taken together with what else we know of Philadelphia reading, provides a case study of how a genre-defying book like Equiano's could synthesize both contemporary abolitionist writing and other categories of print. The history of the Company and its relationship to slavery and abolition, accordingly, may help explain how Dobson could anticipate selling 100 copies of *The Interesting Narrative* while also documenting the reading habits of Philadelphians and of the particular connoisseurs who counted the library as their principal source of taste and status.

I I

The history of the Library Company bears witness to how it not only was the center of reading for colonial Philadelphia, but also the cultural center of the mainland colonies during the colonial period and early Republic. As James Green has established, by the middle and late eighteenth century Philadelphia was a major destination for imported books from London and across Europe, and had a thriving printing and reprinting industry led by such individuals as Benjamin Franklin, David Hall, Robert Bell, and Zachariah Poulson, a printer who also served as the Company's librarian for many years.[33] The city was home to America's second newspaper, and soon had numerous papers and presses serving the area as well as neighboring colonies. Philadelphia had, by 1770, displaced Boston as "the center of book production and distribution" in the colonies, and many printers also worked as booksellers, with imports dominating the Philadelphia book trade by mid-century.[34] Members of the book trade were more likely than not to be members of the Library Company, to the extent that "Philadelphia printers borrowed the English imports and used and abused them to such an extent that a by-law was passed in 1805 declaring that printers would be sued if they took the Library Company's books apart in the course of reprinting the work."[35] There were numerous institutional libraries such as those of churches and large personal libraries among the wealthy, some of which the Company eventually acquired and added to their catalogs, and

[33] James Green, "English Books and Printing in the Age of Franklin." *A History of the Book in America, Volume 1: The Colonial Book in the Atlantic World.* Eds Hugh Amory and David Hall (Chapel Hill: U North Carolina P, 2007), 248–54, 256–60, 271–2, 283–91, 295–6.

[34] David Hall, "The Atlantic Economy in the Eighteenth Century." *A History of the Book in America, Volume 1: The Colonial Book in the Atlantic World.* Eds Hugh Amory and David Hall (Chapel Hill: U North Carolina P, 2007), 155, 156; James Green, "The Book Trade in the Middle Colonies, 1680–1720." *A History of the Book in America, Volume 1: The Colonial Book in the Atlantic World.* Eds Hugh Amory and David Hall (Chapel Hill: U North Carolina P, 2007), 205; Edwin Wolf III, *The Book Culture of a Colonial American City: Philadelphia Books, Bookmen, and Booksellers* (Oxford: Clarendon P, 1988), 37–8, 38–29, 44–5, 39–40, 44, 45–6, 41–3, 54–7; James Raven, "The Importation of Books in the Eighteenth Century." *A History of the Book in America, Volume 1: The Colonial Book in the Atlantic World.* Eds Hugh Amory and David Hall (Chapel Hill: U North Carolina P, 2007), 188; Wolf, 63, 189, 193, 166, 179–80, 185.

[35] Library Company of Philadelphia, *"At the Instance of Benjamin Franklin": A Brief History of the Library Company of Philadelphia* (Philadelphia: Library Company of Philadelphia, 1995), 40.

the city also hosted several other library companies that would eventually be folded into the Company.[36]

In short, almost all Philadelphia reading eventually led back to the Company, establishing it not only as the central space of reading in the city, but also as a powerful social network of the literate and, usually, wealthy population. That this network counted many people connected in some way to slavery provides insight into the economic basis of the library in the hand-press era, as well as the movement away from slavery, evidenced as much by the anti-slavery activities of some members as by the abolitionist titles the library was acquiring. As a civic institution, accordingly, it straddled the worlds of enslavers and those who would end slavery, making it a unique forum among early American libraries for civic engagement not only around economic and political interests, but also for the contemplation and promotion of human rights.

Green has argued that the establishment of the Company stemmed from the fact that many of its founders were tradesmen, and "tradesmen members could neither have afforded such books nor obtained the credit to import them" without pooling their money.[37] But their professions and success cast doubt on this claim. The Library Company, like many of the early American proprietary subscription libraries founded in later years, entered its regional book culture through an intellectual club, the Junto, which was organized by Franklin and which founded the library. The Junto was founded as a masonic organization, the function of which, Franklin "candidly admitted," was both the furtherance of knowledge, particularly scientific knowledge, and the promotion of the business of its members.[38] This dual purpose, as I have been arguing, would be carried over into the library itself over the course of the next century, as members clearly did quite a lot of business with each other in addition to using the library for reading and other intellectual pursuits.

There were about a dozen members of the Junto of diverse backgrounds, according to Franklin's *Autobiography*, and their careers suggest that the poverty that supposedly motivated them to form a library is largely a myth. Joseph Breintnall was a copyist of deeds for a scrivener and helped manage one of Franklin's stationery shops.[39] William Coleman was a merchant's clerk and later a merchant of great wealth and a judge.[40] Thomas Godfrey was a self-taught mathematician and experimenter in optics.[41] William Parsons had a hobby as a mathematician, but was trained as a shoemaker and occasionally worked as a seller of canary wine and surveyor.[42] Nicholas Scull was a tavern-keeper who became surveyor-general and a

---

[36] Wolf, 4–8, 9–13, 11, 12, 19–23, 25–6; Frederick B. Tolles. *Meeting House and Counting House: The Quaker Merchants of Colonial Philadelphia, 1682–1763* (U North Carolina P, 1948), 159–60, 161–2; Wolf, 18–19; Tolles 146–7; Library Company of Philadelphia, 31–6; Tolles, 148; Wolf, 13; Haynes McMullen, "The Founding of Social Libraries in Pennsylvania, 1731–1876." *Pennsylvania History* 32.2 (Apr. 1965): 133; Wolf, 17; James Green, "Subscription Libraries and Commercial Circulating Libraries in Colonial Philadelphia and New York." *Institutions of Reading: The Social Life of Libraries in the United States.* Ed. Thomas Augst and Kenneth Carpenter (Amherst: U Massachusetts P, 2007), 57; Wolf, 33; Tolles, 153–5; McMullen, 133.

[37] Green, "English Books," 262.

[38] Dorothy F. Grimm, "A History of the Library Company of Philadelphia, 1731–1835" (U Pennsylvania dissertation, 1955), 19.

[39] Grimm, 25–6.   [40] Grimm, 26.   [41] Grimm, 26–7.   [42] Grimm, 28.

cartographer.[43] The wealthiest member was Robert Grace, a descendant of British nobles who was also a skilled ironmaster and metallurgist.[44] There was a physician, Thomas Cadwalader, who held the first European medical degree of anyone in America.[45] An Oxford graduate named Thomas Hopkinson was a successful merchant and later an Admiralty Judge and Provincial Councilor.[46] Philip Syng was an Anglican silversmith, and John Jones was a cordwainer.[47] Isaac Penington was the sheriff of Bucks County, and Anthony Nicolls built the first fire engine in Philadelphia in 1730.[48]

These men and others drew up Articles of Agreement to found the library on July 1, 1731, and by February 1733, "Fifty subscribers invested forty shillings each and promised to pay ten shillings a year thereafter to buy books and maintain a shareholder's library."[49] James Logan, "the best Judge of Books in these parts," was asked to form a list of the books the library should order from London.[50] Robert Grace drew a bill of £45 on Peter Collinson, a mercer in Gracious Street in London, in favor of Thomas Hopkinson, who was to buy the books.[51] Hopkinson departed for England in April 1732 with a list of forty-three books and three periodicals to purchase.[52] The books arrived in Philadelphia in October 1732, and were taken to Robert Grace's house, which was being rented by Louis Timothée. That house would serve as the first library building.[53] Most of the books came in sheets, unbound, so they were soon sent to a member of the library for sheathing.[54]

There was a broad range of genres represented in the first collection, and though the Company was unable to obtain some of what it requested, substitutions were made for titles that were unavailable. There were two books that might be classified as general works, three philosophy, five social science, four language, eleven science, two useful arts, two fine arts, nine literature, and nine history.[55] Among these were the *Tatler* and the *Spectator*, as well as literary and political works like Algernon Sidney's *Discourses Concerning Government*, Puffendorf's *Introduction to the History of Europe* and *Of the Law of Nature and Nations*, Addison's *Works*, Marana's *Turkish Spy*, Homer's *Iliad* and *Odyssey*, and Dryden's *Virgil*.[56] In place of unavailable books like Trenchard and Gordon's *Cato's Letters*, the library's London agent sent "*The Hertfordshire Husbandman*, Switzer's *Gardening*, *Life of Charles the 12th King of Sweden*, Allen's *Synopsis*, *Travels of Cyrus*, Ray's *Wisdom of God*, *Lay Monastery*, Milton's *Paradise Lost* and *Regained*, *Historia Literaria*, sixteen pamphlets, Quincey's *Physical Lexicon*, and Philip's *Grammar*."[57]

There were also many gifts to the library early on that enhanced its new collection. The library's agent Peter Collinson, for example, enclosed two gifts with his first 1732 shipment, "Sir Isaac Newton's Philosophy" and "Philip Miller's Gardener's

---

[43] Grimm, 28.   [44] Grimm, 28–9.   [45] Grimm, 29–30.
[46] Grimm, 30.   [47] Grimm, 30.   [48] Grimm, 30–1.
[49] Library Company of Philadelphia, 5; J. Jay Smith (1798–1881), *Notes for a History of the Library Company of Philadelphia* (Philadelphia, 1835), 2; Grimm, 71.
[50] Library Company of Philadelphia, 5; Smith 1; Martin Sable, "The Library Company of Philadelphia: Historical Survey, Bibliography, Chronology." *International Library Review* 18 (1987): 32.
[51] Smith, 1; George Maurice Abbot, *A Short History of the Library Company of Philadelphia* (Philadelphia, 1913), 5; Grimm, 59–60.
[52] Grimm, 61; Sable, 32.   [53] Abbot, 6; Grimm, 62; Smith, 2.   [54] Grimm, 64–5.
[55] Grimm, 56.   [56] Abbot, 5–6.   [57] Grimm, 63.

Dictionary."[58] Members like Timothée, Franklin, and William Rawle also contributed books:

> In February 1733, Librarian Louis Timothée, Secretary Joseph Breintnall, and Franklin presented a number of volumes, including *A Collection of Several Pieces*, by John Locke; *Logic: or, the Art of Thinking*, by the Port Royalists Arnauld and Nicole, which Franklin in his autobiography said he had read at the age of sixteen; Plutarch's *Morals* in the translation of Philemon Holland; Lewis Roberts's *Merchants Mappe of Commerce*; and others. A bit later, William Rawle added a set of Spenser's *Works* to the collection, and Francis Richardson gave several volumes, among them Francis Bacon's *Sylva Sylvarum*.[59]

Indeed, by the time the library's 1741 catalog was published, there were a total of eighty-four books that had been gifted to the library by members and others.[60] The library also continued to acquire books through its own funds, raised through the annual ten shilling assessment. In 1741 there were 375 books in the collection, "114 in history, 60 from literature, 65 in the science fields, 38 in theology, 33 in philosophy, 28 in the social sciences, 13 in the arts, 10 in linguistics, and five of a purely general, all-encompassing nature."[61] This distribution of genres remained fairly constant over the course of the following century.[62] It is significant that about one-third of the works were historical. This category "included geographical books and accounts of voyages and travels," which would have appealed to the merchants, some of whom were engaged in slavery and related enterprises, who quickly began to dominate the Company.[63]

By 1738 the Library Company's membership had grown to seventy-two members, and it obtained a charter in the name of the Penn family from Governor George Thomas on March 24, 1742 that was printed in 1746 with a supplementary catalog and the by-laws of the Company.[64] By this time, Timothée was no longer the librarian; when he resigned in 1733, Franklin took over on an interim basis until 1734. William Parsons then took the role from 1734 to 1746, at which point Robert Greenway assumed the post 1746–63.[65] The library also moved out of the houses of librarians like Parsons and into the West Wing of the state house 1739–72 and then decamped, famously, to Carpenter's Hall, where it served as the library of the Continental Congress in the 1770s and of the Constitutional Convention in 1787, both of which met in that hall.[66] The library eventually moved to a new building of its own that the proprietors built on Fifth Street in 1791.[67] Collinson continued to obtain books for the Company in London and ship them on an annual basis, working mainly through the orders of the secretary of the Company, though he resigned in 1759, complaining of "ill treatment" by the library directors. He was replaced by the London bookseller Thomas Beckett in 1761, with the directors eventually deciding to simply order through David Hall of Philadelphia by the middle of the 1760s.[68] While there continued to be a board of directors,

---

[58] Abbot, 6.   [59] Library Company of Philadelphia, 6–7.
[60] Sable, 32.   [61] Sable, 32.   [62] Library Company of Philadelphia, 9.
[63] Library Company of Philadelphia, 9.
[64] Grimm, 45; Library Company of Philadelphia, 14–15.   [65] Abbot, Appendix.
[66] Grimm, 38; Library Company of Philadelphia, 20.
[67] Library Company of Philadelphia, 30.   [68] Smith, 3; Grimm, 115.

there were certain individuals who can be credited with leading the institution like "the silversmith Philip Syng, Dr. Thomas Cadwalader, the schoolmaster Francis Alison, the builder-architect Samuel Rhoads, secretary Richard Peters of the Governor's Council, and a bit later the merchant-patriot Charles Thomason and John Dickinson, the 'Pennsylvania Farmer.' "[69]

Membership in the library was comparatively expensive and grew more so over the century, and was increased by mergers with various other libraries. By 1738 the number of shareholders had grown to seventy-two; it reached 100 by 1763.[70] Members were added at an average of one a year from 1742 to about 1770, but few members gave up proprietorship: "from 1742, when two members dropped out, no one relinquished his share until 1769, when one share was forfeited."[71] In that year, the Library Company merged with the Union Library, which had been founded in 1746 and which had already incorporated two smaller institutions, the Association Library and Amicable Library.[72] The result of the merger was that the Company now had 400 members who owned shares, the holdings of the libraries were consolidated and duplicate copies of Union Library books already held by the Company were sold, and "A new printed catalogue with 2,033 entries was prepared and published in 1770. On this occasion the books were renumbered by size, beginning an accession series that continues to this day."[73] New directors were elected that were evenly divided between the leaders of both libraries, and at this time three women—Sarah Emlen, Susanna Carmalt, and Sarah Wister—were voted shares in the Company.[74] To be sure, women like Hannah Callendar had availed of their male relatives' memberships prior to 1769 to borrow books, and Ann Bartram, the daughter of famous botanist and shareholder William Bartram, was an early member. The number of women using the library only increased as time went on, and "By the turn of the nineteenth century there were twenty-nine women shareholders, a number that would increase dramatically to nearly 800 by the end of the century."[75] There were also honorary members who did not own a share, such as John Bartram, who was made one at the request of Collinson.[76] Another large influx in members occurred in the early 1790s, as "To pay for the Fifth Street building, 266 shares were sold or given to the carpenters, bricklayers, and others in 1789 to 1793 in partial payment for work done."[77] Though these men could not have afforded to purchase a share, they could enter into membership in this way, or sell the shares that they were given for this work. As the Company's shareholder records show, however, the issuance of shares was not only large scale at key moments; there were individuals either relinquishing or acquiring shares over the course of the late eighteenth century.

The price of shares was also undergoing inflation over the period, as demand for membership in the social network of the Company increased. James Green has commented on how part of the reason for this inflation was that new shareholders

[69] Library Company of Philadelphia, 18.
[70] Grimm, 45; Library Company of Philadelphia, 37.   [71] Grimm, 100.
[72] Library Company of Philadelphia, 18–19.
[73] Library Company of Philadelphia, 37–8, 18–19.
[74] Grimm, 129; Library Company of Philadelphia, 19–20.
[75] Library Company of Philadelphia, 19–20.   [76] Smith, 3.
[77] Library Company of Philadelphia, 37–8.

would not only have to pay the original share price, but also the cumulative annual assessments that had accrued from previous years:

> ...no new member could have a share for less than other members had already invested. Thus someone who bought a Library Company share in 1732 had to pay the original forty shillings plus the ten shillings annual dues the first shareholders had paid in 1731, and so forth year by year. In effect the cost of a share rose automatically ten shillings per year... in 1767, it cost £21 to join the Library Company, plus the 10 shillings annual dues.[78]

This high price of £21 concerned the Company's directors, as they correctly perceived that with the price this high, readers would be driven to competing institutions, such as new commercial circulating libraries. Accordingly, in 1768 they reduced the share price to ten pounds and froze it there.[79] By 1793, the price of a share had increased to £20 in Pennsylvania currency of uncertain value, a situation that led the directors to set the price at $40 in "good Hamiltonian currency" with $2 in annual dues.[80] This price would have been close to $1,000 in today's dollars, and with new shareholders having to pay the cumulative cost of each annual assessment, it is apparent that one had to be quite wealthy to own a share at the Company.

The borrowing rules for the Company also illustrate the migration from low or no cost borrowing to having to pay a fee. In the early days of the library, a borrower was required to leave a promissory note for the cost of a book when he borrowed it, and "promise that he will not lend the Books he borrows to any Person out of his Dwelling House"—a phrase that indicates that the shareholders' wives, children, and servants could borrow at one remove.[81] He would sacrifice his promissory note if the book were returned defaced, but if it were returned in good shape, he would not sacrifice his note unless he failed to return it with a one shilling fine at one week late, or with a two shilling fine at two weeks late.[82] In 1763, the rules were changed because Greenway, the librarian, had been found to have lost many books. After this date one would have to give a promissory note, or bond, before browsing.[83] In 1769, yet another set of rules were issued in which members would still have to post a bond to borrow a book, but now the bond was for double the value of the book, and they could take out one folio for five weeks, one quarto for four weeks, one octavo for three weeks, and two duodecimos or four pamphlets for two weeks.[84] Non-members also would have to post a bond of double the value of the book, but they also were to leave a cash deposit of double the value of the book. Folios were eight pence/week, quartos six pence/week, and octavos, duodecimos, and pamphlets four pence/week.[85] In keeping with the Company's desire to compete with lower-cost libraries, Green has explained, the librarian began to waive deposits of non-members, which drew the ire of the board.[86] Browsing was also liberalized at this time, with non-members being allowed within the rails if they had the

[78] Green, "Subscription," 32.   [79] Green, "Subscription," 64.
[80] Library Company of Philadelphia, 37–8.
[81] Grimm, 67–8.   [82] Grimm, 67–8.   [83] Grimm, 116.
[84] "Minute Book, 1731–2000." Library Company of Philadelphia, 22–4.
[85] "Minute Book," 22–4.   [86] Green, "Subscription," 68.

written permission of a shareholder.[87] Also, a 1770 rule change allowed members of shareholders' families to borrow directly.[88]

These rules were updated yet again in 1789, when existing borrowing regulations for members and non-members were retained, but when fines increased to four shillings per week for each overdue book.[89] A new caveat, however, was introduced: "A member may take out on hire, without a deposit, as many books in value for which his share in the Library shall, by the Librarian, be deemed a sufficient security, on the same terms, in other respects, as persons who are not members."[90] In practical terms this meant that a shareholder still needed to leave a promissory note, but no cash deposit was required unless the value of the books he was borrowing exceeded the value of his or her share. This caveat was reiterated in 1793, though the Library Company's own 1995 history has concluded that "Both members and nonmembers paid a fee for taking out books, but anyone was permitted to read in the library without charge. Penalties were levied for keeping books out overlong."[91] The surviving borrowing receipt book from the 1790s, discussed in greater detail in Section IV of this chapter for its record of titles borrowed and borrowers, lists deposits as high as $40—or $1,000 in today's money—for a folio.[92] The fees for borrowing, in short, could be quite substantial for members and non-members alike.

This high cost of proprietorship and borrowing, I argue, was connected to the wealth created by slavery, which has been acknowledged by some of the historians of the library. In the 1950s, for example, Dorothy Grimm wrote that "Anthony Benezet, who in a few years was to devote his life to the alleviation of the conditions of the Negroes, joined with enthusiasm a group that contained several slave owners."[93] She also cited a newspaper advertisement from early in the library's history showing an original shareholder engaged in a slave sale: "As the advertisements in the *Pennsylvania Gazette* suggest, other members of the Library Company were likewise industrious and enterprising. For the week of October 11 to 18, 1733, for example, appeared the item, 'Three likely young Negroe men fit for Town or Country Business. To be sold by William Plumstead.'"[94] The Library Company itself acknowledges that it received a gift from an Antigua plantation owner: "More generous was the unsolicited gift of £34 sterling that arrived in the summer of 1738 from Walter Sydserfe, a Scottish-born physician and planter of Antigua, who had heard of the establishment of the library from John Sober, one of its original directors."[95] As I explain in Section III of this chapter, these instances were not unique, as many Library Company shareholders were engaged either directly in the slave trade or in the exchange of slave-produced commodities, particularly via the trade between Philadelphia and the West Indies.

---

[87] Grimm, 130.   [88] Green, "Subscription," 68.   [89] "Minute Book," 160–2.
[90] "Minute Book," 160–2.   [91] Library Company of Philadelphia, 37–8.
[92] "Circulation Receipt Books, 1794–1812," Library Company of Philadelphia, 2. All reference to borrowings at the library refer to this note. The receipts have no page numbers, so from here forward they will be cited in the body of the text, rather than in the footnotes, by date, as they are sequential.
[93] Grimm, 73–4.   [94] Grimm, 31–2.   [95] Library Company of Philadelphia, 7.

III

By cross-referencing the Company's shareholder records with secondary works and archival sources that mention their names in relation to trade in enslaved Africans in their products, I have been able to identify some Library Company shareholders who were engaged in that commerce. That Philadelphians were engaged in the trade of slaves both from the West Indies via a coastal trade and directly from Africa cannot be doubted, and their traffic in goods like sugar, molasses, rum, and tobacco indicate their complicity in a slave labor system. Slave ownership was widespread in Philadelphia, and merchants, investors, and ship captains were able to supply that market and others with Africans. Though abolition was obviously of interest to many members of the Company, the sheer quantity of share numbers that I link to slavery below gives us pause as to how widely that sentiment was shared. Share ownership, annual fees, and other aspects of library philanthropy were being supported by proprietors' involvement in slavery to the extent that many of them were clearly using the library as a social network to further their participations in these trades. This fact is evident in the transactions between shareholders that are clearly documented in John Reynell's daybook, William Fisher's letter-book, the Frank M. Etting collection, the Sarah Smith collection, and the Coxe Family Papers, all of which are in Philadelphia archives. The Library Company was made, in part, with slave capital, and its initial civic function seemed to be less about books and more about the social networking necessary to further the business of its members.

The first slave shipment to Philadelphia for which we have evidence arrived in December 1684—only three years after the Quaker founders arrived—on the ship *Isabella*, which had 150 slaves on board who were quickly purchased by Quaker families.[96] Though there were doubtless other such shipments in succeeding years, the next record is of a ship named *Constant Alice* arriving from Barbados in 1701 "with nineteen blacks among the rest of its cargo of rum, molasses, and sugar."[97] The same ship made the same voyage the next year with twenty-three enslaved persons.[98] There were enough slaves being traded to Philadelphia for the Colonial Assembly to order a twenty pounds per head import duty on them not in an abolitionist hope to end the slave trade, but to control the influx of enslaved Africans lest they become rebellious.[99] Though this measure and another legislating a duty of five pounds were vetoed by the Crown, the five-pound duty was re-imposed in 1722.[100] Slave trading died down in the 1720s with the Atlantic-wide recession caused by the South Sea Bubble, but it resumed vigorously shortly thereafter. Aiding in this development was the fact that "importation rates for slaves rose considerably"

---

[96] Maurice Jackson, *Let this Voice be Heard: Anthony Benezet, Father of Atlantic Abolitionism* (Philadelphia: U Pennsylvania P, 2009), 11; Ira Berlin, "Slavery, Freedom, and Philadelphia's Struggle for Brotherly Love, 1685 to 1861." *Anti-slavery and Abolition in Philadelphia: Emancipation and the Long Struggle for Racial Justice in the City of Brotherly Love.* Eds Richard Newman and James Mueller (Baton Rouge: Louisiana State UP, 2011), 20.
[97] Jackson, 11.   [98] Jackson, 11.   [99] Jackson, 11–12.   [100] Jackson, 11–12.

after the reduction in the slave duty to £2 in 1730.[101] Most slaves came from the West Indies in lots of two and three "for the personal use of wealthy Philadelphia merchants," reflecting the fact that Pennsylvania land and climate was not suited to large-scale plantation slavery, but rather to more urban skilled labor.[102]

Quakers, as the colony's primary merchants, "were as active as anyone in the Pennsylvania trade of black cargo," a fact Maurice Jackson documents by discussing the case of Equiano's Quaker master Robert King, who purchased Equiano two years after the Quaker Meeting banned its members from owning slaves.[103] In about 1729–30 Quaker merchants "began to trade slaves in bulk and to import them into the colony in cargoes of up to forty slaves per ship," using mostly "seasoned" slaves directly from the West Indies until the outbreak of the Seven Years War in the middle of the 1750s.[104] The period 1755–65 was the high point of the Philadelphia slave trade, "with most slaves coming directly from Africa" to the extent that 500 arrived in 1762, "many of them from the Gambia."[105] In total, 1,290 slaves were brought to New Jersey and Pennsylvania from both West Africa and the West Indies between 1757 and 1766.[106] The labor and asset status of slaves was certainly important, as craftsmen owned slaves, but slave ownership was also considered fashionable.[107] Quaker slave traders and others were profiting off of this demand, though it was becoming out of vogue by the middle 1760s. There was a decline in slave importations after 1767, at a time when 590 white Philadelphians owned 1,400 slaves. There was a further decline in that ownership by 1775, when fewer than 700 blacks were owned by 376 owners.[108]

Philadelphia did not only directly trade in slaves, but also trafficked in the products of slave labor. In colonial Philadelphia's maritime commerce, as with that of the other cities discussed in this book, one did not need to be a merchant or other individual involved in shipping to be participating in the Atlantic's slavery economy. Because wheat, flour, and bread made up more than half of Philadelphia's exports to the West Indies, which were exchanged for the usual island slave commodities, Pennsylvania farmers and just about everyone else in the colony were benefiting from slavery.[109] One Pennsylvania governor warned that shipbuilders would lose employment if this trade ended, and that " 'Even the farmer, who is too apt to consider the landed and the trading interest in opposition to each other, must confine his produce to the consumption of his own family, if the merchant is disabled from exporting it to foreign markets.' "[110] "Exports from Philadelphia to the West Indies by the time of the Revolution were greater...than those from any other colonial port," wrote Arthur Jensen; by the early 1770s, 262 ships left Philadelphia for the West Indies and 244 left the islands for Philadelphia. From 1768 to 1772 Philadelphia exported 10,524 tons of bread and flour to the islands.[111] In return, they received rum, Muscovado sugar, molasses, woods like mahogany,

---

[101] Jackson, 12; Berlin, 21.   [102] Jackson, 14, 12.   [103] Jackson, 13.
[104] Jackson, 14; Berlin, 21.   [105] Jackson, 14–15; Berlin, 21.   [106] Jackson, 15.
[107] Jackson, 10.   [108] Jackson, 13, 16.
[109] Arthur L. Jensen, *The Maritime Commerce of Colonial Philadelphia* (Madison: U Wisconsin Department of History, 1963), 7.
[110] Jensen, 3.   [111] Jensen, 42, 43, 45.

coffee, cocoa, fruits, and salt.[112] Philadelphians carried on an extensive coastal trade from Newfoundland to Florida, and had considerable commerce with the notable destination for slaves, Charleston, South Carolina, sending flour, bread, and beer for slave products like rice and indigo, which they would often sell in London in a Philadelphia–Charleston–Britain triangular voyage.[113] They also did commerce with co-religionist leaders in slavery such as the Redwoods of Newport; correspondence between John Reynell and William Redwood of Newport "was both commercial and religious in nature" in the way typical of Quaker merchants.[114] Redwood even had one deal in which he exchanged gold he had acquired in the West Indies and Rhode Island rum with a member of Philadelphia's Pemberton family in exchange for a shipment of flour.[115]

Many Library Company shareholders were involved either singly or through partnership in a variety of Atlantic trades. Men like Reynell, who bought share number ninety-five in 1745, would multitask, working as an "importing and exporting merchant" in addition to serving as "wholesaler, retailer, purchasing agent, banker, insurance underwriter, and attorney."[116] The same could be said of the bibliophilic Norris family of merchants, who held share sixty-four from 1734 until at least the middle of the nineteenth century, and of John Gibson, who owned share 120 as of 1768.[117] Abel James, who acquired share ninety-nine in 1747, was in a commercial partnership with Henry Drinker, who bought share 373 in 1776, for the twenty-five years prior to the Revolution.[118] Ezekiel Edwards, share 183 (1773), worked with James Pemberton, relative of the Israel Pemberton, also a merchant, who owned share number seventy-nine as early as 1738.[119] Often, a future library member would work as an apprentice in the firm of an early shareholder, as was the case of Robert Morris, who acquired share 418 in 1769, and who had worked the Jamaica trade both for and in partnership with Charles Willing, who bought share seventy-three in 1736.[120] Similarly, John Reynell brought his nephew Samuel Coates, who acquired share twenty-eight in 1788, into the business.[121] Many younger men started out small as factors and agents for Philadelphia merchants. Richard Waln (share 394) and Clement Biddle (share 150) settled down in Barbados in 1759 until they developed their trade, and others who themselves or their sons would become shareholders like Samuel Powel I, Samuel Rhoads, Anthony Morris, and John Bringhurst started as carpenters, builders, brewers, printers, and coopers before becoming traders.[122] One of the most successful merchants, Thomas Wharton, was dealing with West Indies goods in an extensive and complicated set of voyages that each touched on several Atlantic ports.[123] He acquired share twenty-four in 1768.

There is evidence of current and future Library members engaged in Atlantic trade from the very years that the Library was founded. The 1731–2 daybook of Reynall, for example, shows him trading in corn, sugar, tobacco, indigo, tea, and

[112] Jensen, 46–7.   [113] Jensen, 81.   [114] Jensen, 70.   [115] Jensen, 76.
[116] Shareholder Records, Library Company of Philadelphia. All references to this record book will be in-text by share number, not page; Jensen, 12, 11.
[117] Jensen, 12.   [118] Jensen, 12.   [119] Jensen, 12–13.   [120] Jensen, 19–20.
[121] Tolles, 92.   [122] Tolles, 94, 115.   [123] Tolles, 111.

textiles with various members—and aspiring members—of the library.[124] The letterbook of the merchant William Fisher gives an even more expansive view of Philadelphians involved in the trade in slave-produced goods at mid-century, partly by virtue of his writing several of them while on a trade mission to Barbados, informing them that he had sold their flour for sugar, molasses, and rum. Some of the identifiable names of these Philadelphia correspondents include James and Joseph Morris, Lenard Melken, Joseph King, Daniel Stonmottz, John Rush, Christopher Marshall, Joseph Baker, Jeremiah Warder, Samuel Mifflin, Joseph Stretch, Thomas Leach, Francis Richardson, Jacob Winey, Robert Waln, Evan Morgan, Edward Warner, and Samuel Palmer. Many of these men were current or future Library Company shareholders.[125] Fisher also dealt with other Philadelphia merchants as a partner or insurer.[126]

Several generations of the Wharton family, many of whom were library proprietors, show similar West India and Atlantic trades beginning as early as 1738.[127] Joseph Wharton apparently owned slaves, as a 1733–5 account with a shoemaker, George House, shows that he has bought "Negro boy's shoes," and another with the tailor Albrecht Hase shows "Tom Making 4 Jackets for thy Negro Boy."[128] The business activities of library shareholder number 182, Tench Coxe, a loyalist who was later pardoned, show continuing Atlantic trade during and after the Revolution. He had partnerships and accounts with other current or future merchant Library shareholders such as the Whartons, Morrises, Charles Willing, John Mease, Joseph Snowden, John Duffield, and Joseph Bringhurst.[129] He also dealt with firms all over the East Coast, including New York ones such as Philip Livingston and Schuyler and Company.[130] His letterbook for domestic trade in 1784–5 shows him trading for rum and sugar with Barbados, Jamaica, and St Croix.[131] Coxe was not above dealing in slaves, and while there are doubtless numerous more telling examples in his extensive surviving papers, one in particular shows how he would use his trade contacts to engage in slavery transactions. In June 1785, he wrote Scarborough & Cooke in Charleston, South Carolina, informing the firm that he was willing to circumvent Pennsylvania and European laws to sell a slave for a friend. Interestingly, he penned this letter at a time when he was participating in one of Philadelphia's anti-slavery societies.[132]

---

[124] John Reynell Daybook 1731–1732, MSS.B.R33, 1–2, 3, 70, 27, 31, 35, 66, 36, 47, 44, 55, 71, 60, 17, 80, 36, American Philosophical Society, Philadelphia, Pennsylvania.

[125] William Fisher letterbook, 1750–1751, MS AM.06775, Historical Society of Pennsylvania, Philadelphia, Pennsylvania.

[126] Frank M. Etting Collection, MS 0195 Shelf 54—D03 Box 72. B72, F1, B72 F3 F9, B72 F18, B72 F22, Historical Society of Pennsylvania, Philadelphia, Pennsylvania.

[127] Sarah Smith collection on 18th century Philadelphia Merchants 1705/6–1937 (bulk 1713–1848), Collection 1864, B3 F1, B3 F2, B4 F7, B2 F5; B2 F1, Historical Society of Pennsylvania, Philadelphia, Pennsylvania.

[128] Smith, Box 4, Folder 7.

[129] Coxe Family Papers 1639–1897, MSS 2049, Vol. 24, 10, 29; Vol. 23, 15, 27, 42, 78, Historical Society of Pennsylvania, Philadelphia, Pennsylvania.

[130] Coxe, Vol. 24, 10.   [131] Coxe, Vol. 138; Vol. 139, 1, 15, 16, 106, 205.

[132] Coxe, Vol. 140, 9–10.

While this evidence of library shareholders' involvement in the slavery-based Atlantic economy is compelling, it should be noted that the Library Company was exceptional among America's early proprietary subscription libraries in having abolitionists among its shareholders, even from the earliest days. Anthony Benezet, for example, held share thirty-eight as early as 1734, and though he sold it in 1741, his brother Daniel purchased share seventy-one in 1745 and kept it until 1803, and his brother Philip owned share 368 from 1771 to 1793. The abolitionist Benjamin Rush owned share 267 at some point in the 1770s, forfeited it in May 1781, then purchased another share, number 660, in 1791. Though we can imagine what tensions must have existed between the slavers and the abolitionists in the library, a testament to its enlightened sociability is that members "apparently did not let differences of beliefs and politics interfere with the workings of the library."[133] Though evidence of members' reading habits is lacking for most of the eighteenth century, documented borrowings from the 1790s show readers pushing in an ever-more anti-slavery direction, echoing what was being published around them in abolitionist Philadelphia.

IV

The story of the Library Company and of its relationship to Philadelphia's involvement in slavery provide two historical contexts bearing on Dobson's belief that Equiano's *The Interesting Narrative* would sell well in Philadelphia, but the evidence of reading in an increasingly abolitionist city may provide an additional aesthetic context explaining its anticipated success. The catalogs of the Company are one tool through which the taste for anti-slavery writing can be measured, though they also bear witness to the taste for the other genres, some of them canonical, that Equiano incorporated into his text. A description of the rise of abolitionist writing and institutions in Philadelphia, and how abolitionist writers themselves may have incorporated previous reading into their work, some of it available in the Company, provides an entrée into the city as a site of reading into which the *Narrative* is inserted. Records of donations and acquisitions of anti-slavery writing by the Company, taken together with the sparse record of borrowing in the form of circulation receipt books at the library in the 1790s, show an increasing appetite for this kind of writing (see Figure 5.2). All of these factors bear upon our understanding of how the *Narrative* was doing very different kinds of work in a more abolitionist community like Philadelphia than in New York, where the book had more appeal as a story of the success of a patriotic Protestant entrepreneur and as travel writing.

Philadelphia's abolitionist advocacy was rooted in an anti-slavery strain in Quakerism stemming from its beginnings as a denomination.[134] The first criticism

---

[133] Grimm, 73–4.
[134] Jackson, 35, 36–41; David Waldstreicher, "The Origins of Anti-slavery in Pennsylvania: Early Abolitionists and Benjamin Franklin's Road Not Taken." *Anti-slavery and Abolition in Philadelphia:*

Figure 5.2 *Liberty Displaying the Arts and Sciences, or the Genius of America Encouraging the Emancipation of the Blacks* (1792). By Samuel Jennings. The Library Company of Philadelphia.

of slavery from Pennsylvania came in the form of the Germantown Protest of 1688, a petition signed by the Germantown Quaker meeting, which asked white immigrant readers to imagine being enslaved themselves by Turks in order to understand what they were putting Africans through.[135] A few years later in 1693, George Keith, a Scottish Quaker, protested slavery in *An Exhortation and Caution to Friends Concerning Buying and Keeping of Negroes*, and was disowned by the Quaker meeting for publishing it without their prior approval.[136] In 1696 two Quaker ministers, William Sotheby and Cadwalader Morgan, "called for a ban on slave ownership and the end of the slave trade," which was well received.[137] As discussed in Chapter 1, Sewell's *The Selling of Joseph* of 1700 became a foundational American anti-slavery text, and was appreciated in Philadelphia.[138] In 1713, the Chester, Pennsylvania Quaker meeting "became one of the first bodies to call for the elimination of slavery and requested disciplinary actions against slave-owning

Emancipation and the Long Struggle for Racial Justice in the City of Brotherly Love. Ed. Richard Newman and James Mueller (Baton Rouge: Louisiana State UP, 2011), 50, 52.

[135] Waldstreicher, 46, 47.   [136] Jackson, 43.   [137] Jackson, 43–4.
[138] Jackson, 44–5.

Friends."[139] Two years later, the 1715 Philadelphia Yearly Meeting urged Quakers to treat their slaves with compassion. John Hepburn, a New Jersey Quaker, published *The American Defense of the Christian Golden Rule* (1715), which argued that "the making of slaves is unlawful."[140] In 1729, Franklin agreed to publish the anti-slavery pamphlet of Ralph Sandiford, who had seen the horrors of slavery in the Bahamas and South Carolina.[141] One anti-slavery writer who did receive the approval of the Overseers of the Press was the Nantucket Quaker Elihu Coleman, who published *A Testimony Against that Antichristian Practice of Making Slaves of Men* in 1733 as an address to the Philadelphia Quakers against engaging in the slave trade.[142] Another, Benjamin Lay, had been a merchant in Barbados. He immigrated to Philadelphia in 1731 and was disturbed to see that slavery was as prevalent there as in the islands.[143]

The middle and later part of the century witnessed several developments towards ending slavery in Philadelphia. The Society for the Relief of Free Negroes, which later became the Pennsylvania Abolition Society, was formed in 1775.[144] Franklin became the first president of this organization in 1787, despite having owned slaves up until 1781.[145] A gradual emancipation law was passed in 1780, providing that the children of slaves born after that date would eventually be freed.[146] Richard Allen established the Free African Society in 1787 and soon after founded the African Methodist Episcopal (AME) Church, which emerged from the Philadelphia Union Society congregation.[147] Due to denominational differences, other members of the Union Society formed St Thomas's African Episcopal Church, led by Absalom Jones, in 1794.[148]

John Woolman and Benezet (see Figure 5.3) had initiated some of these anti-slavery developments beginning at mid-century."[149] Woolman published *Considerations on Keeping Negroes* in Philadelphia in 1754 to urge his co-religionists to end the practice. The London Yearly Meeting of 1758 denounced the slave trade, and the Philadelphia Yearly Meeting of the same year condemned slavery in the "Epistle of 1758," drafted by Benezet.[150] Benezet published *Observations on the Inslaving, Importing, and Purchasing of Negroes* the following year.[151] The year 1762 witnessed two publications by this pair, Woolman's *Considerations on Keeping Negroes, Part Second*, and Benezet's *A Short Account of that Part of Africa Inhabited by the Negroes*.[152] Benezet's 1766 *A Caution and Warning to Great Britain and her Colonies, in a Short Representation of the Calamitous State of the Enslaved Negroes in the British Dominions* was so successful that there was another Philadelphia printing

[139] Jackson, 45.   [140] Jackson, 45–6.

[141] Waldstreicher, 56–7; Jackson, 46–8.   [142] Jackson, 48–9.

[143] Waldstreicher, 57–8; Jackson, 49–50.

[144] Berlin, 23.   [145] Jackson, 115.   [146] Berlin, 24.

[147] Richard Newman and James Mueller, "Introduction." *Anti-slavery and Abolition in Philadelphia: Emancipation and the Long Struggle for Racial Justice in the City of Brotherly Love*. Eds Richard Newman and James Mueller (Baton Rouge: Louisiana State UP, 2011), 2.

[148] Berlin, 30.

[149] Waldstreicher, 60; Jackson, 52–4.   [150] Jackson, 55.   [151] Jackson, 61.

[152] Jackson, 55, 63.

Benezet instructing colored children.

ANTHONY BENEZET.

THIS celebrated philanthropist was a native of France. On account of religious persecution in that country, his parents, in 1731, removed to London. While here, the family adopted the religious opinions of the Society of Friends, and in 1731, emigrated to Philadelphia. In his zeal to do good, he left a profitable mercantile business, and devoted himself to the instruction of youth. He was a friend to the poor and distressed of every description, and labored most earnestly for their relief and welfare. He made great exertions to have the slave trade suppressed. The unfortunate and degraded situation of the African race in this country, deeply moved his sympathy, and he made strong efforts for their elevation and improvement. The loss of this benevolent man was deeply felt, and his funeral was attended by all religious denominations. Many hundred colored persons, with tears, followed his remains to the grave. An American officer of the Revolutionary army, in returning from the funeral, pronounced a striking eulogium upon him. "I would rather," said he, "be Anthony Benezet, in that coffin, than the great Washington with all his honors."

Figure 5.3 Wood Carving of Anthony Benezet (1713–84). By J. W. Barber, 1850. New York Public Library. Courtesy, American Antiquarian Society.

of it in 1767 and two London editions in 1767 and 1768.[153] To counter pro-slavery claims about slavery being native to Africa as well as to humanize blacks by discussing West African civilization, Benezet published *Some Historical Account of Guinea, Its Situation, Produce, and the General Disposition of Its Inhabitants, with An Inquiry into the Rise and Progress of the Slave Trade, its Nature, and Lamentable Effects* in 1771.[154]

[153] Jackson, 64.   [154] Jackson, 57.

Benezet had drawn on many previous works to write his tracts, particularly accounts of voyages, geographical, and historical works, some by slave traders.[155] He obtained some of these writings at the Library Company, where his brother was a member, and he "used that connection for borrowing from its holdings," though he had also worked at one point for the Friends Library of Philadelphia and Logan's Library.[156] According to Jonathan Sassi, he incorporated into *Some Historical Account of Guinea* the following works by "men deeply implicated in the slave trade":

> The five works he references repeatedly in *Some Historical Account of Guinea* were the second volume of John Green's four-volume compilation, *A New General Collection of Voyages and Travels* (London, 1745–1747)...Jean Barbot's *A Description of the Coast of North and South-Guinea*...Amsham and John Churchill's six-volume compilation, *A Collection of Voyages and Travels* (London, 1732), William Bosman's *A New and Accurate Description of the Coast of Guinea* (London, 1705), Francis Moore's *Travels into the Inland Parts of Africa* (London, 1738), and William Smith's *A New Voyage to Guinea* (London, 1744). Three other travel narratives that Benezet cited were Michel Adanson's *A Voyage to Senegal, the Isle of Goree, and the River Gambia* (London, 1759), Peter Kolb's *The Present State of the Cape of Good Hope*, 2 vols (London, 1731), and William Snelgrave's aforementioned *A New Account of Some Parts of Guinea and the Slave-Trade* (London, 1734).[157]

The 1770 catalog of the Library Company lists all the travel narratives cited above, so it is clear that Benezet and other readers in Philadelphia were making use of these books, either for furthering their trade with Africa or for abolitionist purposes.[158] Other readers absorbed these books through citing or responding to Benezet's *Some Historical Account of Guinea*. Such readers included the founder of British Methodism John Wesley, who quoted it extensively in *Thoughts Upon Slavery*, and Benjamin Rush, author of *An Address to the Inhabitants of the British Settlements, on the Slavery of the Negroes in America* (1773) and a follow-up pamphlet, *A Vindication of the Address* (1773).[159] Writing in 1808, after the abolition of the slave trade, the British abolitionist Thomas Clarkson deemed Benezet's book "'instrumental, beyond any book ever before published, in disseminating a proper knowledge and detestation of this trade.'"[160] Without ever having been to Africa, Benezet was able to use the familiar travel books that he and other Philadelphians— and literate English speakers all over the Atlantic, for that matter—were reading to write a humanizing account of West African civilization and to advocate for the ending of the slave trade.

Benezet had done other reading that made its way into his works, such as Richard Ligon's *A True & Exact History of the Island of Barbados* (London, 1657).[161] He had also made note of John Randall's book of geography, a document on

---

[155] Jackson, 72.

[156] Jackson, 72; Jonathan D. Sassi, "Africans in the Quaker Image: Anthony Benezet, African Travel Narratives, and Revolutionary-Era Anti-slavery." *Bringing the World to Early Modern Europe: Travel Accounts and their Audiences.* Ed. Peter Mancall (Leiden: Brill, 2007), 102.

[157] Sassi, 101, 100; Jackson, 72–102.   [158] Sassi, 102.

[159] Sassi, 121–2.   [160] Sassi, 120.   [161] Jackson, 73.

Liverpool's slave trading called "the Liverpool Memorandum," the *Gentleman's Magazine* and other periodicals, and the sixty-five-volume *Universal Modern History*.[162] Other travel accounts of Africa included Andre Brue's *Voyages and Travels Along the Western Coasts of Africa*, John Atkins's *A Voyage to Guinea, and the West-Indies in his Majesty's Ships, the Swallow and the Weymouth*, and Richard Jobson's early seventeenth-century account *The Golden Trade*.[163] Jobson's narrative was included in another book Benezet read, Samuel Purchas's *Purchas His Pilgrimage: Or Relations of the World and the Religions Observed in All Ages and Places Discovered, from the Creation to this Present* (1613).[164] Benezet also read about slavery in colonial America in such works as Burke's *An Account of the European Settlements in America* (1757) and Thomas Jeffery's *An Account of Part of North-America* (1761).[165] Benezet's writings suggest that he was familiar with Michel de Montaigne's *Essays*, particularly the cannibal motif for Africa that he wanted to refute.[166] In his earlier work especially, he had also cited the Quaker George Fox, Montesquieu, James Foster, Francis Hutcheson, George Wallace, Jean-Baptiste Labat, Richard Baxter, Sir John Templeton, Sir Hans Sloane, and George Whitefield.[167]

Benezet's work influenced Equiano in the writing of *The Interesting Narrative*, part of a larger two-way exchange of ideas between Philadelphia and British abolitionists. Equiano, who we have recently learned was probably not born in Africa, contrary to his account of his birth and childhood in *The Interesting Narrative*, apparently drew his sympathetic portrait of West African culture from Benezet and, by extension, the travel books that informed his writing. As explained in the introduction to this chapter, in the beginning of the *Narrative*, when describing the putative village of his birth, Equiano includes a footnote to Benezet's *Some Historical Account of Guinea* in a paragraph on tillage, famine, war, and "obtaining slaves."[168] This might explain Equiano's repeated claims that his Ibo people were "like the Jews" and a lost tribe of Israel, as Benezet was trying to make a similar Quaker philosemitic claim: "in Benezet's rendering, Africans enjoyed their continent's abundance in peace and simplicity, and they exhibited numerous other Quaker virtues such as reverence, charity, and industry. Only European slave traders had spoiled this picture of innocence."[169] Equiano, by using the same strategies and arguments as Benezet, was creating a portrait of African civilization and innocence being destroyed by rapacious white slave traders. The two-way traffic in texts and ideas between Philadelphia and Britain, accordingly, helped create the authenticated African textual person "Equiano." This person was formed at three textual removes from Benezet's textual Africa and his textual absorbing of the real experiences of the travel writers upon whom he drew, for the benefit of the "real Equiano" and the abolitionist cause. *The Interesting Narrative*, consequently, seems to have been engineered for people who lived in an imaginary, textual universe of books in several genres rather than the real world: namely, sympathetic readers. Further, it is clear

---

[162] Jackson, 78.   [163] Jackson, 82, 86–7, 95–6.   [164] Jackson, 95–6.
[165] Jackson, 102–3.   [166] Jackson, 100.   [167] Jackson, 64.
[168] Equiano, 39 n. 62.   [169] Equiano, 40–3; Sassi, 129.

that books in Philadelphia, some of which were obtained by Benezet at the Library Company, were being transmitted to Equiano through *Some Historical Account of Guinea.*

Travel books, of course, were not the only genre ventriloquized in the making of this Atlantic imagination of slavery in *The Interesting Narrative.* What we know of Philadelphia reading suggests that Equiano's multi-generic story would have had enough of an appeal for Dobson to believe he could sell 100 copies of it. Ownership of books in some of the personal libraries in the city is one index of taste and reading. Logan and Norris owned works of philosophy and political theory.[170] Some Philadelphians owned works like Giovanni Paolo Marana's *Turkish Spy,* Ramsay's *The Travels of Cyrus,* the *Arabian Nights, Paradise Lost,* Pope's works, Young's *Night Thoughts,* Thomson's *Poems,* Hoadley's *The Suspicious Husband,* Spenser's *Works,* poetry by Chaucer, Shakespeare, Crashaw, Cowley, Denham, Gay, Blackmore, Phillips, and many other English classics.[171] Logan's library contained prose by Sidney, Burton, Browne, Swift, Dryden and Lee, Southerne, Bank, and Tate, and Logan would recommend work to others like the *Tatler* and *Spectator.*[172] Evidence also shows that prominent Philadelphians like Joseph Smith, Lloyd Zachary, John Reynell, Israel Pemberton, Thomas Wharton, James Logan, William Logan, Isaac Norris II, Charles Norris, Abel James, William Griffiths, Joseph Richardson, Benjamin Mifflin, and Joseph Wharton were reading important novels and magazines that marketed books.[173] In short, much of what we now understand as the eighteenth-century British literary canon was being purchased and read in Philadelphia, at least in elite Quaker circles.[174] Surviving common-place books by Elizabeth Graeme Ferguson and John Leacock also provide some evidence of what people were reading. Ferguson had clearly read Benezet, writing a manuscript poem "On the Death of Anthony Benezet" containing the line "All Africa's Sable Hands he Sought to Loose."[175] Leacock mentions purchasing unspecified plays and other books.[176] Leacock also copied out a "Parody on the Tempest by R.H.," a militaristic poem on the American Revolution that is not very Tempest-like at all, and a recipe for a "Preparation of Black Printing Ink for Engravings on copper or other nice purposes."[177] In addition, he copied out sections of the *Transactions of the American Philosophical Society.*[178] By the late 1760s, the commercial lending libraries of Nicola and the Bradfords were stocking history, poetry, plays, voyages, and several forgettable novels, though more canonical texts like Henry Brookes' s *Fool of Quality,* Smollett's *Roderick Random, Peregrine Pickle,* and *Chrysal, or the Adventures of a Guinea* were included.[179] These libraries, however, closed by the middle of the 1770s, and, accordingly, the Library Company became the center of Philadelphia reading.

[170] Tolles, 177–9.   [171] Tolles, 195, 196, 200–1.   [172] Tolles, 202.

[173] Tolles, 198–9, 202–3.   [174] Tolles, 199.

[175] Elizabeth Graeme Ferguson Commonplace Book, Film 1238, American Philosophical Society, Philadelphia, Pennsylvania.

[176] John Leacock Commonplace Book, MSS.B.L463, A, American Philosophical Society, Philadelphia, Pennsylvania.

[177] Leacock, K, O.   [178] Leacock, O.   [179] Wolf, 193–5.

By the time the Library Company's 1789 catalog was published it held most of the above-mentioned works, as well as newer abolitionist writings such as those by Benezet, Hannah More, Thomas Clarkson, and French authors.[180] At around the time of the 1789 London and 1791 New York editions of Equiano's *The Interesting Narrative*, therefore, members of the Library Company would have had access to some of the abolitionist works with which the narrative was in dialogue. The Library also stocked many of the other genres that Carretta identifies as components of Equiano's tale, including spiritual autobiographies, apologia or vindications, captivity narratives, adventure tales, a previous slave narrative by Ignatius Sancho, and economic treatises. Memoirs, however, must be taken as the dominant genre of *The Interesting Narrative*, and there must have been quite an appetite for them because there were at least sixty-three in the library catalog that were either auto-biographical or historical.[181] Closer to Equiano's literary version of the genre, there were also the memoirs of writers like Voltaire and Rousseau, Alexander Pope, Laetitia Pilkington, and Lord Chesterfield.[182] The more historical resonance of the term "memoir" meant that political histories were also included in this category, to the extent that we might regard Equiano's book, in the parlance of the day, as an autobiography that also read like a history, another genre favored by early American readers. In doing so, *The Interesting Narrative* is providing an Atlantic history of the latter half of the eighteenth century—a history in which he has placed himself as a significant, transformative figure.

The novel—particularly the historical novel, an adventure story—is therefore another important genre in understanding Equiano's self-fashioning. The unity of the biographical and historical resonances of the term "memoir" in the period is perhaps most manifest in novels that modeled the life of a character, often in the mode of the *Bildungsroman*. Works in the novel genre often had titles like

---

[180] These holdings include Benezet's *Account of that Part of Africa Inhabited by the Negroes*, his minor works on the innocence of the city of Christianity, on the times, and on the nature of war, *A Caution to Great Britain and Her Colonies*, *An Account of the Baneful Effects of the Use of Distilled Spiritous Liquors, and the Slavery of the Negroes*, and *A Caution and Warning to Great Britain and Her Colonies*. The minutes of the meetings of the library's board of directors show other abolitionist works being acquired. For example, in December 1788 Tench Coxe, on behalf of the Society for Promoting the Abolition of Slavery, donated "four bound volumes" of works containing *Remarks on the Slave-Trade*, *West Indian Eclogues*, *The Wrongs of Africa*, Hannah More's *Slavery, a Poem*, and *Aura*, a poem (Volume 1). Volume 2 contained Day's *Letter on the Slavery of the Negroes*, *An Inquiry into the Effects of the Slave Trade*, Smith's *Letter on the State of the Negro Slaves*, Falconbridge on the slave trade, William Agutter's *A View of the Slave-Trade*, *A Sermon on the Slave Trade*, and William Mason's *A Discourse on the Slave Trade*. The third volume had Thomas Clarkson's *An Essay on the Slavery and Commerce of the Human Species*, and the fourth Wesley's *Thoughts upon Slavery*, Cowper's letter on the slave trade, *A Summary View of the Slave-Trade*, Newton's *Thoughts on the Slave-Trade*, and Nickolls's *Letter on the Slave Trade*. In June 1791, more such books were acquired from the Society, including *La Cause des Esclaves Negres*, by M. Troffard, *Lettre de F. J. Brissot* by A. M. Barnave, *Réflexions sur le Code Noir, Lettre aux Philantropes*, by M. Grégoire, and *Réflexions addressées A Le Assemblée Nationale*, by M. Claviere. Library Company of Philadelphia, *A Catalogue of the Books, Belonging to the Library Company of Philadelphia; to which is Prefixed, a Short Account of the Institution, with the Charter, Laws, and Regulations* (Philadelphia: Poulson, 1789), 110, 147, 156, 160, 161; "Minute Book," 3:119–20; "Minute Book," 3:266.

[181] Library Company of Philadelphia, 1789 *Catalogue*, 16 22, 27, 33, 34, 35, 37.

[182] Library Company of Philadelphia, 1789 *Catalogue*, 59, 64, 67, 335.

The History of Miss Betsy Thoughtless, by Eliza Haywood, or the *The History of Sir Charles Grandison*, by Samuel Richardson, monikers that identified biography as history and often blurred the distinction. Equiano might well have been trying to appeal to readers of such adventurers, in the style of the picaresque novel, as *Don Quixote, Tom Jones, Peregrine Pickle, Roderick Random*, Harry Clinton of Brooke's *The Fool of Quality*, or any number of lucky characters that rise from the fiction of this period. Novels like *Don Quixote, Roderick Random*, and others were in the library catalog and, as noted above, Philadelphians could also find them in the local commercial lending libraries.[183] Equiano's narrative, accordingly, could be read by some audiences for its literary qualities that made him seem like the adventurous protagonist from a form of novel that would have been familiar to both them and the writer.

The ground had been prepared for Equiano to promote his character as an adventurer in previous accounts of shipwreck and military action, and travel literature's sub-genre of "adventure" was represented on the Company's shelves. Equiano's choice to feature an account of his presence at British naval battles, however true, may also have been part of a rhetorical strategy of placing a war adventure narrative in the story to cater to the tastes of male—particularly younger male—readers as part of the packaging of abolitionist sentiment. The exploits of the adventurers in the *Arabian Nights Entertainments*, however, were in the library as they were in so many others, suggesting again that fictional characters from the period's literature may have been a stronger model for the picture of Equiano as hero.[184] Similarly, the adventure subgenre of the captivity narrative would have made readers sympathetic to the condition of enslavement, and many such narratives were also available in the library. It is possible that Equiano's account of his enslavement and re-enslavement after freedom would appeal to men who had been prisoners of war and/or who had read these books.[185]

One aspect of Equiano's novelization of the self that would have appealed to Protestant readers that he sought to convince to end slavery was the spiritual auto-biography. The Company had evangelical accounts of conversion of the type Equiano experienced like John Bunyan's *Grace Abounding to the Chief of Sinners* and seemingly innumerable other Protestant works that would have made the religious aspect of the narrative familiar to readers. *The Interesting Narrative's* anti-Catholicism, manifest in Equiano's resistance to converting to Catholicism and being offered a free Catholic education in Spain, would have been especially appealing to those readers who had read the Company's copy of a book donated by the bookseller-printer David Hall. *The Sufferings of John Coustos, for Free-Masonry, and for his Refusing to Turn Roman Catholic, in the Inquisition at Lisbon* may have provided fodder for readers interested in Equiano's critique of the Inquisition in chapters nine and eleven, parts of the story in which he is quick to assert his credentials as a Protestant Bible reader by writing that the Catholic Church does

---

[183] Library Company of Philadelphia, 1789 *Catalogue*, 306, 322.
[184] Library Company of Philadelphia, 1789 *Catalogue*, 103, 24, 308, 23, 45, 45, 308, 369.
[185] Library Company of Philadelphia, 1789 *Catalogue*, 12, 61, 103, 61.

not allow people to read the Bible, and indeed seizes bibles. In short, Equiano's consistent, and insistent, apologies for and vindications of English Protestantism would have been met well by enthusiasts who had read such books in the library. In all, there are more than 100 listings of books under the category of "theology" in the 1789 catalog.[186]

Many of Equiano's pious readers would also have been merchants and other businessmen, so he was careful to include economic observations and actions in his book. There were economic works in the possession of the Company, including the more theoretical political and commercial works of Charles Davenant and *An Inquiry Into the Principles of Political Economy* by James Stuart. Most works in this vein, though, were about the actual state of trade. To be sure, if one were to search for the term "trade" in the book titles listed in the 1789 catalog today, most titles containing that term would be in reference to the slave trade, but works such as *An Essay on Free Trade and Finance* (Philadelphia, 1779) and other accounts of the commerce of Atlantic nations and colonies would also appear.[187]

The only surviving Library Company borrowing records from this period can tell us something about what genres Philadelphians were reading in the decade of the 1790s, when Equiano's book was widely available, including at the library, which had obtained it by 1793. The borrowing records consist of a receipt book much like the ones at the Redwood Library that they inspired (see Figure 5.4). The names of the borrowers seem to have been cut out of the receipts when a book was returned, but on the reverse side of the receipts, we can see who these borrowers were because they had to sign for a deposit for the books they borrowed. The titles of books on the front of the receipt were also crossed out, but fortunately, the librarian also marked down each book's accession number in the upper left hand corner of the receipt. These accession numbers were a rational system of cataloging and locating books in the library, so the number on the receipt would correspond to a number in the catalog with the book's title next to it.

Borrowing rules had changed five years prior to December 1794, the date the receipts start. This fact affects how we interpret the information on the receipts. Under the new rules, the borrowing terms were that a shareholder could take out one folio for five weeks, one quarto for three weeks, or one octavo or two duodecimos for two weeks. The member would have to leave a bond, but not cash, equivalent to double the value of the book borrowed. Non-members could also borrow by leaving a bond for double the value of the book, but also had to leave a cash deposit for double the value. Crucially, however, a rule was established that exempted shareholders from deposits in some cases. A member could take out on hire, without a deposit, as many books in value for which his share in the Library should be "deemed a sufficient security."[188] This rule change affects how we read the receipt books, as the vast majority of the names remaining on the verso side of

---

[186] Library Company of Philadelphia, 1789 *Catalogue*, 143, 36, 131, 123, 123, 128, 127, 133, 135, 144, 200, 344.
[187] Library Company of Philadelphia, 1789 *Catalogue*, 177, 185, 54, 55, 189, 56, 177, 192.
[188] "Minute Book," 160–2.

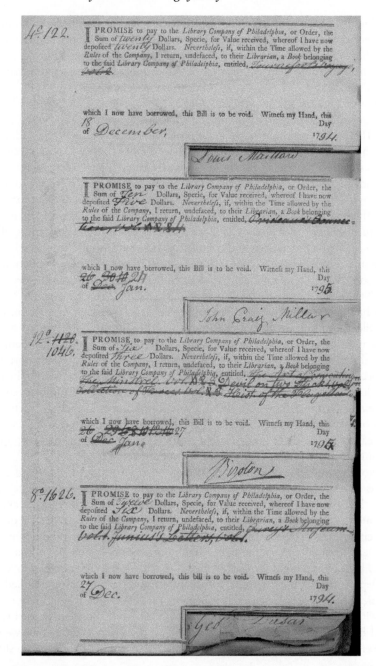

Figure 5.4 Circulation Receipt Book, 1794–1812. The Library Company of Philadelphia.

the receipts do not correspond to those of shareholders listed in the shareholder book, though about twenty names are those of shareholders.

There are two possible reasons for this. The first is that shareholders were not using the library to borrow books so much as a place to conduct business and to network socially. The more likely scenario, however, is the second: that most members borrowed books with a deposit that was less than their share price, probably meaning that they did not have to fill in a receipt at all. From the researcher's perspective, this diminishes our ability to locate the reading tastes of particular shareholders. The twenty-odd member names on the receipts might only be for those members who borrowed books for a deposit greater than the value of their share. Still, the receipt books give evidence about what books were circulating and which titles and genres were most popular, even where we cannot identify information about the reader, the handwriting of whom was often so poor on the verso side of the receipt that his or her name was essentially illegible. And many of the names of non-member borrowers corresponded to those of people who had been a member at one time or were to be in the future, suggesting that an earlier formal membership might lead one to be welcomed as a non-member later, and that non-member borrowing often led to later participation as a shareholder.

For the 1794 to 1800 period, the borrowing record illustrates that works in Equiano's genres that were influencing the reception of his book were circulating. But there is no evidence that the library's copy of *The Interesting Narrative* (accession number "duodecimo 1026") was borrowed in this period.[189] By far the largest category of books being borrowed was voyages and travels, with twenty-three "voyages" and twenty-nine "travels." Of the nine titles of African travels that had gone into Benezet's *Some Historical Account of Guinea*, Green's *New General Collection of Voyages and Travels* was borrowed twice, Smith's *A New Voyage to Guinea* once, and Adanson's *Voyage to Senegal* once. Other such works connected to slavery or Africa that were borrowed included Jerome Lobo's *Voyage to Abyssinia* (translated by Johnson), Alexander Stanislas Wimpffen's *Voyage to St. Domingue*, which was taken out twice, and Stedman's *Surinam*, which was taken out once. Closer to the Atlantic debate over abolition, Jacques Pierre Brissot de Warville's *New Voyage to the United States of America* (1791), a record of a voyage he took on behalf of the French Society of the Friends of the Blacks, was the single most popular travel book borrowed at the library at that time. Warville had already challenged the French general Chastellux's 1786 *Travels in America*, a work borrowed three times, in another book, *A Critical Examination of the Marquis de Chastellux's Travels, in North America, in a Letter Addressed to the Marquis, Principally Intended as a Refutation of His Opinions Concerning the Quakers, the Negroes, the people, and Mankind* (1788). Another member of the Society of the Friends of the Blacks, Nicolas de Condorcet, was also represented in the Library Company's collection with his *Life of Jacques Turgot*, a Physiocrat. Most of the other travel books borrowed concerned Europe, Asia, and the Pacific Rim.

[189] "Circulation."

When we extend the period of analysis of the receipt books to 1794–1812, we can see that several works on slavery and abolition were circulating to patrons. Though these were a very small percentage of all the books that were checked out, they outnumber the amount of such books being borrowed at the other libraries discussed in this book, a fact that confirms that Philadelphia was the most abolitionist city in America. *La Cause des Esclaves et Habitans de la Guinée* was borrowed in August 1795. In July 1796, Clarkson's *Essay on the Impolicy of the Slave Trade, to which is Added, an Oration, Upon Establishing, at Paris, a Society to Promote the Abolition of the Trade and Slavery of the Negroes, by J. P. Brissett* was checked out. The African-American religious leaders Absalom Jones and Richard Allen's *Narrative of the Proceedings of the Black People, During the Late Awful Calamity of Philadelphia, in the year 1793*, a book about the Yellow Fever epidemic, was borrowed in August 1796. Bryan Edwards's pro-slavery *Maroon Negroes*, a work giving a history of the 1694 first Jamaica Maroon War that nonetheless blamed white planters for provoking it, was taken in March 1798. A work simply listed as "Brown on Equality" was borrowed in August 1799. The abolitionist poet William Cowper was popular, with works by or about him circulating in February 1803, August 1805, April 1806, and October 1806. Books on the trade and history of Jamaica, the Congo, and the Cape of Good Hope were borrowed in January 1795 and August 1808, October 1807, and January 1809, respectively. A book by the abolitionist Erasmus Darwin, *Zoonomia*, was checked out in February 1798.

Both the non-fictional memoir and fictional histories of novelistic characters were popular genres. The actor David Garrick's memoirs were borrowed in January 1796, Xenophon's *Memoirs of Socrates* was borrowed in July 1800 and March 1808, Linguet's *Memoirs of the Bastille* was borrowed in December 1798, and two other memoirs with illegible titles were borrowed in January 1796 and July 1800. There were many "lives" borrowed in the middle of the 1790s. The most obvious of these was *Plutarch's Lives*, translated by John Langhorn, several volumes of which were borrowed in the summer of 1798. Others included the *Life of Count Alessandro di Cagliostro*, the *Life of Benvenuto Cellini*, the *Life of George Fox*, the *Life of William Bowyer*, and Nicolas de Condorcet's *Life of Jacques Turgot*. Though the Library Company, like many of the other libraries discussed in this book, did not specialize in novels, some were borrowed in the 1794–1812 period. Hawkesworth's *Telemachus* was checked out from April to June 1795, *Don Quixote* twice in 1795 and once in 1803, Sterne's *Sentimental Journey* in March 1798, Burney's *Evelina* in August 1798, her *Cecilia* in 1804, Fielding's *Works* in 1799, 1804, 1808, 1801, and 1811, and Brooke's *Fool of Quality* from November 1808 to January 1809. *Gulliver's Travels*, to be sure a parody of both the travel narrative and the novel, was borrowed twice in the winter of 1794–5. Even Maria Edgeworth's *Castle Rackrent*, a novel freshly published in London, was taken out in June and July 1801.

Religious works and books about imprisonment were also circulating. *The Sufferings of John Coustos* was borrowed between December 29, 1794 and March 21, 1795. Bunyan's *Pilgrim's Progress* was borrowed in late winter of 1804. George Sale's translation of the *Koran* was borrowed once, between January 30 and March 7, 1795, and his colleague Humphrey Prideaux's *The Old and New Testament Connected in* the *History of the Jews and Neighbouring Nations* was borrowed twice in the winter of 1794–5, with one reader borrowing four volumes sequentially between December 26 and January 24. Joseph Lomas Towers's *Illustrations of Prophecy, in the Course of Which are Illuminated Many Predictions, Which Occur in Isaiah, Daniel, and the Writings of the Evangelists* was borrowed twice, in the winters of 1795 and 1798. John Howard's *The State of Prisons* was of interest to at least one reader in July 1796. These selections suggest that at least a few in Philadelphia would have had an appetite for the spiritual autobiography and captivity genres in Equiano's narrative.

Traditionally masculine genres—adventurous non-fiction like stories of the sea, war and battles, and histories—circulated well. Irvine's *Adventures* were taken out in spring 1795 and Dickinson's *Shipwreck* was checked out twice in that year. Drinkwater's *History of the Late Siege of Gibraltar* was withdrawn once in 1795 and once in 1801, Muller's *Military Treatise* in 1797, and three other military works by Muller in 1798. Ramsey's *History of the American War* was taken in April 1795, Gordon's *History of the American Revolution* in March 1795 and October 1800, and *Buccaneers of America* in May 1808. Clavigero's *History of Mexico* was borrowed once in 1795 and once in 1796, and from December 29, 1794 to March 21, 1795 one reader borrowed Appian's *History*, the *History of Barbary*, the *History of France*, and the *Life of Henry VIII*. The *History of Moravian Missions*, which contained a critique of West Indian slavery, was taken in 1795, as were *Dictionnaire historique* and *History of the Indians*. Histories of the Classical period were popular, with Echard's *Roman History* taken out in 1795, Rollins's *Roman History* in 1795 and 1800, and Gordon's *Tacitus* in 1798. The *History of Inland Navigation, Histoire de la Holland*, and Dunbar's *History of Mankind* were borrowed in 1795, 1796, and 1797, respectively, and Hume's *History of England* was taken out in September 1796 and March 1797. The *History of Spain* was borrowed in the middle of 1800 and Vertot's *History of the Revolution in Spain* over several months from October 1800 through July 1801. A *History of France* was taken in the middle of 1798, while Goldsmith's *History of England* was borrowed in the summer and fall of 1800. Readers were also enhancing their knowledge of areas relevant to the trade in slaves and related products by reading works such as a *History of Guiana*, borrowed in February of 1801, and Jackson's *Morocco*, borrowed in April 1801.

Works on the Atlantic economy also circulated. Whitworth's *State of Trade* was checked out on July 24, 1795, and Adam Smith's *The Wealth of Nations* was taken out in 1807 and 1811. As mentioned above, books on the Congo trade, Jamaica, and the Cape of Good Hope were borrowed by at least one reader each, and many other travel books and histories, because many in the genre were commissioned by companies involved in commerce, were on the economy and trade to these countries. Equiano's embrace of free trade, in fact, was in the spirit of *The Wealth of Nations*, with his plea for honest dealing with black businessmen like himself—and his argument that the slave trade was economically unsound—being in that spirit.

There were many other titles and genres circulating to readers in the late eighteenth and early nineteenth century, but determining who was borrowing which books— and speculating on the reasons—requires attention to the few readers about whom we have some information: the eighteen borrowers listed in the receipt books who were, at one time or another, shareholders. The first volume of Echard's *Roman History* was borrowed by William Govet, share 221, in March 1795. Samuel Morris, share 291, borrowed Emerson's *Mechanics* the same month. Between May and July, 1795, John Craig Miller took out "Rush on the Fever" (Benjamin Rush's book on the Yellow Fever epidemic of 1793), Vattel's *Law of Nations*, a dictionary, and an unidentifiable work. There were three John Millers in the shareholder records, so this borrower was either shareholder 13, 648, or 743. In June 1795, "Mr. B. Patterson," likely shareholder Robert Patterson (number 755), took out "Clark on the Attributes of God." Robert Hare, shareholder thirty-seven, borrowed seven volumes of Rollins's *Roman History* in December 1795. The *Siege of Gibraltar* went out to Robert Pitfield, who was not listed as a member until 1803 (share 658), in October 1795. George Harrison, shareholder number 761, borrowed Hanmer's *Shakespeare* vol. 1 in July 1796. *Handmaid to the Arts* vol. 1 and a text simply listed as "Tracts" were checked out by Richard Lee, share 185, in January and February 1797. Pike's *Arithmetic* was checked out in April 1798 by John Evans, shareholder 465. A book on shorthand was borrowed by Peter A. Brown, shareholder 750, in April 1800. Reese Lloyd, perhaps a grandson of original share-holder Rees Lloyd, borrowed a book on the dropsy in May 1801. In the summer of 1801, Thomas Smith, shareholder 769, borrowed *Doron Medicum, or a Supplement to the London Dispensatory* by William Salmon. The taste of these individuals was clearly omnivorous and varied, and aside from any value these circulating genres have for giving us a general picture of the reading of texts relevant to those bearing on Equiano's book, it is difficult to connect them directly to pro-slavery or abolitionist sentiment.

Several receipts, however, show the circulation to shareholders of books directly relevant to travel, trade, slavery, and abolition. Between January 29 and March 28, 1795, James Robertson, share number 714, borrowed Beckford's *Jamaica* vols 1 and 2 and *Gulliver's Travels*, which contain reflections on slavery. A man named John Palmer, who may have been one who forfeited share 122 in 1770, borrowed the abolitionist Brissot de Warville's book on February 21, 1795, perhaps as a non-member until he became one again by purchasing share 522 a few months later in December 1795. On a receipt that looks like it was reused several times from 1797 to 1800, Joseph Harper, who sold share 309 in 1794, borrowed *Voyage to St. Domingue*. One would think that the famous statesman and abolitionist Dr. Benjamin Rush, who acquired share 660 in 1791, would borrow books on slavery and abolition, but instead he checked out "Cooper's Distiller," a book on making spirituous liquors, in March 1799. The aforementioned copy of the *History of Guiana* was taken out by John Mitchell, who held share 203 until 1783, in February 1801. If shareholders were participating in the Library Company for both business and leisure pursuits, it is clear that these books were supporting both trade interests related to slavery and anti-slavery advocacy.

Dobson, accordingly, may have been correct to speculate that he could sell 100 copies of Equiano's *Interesting Narrative* in Philadelphia in the 1790s. If multi-generic crossover was key to the *Narrative*'s appeal, it is clear that all of that book's genres, particularly travel writing and memoir, were enhancing the already active local market for anti-slavery texts. Because Quakers had a long tradition of abolitionism, particularly in Philadelphia, they might have been Dobson's target audience for sales. Quaker anti-slavery advocates like Woolman and Benezet had built the foundation for that market with their writings of the 1750s through 1770s, and enhanced it with their formation of anti-slavery societies. Benezet's reading about Africa in the Library Company and elsewhere went into his anti-slavery writing, and was in turn to influence Equiano. Philadelphia reading patterns suggest wide uptake of the genres that had made the *Narrative* so appealing. The Library Company's 1789 catalog and its supplements issued in the 1790s indicate the broad availability of these genres, and the circulation receipt books that begin in 1794 suggest that such books were indeed being checked out. Documenting the holdings and reading of Philadelphians, particularly in the Library Company as the center of reading in the city, accordingly, illustrates how a bookseller like Dobson could have the confidence to stock so many copies of the *Narrative*.

V

Clearly, the relationship of Equiano's autobiography to Benezet's account of Africa indicates that there was two-way traffic between Philadelphia and British abolitionists. In fact, it may have been the crucible of the Philadelphia book market and others like it that was formative of Equiano's storytelling technique, reliant as it was on Benezet's reading about Africa, Atlantic trade, and other subjects, which accounts for its success. That book market, centered on the library, might therefore be understood as a microcosm of the English-language book trade that made many of the same books not only available in the other colonial port cities and libraries discussed in this book, but also in London and all over the Atlantic. Equiano himself comes across as a skilled reader of all kinds of Atlantic genres to the extent that his textual identity as an "author" could be understood as the centerpiece and sole support—the "keystone," in Pennsylvania parlance—holding the genres that went into his self-fashioning together. Authorship of the slave narrative might therefore be understood as not merely the former slave reclaiming himself—staking self-possession—but also as modeling that liberated self to the most sophisticated of readers of the print media. To write as Equiano did required great imbibing of the books bearing on the life of a slave, and his autobiography is a construction of the self according to the rules and criteria of the genres of those books—construction that would make him count as a man of taste.

Atlantic abolitionism, due to this traffic in reading and writing, might be understood above all as an eighteenth-century media event taking place in print over the course of several decades. While the suffering described in the slave narrative was real, the way that this suffering was represented in and overcome through such narratives was an act of extremely sophisticated storytelling based on the reading and appropriation of the texts bearing most closely on the subject of Atlantic slavery. The virtual reality inhabited by the reader of the abolitionist text was therefore one in which he would find familiar storylines spun together in a new way. The pattern he would see could only be created through the discernment of a former slave, who could see those storylines as a matrix in which he must find his way in order to represent himself as a modern subject. The transatlantic book market was that matrix of imagination, and is key to understanding not only what was read, but how stories were being told.

By limiting our comprehension of that book market to the confines of an edifice, a library, as I have done throughout this book, this chapter has aimed to further our understanding not only of how anti-slavery was articulated through that edifice as the center of Philadelphia's reading, but also how abolition was politically achieved in that city. The history of the Library Company is therefore, inevitably, also the history of civic engagement in slavery and abolition. Its collections may have been founded with the wealth of men involved in slavery, yet, as its later catalogs and borrowing records show, the library also served as a principal site for abolitionist reading and sentiment. Surveying the shareholders' West Indian commerce has been necessary to elucidate how the wealth to purchase books for the library was accumulated, and a crucial step in explaining colonial Philadelphia's book history. Close-reading *The Interesting Narrative* with attention to the problem of genre, accordingly, requires an understanding of what genres were circulating, an understanding best achieved by studying the Library Company as the center of reading in the Atlantic's most abolitionist city. The Company is thus central to early American cultural history in that it was a civic institution for the mediation of reading that straddled the interpretive communities and reading networks of both enslavers and abolitionists, constituting it as a unique forum for the expression and activities of early American civic engagement.

Conclusion
Philanthropy Recommended—Slavery, the Origins of the "Charitable Industrial Complex," and the Public Sphere

The proprietary subscription libraries examined in this book were multifaceted institutions reflecting the contradictions in American society that still affect us today. They were, first and foremost, inward-facing institutions that served to perpetuate the privilege of their proprietors. As Alexander Hamilton intimated, they may have had the reading of books as their ostensible purpose, but if members sometimes spoke of nothing but "privateering and building of vessels," they were clearly also social networks for business, as the Library Company of Philadelphia explicitly stated from its foundation. That business was mainly in slavery and its products, which provided the wealth to pay for membership in the libraries and to purchase their collections of books. These establishments, however, played an additional role as non-profits in need of these men's cultural philanthropy, with some men like Redwood, whose £500 gift to Newport's library was over and above his membership fees, also funding construction of their buildings and donating to other institutions like universities. Early American libraries were therefore "philanthropic but exclusive," helping to create a wealthy elite, primarily based in shared economic interests in slavery, but also in shared reading—learning that helped form their interpretive communities and their central role in American cultural history.[1] This elite would become the colonies-wide leadership network of the country at the time of the American Revolution. In that capacity, the libraries were also important outward-facing institutions through which their members exercised civic engagement, helping them to influence public policy in their cities and broader regional and national communities. The libraries were therefore private clubs whose members attempted to control the public through that engagement, performing an outsized role in civil society's deliberations and government decisions in a manner that continues to be characteristic of America's unique, but highly contested, model of a privately constituted public sphere.

This model has been triumphant since 1980, as privatization of government functions and public goods has proceeded apace regardless of whether conservatives

---

[1] James Raven, "Social Libraries and Library Societies in Eighteenth-Century North America." *Institutions of Reading: The Social Life of Libraries in the United States.* Eds Thomas Augst and Kenneth Carpenter (Amherst: U Massachusetts P, 2007), 29, 50.

or liberals have been in office. The ideology of this model is "the belief that charities can perform these tasks better and with greater efficiency than government," and that therefore non-profits supported by donations from private individuals, foundations, and other institutions are more successful endeavors than the state.[2] This ideology is essentially turning back the clock to over two centuries ago, before nineteenth- and twentieth-century progressives created most of America's public, taxpayer-supported institutions and goods. That temporal regression is one of the reasons why neo-conservative political action organizations like the Tea Party fetishize the "limited government" of the American eighteenth century. Colonial patriots at that time were protesting taxation from a large imperial British administration, an objection that has contributed to a current conservative historical conviction that the United States was meant to be a low-tax country with a small public sector. This conviction is encapsulated best in the state of New Hampshire's official motto, "live free or die," which translates into the other side of that ideology—private individuals, families, and charities must look after their own without public assistance.

Conservatives, accordingly, often hold up Alexis de Tocqueville's observation, in *Democracy in America* (1835), that one of America's virtues was that it had private associations for the mutual aid of their members without having big government.[3] These had arisen in the eighteenth century in England, where local civic leaders were endowing charity schools, hospitals, and other institutions. Philadelphians and New Yorkers led the way in founding similar institutions in the colonies, with New Englanders following shortly thereafter.[4] By 1820, New England alone had "1,500 Bible societies, missionary societies, masonic lodges, orphanages, and other kinds of charitable institutions."[5] Even de Tocqueville observed, however, that these associations were formed in the context of a slavery economy, yet the eighteenth-century model of a privately constituted public sphere still endures.[6] Our embrace of this old-fashioned system helps explain why we have what the philanthropist Peter Buffett calls a "charitable industrial complex" in which he must negotiate for donations from people who have contributed to the problems his foundation is trying to resolve.[7]

As Ken Stern has argued, the recent privatizations have been proven to be no more successful than the government services that their advocates excoriated, as

[2] Ken Stern, *With Charity for All: Why Charities are Failing and a Better Way to Give* (NY: Anchor Books, 2013), 3.
[3] Elisabeth Bumiller, "Bush Finds Affirmation in a Frenchman's Words," *New York Times*, March 15, 2015. Accessed December 18, 2017. <http://www.nytimes.com/2005/03/14/politics/bush-finds-affirmation-in-a-frenchmans-words.html?_r=0>.
[4] Conrad Edick Wright, *The Transformation of Charity in Postrevolutionary New England* (Boston: Northeastern UP, 1992), 35.
[5] Wright, 5.
[6] The words "slave" or "slavery" are mentioned 248 times in de Toqueville's *Democracy in America* in Part I alone. Accessed December 18, 2017. <https://www.gutenberg.org/files/815/815-h/815-h.htm>.
[7] Peter Buffett, "The Charitable Industrial Complex." *New York Times*, July 26, 2013. Accessed December 6, 2017. <http://www.nytimes.com/2013/07/27/opinion/the-charitable-industrial-complex.html?mtrref=undefined&gwt=pay&assetType=opinion&login=email&auth=login-email>.

"study after study tells the opposite story: of organizations that fail to achieve meaningful impact yet press on with their strategies and services despite significant, at times overwhelming, evidence that they don't work."[8] This fact has not deterred growth; there were 1.1 million charities in the US in 2013, with 50,000 more added every year. Charities take in $1.5 trillion annually, have combined assets of about $3 trillion, and account for 10 percent of the economy.[9] As this has occurred, the portion of state university budgets supplied by government has decreased dramatically. Public higher education tuition has soared to the extent that students at my institution, the University of New Hampshire, pay the highest in-state tuition in America and have the highest levels of student debt. This development is not only happening in higher education, but also at the elementary level, as I have to pay tuition for my six-year-old to attend a kindergarten at a municipal public school in Newburyport, Massachusetts. There are other signs of a lack of commitment to the public good from cash-strapped governments. It is as if the wealthy who are funding political campaigns and demanding low taxes, privatization, and smaller government view themselves as some other species from those in need in an era of growing economic inequality—a tribalism of the elite.

What this book's discussion of slavery philanthropy to early American libraries can teach us about the charitable industrial complex today is not only that many non-profit institutions and associations must account for slavery's role in their establishment and endowments, but also that we have not overcome the country's primitive, colonial method of providing for those in need. Indeed, there already were attempts in the eighteenth century to preserve this method as a means of maintaining capitalism's reputation in the face of the knowledge of slavery's evils. As Philip Gould has explained, awareness of capitalism's dependence on slavery in the eighteenth century spurred efforts to "demarcate the boundary between virtuous and vicious commerce"; some contemporaries were trying to save capitalism from itself in arguing for more moral trade.[10] Quakers George Keith, John Hepburn, Ralph Sandiford, and Benjamin Rush, for example, argued that the slave trade was unchristian, particularly in its tendency to break up families against biblical precept.[11] Pro-slavery advocates like Richard Nisbet, responding to Rush, contended that if abolition of slavery were to happen, Philadelphia would lose her commerce with the West Indies.[12] In turn, anti-slavery advocates often targeted slave products like sugar, rum, tobacco, and indigo by advocating for boycotts.[13] Abolitionists' "commercial jeremiad" regarding slavery encapsulated "the sentimental persona, prophetic and apocalyptic overtones, the ideal connection between trade and enlightened manners, its fear of luxury and decadent consumption, and the simultaneous commodification and feminization of African society."[14] Anti-slavery charity, accordingly, was significant, with Boston's Cotton Mather founding a black self-improvement society as early as 1693 and Providence and

---

[8] Stern, 15.   [9] Stern, 2.
[10] Philip Gould, *Barbaric Traffic: Commerce and Anti-slavery in the Eighteenth-Century Atlantic World* (Cambridge: Harvard UP, 2003), 21.
[11] Gould, 15, 24.   [12] Gould, 24.   [13] Gould, 30–1.   [14] Gould, 42.

Connecticut forming abolition societies in 1789 and 1791, with the Philadelphia and New York societies also participating.[15] Yet these still must be regarded as primitive responses to slavery, as these societies did not always deliver on emancipation; indeed, as my chapter on New York argued, abolitionists were often quite racist and white supremacist. These associations, in short, were too small-scale to respond fully to the larger systemic problem of capitalism's alliance with slavery.

This shortcoming in the associational culture of relief forced it to begin to yield, in the nineteenth century, to "public" establishments in the way that we understand them now—taxpayer-funded organizations for the provision of necessary human services in the form of public universities and other institutions. It was not until the Great Depression and post-World War II period that many of these services became regarded as human rights. The dismal failure of laissez-faire capitalism with the market crash of 1929, and the human misery accompanying it, cast doubt on the ability of neo-liberal economics and policies to privately deliver public goods, so government had to step in, raise taxes on the wealthy, and expand its range of services. Franklin Delano Roosevelt's New Deal initiated many social services, including the social security retirement system, the protection of the right to organize labor, the United States Housing Authority, and other measures to provide a modicum of safety against the downside of modern capitalism. The GI Bill of Rights is the most salient example of this democratic socialism, with government supplying health, education, and other services to veterans. In subsequent years, America's public universities became the envy of the world, medical breakthroughs were accomplished, the interstate highway project was actualized, space exploration was initiated, and a host of other developments in this period that we associate with modernity were made possible by robust government revenue.

To return to Laurence Sterne's "Philanthropy Recommended" sermon, analyzed in Chapter 1, there must be a recognition of the humanity of the unfortunate, the failure of the charitable industrial complex to resolve our problems, and a commitment to providing large-scale public services of the kind only government can deliver. Indeed, this exhortation is rooted in early America, where the parable of the Good Samaritan was the foundation for the belief that charity should extend to people outside of one's race or tribe, such as the enslaved.[16] As New Englanders, particularly clergymen, contemplated the extent of who belonged to their community in the commandment to love thy neighbor, "the consensus was that 'every man breathing' was '...our neighbor.'"[17] Biblical precept was united with the period's movement in literary sentimentalism in regard to African slaves as neighbors, helping religion to work together with capitalism by configuring enlightened commerce as moral and anti-slavery.[18] It could be said that the democratic socialism of the middle of the twentieth century was an extension of this sentimentalized morality, uniting Americans after one of capitalism's worst failures. Sentimental "moral capital" was one of the anti-slavery movement's most utilitarian products for uniting and extending the British empire in the nineteenth century, providing a cultural offensive advertising the human rights benefits of belonging to that

---

[15] Wright, 34, 60.   [16] Wright, 20.   [17] Wright, 20–1.   [18] Gould, 25.

empire. We need that moral capital again now for American purposes.[19] If America's influence in the world is to be sustained, it must advertise more universal and uniting benefits to its own people in the face of what all the world sees as national disunity and inequality.

America's current embrace of the primitive, colonial model of a privately constituted public sphere, with a limited government made possible by private charity rather than public sector investment, works against reestablishing such benefits. This system should be regarded as a failed one for our present needs, and therefore a dangerous historical fantasy in which the violence of slavery that made that model possible is rendered invisible. The long eighteenth century (1660–1830) in which that model arose has indeed served as a template for the projection of such historical fantasies for some time. Patrick O'Brien novels romanticize seafaring life and military service, *Pirates of the Caribbean* films celebrate the golden age of buccaneering, and the current cult of Jane Austen naturalizes the relationship between money and marriage. The American Revolution itself has traditionally captured the imagination to the extent that reenactors of battles dress in period military costume, activity I participated in myself as a Massachusetts school child during the 1976 bicentennial of the Declaration of Independence. Too often, this fantasizing forgets the progress that we have made since that time, and slavery almost never comes up in our fantasies about the Revolution and its associated documents.

To return to the historiographical argument of Chapter 1, the writing of the history of the Revolution is often a literary act making use of storytelling techniques associated with the historical novel and period films, which serve to create and maintain such fantasies about the past. Upon closer analysis, however, the eighteenth century appears to have failed to deliver on the potential for universal rights, for which its Enlightenment books advocated, by excluding enslaved Africans and many others from those rights. To be sure, abolitionists planted the seeds for more inclusivity, but it was not until Roosevelt's New Deal, the Civil Rights Movement, the Women's Rights Movement, the War on Poverty, and other middle twentieth-century initiatives that serious efforts were made to deliver those rights on a public scale. Advocating for the renewal of the idealism of those decades may itself be an anachronistic fantasy projection, but the charitable industrial complex's provision of forgiveness of corporate greed and exploitation around the world in exchange for charitable donations is not delivering a meaningful impact either. A revival of sentimentalism—the affective mode of fiction and rhetoric that helped create an inviting print media environment for rights discourse and advocacy—may be necessary to put Enlightenment ideals into action and resolve inequality in our own day.

---

[19] Christopher Leslie Brown, *Moral Capital: Foundations of British Abolitionism* (Chapel Hill: U North Carolina P, 2006), 11–12, 14.

Bibliography

Abbot, George Maurice. *A Short History of the Library Company of Philadelphia*. Philadelphia: Board of Directors of the Library Company of Philadelphia, 1913.

Allan, David. *A Nation of Readers: The Lending Library in Georgian England*. London: The British Library, 2008.

Altick, Richard D. *The English Common Reader: A Social History of the Mass Reading Public, 1800–1900*. 2nd edn. Chicago: U Chicago P, 1998.

America's Historical Newspapers. Accessed July 1, 2015. <http://infoweb.newsbank.com. libproxy.unh.edu>.

Amory, Hugh. "Printing and Bookselling in New England, 1638–1713." In *A History of the Book in America, Volume 1: The Colonial Book in the Atlantic World*, edited by Hugh Amory and David Hall, 83–116. Chapel Hill: U North Carolina P, 2007.

Amory, Hugh. *Bibliography and the Book Trades: Studies in the Print Culture of Early New England*, edited by David Hall. Philadelphia: U Pennsylvania P, 2005.

An Account of the Rise and Progress of the Paper Bills of Credit in South Carolina etc. 1739.

Andrews, Charles M. "The Boston Merchants and the Non-importation Movement." *Publications of the Colonial Society of Massachusetts* 19 (Transactions 1916–1917): 159–259.

Apter, Emily. *The Translation Zone: A New Comparative Literature*. Princeton: Princeton UP, 2006.

Aravamudan, Srinivas. *Tropicopolitans: Colonialism and Agency, 1688–1804*. Durham: Duke UP, 1999.

Aravamudan, Srinivas. *Guru English: South Asian Religion in a Cosmopolitan Language*. Princeton: Princeton UP, 2006.

Armitage, David. "John Locke, Carolina, and the *Two Treatises of Government*." *Political Theory* 32.5 (Oct. 2004): 602–27.

Arneil, Barbara. *John Locke and America: The Defence of English Colonialism*. Oxford: Clarendon P, 1996.

Baenen, Michael A. "Books, Newspapers, and Sociability in the Making of the Portsmouth Athenaeum." *The New England Quarterly* 76.3 (Sept. 2003): 378–412.

Bailyn, Bernard. *The Ideological Origins of the American Revolution*. Cambridge: Harvard UP, 1992.

Bartlett, John R. *Census of the Inhabitants of the Colony of Rhode Island and Providence Plantations, Taken by Order of the General Assembly, in the Year 1774; and by the General Assembly of the State ordered to be Printed*. Providence: Knowles, Anthony & Co., State Printers, 1858.

Barton Family Papers. Phillips Library, MSS 110. Peabody Essex Museum, Salem, Massachusetts.

Basker, James. "Intimations of Abolition in 1759." *Age of Johnson* 12.1 (2001): 47–66.

Baucom, Ian. *Specters of the Atlantic: Finance Capital, Slavery, and the Philosophy of History*. Durham: Duke UP, 2005.

Beales, Ross W. and E. Jennifer Monaghan, "Literacy and Schoolbooks." *A History of the Book in America, Volume 1: The Colonial Book in the Atlantic World*, edited by Hugh Amory and David Hall, 380–7. Chapel Hill: U North Carolina P, 2007.

Beckert, Sven. *Empire of Cotton: A Global History.* NY: Vintage Books, 2015.

Beckert, Sven and Seth Rockman, eds. *Slavery's Capitalism: A New History of American Economic Development.* Philadelphia: U Pennsylvania P, 2016.

Bellamy, Liz. *Commerce, Morality and the Eighteenth-Century Novel.* Cambridge: Cambridge UP, 1998.

Benes, Peter. "Slavery in Boston Households, 1647–1770." *Slavery/Anti-slavery in New England, the Dublin Seminar for New England Folklife Annual Proceedings* (June 2003), 12–30.

Berkeley, George. *The Querist, Containing Several Queries, Proposed to the Consideration of the Public.* Dublin: Reilly, 1725 & 1735.

Berlin, Ira. "Slavery, Freedom, and Philadelphia's Struggle for Brotherly Love, 1685 to 1861." In *Anti-slavery and Abolition in Philadelphia: Emancipation and the Long Struggle for Racial Justice in the City of Brotherly Love*, edited by Richard Newman and James Mueller, 19–41. Baton Rouge: Louisiana State UP, 2011.

Bhabha, Homi K. "Signs Taken for Wonders: Questions of Ambivalence and Authority under a Tree Outside Delhi, May 1817." *Critical Inquiry* 12.1 (Autumn 1985): 144–65.

Bilder, Mary Sarah. *The Transatlantic Constitution: Colonial Legal Culture and the Empire.* Cambridge: Harvard UP, 2004.

Blackburn, Robin. *The American Crucible: Slavery, Emancipation and Human Rights.* London: Verso, 2011.

Bolhouse, Gladys E. "Abraham Redwood: Reluctant Quaker, Philanthropist, Botanist." In *Redwood Papers: A Bicentennial Collection*, edited by Lorraine Dexter and Alan Pryce-Jones, 1–11. Newport: Redwood Library and Athenaeum, 1776.

Boston Library. "Books Borrowed Volume 1, 1793–1797." Archives of the Boston Library Society. Boston Athenaeum, Boston, Massachusetts. Accessed September 9, 2018. <http://cdm16057.contentdm.oclc.org/cdm/ref/collection/p16057coll21/id/7>, 99, 196, 280, 368, 428, 474, 518, 539.

Boulokos, George. *The Grateful Slave: The Emergence of Race in Eighteenth-Century British and American Culture.* Cambridge: Cambridge UP, 2008.

Bourdieu, Pierre. *Distinction: A Social Critique of the Judgment of Taste.* Trans. Richard Nice. Cambridge: Harvard UP, 1984.

Bowditch, Joseph Papers. Phillips Library, MSS 156. Peabody Essex Museum, Salem, Massachusetts.

Brantlinger, Patrick. *Crusoe's Footprints: Cultural Studies in Britain and America.* London: Routledge, 1990.

Breen, T. H. "'Baubles of Britain': The American and Consumer Revolutions of the Eighteenth Centuries." *Past and Present* 119 (May 1988): 73–104.

Breen, T. H. *Marketplace of Revolution: How Consumer Politics Shaped America Independence.* Oxford: Oxford UP, 2005.

Brewer, John. *The Pleasures of the Imagination: English Culture in the Eighteenth Century.* NY: Farrar Straus Giroux, 1997.

Brown, Christopher Leslie. *Moral Capital: Foundations of British Abolitionism.* Chapel Hill: U North Carolina P, 2006.

Brown, Gillian. *The Consent of the Governed: The Lockean Legacy in Early American Culture.* Cambridge: Harvard UP, 2001.

Brown, James. "Papers of James Brown (1761–1834)," MSS 310. Rhode Island Historical Society (RIHS), Providence.

Brown, Laura. *Alexander Pope*. Oxford: Blackwell, 1985.

Brown University Steering Committee on Slavery and Justice. Accessed June 16, 2018. <http://www.brown.edu/Research/Slavery_Justice/>.

Bruns, Roger, ed. *Am I Not a Man and a Brother: The Anti-slavery Crusade of Revolutionary America, 1688–1788*. NY: Chelsea House Publishers, 1977.

Buffett, Peter. "The Charitable Industrial Complex." *New York Times*, July 26, 2013. Accessed December 6, 2017. <http://www.nytimes.com/2013/07/27/opinion/the-charitable-industrial-complex.html>.

Bumiller, Elisabeth. "Bush Finds Affirmation in a Frenchman's Words," *New York Times*, March 15, 2005. Accessed December 18, 2017. <http://www.nytimes.com/2005/03/14/politics/bush-finds-affirmation-in-a-frenchmans%20-words.html_r=0>.

Burghardt Du Bois, W. E. *The Suppression of the African Slave-Trade to the United States of America, 1638–1870*. NY: Longmans, 1904.

Bushman, Richard. *The Refinement of America: Persons, Houses, Cities*. NY: Vintage, 1993.

Bussing, John Stuyvesant. *The National Cyclopedia of American Biography*. Vol. 17 NY: White, 1920.

Butler, Judith and Athena Athanasiou. *Dispossession: The Performative in the Political*. Cambridge: Polity P, 2013.

Cabot Family Papers. Phillips Library, MSS 161. Peabody Essex Museum, Salem, Massachusetts.

Care, Henry. *English Liberties, or, the Freeborn Subject's Inheritance*. Providence: Carter, 1774.

Carens, Joseph H. "Possessive Individualism and Democratic Theory: MacPherson's Legacy." In *Democracy and Possessive Individualism: The Intellectual Legacy of C. B. MacPherson*, Joseph H. Carens, 1–18. Albany: SUNY P, 1993.

Carey, Brycchan. "To Force a Tear: Anti-Slavery on the Eighteenth-Century London Stage." In *Affect and Abolition in the Anglo-Atlantic, 1770–1830*, edited by Stephen Ahern, 109–28. Farnham: Ashgate, 2013.

Carey, Dan. "Reading Contrapuntally: Robinson Crusoe, Slavery, and Postcolonial Theory." In *The Postcolonial Enlightenment*, edited by Dan Carey and Lynn Festa, 105–36. Oxford: Oxford UP, 2009.

Carretta, Vincent. "Anne and Elizabeth: The Poet as Historian in *Windsor Forest*." *SEL* 21.3 (Summer 1981): 425–37.

Carretta, Vincent. *Equiano the African*. Athens: U Georgia P, 2005.

Carter, John. John Carter Ledger #1 1768–1775. MSS 336 Vol. 2. Rhode Island Historical Society. Providence, RI.

Casper, Scott E., Jeffrey D. Groves, Stephen W. Nissenbaum, and Michael Winship, eds. *A History of the Book in America, Volume 3: The Industrial Book, 1840–1880*. Chapel Hill: U North Carolina P, 2007.

"Catalogue and Donation Book, 1761–1782." Salem Athenaeum Records, 1760–1889, MSS 56. Phillips Library, Peabody Essex Museum, Salem, Massachusetts.

"Charge Book, 1760–1768." Salem Athenaeum Records, 1760–1889, MSS 56. Phillips Library, Peabody Essex Museum. Salem, Massachusetts.

Charter, Rules, & Regulations of the Social Library. Salem Athenaeum Papers, 1760–1889, MSS 56 B2 F1, 4–6. Phillips Library, Salem, Massachusetts.

Chomsky, Aviva. "Salem as a Global City, 1850–2004." In *Salem: Place, Myth, Memory*, edited by Dane Anthony Morrison and Nancy Lusignan Schultz, 219–47. Boston: Northeastern UP, 2004.

Choudhury, Mita. "Race, Performance, and the Silenced Prince of Angola." In *A Companion to Restoration Drama*, edited by Susan J. Owen, 161–76. Oxford: Blackwell, 2001.

"Circulation Receipt Books, 1794–1812." Library Company of Philadelphia. Philadelphia, Pennsylvania.

"Circulation Receipt Books, 1756–1761." Redwood Archives, Redwood Library and Athenaeum. Newport, Rhode Island.

"Circulation Records." Charleston Library Society Records, MS 29. Charleston, South Carolina.

Cist, Charles, ed. *The Wonderful Life, and Surprizing Adventures of that Renowned Hero, Robinson Crusoe*. Philadelphia: Cist, 1787.

City Readers, New York Society Library. Accessed September 20, 2017. <http://cityreaders.nysoclib.org>.

Codr, Dwight. *Raving at Usurers: Anti-Finance and the Ethics of Uncertainty in England, 1690–1750*. Charlottesville: U Virginia P, 2016.

Cohen, Lara Langer and Jordan Alexander Stein. "Introduction: Early African American Print Culture." *Early African American Print Culture*, edited by Lara Langer Cohen and Jordan Alexander Stein, 1–16. Philadelphia: U Pennsylvania P, 2012.

Cohen, Matt. *The Networked Wilderness: Communicating in Early New England*. Minneapolis: U Minnesota P, 2010.

Collins, John Daniel. "American Drama in Anti-slavery Agitation, 1792–1861." Ph.D. Dissertation, State University of Iowa, 1976.

Columbia University and Slavery. Accessed December 11, 2017. <https://columbiaandslavery.columbia.edu>.

Condy, Jeremiah. "Account Book, 1759–1770." American Antiquarian Society. Worcester, Massachusetts, MSS Folio Vol. C.

Coughtry, Jay. *The Notorious Triangle: Rhode Island and the African Slave Trade 1700–1807*. Philadelphia: Temple UP, 1981.

Coveely, N., ed. *The Wonderful Life, and Surprizing Adventures of that Renowned Hero, Robinson Crusoe. By Daniel Defoe*. Boston: Coveely, 1784.

Coxe Family Papers 1639–1897. MSS 2049, Historical Society of Pennsylvania.

Crousaz, Jean Pierre de. *An Examination of Mr. Pope's Essay on Man*. Trans. Elizabeth Carter. London: Dodd, 1739.

Curwen Family Papers. Phillips Library, MSS 45. Peabody Essex Museum, Salem, Massachusetts.

Darnton, Robert. "What is the History of Books?" In *The Book History Reader*, edited by David Finkelstein and Alistair McCleery, 9–26. London: Routledge, 2002.

Davidson, Cathy N. *Revolution and the Word: The Rise of the Novel in America*. Oxford: Oxford UP, 2004.

Davis, David Brion. *The Problem of Slavery in the Age of the Revolution, 1770–1823*. Ithaca: Cornell UP, 1975.

Deane, Charles. "The Connection of Massachusetts with Slavery and the Slave Trade." *Proceedings of the American Antiquarian Society* New Series, Vol. IV (Oct. 1885–Apr. 1887): 178–222.

The Declaration of the reasons and motives for the present appearing in arms of Their Majesties Protestant subjects in the Province of Maryland. Licens'd, November 28th 1689. London 1689.

Defoe, Daniel. *The Life and Adventures of Robinson Crusoe*, edited by Angus Ross. London: Penguin, 1965.

Derby Family Papers. Phillips Library, MSS 37. Peabody Essex Museum, Salem, Massachusetts.

Derrida, Jacques. *Of Grammatology*. Trans. Gayatri Chakravorty Spivak. Baltimore: Johns Hopkins UP, 1997.

Desrochers, Robert E., Jr. "Slave-for-Sale Advertisements and Slavery in Massachusetts, 1704–1781." *The William and Mary Quarterly* 59.3 (July 2002): 623–64.

DeWolfe, Thomas Norman. *Inheriting the Trade: A Northern Family Confronts its Legacy as the Largest Slave-Trading Dynasty in American History*. Boston: Beacon P, 2008.

Dharwadker, Aparna. "Nation, Race, and the Ideology of Commerce in Defoe." *The Eighteenth Century: Theory and Interpretation* 39.1 (1998): 63–84.

Dillon, Elizabeth Maddock. *New World Drama: The Performative Commons in the Atlantic World, 1649–1849*. Durham: Duke UP, 2014.

Dimunation, Mark. "'The Whole of Recorded Knowledge': Jefferson as Collector and Reader." In *The Libraries, Leadership, & Legacy of John Adams and Thomas Jefferson*, edited by Robert C. Baron and Conrad Edick Wright, 21–40. Golden: Fulcrum, 2010.

Dottin, Paul. "The Life of Charles Gildon." In *Robinson Crusoe Examin'd and Criticis'd*, edited by Paul Dottin, 5–46. London: Dent, 1923.

Douglas, Aileen. "Brittania's Rule and the It-Narrator." *Eighteenth-Century Fiction* 6.1 (Oct. 1993): 65–82.

Doyle, Laura. *Freedom's Empire: Race and the Rise of the Novel in Atlantic Modernity, 1640–1940*. Durham: Duke UP, 2008.

Du Bois, W. E. Burghardt. *The Suppression of the African Slave-Trade to the United States of America, 1638–1870*. NY: Longmans, 1904.

Ducykinck, Evert A. *A Memorial of John David Wolfe*. NY: New York Historical Society, 1872.

Dworetz, Steven. "'See Locke on Government': The Two Treatises and the American Revolution." *Studies in Eighteenth Century Culture* 21 (1992): 101–27.

Earle, Peter. *The World of Daniel Defoe*. NY: Atheneum, 1977.

ECCO (Eighteenth-Century Collections Online). Accessed July 16, 2015. <http://find.galegroup.com.>.

Edwards, Pamela. *The Statesman's Science: History, Nature, and Law in the Political Thought of Samuel Taylor Coleridge*. NY: Columbia UP, 2004.

Elford, Jana Smith. "Recovering Women's History with Network Analysis: A Case Study of the Fabian News." *The Journal of Modern Periodical Studies* 6.2 (2015): 191–213.

Ellis, Markman. "Suffering Things: Lapdogs, Slaves, and Counter-Sensibility." In *The Secret Life of Things: Animals, Objects, and It-Narratives in Eighteenth-Century England*, edited by Mark Blackwell, 92–114. Lewisburg, Bucknell UP, 2007.

Equiano, Olaudah. *The Interesting Narrative and Other Writings*, edited by Vincent Carretta. NY: Penguin, 1995.

Erskine-Hill, Howard. "Pope and Slavery." In *Alexander Pope: World and Word*, edited by Howard Erskine-Hill, 27–53. Oxford: Oxford UP, 1998.

An Essay on Currency, Written in August 1732. Charlestown: Lewis Timothy, 1732.

ESTC (English Short Title Catalogue). Accessed July 16, 2015. <http://estc.bl.uk>.

Etting, Frank M. "Collection." MS 0195 Shelf 54 – D03 Box 72. Box 72, Folder 1. Historical Society of Pennsylvania, Philadelphia, Pennsylvania.

Eustace, Nicole. *Passion is the Gale: Emotion, Power, and the Coming of the American Revolution*. Chapel Hill: U North Carolina P, 2008.

Fanon, Frantz. *Black Skin White Masks*. Trans. Charles Lam Markmann. NY: Grove Press, 1967.

Farrow, Anne, Joel Lang, and Jennifer Frank. *Complicity: How the North Promoted, Prolonged, and Profited from Slavery*. Hartford: Hartford Courant Co., 2005.

Feather, John. *The Provincial Book Trade in Eighteenth-Century England*. Cambridge: Cambridge UP, 1985.

Feather, John. *A History of British Publishing*. 2nd edn. London: Routledge, 2006.

Felt, Joseph B. *Annals of Salem, Volume 2*. Salem: W & S. B. Ives, 1849.

Fergus, Jan. *Provincial Readers in Eighteenth-Century England*. Oxford: Oxford UP, 2007.

Ferguson, Elizabeth Graeme. "Commonplace Book." Film 1238. American Philosophical Society. Philadelphia, Pennsylvania.

Festa, Lynn. *Sentimental Figures of Empire in Eighteenth-Century Britain and France*. Baltimore: Johns Hopkins UP, 2006.

Finkelstein, David and Alistair McCleery, eds. *An Introduction to Book History*. London: Routledge, 2005.

Fish, Stanley. "Interpreting the Variorum." *Critical Inquiry* 2.3 (Spring 1976): 465–85.

Fisher, William. "Letterbook, 1750–1751." MS AM.06775. Historical Society of Pennsylvania, Philadelphia, Pennsylvania.

Fiske, Jane Fletcher. *Gleanings from Newport Court Files 1659–1783*. Boxford: Self-Published, 1998.

Fitch, Timothy. *The Medford Slave Trade Letters, 1759–1765*. Medford Historical Society & Museum. Accessed May 2, 2016. <http://www.medfordhistorical.org/collections/slave-trade-letters/voyage-one>.

Flavel, Julie. *When London was Capital of America*. New Haven: Yale UP, 2010.

Fleck, Andrew. "Crusoe's Shadow: Christianity, Colonization and the Other." In *Historicizing Christian Encounters with the Other*, edited by John C. Hawley, 74–89. Basingstoke: Macmillan, 1998.

Fliegelman, Jay. *Prodigals and Pilgrims: The American Revolution Against Patriarchal Authority 1750–1800*. Cambridge: Cambridge UP, 1982.

Ford, Worthington Chauncey. *The Boston Book Market, 1689–1700*. Boston: The Club of Odd Volumes, 1917.

Foster, Theodore. "Theodore Foster Papers." MSS 424. Rhode Island Historical Society (RIHS), Providence.

Fraser, Robert. *Book History Through Postcolonial Eyes: Rewriting the Script*. London: Routledge, 2008.

Gaine, Hugh, ed. *The Wonderful Life, and Surprizing Adventures of that Renowned Hero, Robinson Crusoe. By Daniel Defoe*. NY: Gaine, 1774.

Gardner Family Papers. Phillips Library, MSS 147. Peabody Essex Museum, Salem, Massachusetts.

Gautier, Gary. "Slavery and the Fashioning of Race in 'Oroonoko,' 'Robinson Crusoe,' and Equiano's 'Life.'" *The Eighteenth Century* 42.2 (Summer 2001): 161–79.

Gentleman's Magazine, by Sylvanus Urban, Gent 29 (Dec. 1759).

The Georgetown Slavery Archive. Accessed December 11, 2017. <https://slaveryarchive.georgetown.edu/>.

Gikandi, Simon. *Slavery and the Culture of Taste*. Princeton: Princeton UP, 2011.

Gikandi, Simon. "Editor's Column: The Fantasy of the Library." *PMLA* 128.1 (Jan. 2013): 9–20.

Gildon, Charles. *An Epistle to D......D' F..e, the Reputed Author of Robinson Crusoe. Robinson Crusoe Examin'd and Criticis'd*. edited by Paul Dottin, 81–128. London: Dent, 1923.

Giles, Paul. *Transatlantic Insurrections: British Culture and the Formation of American Literature, 1730–1860*. Philadelphia: U Pennsylvania P, 2001.

Glynn, Tom. *Reading Publics: New York City's Public Libraries, 1754–1911*. NY: Fordham UP, 2015.

Goebel, Jules, Jr., ed. *The Law Practice of Alexander Hamilton: Documents and Commentary.* Vol. 2. NY: Columbia UP, 1969.

Goffin, Jordan. *Atlas of the Rhode Island Book Trade in the Eighteenth Century.* Accessed July 15, 2014. <http://www.rihs.org/atlas/>.

Goldberg, Isaac. *Tin Pan Alley: A Chronicle of American Popular Music.* NY: F. Ungar, 1961.

Gould, Philip. *Barbaric Traffic: Commerce and Anti-slavery in the Eighteenth-Century Atlantic World.* Cambridge: Harvard UP, 2003.

Gould, Philip. *Writing the Rebellion: Loyalists and the Literature of Politics in British America.* Oxford: Oxford UP, 2013.

Grafton, Anthony. "Is the History of Reading a Marginal Enterprise? Guillaume Budé and His Books." *The Papers of the Bibliographical Society of America* 91.2 (June 1997): 139–57.

Green, James. "English Books and Printing in the Age of Franklin." In *A History of the Book in America, Volume 1: The Colonial Book in the Atlantic World,* edited by Hugh Amory and David Hall, 248–98. Chapel Hill: U North Carolina P, 2007.

Green, James. "Subscription Libraries and Commercial Circulating Libraries in Colonial Philadelphia and New York." In *Institutions of Reading: The Social Life of Libraries in the United States,* edited by Thomas Augst and Kenneth Carpenter, 53–71. Amherst: U Massachusetts P, 2007.

Green, James. "The Book Trade in the Middle Colonies, 1680–1720." In *A History of the Book in America, Volume 1: The Colonial Book in the Atlantic World,* edited by Hugh Amory and David Hall, 199–223. Chapel Hill: U North Carolina P, 2007.

Green, James. "The Publishing History of Olaudah Equiano's Interesting Narrative." *Slavery and Abolition* 16.3 (1995): 362–75.

Greene, Jack P. *Pursuits of Happiness: The Social Development of Early Modern British Colonies and the Formation of American Culture.* Chapel Hill: U North Carolina P, 1988.

Greene, Lorenzo Johnston. *The Negro in Colonial New England 1620–1776.* NY: Columbia UP, 1942.

Grimm, Dorothy F. "A History of the Library Company of Philadelphia, 1731–1835." U Pennsylvania dissertation, 1955.

Hall, David. "The Atlantic Economy in the Eighteenth Century." In *A History of the Book in America, Volume 1: The Colonial Book in the Atlantic World,* edited by Hugh Amory and David Hall, 152–62. Chapel Hill: U North Carolina P, 2007.

Hall, David D. "Readers and Writers in Early New England." In *A History of the Book in America, Volume 1: The Colonial Book in the Atlantic World,* edited by Hugh Amory and David Hall, 117–51. Chapel Hill: U North Carolina P, 2007.

Hall, David D. and Elizabeth Carroll Reilly. "Practices of Reading: Introduction." In *A History of the Book in America, Volume 1: The Colonial Book in the Atlantic World,* edited by Hugh Amory and David Hall, 377–80. Chapel Hill: U North Carolina P, 2007.

Hancock, David. *Citizens of the World: London Merchants and the Integration of the British Atlantic Community, 1735–1785.* Cambridge: Cambridge UP, 1995.

Hancock, David. *Oceans of Wine: Madeira and the Emergence of American Trade and Taste.* New Haven: Yale UP, 2009.

Harrington, Virginia D. "The Place of the Merchant in New York Life." *New York History* 13.4 (Oct. 1932): 366–80.

Harrington, Virginia D. *The New York Merchant on the Eve of the Revolution.* NY: Columbia UP, 1935.

Harris, Leslie M. *In the Shadow of Slavery: African-Americans in New York City, 1626–1863.* Chicago: U Chicago P, 2003.

Hart, James D. *The Popular Book: A History of America's Literary Taste*. NY: Oxford UP, 1950.

Hawkesworth, John and Thomas Southerne. *Oroonoko, a Tragedy, as it is Now Acted at the Theatre-Royal in Drury Lane*. London: Bathurst, 1759.

Hayes, Kevin. *A Colonial Woman's Bookshelf*. Knoxville: U Tennessee P, 1996.

Hayes, Kevin. *The Road to Monticello: The Life and Mind of Thomas Jefferson*. Oxford: Oxford UP, 2008.

Hicks, Rob. *Amelia Island*. Charleston: Arcadia Publishing, 2014.

Holyoke Family Papers. Phillips Library, MSS 49. Peabody Essex Museum, Salem, Massachusetts.

Hopkins, Samuel. *A Dialogue Concerning the Slavery of the Africans, Showing it to be the Duty and Interest of the American States to Emancipate all their African Slaves*. Norwich: Spooner, 1776.

Horne, Gerald. *The Counter-Revolution of 1776: Slave Resistance and the Origins of the United States of America*. NY: NYU P, 2014.

Howsam, Leslie and James Raven, "Introduction." *Books Between Europe and the Americas: Connections and Communities, 1620–1860*. Basingstoke: Palgrave Macmillan, 2011. Accessed December 9, 2014. <http://rotunda.upress.virginia.edu/PinckneyHorry/ELP0316>.

Hudson, Nicholas. "Social Rank, 'The Rise of the Novel,' and Whig Histories of Eighteenth Century Fiction." *Eighteenth-Century Fiction* 17.4 (2005): 563–98.

Hulme, Peter. *Colonial Encounters: Europe and the Native Caribbean, 1492–1797*. London: Methuen, 1986.

Hume, Robert D. "The Value of Money in Eighteenth-Century England: Incomes, Prices, Buying Power—and Some Problems in Cultural Economics." *Huntington Library Quarterly* 77.4 (Winter 2014): 373–16.

Hunt, Lynn. *Inventing Human Rights: A History*. NY: Norton, 2007.

Hunter, J. Paul. *The Reluctant Pilgrim: Defoe's Emblematic Method and Quest for Form in Robinson Crusoe*. Baltimore: Johns Hopkins UP, 1966.

Hunter, J. Paul. *Before Novels: The Cultural Contexts of Eighteenth-Century Fiction*. NY: Norton, 1992.

Hunter, Phyllis Whitman. *Purchasing Identity in the Atlantic World: Massachusetts Merchants, 1670–1780*. Ithaca: Cornell UP, 2001.

Hunter, Phyllis Whitman. "Transatlantic News: American Interpretations of the Scandalous and Heroic." In *Books Between Europe and the Americas: Connections and Communities, 1620–1860*, edited by Leslie Howsam and James Raven, 64–82. Basingstoke: Palgrave Macmillan, 2011.

Islam, Syed Manzurul. *The Ethics of Travel: From Marco Polo to Kafka*. Manchester: Manchester University Press, 1996.

Ito, Akiyo. "Olaudah Equiano and the New York Artisans: The First American Edition of *The Interesting Life of Olaudah Equiano, or Gustavus Vassa, the African*." *Early American Literature* 32.1 (1997): 82–101.

Jackson, Leon. "The Talking Book and the Talking Book Historian: African American Cultures of Print—the State of the Discipline." *Book History* 13 (2010): 251–308.

Jackson, Maurice. *Let this Voice be Heard: Anthony Benezet, Father of Atlantic Abolitionism*. Philadelphia: U Pennsylvania P, 2009.

Jameson, Fredric. *The Political Unconscious: Narrative as a Socially Symbolic Act*. Ithaca: Cornell UP, 1981.

Jardine, Lisa and Anthony Grafton, "'Studied for Action': How Gabriel Harvey Read his Livy." *Past & Present* 129 (Nov. 1990): 30–78.

Jefferson, Thomas. *The Papers of Thomas Jefferson Digital Edition*, edited by Barbara B. Oberg and J. Jefferson Looney. Charlottesville: University of Virginia Press, Rotunda, 2008.

Jeffries Papers 1622–1880. MSS MsN-2067 (XT). Massachusetts Historical Society, Boston, Massachusetts.

Jensen, Arthur L. *The Maritime Commerce of Colonial Philadelphia*. Madison: U Wisconsin Department of History, 1963.

Johnson, Samuel. *Taxation No Tyranny: An Answer to the Resolution and Address of the American Congress*. London: Cadell, 1775.

Johnstone, Charles. *Chrysal, or, the Adventures of a Guinea*, edited by Kevin Bourque, Four Volumes in Two. Kansas City: Valancourt Books, 2011.

Joshi, Priya. *In Another Country: Colonialism, Culture, and the English Novel in India*. NY: Columbia UP, 2002.

Kaul, Suvir. "Reading Literary Symptoms: Colonial Pathologies and the *Oroonoko* Fictions of Behn, Southerne, and Hawkesworth." *Eighteenth-Century Life* 18.3 (Nov. 1994): 80–96.

Keane, John. "Stretching the Limits of the Democratic Imagination." In *Democracy and Possessive Individualism: The Intellectual Legacy of C. B. MacPherson*, edited by Joseph H. Carens, 105–35. Albany: SUNY P, 1993.

Keep, Austin Baxter, A. M. *History of the New York Society Library. With an Introductory Chapter on Libraries in Colonial New York, 1698–1776*. NY: De Vinne P, 1908.

Kilbourne, Richard, Jr. *Debt, Investment, Slaves: Credit Relations in East Feliciana Parish, Louisiana, 1825–1885*. London: Pickering and Chatto, 1995.

Knott, Sarah. *Sensibility and the American Revolution*. Chapel Hill: U North Carolina P, 2009.

Knox, Henry. "Henry Knox Papers II, 1736–1823." Microfilm P-467. Massachusetts Historical Society, Boston, Massachusetts.

Lancaster, Jane. *Inquire Within: A Social History of the Providence Athenaeum since 1753*. Providence: The Providence Athenaeum, 2003.

Leacock, John. "Commonplace Book." MSS.B.L463. American Philosophical Society.

Lehuu, Isabelle. "Reconstructing Reading Vogues in the Old South: Borrowings from the Charleston Library Society, 1811–1817." In *The History of Reading, Volume 1: International Perspectives c.1500–1990*, edited by Shafquat Towheed and W. R. Owens, 64–84. Basingstoke: Palgrave Macmillan, 2011.

Leiss, William. "The End of History and Its Beginning Again; or, The Not-Quite-Yet Human Stage of Human History." In *Democracy and Possessive Individualism: The Intellectual Legacy of C. B. MacPherson*, edited by Joseph H. Carens, 263–74. Albany: SUNY P, 1993.

Library Company of Philadelphia. *A Catalogue of the Books, Belonging to the Library Company of Philadelphia; to which is Prefixed, a Short Account of the Institution, with the Charter, Laws, and Regulations*. Philadelphia: Poulson, 1789.

Library Company of Philadelphia. *"At the Instance of Benjamin Franklin": A Brief History of the Library Company of Philadelphia*. Philadelphia: Library Company of Philadelphia, 1995.

Lin, Rachel Chernos. "The Rhode Island Slave Traders: Butchers, Bakers, and Candlestick Makers." *Slavery and Abolition* 23.3 (Dec. 2002): 21–38.

Lippincott, Bertram III, ed. "Genealogy of the Redwood Family." Unpublished Manuscript. Property of the Author and the Board for Certification of Genealogists, Washington, DC. Jamestown, RI, 1986.

Locke, John. *Two Treatises of Government*, edited by Peter Laslett. Cambridge: Cambridge UP, 1996.

London Magazine, or Gentleman's Monthly Intelligencer 28 (Dec. 1759).

Lowndes, Thomas. *A New Catalogue of Lownds Circulating Library*. London, 1761.

Lydon, James G. "New York and the Slave Trade, 1700 to 1774." *William and Mary Quarterly* 35.2 (Apr. 1978): 375–94.

Lynch, Deidre. *The Economy of Character: Novels, Market Culture, and the Business of Inner Meaning*. Chicago: U Chicago P, 1998.

Lyon, Joseph Family Papers. MS A2012.031 Hay Library. Brown University, Providence, Rhode Island.

MacPherson, C. B. *The Political Theory of Possessive Individualism: Hobbes to Locke*, edited by Frank Cunningham. Oxford: Oxford UP, 2011.

Madison, James. *The Papers of James Madison Digital Edition*, edited by J. C. A. Stagg. Charlottesville: University of Virginia Press, Rotunda, 2010. Accessed June 25, 2014. <http://rotunda.upress.virginia.edu/founders/JSMN-01-04-02-0057>.

Maier, Pauline *American Scripture: Making the Declaration of Independence*. NY: Vintage, 1997.

Majewski, John. *Modernizing a Slave Economy: The Economic Vision of the Confederate Nation*. Chapel Hill: U North Carolina P, 2009.

Mallipeddi, Ramesh. *Spectacular Suffering: Witnessing Slavery in the Eighteenth-Century British Atlantic*. Charlottesville: U Virginia P, 2016.

Manegold, C. S. *Ten Hills Farm: The Forgotten History of Slavery in the North*. Princeton: Princeton UP, 2010.

Mansbridge, Jane. "MacPherson's Neglect of the Political." In *Democracy and Possessive Individualism: The Intellectual Legacy of C. B. MacPherson*, edited by Joseph H. Carens, 155–73. Albany: SUNY P, 1993.

Marcus, Jacob Rader. "Light on Early Connecticut Jewry." In *American Jewish History: The Colonial and Early National Periods, 1654–1840*, edited by Jeffrey S. Gurock, 3–52. NY: Routledge, 1998.

Martin, Bonnie. "Slavery's Invisible Engine: Mortgaging Human Property." *The Journal of Southern History* 76.4 (Nov. 2010): 817–66.

Martin, Bonnie. "Neighbor-to-Neighbor Capitalism: Local Credit Networks and the Mortgaging of Slaves." In *Slavery's Capitalism: A New History of American Economic Development*, edited by Sven Beckert and Seth Rockman, 107–21. Philadelphia: U Pennsylvania P, 2016.

Mason, George Champlin. *Annals of the Redwood Library and Athenaeum*. Newport: Redwood, 1891.

Matson, Cathy. *Merchants and Empire: Trading in Colonial New York*. Baltimore: Johns Hopkins UP, 1998.

McCorison, Marcus A., ed. *The 1764 Catalogue of the Redwood Library Company at Newport, Rhode Island*. New Haven: Yale UP, 1965.

McCrady, Edward. *The History of South Carolina Under the Proprietary Government 1670–1719*. NY: Macmillan, 1901.

McDonald, Joyce Green. "The Disappearing African Woman: Imoinda in 'Oroonoko' after Behn." *ELH* 66.1 (Spring 1999): 71–86.

McDowell, Tremaine. "An American Robinson Crusoe." *American Literature* 1.3 (Nov. 1929): 307–9.

McInelly, Brett C. "Expanding Empires, Expanding Selves: Colonialism, the Novel, and Robinson Crusoe." *Studies in the Novel* 35.1 (2003): 1–21.

McKenzie, Donald F. *Bibliography and the Sociology of Texts*. Cambridge: Cambridge UP, 1999.

McKeon, Michael. *The Origins of the English Novel 1600–1740*. Baltimore: Johns Hopkins UP, 1987.

McManus, Edgar J. *A History of Negro Slavery in New York*. Syracuse: Syracuse UP, 1970.

McManus, Edgar J. *Black Bondage in the North*. Syracuse: Syracuse UP, 1973.

McMullen, Haynes. "The Founding of Social Libraries in Pennsylvania, 1731–1876." *Pennsylvania History* 32.2 (Apr. 1965): 130–52.

Meehan, Thomas. "Some Pioneer Catholic Laymen in New York." *United States Catholic Historical Society Historical Records and Studies* 4.1–2 (Oct. 1906): 285–301.

Melish, Joanne Pope. *Disowning Slavery: Gradual Emancipation and "Race" in New England, 1780–1860*. Ithaca: Cornell UP, 1998.

Mills, Charles. *The Racial Contract*. Ithaca: Cornell UP, 1997.

Minute Book, 1731–2000. Library Company of Philadelphia. Philadelphia, Pennsylvania.

Monaghan, E. Jennifer. *Learning to Read and Write in Colonial America*. Amherst: U Massachusetts P, 2005.

Montesquieu, Baron de La Bréde et de. *Spirit of the Laws*. London: Nourse & Vaillant, 1758.

Moore, George H. *Notes on the History of Slavery in Massachusetts*. NY: Appleton, 1866.

Moore, John Robert. *Daniel Defoe: Citizen of the World*. Chicago: U Chicago P, 1958.

Moore, Sean. " 'Our Irish Copper-Farthen Dean': Swift's *Drapier's Letters*, the 'Forging' of a Modernist Anglo-Irish Literature, and the Atlantic World of Paper Credit." *Atlantic Studies* 2.1 (2005): 65–92.

Moore, Sean. "The Irish Contribution to the Ideological Origins of the American Revolution: Non-importation and the Reception of Jonathan Swift's Irish Satires in Early America." *Early American Literature* 52.2 (Spring 2017): 333–62.

Morgan, Edmund S. and Helen M. Morgan. *The Stamp Act Crisis: Prologue to Revolution*. Chapel Hill: U North Carolina P, 1953.

Morgan, Edmund S. *American Slavery, American Freedom: The Ordeal of Colonial Virginia*. NY: Norton, 1975.

Mulford, Carla, ed. *Only for the Eye of a Friend: The Poems of Annis Boudinot Stockton*. Charlottesville: UP of Virginia, 1995.

Murphy, Sharon Ann. *Investing in Life: Insurance in Antebellum America*. Baltimore: Johns Hopkins UP, 2010.

Nathans, Heather S. *Early American Theatre from the Revolution to Thomas Jefferson: Into the Hands of the People*. Cambridge: Cambridge UP, 2003.

National Park Service. *Salem: Maritime Salem in the Age of Sail*. Washington: US Department of the Interior, 1987.

National Park Service. *African-American Heritage Sites in Salem: A Guide to Salem's History*. Washington: US Department of the Interior, 1998.

Nelson, Eric. *The Royalist Revolution: Monarchy and the American Founding*. Cambridge: Belknap P, 2014.

Newman, Richard and James Mueller. "Introduction." In *Anti-slavery and Abolition in Philadelphia: Emancipation and the Long Struggle for Racial Justice in the City of Brotherly Love*, edited by Richard Newman and James Mueller, 1–16. Baton Rouge: Louisiana State UP, 2011.

New York Society Library. *The Charter, Bye-laws, and Names of the Members of the New-York Society Library: With a Catalogue of the Books Belonging to the Said Library*. NY: Gaine, 1789.

Novak, Maxmillian. "Robinson Crusoe's Original Sin." *SEL* 1.3 (1961): 19–29.

Novak, Maximillian E. *Realism, Myth, and History in Defoe's Fiction.* Lincoln: U Nebraska P, 1983.

Nussbaum, Frederick L. "American Tobacco and French Politics, 1783–1789." *Political Science Quarterly* 40 (1925): 497–516.

O'Malley, Gregory E. *Final Passages: The Intercolonial Slave Trade of British America, 1619–1807.* Chapel Hill: U North Carolina P, 2014.

Oldfield, J. R. "Ties of Soft Humanity: Slavery and Race in British Drama, 1760–1800." *Huntington Library Quarterly* 56.1 (Winter 1993): 1–14.

Oldfield, J. R. *Transatlantic Abolitionism in the Age of Revolution: An International History of Anti-slavery, c.1787–1820.* Cambridge: Cambridge UP, 2013.

Orne Family Papers. Phillips Library, MSS 41. Peabody Essex Museum, Salem, Massachusetts.

Osgood, Charles S. and H. M. Batchelder. *Historical Sketch of Salem 1626–1879.* Salem: Essex Institute, 1879.

Otis, James. "Against Writs of Assistance." National Humanities Institute. Accessed May 2, 2016. <http://www.nhinet.org/ccs/docs/writs.htm>.

Otis, James. "Rights of the British Colonies." In *Am I Not a Man and a Brother: The Anti-slavery Crusade of Revolutionary America, 1688–1788.* Ed. Roger Bruns. NY: Chelsea House Publishers, 1977.

Overton, Bill. "Countering Crusoe: Two Colonial Narratives." *Critical Survey* 4.3 (1992): 302–10.

Paine, Thomas. *Common Sense: Addressed to the Inhabitants of America.* Philadelphia: Bell, 1776.

Parker, Katherine. "London's Geographic Knowledge Network and the Anson Account (1748)." In *The Global Histories of Books: Methods and Practices*, edited by Elleke Boehmer, Rouven Kunstmann, Priyasha Mukhopadhyay, and Asha Rogers, 23–46. London: Palgrave Macmillan, 2017.

Pearson, Edward. "'Planters Full of Money': The Self-Fashioning of South Carolina's Plantation Society." In *Money Trade and Power: The Evolution of South Carolina's Plantation Society*, edited by Jack P. Greene, Rosemary Brana-Shute, and Randy J. Sparks, 299–321. Columbia: U South Carolina P, 2001.

Phillips, James Duncan. *Salem in the Eighteenth Century.* Boston: Houghton Mifflin, 1937.

Pickering Family Papers. Phillips Library, MSS 400. Peabody Essex Museum. Salem, Massachusetts.

Pickman, Benjamin Papers. Phillips Library, MSS 5. Peabody Essex Museum, Salem, Massachusetts.

Piecuch, Jim. "'Of Great Importance Both to Civil and Religious Welfare': The Portsmouth Social Library, 1750–1786." *Historical New Hampshire* 57 (2002): 67–84.

Pinckney, Elise, ed. *The Letterbook of Eliza Lucas Pinckney 1739–1762.* Columbia: U South Carolina P, 1997.

Pocock, J. G. A. *Three British Revolutions: 1641, 1688, 1776.* Princeton: Princeton UP, 1980.

Pocock, J. G. A. *Virtue, Commerce, and History: Essays on Political Thought and History, Chiefly in the Eighteenth Century.* Cambridge: Cambridge UP, 1985.

Pollack, Thomas Clark. *The Philadelphia Theatre in the Eighteenth Century.* NY: Greenwood P, 1968.

Pope, Alexander. *Essay on Man*, edited by Tom Jones. Princeton: Princeton University Press, 2016.

Pope, Alexander. *Windsor Forest.* Accessed July 15, 2015. <https://andromeda.rutgers.edu/~jlynch/Texts/windsor.html>.

Price, Leah. "Reading: The State of the Discipline." *Book History* 7 (2004): 303–20.

Prince Family Papers. Phillips Library, MSS 72. Peabody Essex Museum, Salem, Massachusetts.

Princeton & Slavery. Accessed December 11, 2017. <https://slavery.princeton.edu/>.

Providence Library. *Catalogue of all the Books, Belonging to the Providence Library.* Providence: Waterman and Russell, 1768.

Pruitt, Bettye Hobbs. *The Massachusetts Tax Valuation List of 1771.* Boston: G. K. Hall, 1978.

Pujara-Clark. Christy. *Dark Work: The Business of Slavery in Rhode Island.* NY: NYU P, 2016.

Pynchon, William Papers. Phillips Library, MSS 236. Peabody Essex Museum, Salem, Massachusetts.

Ravela, Christian. "'Turning Out' Possessive Individualism: Freedom and Belonging in Samuel R. Delany's *The Mad Man.*" *Modern Fiction Studies* 62.1 (Spring 2016): 92–110.

Raven, James. *London Booksellers and American Customers: Transatlantic Literary Community and the Charleston Library Society, 1748–1811.* Columbia: U South Carolina P, 2002.

Raven, James. "Social Libraries and Library Societies in Eighteenth-Century North America." In *Institutions of Reading: The Social Life of Libraries in the United States,* edited by Thomas Augst and Kenneth Carpenter, 24–52. Amherst: U Massachusetts P, 2007.

Raven, James. "The Importation of Books in the Eighteenth Century." In *A History of the Book in America, Volume 1: The Colonial Book in the Atlantic World,* edited by Hugh Amory and David Hall, 183–98. Chapel Hill: U North Carolina P, 2007.

"Redwood, Abraham." *DNB (Dictionary of National Biography).* Accessed July 16, 2015. <http://www.oxforddnb.com.libproxy.unh.edu/view/article/68736>.

Reilly, Elizabeth Carroll and David D. Hall. "Customers and the Market for Books." In *A History of the Book in America, Volume 1: The Colonial Book in the Atlantic World,* edited by Hugh Amory and David D. Hall, 387–98. Chapel Hill: U North Carolina P, 2007.

Reynell, John. "Daybook 1731–1732." MSS.B.R33, 1–2, 3, 70. American Philosophical Society.

Richardson, John. "Alexander Pope's 'Windsor Forest': Its Context and Attitudes Towards Slavery." *Eighteenth-Century Studies* 35.1 (Fall 2001): 1–17.

Richardson, John. *Slavery and Augustan Literature: Swift, Pope, Gay.* London: Routledge, 2004.

Richetti, John. *Philosophical Writing: Locke, Berkeley, Hume.* Cambridge: Harvard UP, 1983.

Richetti, John. "Introduction." In *The Cambridge Companion to the Eighteenth-Century Novel,* edited by John Richetti, 1–8. Cambridge: Cambridge UP, 1996.

Richetti, John. *The English Novel in History 1700–1780.* London: Routledge, 1999.

Ridley, Hugh. *Images of Imperial Rule.* London: Croom Helm, 1983.

Roach, Joseph. *Cities of the Dead: Circum-Atlantic Performance.* NY: Columbia, 1996.

Roberts, Arthur. *Redwood Library and Athenaeum Newport, Rhode Island.* Providence: Privately Printed, 1948.

Roberts, Arthur S. "Redwood Library: Two Centuries: Excerpts from an article written in 1946." In *Redwood Papers: A Bicentennial Collection,* edited by Lorraine Dexter and Alan Pryce-Jones, 13–26. Newport: Redwood Library and Athenaeum, 1776.

Ropes, Nathaniel Papers. Phillips Library, MSS 190. Peabody Essex Museum, Salem, Massachusetts.

Ross, Angus. "Introduction." *The Life and Adventures of Robinson Crusoe. Daniel Defoe.* London: Penguin, 1965.

Rothman, Joshua, Edward Baptist, and Gavin Wright. *Slavery and Economic Development.* Baton Rouge: Louisiana State UP, 2006.

Round, Phillip H. *Removable Type: Histories of the Book in Indian Country, 1663–1880.* Chapel Hill: U North Carolina P, 2010.

Sable, Martin. "The Library Company of Philadelphia: Historical Survey, Bibliography, Chronology." *International Library Review* 18 (1987): 29–46.

Said, Edward. *Culture and Imperialism.* NY: Knopf, 1993.

Sammons, Mark J. and Valerie Cunningham. *Black Portsmouth: Three Centuries of African American Heritage.* Durham: U New Hampshire P, 2004.

Samuels, Wilfred D. "Disguised Voice in *The Interesting Narrative of Olaudah Equiano, or Gustavus Vassa, the African.*" *Black American Literature Forum* 19.2 (Summer 1985): 64–9.

Sassi, Jonathan D. "Africans in the Quaker Image: Anthony Benezet, African Travel Narratives, and Revolutionary-Era Anti-slavery." In *Bringing the World to Early Modern Europe: Travel Accounts and Their Audiences,* edited by Peter Mancall, 95–130. Leiden: Brill, 2007.

Schermerhorn, Calvin. *The Business of Slavery and the Rise of American Capitalism, 1815–1860.* New Haven, Yale UP, 2015.

Schmidgen, Wolfram. *Eighteenth-Century Fiction and the Law of Property.* Cambridge: Cambridge UP, 2002.

Schulz, Constance, ed. *The Papers of Eliza Lucas Pinckney and Harriott Pinckney Horry Digital Edition.* Charlottesville: University of Virginia Press, Rotunda, 2012. Accessed December 9, 2014. <http://rotunda.upress.virginia.edu/PinckneyHorry/ELP0869>.

Shareholder Records. Library Company of Philadelphia. Philadelphia, Pennsylvania.

Shields, David S. *Oracles of Empire: Poetry, Politics, and Commerce in British America, 1690–1750.* Chicago: U Chicago P, 1990.

Shields, David S. *Civil Tongues and Polite Letters in British America.* Chapel Hill: U North Carolina P, 1997.

Sibley, Agnes Marie. *Alexander Pope's Prestige in America, 1725–1835.* NY: Columbia UP, 1949.

Simmons, John. *The Lockean Theory of Rights.* Princeton: Princeton UP, 1992.

Slauter, Eric. *The State as a Work of Art: The Cultural Origins of the Constitution.* Chicago: U Chicago P, 2009.

Slauter, Eric. "Reading and Radicalization: Print, Politics, and the American Revolution." *Early American Studies* 8.1 (Winter 2010): 5–40.

"Slavery in Rhode Island." Slavery in the North Website. Accessed December 23, 2015. <http://slavenorth.com/rhodeisland.htm>.

Smith, Adam. *The Theory of Moral Sentiments.* Library of Economics and Liberty. Accessed April 30, 2016. <http://www.econlib.org/library/Smith/smMS1.html>.

Smith, J. Jay. *Notes for a History of the Library Company of Philadelphia.* Philadelphia, 1835.

Smith, Sarah. "Collection on 18th century Philadelphia Merchants 1705/6–1937 (bulk 1713–1848)." Collection 1864, Box 3, Folder 1. Historical Society of Pennsylvania, Philadelphia, Pennsylvania.

Solow, Barbara. "Slavery and Colonization." In *Slavery and the Rise of the Atlantic System,* edited by Barbara Solow, 21–42. Cambridge: Cambridge UP, 1991.

Solow, Barbara L. *The Economic Consequences of the Atlantic Slave Trade.* Lanham: Lexington Books, 2014.

Spencer, Jane. *Aphra Behn's Afterlife.* Oxford: Oxford UP, 2000.

Spencer, Mark G. *David Hume and Eighteenth-Century America.* Rochester: U Rochester P, 2005.

Starr, George A. *Defoe and Spiritual Autobiography.* Princeton: Princeton UP, 1965.

The Statutes at Large of South Carolina, edited by Thomas Cooper and David J. McCord. 10 vols. Columbia: A. S. Johnston, 1836–41.

Stern, Ken. *With Charity for All: Why Charities are Failing and a Better Way to Give*. NY: Anchor Books, 2013.

Sterne, Laurence. *The Sermons of Mr. Yorick*. London: Dodsley, 1764.

Stewart, Garrett. *The Look of Reading: Book, Painting, Text*. Chicago: U Chicago P, 2006.

Stewart, Peter, ed. *The Most Surprising Adventures, and Wonderful Life of Robinson Crusoe, of York, Mariner*. Philadelphia: Stewart, 1789.

Stiles, Ezra. *The Literary Diary of Ezra Stiles, D.D., LL.D*, edited by Franklin Bowditch Dexter. 3 vols. NY: Scribner's Sons, 1901.

Stockdale, Eric. "John Stockdale, London Bookseller and Publisher of Adams and Jefferson." In *The Libraries, Leadership, & Legacy of John Adams and Thomas Jefferson*, edited by Robert C. Baron and Conrad Edick Wright, 41–55. Golden: Fulcrum, 2010.

Sudan, Rajani. *Fair Exotics: Xenophobic Subjects in English Literature, 1720–1850*. Philadelphia: U Pennsylvania P, 2002.

Swaminathan, Srividhya and Adam R. Beach, eds. *Invoking Slavery in the Eighteenth-Century British Imagination*. Farnham: Ashgate, 2013.

Swift, Jonathan. *The Prose Works of Jonathan Swift*, edited by Herbert Davis. 14 vols. Oxford: Blackwell, 1939–68.

Thomas, Hugh. *The Slave Trade: The Story of the Atlantic Slave Trade: 1440–1870*. NY: Simon & Schuster, 1997.

Thomas, Isaiah, ed. *Travels of Robinson Crusoe. By Daniel Defoe*. Worcester: Thomas, 1786.

Thomas, Isaiah, ed. *Travels of Robinson Crusoe. By Daniel Defoe*. Worcester: Thomas, 1789.

Thomson, James. *The Works of Mr. Thomson*. 2 vols. London: Millar, 1744/1738.

Tiffin, Helen. "Postcolonial Literature and Counter-Discourse." In *The Post-Colonial Studies Reader*, 2nd edition, edited by Bill Ashcroft, Gareth Griffith, and Helen Tiffin, 99–101. NY: Routledge, 2006.

Todd, Dennis. *Defoe's America*. Cambridge: Cambridge UP, 2010.

Tolles, Frederick B. *Meeting House and Counting House: The Quaker Merchants of Colonial Philadelphia, 1682–1763*. Chapel Hill: U North Carolina P, 1948.

Toqueville, Alexis de. *Democracy in America*. Part I. Accessed December 18, 2017. <https://www.gutenberg.org/files/815/815-h/815-h.htm>.

Towsey, Mark and Kyle B. Roberts, "Introduction." *Before the Public Library: Reading, Community, and Identity in the Atlantic World, 1650–1850*, edited by Mark Towsey and Kyle B. Roberts, 1–30. Leiden: Brill, 2017.

The Transatlantic Slave Trade Database. Accessed May 2, 2016. <http://www.slavevoyages.org/voyage/search>.

Tully, James. "The Possessive Individualism Theses: A Reconsideration in the Light of Recent Scholarship." In *Democracy and Possessive Individualism: The Intellectual Legacy of C. B. MacPherson*, edited by Joseph H. Carens, 19–44. Albany: SUNY P, 1993.

Turley, Hans. "Protestant Evangelicalism, British Imperialism, and Crusonian Identity." *A New Imperial History: Culture, Identity, and Modernity in Britain and the Empire, 1660–1840*, edited by Kathleen Wilson, 176–93. Cambridge: Cambridge University Press, 2004.

Van Cleve, George William. *A Slaveholder's Union: Slavery, Politics, and the Constitution in the Early American Republic*. Chicago: U Chicago P, 2010.

Wait, Thomas, ed. *The Most Surprising Adventures, and Wonderful Life of Robinson Crusoe, of York, Mariner*. Portland: Wait, 1789.

Waldstreicher, David. *Slavery's Constitution: From Revolution to Ratification*. NY: Hill and Wang, 2009.

Waldstreicher, David. "The Origins of Anti-slavery in Pennsylvania: Early Abolitionists and Benjamin Franklin's Road Not Taken." In *Anti-slavery and Abolition in Philadelphia: Emancipation and the Long Struggle for Racial Justice in the City of Brotherly Love*, edited by Richard Newman and James Mueller, 45–65. Baton Rouge: Louisiana State UP, 2011.

Ward, Lee. *The Politics of Liberty in England and Revolutionary America*. Cambridge: Cambridge UP, 2004.

Warner, Michael. *The Letters of the Republic: Publication and the Public Sphere in Eighteenth Century America*. Cambridge: Harvard UP, 1990.

Warren, Austin. "To Mr. Pope: Epistles from America." *PMLA* 48.1 (Mar. 1933): 61–73.

Washington, George. *The Papers of George Washington Digital Edition*, edited by Theodore J. Crackel. Charlottesville: University of Virginia Press, Rotunda, 2008. Accessed June 23, 2014. <http://rotunda.upress.virginia.edu/founders/GEWN-05-10-02-0180>.

Waterman, Zuriel. "Zuriel Waterman Memorandum Book." "Benoni and John Waterman Family Papers." MSS 787. Rhode Island Historical Society (RIHS), Providence, Rhode Island.

Watt, Ian. *The Rise of the Novel: Studies in Defoe, Richardson and Fielding*. Berkeley: U California P, 1957.

West, Benjamin. "Account Book 1758–1773." MSS 794. Rhode Island Historical Society, Providence, Rhode Island.

Wheatland, Dr. H. "Sketch of the Social and Philosophical Libraries." *Proceedings of the Essex Institute* 2 (1856–60): 140–6.

Wheeler, Roxann. "'My Savage, My Man': Racial Multiplicity in Robinson Crusoe." *ELH* 62.4 (Winter 1995): 821–61.

Wheeler, Roxann. "Powerful Affections: Slaves, Servants, and Labours of Love in Defoe's Writing." In *Defoe's Footprints: Essays in Honour of Maximillian E. Novak*, edited by Robert M. Maniquis and Carl Fisher, 126–52. Toronto: U Toronto P, 2009.

White, Hayden. "The Historical Text as Literary Artifact." In *Narrative Dynamics: Essays on Time, Plot, Closure, and Frames*, edited by Brian Richardson, 191–210. Columbus: Ohio State UP, 2002.

White, Philip L. *The Beekmans of New York in Politics and Commerce, 1647–1877*. New York: New York Historical Society, 1956.

White, Shane. *Somewhat More Independent: The End of Slavery in New York City, 1770–1810*. Athens: U Georgia P, 1991.

Whitridge, Arnold. "The New York Society Library: A Comparison." In *Redwood Papers: A Bicentennial Collection*, edited by Lorraine Dexter and Alan Pryce-Jones, 111–18. Newport: Redwood Library and Athenaeum, 1976.

Widmayer, Anne F. "The Politics of Adapting Behn's *Oroonoko*." *Comparative Drama* 37.2 (Summer 2003): 189–223.

Wiggin, Cynthia B. *A Short History of the Salem Athenaeum*. Salem: Forest River P, 1972.

Wilder, Craig Steven. *Ebony and Ivy: Race, Slavery, and the Troubled History of America's Universities*. NY: Bloomsbury P, 2013.

William III. *The first declaration of His Highness William Henry, by the grace of God Prince of Orang. &c.* Boston: B. Harris, 1689.

Williams, Abigail. *The Social Life of Books: Reading Together in the Eighteenth-Century Home*. New Haven: Yale UP, 2017.

Williams, Eric. *Capitalism and Slavery*. Chapel Hill: U North Carolina P, 1944.

Winterer, Caroline. *The Mirror of Antiquity: American Women and the Classical Tradition, 1750–1900*. Ithaca: Cornell UP, 2007.

Winton, Calhoun. "The Southern Book Trade in the Eighteenth Century." In *A History of the Book in America, Volume 1: The Colonial Book in the Atlantic World*, edited by Hugh Amory and David D. Hall, 224–46. Chapel Hill: U North Carolina P, 2007.

Wolf, Edwin III. *The Book Culture of a Colonial American City: Philadelphia Books, Bookmen, and Booksellers*. Oxford: Clarendon P, 1988.

Wood, Peter H. *Black Majority: Negroes in Colonial South Carolina from 1670 to the Stono Rebellion*. NY: Knopf, 1974.

Woolf, Virginia. *A Room of One's Own*. London: Vintage, 1996.

Wright, Conrad Edick. *The Transformation of Charity in Post-revolutionary New England*. Boston: Northeastern UP, 1992.

Yale, Slavery & Abolition: Yale University and Its Legacy. Accessed December 11, 2017. <http://www.yaleslavery.org/>.

Yokota, Kariann Akemi. *Unbecoming British: How Revolutionary America Became a Postcolonial Nation*. Oxford: Oxford UP, 2011.

Zhang, Xudong. "Modernity as Cultural Politics: Jameson and China." In *Fredric Jameson: A Critical Reader*, edited by Sean Homer and Douglas Kellner, 169–94. Basingstoke: Palgrave, 2004.

Zimmet, Tyler, "Joseph Murray, Edward Antill, and New York City's Interlocking Elite." Columbia University and Slavery website. Accessed July 10, 2017. <https://columbiaandslavery.columbia.edu/content/joseph-murray-edward-antill-and-new-york-citys-interlocking-elite>.

Zizek, Slavoj. *First as Tragedy, Then as Farce*. London: Verso, 2009.

Index